FAITH AND POWER

Faith and Power

Latino Religious Politics Since 1945

Edited by
Felipe Hinojosa, Maggie Elmore, *and* Sergio M. González

NEW YORK UNIVERSITY PRESS
New York

NEW YORK UNIVERSITY PRESS
New York
www.nyupress.org

© 2022 by New York University
All rights reserved

References to Internet websites (URLs) were accurate at the time of writing. Neither the author nor New York University Press is responsible for URLs that may have expired or changed since the manuscript was prepared.

Library of Congress Cataloging-in-Publication Data
Names: Hinojosa, Felipe, 1977– editor. | Elmore, Maggie, editor. | González, Sergio M., 1987– editor.
Title: Faith and power : Latino religious politics since 1945 / edited by Felipe Hinojosa, Maggie Elmore, and Sergio M. González.
Description: New York : New York University Press, [2022] | Includes bibliographical references and index.
Identifiers: LCCN 2021011944 | ISBN 9781479804511 (hardback) | ISBN 9781479804528 (paperback) | ISBN 9781479804559 (ebook) | ISBN 9781479804542 (ebook other)
Subjects: LCSH: Hispanic Americans—Religion. | Hispanic Americans—Political activity. | Hispanic Americans—Civil rights. | Religion and politics—United States—History—20th century. | United States—Ethnic relations—History—20th century. | United States—Race relations—History—20th century. | United States—Religion—1945- | United States—Politics and government—20th century.
Classification: LCC BR563.H57 F35 2021 | DDC 322/.108968073—dc23
LC record available at https://lccn.loc.gov/2021011944

New York University Press books are printed on acid-free paper, and their binding materials are chosen for strength and durability. We strive to use environmentally responsible suppliers and materials to the greatest extent possible in publishing our books.

Manufactured in the United States of America

10 9 8 7 6 5 4 3 2 1

Also available as an ebook

CONTENTS

Introduction: Latino Religious Politics: Mapping the Field   1
Felipe Hinojosa, Maggie Elmore, and Sergio M. González

PART I. PLACE AND POLITICS

1. Catholics, the State, and Latino Advocacy in World War II   21
   Maggie Elmore

2. Chicago's Catholic Archdiocese and the Challenges of Serving a Multiethnic Latino Population   42
   Lilia Fernández

3. Pan-Latino Placemaking and Housing Dynamics: St. Joseph the Worker in Grand Rapids, Michigan, 1956–2000   70
   Delia Fernández-Jones

4. Latina/o Mormons: Spanish-Speaking Saints Negotiating Identity in the Deseret   94
   Sujey Vega

PART II. FREEDOM MOVEMENTS

5. Pentecostalism's Instrumental Faith and Alternative Power: César Chávez and Reies López Tijerina among Pentecostal Farmworkers, 1954–1956   121
   Lloyd D. Barba

6. Lived Religion in East Harlem: The New York Young Lords Occupy First Spanish—The People's Church   145
   Jorge Juan Rodríguez V

7. From the Fields to the Cities: The Rise of Latina/o Religious Politics in the Civil Rights Era   166
   Felipe Hinojosa

8. The Legacy of Las Hermanas for Latina/o Religious Politics
in the Twenty-First Century 188
Lara Medina

PART III. IMMIGRANT TRANSFORMATIONS

9. Political Fellowship and the Sanctuary Movement: Central
American Refugees and Practices of Religiopolitical
Accompaniment, 1982–1990 211
Sergio M. González

10. "The Needs of Migrant People": Catholics and Immigrants'
Rights in the Twentieth Century 233
Eladio B. Bobadilla

11. The Spiritual Is Political: The Pilsen Via Crucis as a
Path to Resistance 253
Anne M. Martínez

12. "Two Churches in One Building": Holy Cross Catholic
Church, Latino Immigration, and New Geographies
of Resistance, 1988–1997 273
Yuridia Ramírez

Afterword 299
Geraldo L. Cadava

Acknowledgments 309

Suggested Readings 313

About the Editors 321

About the Contributors 323

Index 325

Introduction

Latino Religious Politics: Mapping the Field

FELIPE HINOJOSA, MAGGIE ELMORE, AND
SERGIO M. GONZÁLEZ

Since its opening in 2014, the Humanitarian Respite Center at the Sacred Heart Church in McAllen, Texas, has aided more than 100,000 refugees. At the center of this work is Sister Norma Pimentel, a member of the order of the Missionaries of Jesus, who in September 2020 *Time* magazine named one of the hundred most influential people in the world. In 2018 she was honored with the Laetare Medal, the highest honor an American Catholic can receive. That recognition is fitting. For more than thirty years, the "Mother Teresa of South Texas" and "the pope's favorite nun" has worked with immigrants, refugees, and asylum seekers at the US-Mexico border. The daughter of Mexican immigrants, Sister Pimentel was raised in Brownsville, Texas, but like many border residents grew up crossing the border to Matamoros, Mexico, to visit family.[1] This soft-spoken nun has testified before the United Nations and the US Congress, and been a frequent visitor to the White House, each time sharing the stories of those who are suffering as they seek refuge in the United States. Throughout her career, Pimentel has carefully struck a largely apolitical stance, though she rarely minces words. Her defense of refugees is grounded in what she once called the social mission of the Catholic Church—the obligation of people of faith to care for the most vulnerable. Pimentel's commitment to those pushed to the margins of society draws upon a half-century-long tradition within Latino communities that has fused religion and politics.[2]

That tradition is at the heart of this book. For over half a century, Latino communities have drawn from their faith and spirituality to build networks of mutual aid, demand self-determination within institutions and social agencies tasked with serving them, organize movements for freedom, and, like Sister Pimentel, provide sanctuary for those seeking refuge. In recent years, historians including Mario T. García, Lara Medina, and Gastón Espinosa have acknowledged this history and woven together religion's power in shaping political engagement, community formation, and cultural production in Latino history.[3] These scholars have slowly started to piece together strands that extend all the way back to the early and middle decades of the twentieth century, when historians Carlos Castañeda and Samuel Ortegón first wrote about the Mexican American religious experience in the United States.[4] Ortegón's and Castañeda's scholarship provided important insights about Mexican-descent Catholics and Protestants even as they presented a romanticized view of Christianity and stressed the connections between religion and social uplift. That approach shifted significantly in the 1960s and 1970s. When the fields of Chicano and Puerto Rican studies emerged, they did so out of an urgency to tell the stories of exploitation, segregation, and political oppression that people of Latin American descent suffered in the United States. To that end, questions of race, colonialism, and the economies of migration and labor were paramount for fields in search of justice for their communities. As Gastón Espinosa, Virgilio Elizondo, and Jesse Miranda have argued, religion's absence in early Chicano historical scholarship is due at least in part to the "Marxist and socialist" analytical perspectives of scholars from the era.[5] For many of these scholars, working to recover generations of marginalized and oft-forgotten history within the milieu of social movements for Chicano and Puerto Rican self-determination, the role and place of religion, and especially the Catholic Church, factored in most prominently as a tool of empire and as an infinitely powerful institution committed to the subjugation of Latinos in Latin America and the United States.

These early perspectives, while certainly dominating the fields of Chicano and Puerto Rican studies, were never monolithic. Latino and Latina theologians of this period presented an alternative interpretation, one that recognized the institutional importance of the church as well as the role that faith played in the quotidian struggles of Latin American-descent peoples across the Americas. Inspired by the writings of liberation theologians in Latin America and the Latino freedom movements, Justo González, Ada María Isasi-Díaz, Virgilio Elizondo, and Orlando

Costas laid the groundwork for what Anthony M. Stevens-Arroyo called the "Latino religious resurgence" of the 1970s.[6] For them, the faith and power of oppressed communities had informed political mobilizations, church reform movements, and theological writings that emerged in the 1960s and 1970s, all of which marked a new era in Latino religious politics. In the 1980s the Catholic journalist Moises Sandoval and Stevens-Arroyo advanced the field by engaging theology and history in order to account for the political movements of Latino religious communities.[7] Sandoval and Stevens-Arroyo combined biography, theology, and history to tell the dynamic story of Latino religion in the United States, from Catholicism to storefront Pentecostal churches. One of the most important developments was the creation of the Program for the Analysis of Religion Among Latinos (PARAL). The program created new opportunities for scholars and helped further social scientific research on Latino religion in the 1990s.[8]

In the early 2000s a new generation of scholars emerged determined to cross disciplinary borders and bring religious history into conversation with fields such as ethnic and cultural studies. While they remained committed to the political dimensions of faith, these scholars published important work that focused on topics that had remained understudied across the field of Latino studies: religious identities, religious activism, Pentecostals and politics, the confluence of faith and immigration, and the politics of urban religious institutions. These works amplified religion in Latino history and brought much-needed attention to an area of study that had long remained siloed and separate from other areas of Latino history, including education, labor, and social movement history.[9]

Latino Religious Politics

This book continues the effort to excavate and recenter this long and somewhat neglected history. It presents new scholarship that rethinks the major ideas, arguments, periodization, and historical figures in the disciplinary fields of Latino history and Latino studies, doing so while recovering the history of the often misunderstood and ignored but, as we argue, vital component of faith and religiosity. Incorporating this innovative and rising crop of new research in the field—grounded in a comparative approach and focused on multiple Latino groups across space and place—demands that we work to define a term as capacious as "Latino religious politics." While in its simplest form Latino religious politics are political engagements by Latinos grounded in a particular form of religiosity, we take this one step further to consider what we might learn from thinking about Latino political participation and faith from the outside-in as much as the inside-out. This form of political contestation, we argue, has historically manifested at different scales, in distinct locations, and with a variety of actors professing varying commitments to faith traditions.

Several chapters in this volume examine the expanding institutional power of Latinos in religious organizations—be they in large agencies like the National Catholic Welfare Conference or smaller regional bodies like Latter-day Saints wards in the US Southwest—in matters directly affecting many Latino communities, including issues related to immigration, economic justice, and social integration. Others, however, expand our frame into yet under-explored aspects of Latino religious and political history. We consider, for example, social movements that may not necessarily have acknowledged adherence to any particular faith tradition but that were nonetheless engaged in building power and capacity through religious sites and organizations. In this sense, this volume examines Latino religious politics panoramically, identifying the way Latinos have engaged with systems of political power (often beyond the realm of electoral politics) and social movements that are steeped in faith, but with expressions that varied from the popular and institutional to the nonreligious. In other words, we understand the "religious" in Latino religious politics broadly as both a history of action and a shared culture, a way of understanding how injustice operates, and a belief that God is on the side of those who suffer, of those who struggle.

While our contributors recognize the importance of institutional reforms such as the Second Vatican Council and liberation theology as it developed in Latin America and the United States, we are intentional in leaving room for the varied manifestations of religious politics by considering how the outer edges of Latino religion reveal its inner workings; how social movements like the Young Lords and the United Farm Workers shaped Latino Catholic and Protestant activism; and how the politics of immigration and refugee admittance shaped an entire current of Latino theological thought. This volume thus argues that Latino religious politics must be defined as much by forces not normally considered religious as by institutional and doctrinal reforms. From this vantage point, the book takes on long-held assumptions about what constitutes Latino religious politics, where they take place, and their multiple streams of influence.

Part of the frustration that has led us—historians who write and research on Latino religious politics—to write this volume is that too often many in our field have ignored religion or have minimized the significant bearing faith has on the dynamics of community formation in the United States. Historians of Latino communities have for too long misunderstood religion as solely manifesting through spirituality, belief systems, cosmology, or cultural expressions and practices of faith.[10] Media pundits and cultural observers, meanwhile, often simplistically tag the religious political orientations of Latinos as being either inherently conservative or strictly tied to denominational associations, ignoring the reality that Latino religious politics in fact fluctuate across time and community and are not neatly tied to political affiliations. Our work instead joins that of other scholars who have recently begun to challenge the focus on a conservative thrust of postwar religious politics. This corrective to the dominant historiography argues that a progressive strain of faith politics centered around questions of justice, human dignity, and the common good remained vibrant and also motivated religious communities throughout the period.[11]

Faith and Power in Postwar America

This book seeks to correct these misinterpretations by focusing on the post–World War II era, a period in which a formal political engagement began among Latino religious leaders and laity. World War II and the immediate postwar period profoundly disrupted ideas about race, the role of the state in protecting and securing civil rights, and interfaith cooperation. While, on the one hand, World War II represented a global fight to defend democracy, to many Americans it was also a moment in which the country's racial ideology was suddenly in flux. The explosive growth of the state—which we take as both the governmental institutions at various local, state, and federal levels, as well as the agencies and bureaucrats that represented the government and implemented or influenced policy—provided new possibilities for the United States to wage war, but it also offered new opportunities for different groups to make claims on the state.[12] Racial liberalism presented one potential solution, by harnessing the power of the state to address long-standing issues of racial inequality. For the first time since Reconstruction, the federal government created agencies tasked with rooting out racial discrimination and preparing women and people of color to join the industrial workforce. African American civil rights leaders seized this opportunity. If the federal government could wage a war to defend democracy abroad, they reasoned, then it certainly had the power to instill it at home.[13]

Like African Americans, Latinos saw World War II as a golden opportunity. Sensitive to the ways Nazi Germany propagandized the United States' race problem and the impact of Nazi propaganda on hemispheric relations, the US federal government set about trying to learn as much as it could and as quickly as it could about a population that it suddenly saw as crucial to the war effort. Not only did federal officials worry that Latinos, especially Mexican Americans, might fall prey to fascist propaganda, they also considered how to convince them to join a war economy that consistently refused to offer them fair employment opportunities. Mexican American leaders capitalized on this moment. As historians, including Emilio Zamora, Elizabeth Escobedo, Luis Alvarez, and others, have demonstrated, Mexican American civil rights leaders drew the federal government's attention to the incongruity between asking Latino soldiers to sacrifice their lives abroad while subjecting them to "Juan Crowism" and racial violence at home. And in many instances, the new international attention to race relations in the United States forced the federal government and its quickly expanding bureaucratic agencies to reckon with the political, social, and labor structures that often shuttled Latino Americans into a loose category of second-class citizenship. But as much promise as the World War II period had shown, the decade following the war saw a period of marked indifference on the part of the US federal government in Latinos' struggle for full inclusion in the country's political and economic mainstream.[14]

Faith leaders occupied a unique space in the postwar political landscape. Their resolute support of US military interventions during World War II and their staunch attacks against communism in the postwar period inoculated them from accusations of subversive activity levied by critics. It would be a mistake to assume that divisions between religious groups simply melted away in the postwar period. Yet, as historians such as Kevin Schultz have noted, the years leading up to and immediately following the war marked a period of increased collaboration between the three largest faith groups in the United States: Protestants, Catholics, and Jews. In the postwar years, religious tribalism did not entirely disappear, but it was subsumed by the durability of a "tri-faith America" that pitted its religious and political commitments to democracy against the godless communism of the Soviet Union. Moreover, the bringing together of the three most prominent faith traditions in the country offered those communities seeking social justice, including African Americans and Latinos, new tools to resist discrimination in housing and employment.[15]

If a domestic embrace of religious pluralism opened new avenues for advancing the objectives of Black and Latino communities, developments in the burgeoning field of "human rights" offered the language and purchase to gain support for their struggles abroad. Historians including Gene Zubovich, Carol Anderson, Samuel Moyn, and others have shown that civil rights activists in the post–World War II period linked their struggle to dismantle Jim Crow in the United States to an emerging international commitment to human rights.[16] Historians of the mid-twentieth-century Black freedom movement, including David Chappell, Rosetta Ross, and Charles Marsh, have likewise shown how church leaders deployed a universal language of human rights in the development of civil rights movements, offering their movement an irrefutable moral high ground.[17] These tactics influenced many of the activists in this book. Latino Catholics and Protestants understood the power of drawing upon the language of human rights in their efforts to overturn centuries of racial nativism and economic subjugation.

The postwar period, however, is only one part of a longer evolution with roots in the pre-Columbian and colonial eras. Our aim here is to examine one part of this long history. Although it lies beyond the chronological scope of this volume, it is important to note that understanding Latino religion requires a recognition of how colonialism spurred on religious syncretism, new symbols, prayers, and festivals rooted in the Indigenous, Iberian, and African past of the Americas.

As cultural theorist Gloria Anzaldúa once argued, "The religion of the Mexicans—Catholicism—is just a veneer . . . people only go to church, believe in Christ, and eat the host because that was happening in Aztec religion."[18] Latino religion, in other words, has a long and storied tradition grounded in the experiences, miracles, cultures, and worldviews of Indigenous and African groups across the Americas.

Consider, for example, that Latino Catholicism originated in the sixteenth century with the first diocese established in 1511 in San Juan, Puerto Rico. Its evolution from there followed complex patterns of violence and cultural exchange, land theft, and religious innovation. As a result, Latino religion is a faith tradition steeped in the resistance and dignity of peoples across the Americas whose religious innovations— the blending of European, Indigenous, and African spiritualities—were critical to their survival. Colonialism, in other words, was not an all-encompassing project. In independence movements across Latin America, religion served as a major force of inspiration. The Catholic priest Miguel Hidalgo y Costilla appealed to the unifying symbol of the Virgen de Guadalupe to promote Mexican independence as he shouted *el grito de Dolores* on the morning of September 16, 1810. In the twentieth century, Puerto Rican nationalists advocated for native priests as a way to bolster national consciousness on the island and link Christianity with revolution in the fight for independence.[19] That spirit reemerged in the years after World War II buoyed by increased immigration, freedom movements across the globe, and the rise of liberation theology in Latin America. This religious diversity offers us new clues into the ways Latinos have forged transnational networks, participated in electoral politics and immigrant rights' movements, and transformed public space via storefront churches or sidewalk shrines. This centuries-long history undergirds the narratives of each chapter in this volume.

The chapters in this book take it as their starting point that movements are not religious simply because they originate in the church or are led by clergy. The farmworker movement, for example, was not a religious movement because of César Chávez's spirituality, but because churches provided structure and resources and the workers themselves employed religious imagery and structures. The im/migrants who mobilized their faith to make a home in the frigid Midwest or the New York Young Lords who in 1969 occupied the First Spanish United Methodist

Church were each driven by a need for survival in the midst of new environments and anti-Latino sentiments. Latino history is full of stories of ordinary folks who drew upon scripture or moral systems to center their activism and to inspire, critique, and bring people into their movements as they created opportunities for themselves and for others.

Book Outline

This book brings together historians whose work focuses on Latinos, race, migration, social movements, and, in some cases, religion. For some contributors, this is the first time that they are writing about religion so directly. That is by design. In order to both conceptualize and make sense of the history of Latino religious politics in the United States since 1945, we sought out fresh perspectives, new ideas, and scholars who themselves are finding it increasingly important to write about religious politics. In other words, we wanted to shake things up a bit and expand what is often taken for granted as religious politics. Our first goal here is to make known the significant role that religion has played in the lives of Latinos in the postwar era. From being a point of orientation to new im/migrants to providing a moral voice in the fight for civil rights, religion is intimately tied to how Latinos have practiced politics in the United States. But more importantly, we hope to provide the reader with a sense of religion's place in history as a political and organizing force. To that end, this book is organized chronologically, and divided into three parts that cover significant moments in Latino history and religious history: "Place and Politics," "Freedom Movements," and "Immigrant Transformations."

In part 1, "Place and Politics," four scholars take a critical look at how Latino im/migration shaped religious politics across a wide range of institutional and community spaces throughout the United States in the years following World War II. The authors in this section understand the concept of "place" across a number of settings, including in its geographic interpretations (local, regional, and national) as well as in the ways religious actors occupied space in institutional settings. Collectively, these chapters remind readers that the manifestations of Latino faith and politics can be analyzed at different scales and within different sites throughout the second half of the twentieth century. Maggie

Elmore opens part 1 by guiding us through the complex and often hidden relationships between the state, Mexican American leaders, and Catholic leaders as the Office of the Coordinator of Inter-American Affairs came to be during the middle part of the twentieth century. Lilia Fernández's "Chicago's Catholic Archdiocese and the Challenge of Serving a Multiethnic Latino Population" shifts the conversation from discussions of political maneuvering at the national level to more regional colorings as she explores the prominent role that the Catholic Church played in the lives of new Latino im/migrants (Mexican, Puerto Rican, and Cuban) to Chicago in the 1950s. In chapter 3, Delia Fernández-Jones moves us further north to Grand Rapids, Michigan, where in the 1950s Latino im/migrants transformed the Grandville Avenue corridor and St Joseph the Worker Parish into a neighborhood they called home. It is a story about placemaking and religion as much as it is about how im/migrant communities adapted to and were changed by the American Midwest. In chapter 4, we move out west, where Sujey Vega writes about the role of politics, political rhetoric, and community activism in the lives of Latinos in the Mormon Church. This chapter shifts our regional focus westward while also integrating Latino history, Mormon studies, and studies on the American West. Vega's particular focus on women and on culturally familiar networks of *comadrazgo* in the Mormon Church provides a fresh new angle on the history of Latino religious history by covering an area of research that up until now has rarely been studied.

In part 2, "Freedom Movements," we focus on the roles of mainline Protestants, Pentecostals, and Catholics in the Latino freedom movement—from central California to New York City—from the 1950s to the 1970s. We begin with Lloyd D. Barba, whose chapter on the often overlooked contributions of Pentecostals to the farmworker movement provides a much-needed corrective to the role of religion in the Chicano movement. His chapter expands the chronology of this history by interrogating early farmworker activism in church spaces in the mid-1950s, while also emphasizing the way evangelical faith practices influenced the maturation of central movement figures such as César Chávez and Reies López Tijerina. From there we jump to the streets of East Harlem in New York City, where Jorge Juan Rodríguez V writes about the revolutionary politics of the Puerto Rican Young Lords in the late 1960s. Here, Rodríguez pieces together the religious dynamics that propelled the Young Lords to occupy the First Spanish United Methodist Church (FSUMC) in 1969 and then again in 1970. This chapter pays particular attention not just to the Young Lords, but also to the church's own history and its members who witnessed both occupations. Next we move to Felipe Hinojosa's chapter, "From the Fields to the Cities," where he traces the narrative arc of Latino Protestant and Catholic activism from the farmworker movement in the 1960s to the rise of faith-based organizations since the late 1970s. We end part 2 with the Catholic Church, where Lara Medina carefully walks us through the radical and transformative politics of Las Hermanas. As a Latina feminist movement that emerged in a moment in the early 1970s, Las Hermanas played a paramount role in Latino religious politics. In this chapter, Medina recounts this history but also moves us forward to what the politics of Las Hermanas can teach us about contemporary movements for immigrant and women's rights.

In part 3, "Immigrant Transformations," we take a critical look at how migration, immigration, and refugee movements from Latin America have fundamentally transformed the United States since the 1970s. Sergio M. González begins with a chapter on the social and political movements for immigrant and refugee sanctuary within religious spaces from the 1980s to the present. Drawing on his research on the sanctuary movement in the US Midwest, González connects the histories of movements to aid Central American refugees fleeing persecution in their homelands and arbitrary deportation from the United States in the 1980s with the growth of the nascent New Sanctuary Movement of the twenty-first century. From there we focus on the role of the Catholic Church in mediating the passage and implementation of the Immigration Reform and Control Act of 1986. Here Eladio B. Bobadilla explores how Catholic hierarchy and clergy sought to expand their moral vision and political will in the service of immigration reform policy and advocacy for Latino immigrants in the late twentieth century. The moral vision and political will of Latino Catholics are also evident in religious rituals and performances. In Anne M. Martínez's chapter, we are treated to the Pilsen Via Crucis—a dramatic reenactment of the Stations of the Cross—in one of Chicago's most iconic neighborhoods. Martínez historicizes this reenactment and the role that important rituals like this have had on Latino community formation and immigration politics. The final chapter in part 3 takes us to the US South, where Yuridia Ramírez examines the confluence between faith spaces, organizing, and Latino Indigenous identity.

The book ends with an afterword by Geraldo L. Cadava, who provides concluding comments and sets forth some ideas about the future of Latino religious history. Cadava, a leading historian of Latino politics, lends particular attention to what lies ahead for scholars of Latino communities, pointing to potential areas of study in understanding the interplay between progressive and conservative politics, political party, and faith. He reminds readers and future scholars that whether it's analyzing community formation and progressive politics, as we do in this volume, or focusing on the faith commitments of conservative Latino voters, historians must continue to disentangle normative assumptions that treat "religious politics" as either inherently conservative or liberal.

The scholars in this volume foreground their analysis within a historical context, arguing that Latino religious politics are not a fixed project or solely based on religious affiliation, but rather have evolved and changed over time. Each chapter in this book then builds on this thesis by engaging important moments in Latino religious politics that are framed within the larger processes of immigration, refugee policies, deindustrialization, and the Chicano, Puerto Rican, and immigrant freedom movements. That is, this book explores religion and religious politics as part of the larger ecosystem that has shaped Latino communities specifically and American politics in general. While this project acknowledges that Latino religious politics have never been only radical, instead involving both conservative and progressive politics, we do contend that they reveal how ordinary people—religious and nonreligious—have made sense of their present and worked to build a better future for their churches, neighborhoods, and nation. This book aims to offer breadth and nuance to the history of Latino religions in the United States by incorporating studies of previously under-acknowledged dynamics such as Pentecostals in the farmworker movement, Protestants in the Midwest, and Catholics in the US South. The studies of religion that we and our collaborators offer in these pages not only encompass a set of religious beliefs and rituals, but also seek to highlight the political and sometimes contradictory crossings of faith and power.

NOTES

1 Julián Castro, "The 100 Most Influential People of 2020: Sister Norma Pimentel," *Time*, September 22, 2020; "World's 50 Greatest Leaders: Sister Norma Pimentel," *Fortune*, 2020, https://fortune.com; Carol Zimmermann, "Sister Norma Pimentel Is One of Time Magazine's 100 Most Influential People of 2020," *Angelus*, September 23, 2020, https://angelusnews.com.

2 In the book title and introductory chapter, the editors use the term *Latino* as a broad way to identify people of Latin American descent in the United States. As we prepared this volume, we discussed the limits of this term, when writing about a diverse population of women, men, and gender nonconforming people, and we acknowledge the significance of gender in everyday life and especially in religious politics. For this reason, we use *Latina* and *Latino* when addressing gendered experiences specifically. Throughout the volume, contributors were encouraged to employ their own choice of terms. They've done so, using identifiers ranging from *Latino* to *Latina/o* to *Latine* to *Latinx*, and have explained their own processes to deploy these terms in accompanying endnotes to their chapters.

3 Mario T. García, *Católicos: Resistance and Affirmation in Chicano Catholic History* (Austin: University of Texas Press, 2008); Lara Medina, *Las Hermanas: Chicana/Latina Religious-Political Activism in the US Catholic Church* (Philadelphia: Temple University Press, 2004); Mario T. García and Gastón Espinosa, *Mexican American Religions: Spirituality, Activism, and Culture* (Durham: Duke University Press, 2008); Gastón Espinosa, *Latino Pentecostals in America: Faith and Politics in Action* (Cambridge: Harvard University Press, 2014). Virgilio Elizondo, a theologian by training, provided an essential framework for understanding the history of Mexican American religion decades earlier. See Virgilio Elizondo, *Galilean Journey: The Mexican-American Promise* (Maryknoll, NY: Orbis, 1983).

4 Jean Baptiste Salpointe, *Soldiers of the Cross: Notes on the Ecclesiastical History of New Mexico, Arizona, and Colorado* (Banning, CA: St. Boniface's Industrial School, 1898); Thomas Harwood, *History of Spanish and English Missions of the New Mexico Methodist Episcopal Church from 1850–1910*, 2 vols. (Albuquerque, N.M., El Abogado Press, 1908, 1910); Jay S. Stowell, *A Study of Mexicans and Spanish Americans in the United States* (New York : Council of Women for Home Missions, 1920); Theodore Abel, *Protestant Home Missions to Catholic Immigrants* (Institute of Social and Religious Research, 1933); Samuel M. Ortegón, "The Religious Thought and Practice among Mexican Baptists of the United States, 1900–1947," PhD diss., USC (1950); Juan Lugo, *Pentecostes en Puerto Rico: o, La Vida de un Misionero* (San Juan, PR: Puerto Rico Gospel Press, 1951); Carlos Castañeda, *Our Catholic Heritage in Texas, 1519–1936* (Austin: Von Boeckmann-Jones, 1938). These works emphasized an adaptation approach to the study of

Mexicans and Puerto Ricans. For a review of this scholarship and the trajectory of Mexican American religious history, see Gastón Espinosa, "History and Theory in the Study of Mexican American Religions," in *Rethinking Latino(a) Religion and Identity*, ed. Gastón Espinosa and Miguel De La Torre (Cleveland: Pilgrim, 2006).

5 Gastón Espinosa, Virgilio Elizondo, and Jesse Miranda, "Introduction: US Latino Religions and Faith-Based Political, Civic, and Social Action," in *Latino Religions and Civic Activism in the United States*, ed. Gastón Espinosa, Virgilio Elizondo, and Jesse Miranda (New York: Oxford University Press, 2005), 3; Alberto Carrillo, "The Sociological Failure of the Catholic Church towards the Chicano," *Journal of Mexican American Studies 1*, no. 2 (Winter 1971): 75–83.

6 Ana María Díaz and Anthony M. Stevens-Arroyo, *Recognizing the Latino Resurgence in US Religion: The Emmaus Paradigm* (Boulder: Westview, 1998). See also Anthony M. Stevens-Arroyo, "From Barrios to Barricades: Religion and Religiosity in Latino Life," in *The Columbia History of Latinos in the United States since 1960*, ed. David Gutiérrez (New York: Columbia University Press, 2006), 303–54.

7 Moises Sandoval, *Fronteras: A History of the Latin American Church in the USA since 1513* (Austin: Mexican American Cultural Center, 1983); Antonio M. Stevens-Arroyo, ed., *Prophets Denied Honor: An Anthology on the Hispano Church in the United States* (Maryknoll, NY: Orbis, 1980).

8 One of the most important first books to come from the support of PARAL was Díaz-Stevens's *Oxcart Catholicism*. Ana María Díaz-Stevens, *Oxcart Catholicism on Fifth Avenue: The Impact of the Puerto Rican Migration upon the Archdiocese of New York* (Notre Dame, IN: University of Notre Dame Press, 1993); Carlos Vargas-Ramos and Anthony M. Stevens-Arroyo, eds., *Blessing la Política: The Latino Religious Experience and Political Engagement in the United States* (Santa Barbara, CA: Praeger, 2012).

9 Timothy Matovina, *Guadalupe and Her Faithful: Latino Catholics in San Antonio, from Colonial Origins to the Present* (Baltimore: Johns Hopkins University Press, 2005); Arlene M. Sánchez-Walsh, *Latino Pentecostal Identity: Evangelical Faith, Self, and Society* (New York: Columbia University Press, 2005); David Badillo, *Latinos and the New Immigrant Church* (Baltimore: Johns Hopkins University Press, 2006); Theresa Delgadillo, *Spiritual Mestizaje: Religion, Gender, Race, and Nation in Contemporary Chicana Narrative* (Durham: Duke University Press, 2011). For more on the histories and meanings of Latino religious politics, see Medina, *Las Hermanas*; Kristy Nabhan-Warren, *The Virgin of El Barrio: Marian Apparitions, Catholic Evangelizing, and Mexican American Activism* (New York: New York University Press, 2005); Roberto Treviño, *The Church in the Barrio: Mexican American Ethno-Catholicism in Houston* (Chapel Hill: University of North Carolina Press, 2006); Espinosa, Elizondo, and Miranda, *Latino Religions and Civic Activism*; Catherine Wilson, *The Politics of Latino Faith: Religion, Identity, and Urban Community* (New York: New York University Press, 2008); Elaine A. Peña, *Performing Piety: Making Space Sacred with the Virgin of Guadalupe* (Chapel Hill:

University of North Carolina Press, 2011); Felipe Hinojosa, *Latino Mennonites: Civil Rights, Faith, and Evangelical Culture* (Baltimore: Johns Hopkins University Press, 2014); Daniel Ramírez, *Migrating Faith: Pentecostalism in the United States and Mexico in the Twentieth Century* (Chapel Hill: University of North Carolina Press, 2015); Mario T. García, *Father Luis Olivares, a Biography: Faith Politics and the Origins of the Sanctuary Movement in Los Angeles* (Chapel Hill: University of North Carolina Press, 2018); Deborah E. Kanter, *Chicago Católico: Making Catholic Parishes Mexican* (Urbana: University of Illinois Press, 2020); and Felipe Hinojosa, *Apostles of Change: Latino Radical Politics, Church Occupations, and the Fight to Save the Barrio* (Austin: University of Texas Press, 2021).

10 For critiques of past treatments of Latino history and faith, see Sánchez-Walsh, *Latino Pentecostal Identity*, 1–47; Espinosa, Elizondo, and Miranda, "Introduction," 3–18; David Gutiérrez, "The New Turn in Chicano/Mexican History: Integrating Religious Belief and Practice," in *Catholics in the American Century: Recasting Narratives of US History*, ed. R. Scott Appleby and Kathleen Sprows Cummings (Ithaca: Cornell University Press, 2012), 109–34; and Felipe Hinojosa, "Sacred Spaces: Race, Resistance, and the Politics of Chicana/o and Latina/o Religious History," in *A Promising Problem: The New Chicana/o History*, ed. Carlos Kevin Blanton (Austin: University of Texas Press, 2016), 111–34.

11 This volume joins in a growing scholarship that has sought to recover the history of progressive religious movements in the United States and Latin America. R. Marie Griffith, *Moral Combat: How Sex Divided American Christians and Fractured American Politics* (New York: Basic Books, 2017); Christopher D. Cantwell, Heath W. Carter, and Janine Giordano Drake, eds., *The Pew and the Picket Line: Christianity and the American Working Class* (Urbana: University of Illinois Press, 2016); David Hollinger, *Protestants Abroad: How Missionaries Tried to Change the World but Changed America* (Princeton: Princeton University Press, 2019); David C. Kirkpatrick, *A Gospel for the Poor: Global Social Christianity and the Latin American Evangelical Left* (Philadelphia: University of Pennsylvania Press, 2019).

12 Margot Canaday, *The Straight State: Sexuality and Citizenship in Twentieth-Century America* (Princeton: Princeton University Press, 2009); James Sparrow, *Warfare State: World War II Americans and the Age of Big Government* (New York: Oxford University Press, 2013); Cybelle Fox, *Three Worlds of Relief: Race, Immigration, and the American Welfare State from the Progressive Era to the New Deal* (Princeton: Princeton University Press, 2012).

13 See, for instance, Mark Brilliant, *The Color of America Has Changed: How Racial Diversity Drove Civil Rights Reform in California, 1941–1978* (New York: Oxford University Press, 2010); James H. Merriwether, *Proudly We Can Be Africans: Black Americans and Africa, 1935–1961* (Chapel Hill: University of North Carolina Press, 2002); Penny M. Von Eschen, *Race against Empire: Black Americans and Anticolonialism, 1937–1957* (Ithaca: Cornell University Press, 1997); Justin Hart, *Empire of Ideas: The Origins of Public Diplomacy and the Transformation of US Foreign Policy* (New York: Oxford University Press, 2012).

14 Emilio Zamora, *Claiming Rights and Righting Wrongs in Texas: Mexican Workers and Job Politics during World War II* (College Station: Texas A&M University Press, 2008); Elizabeth R. Escobedo, *From Coveralls to Zoot Suits: The Lives of Mexican American Women on the World War II Home Front* (Chapel Hill: University of North Carolina Press, 2013); Luis Alvarez, *The Power of the Zoot: Youth Culture and Resistance during World War II* (Berkeley: University of California Press, 2008). See also David Kryder, *Divided Arsenal: Race and the American State during World War II* (New York: Cambridge University Press, 2000); Ruben Flores, *Backroads Pragmatists: Mexico's Melting Pot and Civil Rights in the United States* (Philadelphia: University of Pennsylvania Press, 2013); Zaragosa Vargas, *Labor Rights Are Civil Rights: Mexican American Workers in Twentieth-Century America* (Princeton: Princeton University Press, 2007); Clete Daniel, *Chicano Workers and the Politics of Fairness: The FEPC in the Southwest, 1941–1945* (Austin: University of Texas Press, 1991); Max Paul Freidman, *Nazis and Good Neighbors: The United States Campaign against the Germans of Latin America in World War II* (New York: Cambridge University Press, 2003); and Veronica Martínez-Matsuda, *Migrant Citizenship: Race, Rights, and Reform in the US Farm Labor Camp Program* (Philadelphia: University of Pennsylvania Press, 2020).

15 Kevin M. Schultz, *Tri-Faith America: How Catholics and Jews Held Postwar America to Its Protestant Promise* (New York: Oxford University Press, 2013). See also David Sehat, *The Myth of American Religious Freedom* (New York: Oxford University Press, 2011); Matthew Avery Sutton, *Double Crossed: The Missionaries Who Spied for the United States during the Second World War* (New York: Basic Books, 2019); Hollinger, *Protestants Abroad*; Patrick McNamara, *A Catholic Cold War: Edmund A. Walsh, SJ, and the Politics of American Anticommunism* (New York: Fordham University Press, 2005); and Tisa Wenger, *Religious Freedom: The Contested History of an American Ideal* (Chapel Hill: University of North Carolina Press, 2017).

16 Mary Ann Glendon, *A World Made Anew: Eleanor Roosevelt and the Universal Declaration of Human Rights* (New York: Random House, 2001); Samuel Moyn, *Christian Human Rights* (Philadelphia: University of Pennsylvania Press, 2015); Sarah Shortall and Daniel Steinmetz-Jenkins, *Christianity and Human Rights Reconsidered* (New York: Cambridge University Press, 2020); Carol Anderson, *Eyes off the Prize: The United Nations and the African American Struggle for Human Rights, 1944–1955* (New York: Cambridge University Press, 2013); Mark Phillip Bradley, *The World Reimagined: Americans and Human Rights in the Twentieth Century* (New York: Cambridge University Press, 2016).

17 These scholars have adeptly explored the internal logic of civil rights leaders' beliefs and actions, seamlessly incorporating religion into the history of protests against racial subjugation, voter suppression, and economic injustice. Their work asks historians to envision how faith informs action, never separating the belief of individuals from their motivations. David Chappell, *A Stone of Hope: Prophetic Religion and the Death of Jim Crow* (Chapel Hill: University of North Carolina

Press, 2005); Rosetta Ross, *Witnessing and Testifying: Black Women, Religion, and Civil Rights* (Minneapolis: Augsburg Fortress Press, 2003); Charles Marsh, *God's Long Summer: Stories of Faith and Civil Rights* (Princeton: Princeton University Press, 2008). See also Paul Harvey, *Freedom's Coming: Religious Culture and the Shaping of the South from the Civil War through the Civil Rights Era* (Chapel Hill: University of North Carolina Press, 2007).
18 Gloria Anzaldúa, interview with AnaLouise Keating, in *Interviews/Entrevistas*, ed. AnaLouise Keating (New York: Routledge, 2000), 96.
19 Padre Antonio José Martínez, "Padre Hidalgo," in Stevens-Arroyo, *Prophets Denied Honor*, 85; Pedro Albizu Campos, "Columbus Day Speech, Ponce, Puerto Rico, October 12, 1933," in Stevens-Arroyo, *Prophets Denied Honor*, 89.

PART I

Place and Politics

1

Catholics, the State, and Latino Advocacy in World War II

MAGGIE ELMORE

The envelope's arrival at 1317 F Street NW, a leisurely ten-minute walk from the White House, likely came as no surprise to the priest. It was, after all, addressed to him, even if its contents were not. That late fall afternoon, nearly a year after the United States had entered World War II, Monsignor John O'Grady sat down at his desk to find a letter from the Mexican ambassador to the United States to US officials overseeing the nation's integration of racial minority workers into the defense industry. Attached to the letter was a report detailing the Mexican embassy's request for the US federal government's aid in combatting employment discrimination against Mexican Americans. If the sender included instructions telling the priest what he should do with the information, they did not make it into the historical record. Regardless, O'Grady must have known what to do next. He submitted a memo of recommendations to the US State Department, urging the federal government to immediately address discrimination against Mexican Americans working in the shipyards of Houston, Texas. It helped that O'Grady was a close friend to assistant secretaries of state Howland Shaw and Adolf Berle Jr. When the anonymous letter writer contacted O'Grady, they tapped into a Catholic network that by the 1940s had closely allied itself with President Franklin Roosevelt's administration.[1]

In the years since O'Grady first received that cryptic request for assistance in 1942, the collaboration between US federal agencies and Catholic organizations has expanded exponentially, particularly in moments of national crisis. This partnership has proven lucrative for both the Catholic Church—and its various affiliated agencies—and the federal government. Consider for a moment the more than $1.4 billion in federal monies that flowed into Catholic Charities USA (an organization that O'Grady directed in the 1940s) from 2008 to 2010. During this two-year period, the United States battled its worst economic disaster since the Great Depression. Catholic organizations were at the forefront of this fight, providing a range of housing and anti-poverty programs to millions of Americans. On their own, federal agencies could not have met these needs.[2]

So how and why did Catholic-affiliated organizations become the recipients of so much federal money? Answering this question requires looking back to a different national crisis, a moment in time when the existential threat to democracy required politicians and religious leaders to become strange if not pragmatic bedfellows in their shared fight to defeat Nazism. World War II marked the beginning of a church-state collaboration between Catholic-affiliated organizations and the federal government that continues today.

To be clear, I am not arguing that Catholics merely influenced American politics. Certainly, they did and continue to do so. But what I am contending is that politics influence religion—particularly religious institutions—as much as religious actors influence politics. Rather than focusing solely on how religious actors shaped their political reality, we need also to consider how key political moments and state actors remake religious institutions. In the case of World War II, the US federal government's pressing needs to leverage a full war economy dictated how and when the US Catholic Church created a nationally coordinated ministry for Latino Catholics. By embracing the opportunity to work closely with the federal government, Catholic leaders created a model of advocacy on behalf of, but not alongside, Latinos. In short, Catholic advocacy during World War II and in the immediate postwar period was based not on an understanding of mutual power with Latino leaders, but on a partnership with the US federal government.

Two illuminating cases help to paint this picture further. The first involves the creation of the first sustained Catholic Latino ministry effort during World War II, the Bishops' Committee for the Spanish Speaking. The second relates to the collaboration between the Bishops' Committee and the US Department of Labor to enforce a bilateral labor program during the 1950s. In each of these instances, Catholic leaders were able to provide an essential service to the US federal government in the form of moral authority and community access.

* * *

In the 1940s the US federal government became interested in the status of Latinos in the Southwest for two key reasons: first, because of their potential contributions to the labor force, and second, because of the strategic diplomatic position they held in hemispheric politics.[3] Race relations in the US Southwest threatened to create a diplomatic crisis on the eve of World War II. Reports of violence against Mexicans and Mexican Americans in the US Southwest quickly overshadowed Roosevelt's pledge to hemispheric collaboration. Early in his presidency, FDR had committed the United States to a course of non-intervention in Latin America, and later to an understanding of collaboration, to prevent the specter of fascism from creeping into the Western Hemisphere. Roosevelt called his foreign policy the Good Neighbor Policy. The Good Neighbor Policy and the need for hemispheric solidarity in the face of Nazism drove a new attention to domestic race relations. In the eyes of the US federal government, integrating Latinos, especially Mexicans and Mexican Americans, into the war economy became a matter of providing employment and training opportunities, as well as an issue of national and hemispheric security.[4]

The Good Neighbor Policy's diplomatic success depended at least in part on the FDR administration's ability to persuade Latin American countries that the United States would work to protect the civil rights of Mexicans and Mexican Americans already residing within US borders.[5] The US record on race relations in the Southwest, however, was less than reassuring. Mexican consuls throughout the US West and Southwest regularly received reports of violence and employment discrimination against Mexicans and Mexican Americans and petitioned local and federal officials to investigate these claims, often to no avail. Beginning in the 1940s, Roosevelt used the Office of the Coordinator of Inter-American Affairs to salvage the hemorrhaging Good Neighbor Policy.[6]

Roosevelt's use of the Office of the Coordinator to address domestic concerns of international importance brought a dramatic new attention to Latino communities in the US Southwest. Until World War II, the US federal government had largely ignored Latino community concerns.

That changed during World War II, when issues such as employment discrimination and racial violence suddenly had national security and diplomatic consequences. One reason that Mexican Americans had a difficult time directing federal resources prior to World War II stemmed from the fact that Mexican Americans lacked a national organization powerful enough to pressure the federal government into action. While African Americans could rely on multiple national organizations, including the National Association for the Advancement of Colored People (NAACP), the Brotherhood of Sleeping Car Porters, and the National Negro Congress, Mexican Americans relied primarily on regional organizations, such as the League of United Latin American Citizens (LULAC), and other community stakeholders such as the Mexican consulate. LULAC, the leading Mexican American civil rights organization of its day, enjoyed prominence in Texas and New Mexico, but during World War II, its reach did not expand much beyond these two states. More importantly, the federal government recognized leaders of organizations such as the NAACP as the spokespersons for African Americans but did not always grant LULAC the same recognition. The federal government viewed LULAC as a nascent organization, one with the potential to become a national organization akin to the NAACP. Instead of looking to civil rights organizations, the federal government relied on a variety of stakeholders, including the Catholic Church, to provide information about Latino communities in the US Southwest.[7]

In the early 1940s the emerging alliance between the US federal government and Catholic leadership was not a foregone conclusion, but it would have hardly come as a surprise to the closest observers of Washington's backroom politics. In the 1940s many Americans still regarded Catholics with a great deal of suspicion and mistrust, though Roosevelt did not. The New Deal coalition that elected him president in 1932, and again in 1936 and 1940, relied on Catholic support. Catholic intellectuals' defense of the New Deal had won Roosevelt's open admiration. Indeed, Catholic clergymen received appointments at all levels in the New Deal administration. Members of Roosevelt's administration regularly met with top Catholic leaders, particularly on matters related to Latin America and Mexico.

For their part, Catholic leaders had sought a warmer relationship with federal officials in Washington since the 1910s, when a loose coalition of

Catholic-affiliated charity organizations first consolidated itself into the National Conference of Catholic Charities. During World War I, Catholic leaders further consolidated these efforts when the National Catholic War Council channeled virtually all political activities of the US Catholic Church into a single bureaucratic organization. In the years following World War I, the hierarchy remade the war council into the National Catholic Welfare Conference (NCWC). The NCWC channeled and coordinated the US Catholic Church's political and financial resources. By the early 1940s, the NCWC believed that it had an important role to play in fighting wartime racial discrimination.[8]

Enforcing the federal government's rhetoric of equality was a tall order. Mexicans and Mexican Americans occupied an ambiguous place in the World War II racial landscape. Legally white, or at least not classified as "colored" by most state and federal laws, Mexicans and Mexican Americans found that their racial status fluctuated depending on the time and place. Technically, they voted in white Democratic primaries. At times, their children attended white schools (though usually of a far lesser quality than those of their Euro-American neighbors). This liminal white status did not hold in all places. Communities across the Southwest regularly practiced *de facto* forms of segregation and denied Mexicans and Mexican Americans access to public places. Signs reading "No Mexicans, Whites Only" decorated storefronts. Hospitals and prisons held separate visiting days for "coloreds and Mexicans." Employers in wartime industries such as shipbuilding or mining often refused to hire Mexicans and Mexican Americans or offered them significantly lower wages than those of their white counterparts. Consequently, public accommodations and equal employment opportunities anchored Mexicans' and Mexican Americans' wartime campaign for greater equality.[9]

To demonstrate the nation's commitment to racial equality, the FDR administration commissioned numerous studies on the status of Latinos in the Southwest.[10] From these initial reports, federal investigators learned that Mexicans and Mexican Americans across the region shared a set of overlapping problems. One investigator described the population as the nation's "most submerged class," a population set apart by poor wages, slums, disease, poverty, delinquency, and other forms of economic and social discrimination. Most disconcertingly to investigators, Mexican Americans also lacked a highly visible national organization, similar to the NAACP for African Americans, that could provide national representation. The closest relative to a national organization appeared to be the Catholic Church.[11]

If in the eyes of the federal government the Mexican-descent communities across the Southwest were connected through a common set of problems, rather than a racial or ethnic identity, then as federal investigators revealed, many were also connected by their shared affiliation with the Catholic Church.[12] The church's position, one federal investigator noted, was "strengthened further because it is the only group which is successful in furnishing education and social services to the Spanish-speaking people." Federal investigators recommend strengthening relations with Catholic leaders in order to develop a leadership program for Mexican Americans.[13]

Catholic leaders were keen to play a role in any federal effort to develop a leadership program for Mexican Americans. When assistant secretary of state Adolf Berle shared news of the proposed leadership program, O'Grady saw an opportunity to secure a piece of the pie for the NCWC. "For some time past there has been a considerable amount of talk about the desirability of developing a national organization of Spanish-Americans," O'Grady explained to San Antonio archbishop Robert Lucey. The Office of the Coordinator of Inter-American Affairs (OCIAA), O'Grady knew, funded various community programs aimed at intercultural dialogue. O'Grady believed that the OCIAA's interest in developing a Mexican American leadership program would provide the NCWC for the opportunity to create a federally funded Catholic program. "A good deal can be done in steering this program if we proceed carefully," O'Grady noted.[14]

In February 1943 representatives of the OCIAA requested a meeting with the NCWC. They met with William Montavon, who served as a personal advisor to Nelson Rockefeller, coordinator of inter-American affairs, as well as the director of the NCWC's legal department. Meeting with Montavon, then, would have been seen as a normal part of the OCIAA's administrative functions. At the time, NCWC leadership feared being shut out of program development in the Southwest. They need not have worried. During their visit to NCWC headquarters, OCIAA representatives promised to ask Rockefeller for a list of bishops and archbishops with whom they might meet during an upcoming trip to the Southwest. Rockefeller directed field agent Victor Borella to head to the Southwest and investigate conditions among Spanish-speaking Americans.[15]

The purpose of Borella's trip would be to identify which local agencies might aid in the development of a federally sponsored social service program. Borella had already worked closely in Los Angeles with Catholic officials and civil rights leader Manuel Ruiz Jr. on the Latin American Youth Committee and anticipated further fruitful collaborations with other Catholic representatives. He hoped to use existing Catholic-affiliated organizations in the creation of educational and community health programs in cities across the Southwest. Montavon provided Victor Borella with a letter of introduction to Archbishop Robert Lucey.[16]

When Borella returned to Washington, OCIAA representatives and NCWC leaders met to discuss implementing a social service program in key sites across the Southwest. Just before the scheduled meeting, the archbishop of Los Angeles, wrote to the OCIAA telling the office that field representatives in Los Angeles refused to cooperate with Catholic leaders. The NCWC, already aware of the complaint, raised the issue of OCIAA-Catholic cooperation during the meeting. The OCIAA assured the Los Angeles archbishop and the NCWC that he would personally instruct the office's representative in Los Angeles to cooperate with Catholic leadership in Los Angeles. The OCIAA also maintained that Catholic cooperation was essential for integrating Mexicans and Mexican Americans into "the national body of the United States" and avoiding any disruption in defense production.[17] The men also considered the possibility of a conference to be held in a southwestern city for the purposes of discussing the economic and sociological questions concerning Mexicans and Mexican Americans. The conference would eventually give birth to the Catholic Church's first national effort to provide greater social services and leadership opportunities for the population, the Bishops' Committee for the Spanish Speaking.

The National Catholic Welfare Conference relished the idea of a conference bringing together leaders in community action from areas across the Southwest, which it saw as an opportunity to address religious education and social action. The NCWC's general secretary nominated Father Raymond McGowan as a point person on the conference. In addition to his involvement with the Catholic labor movement, McGowan also directed the NCWC's social action department. A former student of New Deal intellectual John Ryan, McGowan had a special interest in both the labor movement and the status of Mexicans and Mexican Americans. He contacted his former seminary chum, San Antonio archbishop Robert Lucey, and the two men devised a plan. Within just three weeks of the meeting between OCIAA and NCWC representatives, McGowan had drafted a proposal for the OCIAA, created a four-day conference schedule, and secured a location for the conference.[18]

The OCIAA had all but guaranteed some level of funding for the conference. McGowan proposed an event that would bring together "the chief people in the Southwest working to help" the Mexican-descent population. The NCWC provided facilities under the auspices of the San Antonio Archdiocese. McGowan described the conference as one in which the leaders in the Southwest had come together to learn which agencies were conducting work among the population across the region. In other words, the NCWC proposed what it believed to be the first region-wide meeting of social workers, community leaders, youth leaders, labor organizers, economists, sociologists, business leaders, religious leaders, educators, and government administrators, working to integrate Mexican and Mexican American workers into the war program and to solve problems of economic and social inequality.[19] Borella worked closely with McGowan to develop a grant proposal that would pass OCIAA funding muster. In the end, the NCWC requested $7,500 from the OCIAA to cover the cost of publications, travel, and guest speakers. The OCIAA approved the funding request and the NCWC sent invitations to approximately forty-five delegates for a meeting to be held in the summer of 1943.

Catholic leaders like McGowan, O'Grady, and Montavon saw the upcoming seminar as a victory in securing federal funding in pursuit of Catholic aims. The federal government, however, agreed to sponsor the four-day conference in order to address its own strategic initiatives. These aims were threefold and included "integrating Spanish speaking American labor more effectively into the war program," addressing racial tensions and the "causes and conditions which cause friction or prevent unity among English speaking and Spanish speaking Americans," and the creation of a long-term program to address the structural causes of inequality.[20]

On an early summer morning in 1943, San Antonio archbishop Robert Lucey's voice rang out before a small crowd. "Can we keep our self-respect if we demand that the colored American fight for freedom in Africa and deny him freedom at home? Can we make the western hemisphere a bulwark of liberty and law while we maim and mangle our Mexican youth in the streets of our cities?" Lucey demanded. "Can we," he continued, "the greatest nation on earth, assume the moral leadership of the world when race riots and murder, political crimes and economic injustices disgrace the very name of America?" Often remembered by friends and detractors as a quiet man who nevertheless liked to hear himself talk, Lucey was not a likable man. His contemporaries described him as "cold," "pompous," and "self-righteous," but he knew how to stir a crowd. The conference at which he spoke received billing from local media and national Catholic press outlets. Excerpts of Lucey's speech, "Are We Good Neighbors?," appeared in print form across the nation, stirring religious and secular audiences alike. Among the attendees at the July 1943 conference were numerous Catholic leaders, representatives from various US federal agencies, and newly appointed Fair Employment Practice Committee chairman Monsignor Francis Haas.[21]

The event was something of a marvel for its time, hosted by the Catholic Church and funded by the Office of the Coordinator of Inter-American Affairs, a federal agency charged with promoting cooperation across the Americas during World War II.[22] The group that Lucey addressed at the July 1943 Conference on Spanish-Speaking People of the Southwest had gathered under the auspices of the Catholic Church in San Antonio to discuss the problems preventing Mexicans and Mexican Americans from fully participating in the war effort. Among the attendees were numerous Catholic leaders, Mexican American civil rights activists, and representatives from the federal government. The following year, the NCWC organized a second seminar. Like the first meeting, this second meeting received funding from the OCIAA.[23] The OCIAA conferences solidified the role of Catholic-affiliated agencies as conduits of federal resources.

In response to the inter-American seminars, the NCWC created a standing national committee comprised of bishops in the southwestern United States. The new committee, the Bishops' Committee for the

Spanish-Speaking (BCSS), represented the first time the US Catholic Church had attempted to coordinate a national response to the needs of its Latino members. Led by Archbishop Lucey, the Bishops' Committee guided the NCWC's efforts among the population and spoke for the conference on matters of public interest concerning Spanish-speaking Americans.

Though the committee took cues from Mexican American leaders and labor organizers, the BCSS remained under Archbishop Lucey's directorship throughout its existence. The BCSS encouraged local priests to advocate for fair wages and employment practices by reaching out to local divisions of the Farm Security Administration and the Fair Employment Practice Committee. Lucey believed that economic and social improvement depended heavily upon worker organization. He insisted that "unions [are] needed for farm workers" and the "law should be extended to protect [the] organization of farm workers."[24] Consequently, the goal of extending economic equality to domestic migratory farm labor through unionism drove half of the BCSS's agenda. The Bracero Program drove the second half.

First enacted as a wartime program in 1942, the bilateral labor agreement between the United States and Mexico eventually morphed into one of the largest and longest-running imported labor programs in US history. From 1942 until the program's close in 1964, the US government issued between 4.6 and 5.2 billion labor contracts. The Bracero Program fundamentally reshaped the fabrics of US and Mexican society. Families in both countries experienced relocation and dislocation, as millions of workers joined the migrant labor stream.[25]

Catholics, particularly those in the agricultural meccas of central California and Texas, championed the program, but the NCWC's position was more complicated. Many Catholics and non-Catholics alike viewed the NCWC's tepid resistance as tacit support. But numerous Catholic leaders, including Archbishop Lucey, were determined to take a more forceful stand. Lucey hoped to use the BCSS to lobby for an end to the Bracero Program. Echoing the position of labor unions and Mexican American civic organizations, the BCSS argued that the presence of braceros undermined the political advancement and economic security of Mexican Americans. Lucey hoped that the BCSS would be able to bring the New Deal to Mexican Americans in the Southwest by improving their social and economic conditions through mission work and the expansion of collective bargaining rights to agricultural workers, a position that he maintained throughout the 1940s and 1950s.[26]

Lucey's commitment to labor unionism and his work with the federal government during the 1940s would win him a seat on President Truman's Commission on Migratory Labor in 1950.[27] Lucey's service on the President's Commission on Migratory Labor expanded church-state coordination with regard to the Bracero Program. As a leading figure in a labor-liberal coalition, which actively sought to root out communism even as it attempted to stabilize the economic position of Mexican American farm laborers, Archbishop Lucey cemented the status of the BCSS and the National Catholic Welfare Conference as leading nongovernmental migrant labor advocacy groups. Moreover, the commission's final report fundamentally shaped the programs and advocacy of leading Catholic agencies throughout the remainder of the Bracero Program. Following Lucey's service on the commission, church-state cooperation entered a new chapter as both the Department of Labor and the BCSS began to rely on one another to regulate the Bracero Program.[28]

* * *

The nomination of James Mitchell to secretary of labor in 1953 offered Catholics a new opportunity to collaborate, especially in areas regarding migrants and farmworkers. Born in New Jersey in 1900, Mitchell was raised in a Catholic household and educated in parish schools. He began his career as a grocer and industrial worker. In 1942 Mitchell started working in labor relations and in 1953 received a nomination as secretary of labor. Although his record on industrial labor relations was somewhat mixed, Mitchell was an active supporter of domestic migrant laborers. Known as the "moral conscience" of the Eisenhower administration, Mitchell's commitment to domestic workers (agricultural workers who were either US citizens or long-term residents of the United States) was nothing short of a personal, moral obligation. Mitchell believed that by gradually stabilizing wages and employment for domestic workers, he might relieve growers of their dependency on foreign labor.[29]

These efforts pleased neither labor organizers nor growers. Labor leaders insisted that the Labor Department, from the secretary himself down to its regional representatives, belonged to the growers. Growers held that Mitchell bent under the influence of organized labor and mandated an unconstitutional minimum wage. And there was some evidence for each of these claims. Although he attempted to set a minimum wage for agricultural workers, the labor secretary lacked the legal authority to do so. At the same time, the Department of Labor regularly failed to enforce the terms of the bilateral agreement governing the Bracero Program. Regional United States Employment Services representatives, employees technically under Mitchell's supervision, often refused to recognize strike conditions, ignored the use of braceros and undocumented workers as strikebreakers, and certified labor shortages where none existed.[30]

The practice of ignoring the secretary of labor's orders at the regional level frustrated labor leaders, who watched helplessly as union jobs evaporated. National Agricultural Workers Union organizer and BCSS ally Ernesto Galarza noted one such instance in 1954. "The CIO Fruit and Vegetable Workers Union 78 which based contracts in the packing shed of both Arizona and California has lost over 2,500 jobs in the Imperial Valley to Mexican nationals who perform the work formerly done in the sheds directly in the fields. AF of L Unions of processing workers are similarly affected," Galarza complained to fellow union leader H. L. Mitchell (no relation to the secretary).[31] To Galarza, the Labor Department was directly responsible for the displacement of the Local 78 workers, and he wasted no time in clarifying his position.

Though many of his colleagues hesitated to attack the Department of Labor directly, Galarza had no such qualms. Galarza held the Labor Department, which he considered "less an advocate of workers than a sensitive barometer of the powerful forces that focus in the national capital," at least partially responsible for labor's inability to secure economic rights for workers.[32] One expression of the Labor Department's moral failings in Galarza's mind was its decision "to leave to growers the determination of housing policy, public or private. Denied a place to live, domestic farm laborers discover yet again that their powerlessness economically [is] matched by their powerlessness politically."[33] If the mandate of the Department of Labor was to "oversee labor-management relations and to provide an institutional arena in which the interests of American workers [could] be voiced, if not always realized," then, according to Galarza, it had failed on both counts.[34]

Growers had a different opinion. Even before Congress first enacted the Bracero Program in 1942, they had clamored for Mexican labor. Growers cast Mexican farmworkers as biologically suited for agricultural labor. Charles Teague, a citrus and walnut grower from California, for instance, described his laborers as "naturally adapted to agricultural work, particularly in the handling of fruits and vegetables.... Many of them have a natural skill in the handling of tools." Teague and other growers saw themselves as defenders of American democracy and providers of an essential service to the American public. "The American farmer is engaged in producing the foods and fibres which are absolutely essential to life," Teague said. "Any delays in production or harvesting are not merely an economic loss to the farmer—they are a loss of essentials to the consuming public."[35] Other growers insisted that Galarza and his colleagues had it backwards. The presence of Mexican nationals did not decrease wages for domestic workers, defenders of the Bracero Program argued. Instead, the influx of foreign workers led to wage increases. In California, one grower, William Tolbert, testified that "the wage rate has increased 189 percent" since 1943.[36]

Tasked with protecting domestic farmworkers while securing the interests of their employers, the Department of Labor found itself in an impossible situation. Whenever the department sought to intervene on behalf of domestic workers by way of wage increases or by cracking down on grower abuses of the contract labor system, it faced the unenviable task of staring down growers and their congressional defenders in budget hearings.[37] To get to the heart of the matter, secretary of labor James Mitchell created an elaborate network of farm labor advocates charged with monitoring the Bracero Program and reporting violations to local and regional Department of Labor offices.[38]

Part of Mitchell's decision to rely on voluntary organizations like the Bishops' Committee stemmed from his own limited political realities. In 1955 Congress slashed funding for the Department of Labor's enforcement program, resulting in a significant reduction in the number of enforcement officers. In light of the staff shortage, the Department of Labor began to rely upon voluntary organizations, particularly Catholic clergy represented by the Bishops' Committee for the Spanish-Speaking, to report violations of housing, wages, and substandard living standards.[39]

In the spring of 1956, for instance, regional Labor Department director Ed McDonald instructed farm placement representative W. B. McFarland to meet with representatives of the BCSS. During the meeting, McFarland informed the BCSS that "due to our limited staff, of field men we [can] not check every employer regularly and that in the event the Pastors in the area should receive any information regarding immoral and illegal activities they should immediately notify the appropriate Regional Office." McFarland promised that following such reports, "an investigation would be authorized, completed and necessary action taken."[40] In exchange for Catholic cooperation, McFarland promised that regional Labor Department offices would assist in the church's effort to provide spiritual services for braceros.

In addition to striking a deal with the BCSS, McFarland furnished the organization with a directory of regional offices and a copy of the most recent contract offered to braceros so that priests might be better aware of potential contract violations. Father R. A. Goddard of Stamford, Texas, noticed such violations during his weekly visit to labor camps in his district of Northwest Texas. October 1957 was a bitterly cold month in North Texas, with nightly temperatures dropping below freezing. Concerned about the poor conditions at the camp, Goddard contacted the BCSS. "The migrants are living in inhumane conditions," Goddard wrote. "It would take pages to describe the lack of sanitation, overcrowding, etc., but what they complain mostly about is cold. . . . Some talk of leaving but they did not make any money up to now and the situation in Mexico is so poor. . . . I read their contract. It is a revolting joke."[41] The BCSS quickly forwarded Goddard's report to local Labor Department representatives and instructed Goddard to file a notice of a contract violation with the same office. When the Labor Department area supervisor visited the camps in question, he too noted the violations and ordered the labor camps' directors to provide sufficient heating facilities and additional blankets or risk losing their contracts.[42]

Coordinating with the BCSS provided concrete benefits for the understaffed Labor Department regional offices in other ways as well. As part of his plan to alleviate periods of unemployment among domestic farmworkers, Secretary Mitchell created a centralized network that would communicate available jobs to job seekers early in the harvest season. In July 1956, Texas employment commissioner James Strauss traveled throughout the central and southeastern regions of Texas, introducing himself to various bishops and explaining the function of the Texas Employment Commission.[43] Strauss intended for priests to convey the purpose of the Texas Employment Commission to migrant laborers. Strauss provided the BCSS with a list of six hundred crew leaders, and the BCSS regional office wrote a letter to each crew leader "pointing out their obligations to the migrants that they transport to different areas to work in the beet fields and to harvest other crops."[44]

One result of the coordination between the Texas Employment Commission and the BCSS was that the commission received fewer complaints from workers than ever before. The BCSS considered the decline in migrants' complaints to the Texas Employment Commission to be the result of its efforts to "reach migrants through their crew leaders." In a series of interviews conducted by Strauss and other representatives, crew bosses overwhelmingly related that their work plans depended directly on the information they received from local priests and during Sunday mass.

The collaboration between the state employment commission office and the Catholic Church reached well beyond Texas. One crew leader, Vicente Chavarria, advised that he did not leave the state with his crew unless he had received a referral from the employment commission office. Chavarria also reported that the "Catholic Churches where we attend Sunday Mass in Laredo and other places of the United States . . . strongly emphasize for us to use the services of the Employment Offices." Another crew leader, Rafael Cantu, recalled that his crew planned their seasonal work all the way to Wisconsin through the state employment commission and that he learned of the state employment commission from his local priest during Sunday mass.[45]

* * *

Since the 1950s, church-state collaboration between various Catholic organizations and the branches of the federal government have continued. But in 2020 the partnership took on a new tone. Faced with the possibility of closing hundreds of Catholic-affiliated organizations in the early months of the COVID-19 pandemic, US Catholic bishops turned to the federal government for financial help. In late spring 2020, the

US Catholic Church received an estimated $1.4 to $3.5 billion in funding from the Paycheck Protection Program, a $659 billion program. The Paycheck Protection Program was created to counteract the economic devastation wrought by the COVID-19 pandemic, by providing funding to small businesses and nonprofit organizations. Pundits and analysts pointed to behind-the-scenes negotiations between President Trump and various Catholic leaders, such as Cardinal Timothy Dolan, as the reason for the church's PPP funding. The truth, however, is that the distribution of federal monies to Catholic agencies is hardly a new practice. Catholic agencies have long partnered with the federal government to carry out their own strategic goals, often with profound implications for Latino communities.[46]

This history is but one short chapter in the story of US Latino religious politics. The diversity of Latino communities and their politics requires us to consider the national as well as the local—to look from the outside in as much as from the inside out—if we are to understand religious politics in all their complexity. Relationships of power, often cloaked in the language of bureaucracy, offer a window into how institutions confront political realities that imperil their moral purpose. From this vantage, we can also imagine the possibilities that Robert Lucey or Ernesto Galarza saw when they sought to harness the power of the church and the state to right a world that seemed to them to have turned upside down. Even in their failures, they believed that God was on their side. Of course, this is not the whole story. But it can help us to make sense of the strategic and seemingly contradictory choices that community and national leaders sometimes make in the name of creating a more equitable and just society, and how religion can drive that charge.

NOTES

1 Will Alexander to John O'Grady, December 7, 1942; "Report from Los Angeles," November 25, 1942; John O'Grady to G. Howland Shaw, October 12, 1942; John O'Grady, "A More Considered Policy in the Employment of Mexicans in Industry in Houston Area"; Francisco Castillo Najera to Will Alexander, October 2, 1942; Adolfo Domínguez, "Memorandum on Racial Discrimination: Houston, Texas," all in Box 37, Folder 10, Catholic Charities of the United States of America Records, American Catholic Research Center and University Archives, Catholic University of America, Washington, DC (hereafter CCUSA).

2 Tom Gallagher, "Following the Money from the White House," *National Catholic Reporter*, March 22, 2013, www.ncronline.org.
3 During the 1940s and 1950s, the US federal government used a variety of terms to describe Latina/os, including but not limited to "Spanish-speaking," "Latin American," "Mexican," "Americans of Mexican descent," and "people of Latin descent." I use the terms "Mexican American" to denote US citizens of Mexican descent; "Mexican" to denote citizens of Mexico (regardless of residency); and "Latino" as a broad term to describe the larger pan-ethnic and pan-racial population who reside in the contemporary United States, but whose heritage includes familial roots in South America, Latin America, parts of North America, and/or the Caribbean, and who share an ethno-linguistic pre-Columbian ancestry.
4 See, for instance, James H. Merriwether, *Proudly We Can Be Africans: Black Americans and Africa, 1935–1961* (Chapel Hill: University of North Carolina Press, 2002); Penny M. Von Eschen, *Race against Empire: Black Americans and Anticolonialism, 1937–1957* (Ithaca: Cornell University Press, 1997); Justin Hart, *Empire of Ideas: The Origins of Public Diplomacy and the Transformation of US Foreign Policy* (New York: Oxford University Press, 2012); Emilio Zamora, *Claiming Rights and Righting Wrongs in Texas: Mexican Workers and Job Politics during World War II* (College Station: Texas A&M University Press, 2009); Thomas Borstelmann, *The Cold War and the Color Line: American Race Relations in the Global Arena* (Cambridge: Harvard University Press, 2001); Mary L. Dudziak, *Cold War Civil Rights: Race and the Image of American Democracy* (Princeton: Princeton University Press, 2001); Mark Brilliant, *The Color of America Has Changed: How Racial Diversity Shaped Civil Rights Reform in California, 1941–1978* (New York: Oxford University Press, 2010); David Gutiérrez, *Walls and Mirrors: Mexican Americans, Mexican Immigrants, and the Politics of Ethnicity* (Berkeley: University of California Press, 1995).
5 A portion of this section previously appeared in Maggie J. Elmore, "Fighting for Hemispheric Solidarity: The National Catholic Welfare Conference and the Quest to Secure Mexican American Employment Rights during World War II," *US Catholic Historian* 35, no. 2 (Spring 2017): 125–49.
6 David J. Saposs, "Report on Rapid Survey of Resident Latin American Problems and Recommended Program," Box 339, Additional Hearing Materials, RG 228, Fair Employment Practice Committee, National Archives, College Park, MD (hereafter FEPC); "Spanish-Americans in the Southwest and the War Effort," August 18, 1942, Special Collections Library, University of Wisconsin, Milwaukee; "Report on the Spanish-Speaking Peoples in the Southwest, Field Survey March 14 to April 7, 1942," Box 371, Folder: Mexican Study, RG 228, FEPC; "Program for Cooperation with Spanish-Speaking Minorities in the United States: Progress Report," Office of the Coordinator of Inter-American Affairs, Division of Inter-American Activities in the United States, July 1, 1942 (report is labeled July 1, 1942, but all indications are that the report was released July 1, 1943), Box 35, Folder 9, United States Conference of Catholic Bishops General Counsel/

Legal Department, American Catholic Research Center and University Archives, Catholic University of America, Washington, DC (hereafter Legal Department Papers).

7   For an account of LULAC's limitations, see Cynthia Orozco, *No Mexicans, Women, or Dogs Allowed: The Rise of the Mexican American Civil Rights Movement* (Austin: University of Texas Press, 2009).

8   Kevin Schultz, *Tri-Faith America: How Catholics and Jews Held Postwar America to Its Protestant Promise* (New York: Oxford University Press, 2013).

9   Alice Kahn to Marjorie Lawson, "Summary of Various Articles Dealing with Spanish-Speaking People in the Southwest," September 23, 1942; Alice Kahn to Marjorie Lawson, "Summary of Spanish-Americans in the Southwest" (Report #25, OWI) and "The War Effort and War Attitudes of Spanish-speaking people in the Southwest" (Special Report #19, OWI); Alice Kahn to John A. Davis, "Summary of an Evaluation of Media for Reaching the Spanish-Americans of the Southwest" (Report #23A, OWI), September 23, 1943; unsigned memo to Malcolm Ross, Mr. Johnson, Mr. Bourne, John Davis, and Barbara Wright, December 8, 1943, all in Box 371, Folder: Mexican Study, RG 228, FEPC.

10 Clete Daniel, *Chicano Workers and the Politics of Fairness* (Austin: University of Texas Press, 1991), 21; Matthew Gritter, *Mexican Inclusion: The Origins of Anti-Discrimination Policy in Texas and the Southwest* (College Station: Texas A&M University Press, 2012), 25; Zamora, *Claiming Rights and Righting Wrongs*, 66; Neil Foley, *Mexicans in the Making of America* (Cambridge: Harvard University Press, 2014), 69; Justin Hart, "Making Democracy Safe for the World: Race, Propaganda, and the Transformation of US Foreign Policy during World War II," *Pacific Historical Review* 73, no. 1 (February 2004): 60.

11 Saposs, "Report on Rapid Survey"; "Spanish-Americans in the Southwest"; "Report on the Spanish-Speaking Peoples."

12 "Program for Cooperation."

13 Kahn to Lawson, "Summary of Spanish-Americans" and "War Effort."

14 John O'Grady to Robert Lucey, February 11, 1942, Box 37, Folder 11, CCUSA.

15 William Montavon to Michael Ready, February 3, 1943, Box 35, Folder 9, Legal Department Papers.

16 Montavon to Ready, February 3, 1943; Ignacio L. Lopez to Joseph T. McGuckin, July 7, 1943, Carton 4, Folder: Mexican Division, Alan Cranston Papers, BANC MSS 88/214 c, Bancroft Library, University of California, Berkeley; William Montavon to Carmen Tranchese, February 26, 1943; Nelson Rockefeller to William Montavon, March 23, 1943, Box 35, Folder 9, Legal Department Papers.

17 Walter Prendergast to Joseph McGucken, March 24, 1943, Box 90, Folder 17, Records of the Office of the General Secretary, American Catholic History Research Center and University Archives, Catholic University of America, Washington, DC (hereafter OGS Papers).

18 Raymond McGowan to Michael Ready, April 19, 1943; Michael Ready to Raymond McGowan, April 13, 1943; Michael Ready to Walter Prendergast, April 13, 1943;

Walter Prendergast to Michael Ready, March 25, 1943, Box 90, Folder 17, OGS Papers.
19 "Proposal of a Conference on Spanish-Americans in the Southwest," April 28, 1943, Box 90, Folder 17, OGS Papers.
20 Percy L. Douglas to Michael J. Ready, June 21, 1943, Box 90, Folder 17, OGS Papers.
21 Robert Lucey, "Are We Good Neighbors? Opening Address of His Excellency, the Most Reverend Robert E. Lucey, STD, Archbishop of San Antonio, the Conference on Spanish-Speaking People of the Southwest," Incarnate Word College, San Antonio, TX, July 20, 1943, Box 90, Folder 17, OGS Papers; Carey McWilliams, *North from Mexico: The Spanish Speaking People of the United States*, rev. ed. (New York: Praeger, 1990), 247.
22 Howard Carroll to Eugene Butler, September 13, 1943, Box 35, Folder 9, Legal Department Papers.
23 Social Action Department, National Catholic Welfare Conference, *The Spanish Speaking of the Southwest and West: Second Report* (Washington, DC: National Catholic Welfare Conference, 1944), 3.
24 "Recommendations of the Seminars on Spanish Speaking People, 1945"; "Actas de la junta de la mesa directive del comité episcopal a para los fieles de habla española que se celebro en El Paso, Texas, el 21 de Febrero, 1945," Robert Emmet Lucey Papers, University of Notre Dame Archives (UNDA), Notre Dame, IN (hereafter Lucey Papers).
25 For a discussion on the Bracero Program, as well as its impact on braceros and lasting impact on US and Mexican society, see Lori Flores, *Grounds for Dreaming: Mexican Americans, Mexican Immigrants, and the California Farmworker Movement* (New Haven: Yale University Press, 2016); Mioslava Chávez-García, *Migrant Longing: Letter Writing across the US-Mexico Borderlands* (Chapel Hill: University of North Carolina Press, 2018); Mireya Loza, *Defiant Braceros: How Migrant Workers Fought for Racial, Sexual, and Political Freedom* (Chapel Hill: University of North Carolina Press, 2016); Deborah Cohen, *Braceros: Migrant Citizens and Transnational Subjects in the Postwar United States and Mexico* (Chapel Hill: University of North Carolina Press, 2011); Ana Raquel Minian, *Undocumented Lives: The Untold Story of Mexican Migration* (Cambridge: Harvard University Press, 2018).
26 Robert Lucey to John Wagner, October 2, 1958, Box 16, Folder 5, Lucey Papers.
27 President Harry Truman created the President's Commission on Migratory Labor in 1949. He hoped that a thorough investigation of the Bracero Program would allow for the program's elimination. Lucey was one of five commissioners, and the only clergyman. The President's Commission on Migratory Labor met during the summer and fall of 1950. After gathering thirty volumes of testimony from twelve public hearings held across the country, the commission released a 188-page report, full of recommendations that included terminating the Bracero Program, organizing farm labor, criminalizing the hiring of undocumented workers, and

establishing a permanent committee staffed by the secretaries of labor and agriculture to advise the president on matters related to migratory labor.

28 Peter Kirstein, "Anglo over Bracero: A History of the Mexican Worker in the United States, from Roosevelt to Nixon" (PhD diss., Saint Louis University, 1973), 173; Jim Norris, *North for the Harvest: Mexican Workers, the Bracero Program, and the Sugar Beet Industry* (St. Paul: Minnesota Historical Society Press, 2009), 88; "The New Dealing Archbishop," *Time*, April 7, 1941, 73–74; Harry S. Truman, "Executive Order 10129—Establishing the President's Commission on Migratory Labor," June 3, 1950, Box 39, Folder: Migratory Labor Committee 1949, NC-58, Entry 30, Office of the Secretary, Subject File of Secretary Maurice J. Tobin, 1949–52, RG 174, General Records of the Department of Labor, National Archives, College Park, MD.

29 Andrew J. Hazelton, "Farmworker Advocacy through Guestworker Policy: Secretary of Labor James P. Mitchell and the Bracero Program," *Journal of Policy History* 29, no. 3 (2017): 431–61.

30 Hazelton, "Farmworker Advocacy."

31 Ernesto Galarza to H. L. Mitchell, May 30, 1954, Reel 38, Southern Tenant Farmers' Union Records #3472, Southern Historical Collection, Wilson Library, University of North Carolina at Chapel Hill.

32 Ernesto Galarza, *Farm Workers and Agri-Business in California, 1947–1960* (Notre Dame: University of Notre Dame Press, 1977), 82.

33 Galarza, *Farm Workers and Agri-Business*, 66.

34 Francis E. Rourke, *Bureaucracy, Politics, and Public Policy* (Boston: Little, Brown, 1969), 20, quoted in Kitty Calavita, *Inside the State: The Bracero Program, Immigration, and the INS* (New York: Quid Pro Books, 2010), 136.

35 Charles C. Teague, *Fifty Years a Rancher: Recollections of a Half a Century Devoted to the Citrus and Walnut Industries of California and to Furthering the Cooperative Movement in Agriculture* (n.p.: Charles Teague, 1944), 150.

36 "Statement of William H. Tolbert, National Farm Labor Users Conference and California Farm Labor Association, Accompanied by Bruce Sanborn, California Production Association; George Lyons, Vegetable Industry, California and Arizona; and Leland J. Yost, Coachella Valley Farmers Association, Thermal, Calif.," *Hearings before the Subcommittee of Equipment, Supplies, and Manpower of the Committee on Agriculture, House of Representatives, Eighty-Fourth Congress, First Session on H.R. 3822, March 16–22, 1955, Serial H* (Washington, DC: US Government Printing Office, 1955), 115. For an in-depth discussion on growers' changing views of agricultural labor, see Cohen, *Braceros*.

37 Calavita, *Inside the State*, 136.

38 "Proposed Migratory Labor Program," 1954, Box 54, Folder: 1954 Migrant Labor Program, NC-58, Entry 36, Office of the Secretary, 1954 Subject Files, Messages-Solicitor's Office, RG 174, General Records of the Department of Labor, National Archives, College Park, MD.

39 W. B. McFarland, Regional Farm Placement Representative, to Ed McDonald, Regional Director, Department of Labor, May 29, 1956, Box 16, Folder 5, Lucey Papers; "Significant Improvements in the Mexican Program—1956–1958," April 9, 1958, Box 32, Folder 1958, July 28–30—Session on "Specials," Mexico City, Robert C. Goodwin Papers, Department of Labor File, Harry S. Truman Presidential Library, Independence, MO.
40 McFarland to McDonald, May 29, 1956; "Significant Improvements."
41 Raphael Goodard to William O'Connor, October 27, 1957, Box 16, Folder 4, Lucey Papers.
42 Ed McDonald to William D. O'Connor, November 13, 1957, attached report, Box 16, Folder 4, Lucey Papers.
43 The Texas State Employment Commission was part of a federal-state employment office system that fell under the Department of Labor.
44 William O'Connor, "Results of Last Year's Activities in the Regional Office," October 1957, Box 16, Folder 4, Lucey Papers.
45 R. Garcia, Office Manager, to James H. Strauss, District Director, Texas Employment Commission, October 4, 1957; James H. Strauss to William O'Connor, BCSS, San Antonio, October 10, 1957, Box 16, Folder 4, Lucey Papers.
46 Michael Rezendes and Reese Dunklin, "Catholic Church Lobbied for Taxpayer Funds, Got $1.4B," *Associated Press*, July 10, 2020, https://apnews.com; Public Affairs Office, "Bishop Chairman Comments on Paycheck Protection Program," United States Conference of Catholic Bishops, July 10, 2020, www.usccb.org.

2

Chicago's Catholic Archdiocese and the Challenges of Serving a Multiethnic Latino Population

LILIA FERNÁNDEZ

Spirituality is nothing if it's not solidarity. Solidarity is very special.
—Father Donald J. Headley[1]

There is a growing browning of America, and the Catholic Church must look inward to find the power in itself to join the social revolution that this phenomenon demands. In the process, there has to be a browning of the American church—it has already begun. Hispanics cannot be a "problem" for the American church. They are the way to its future.
—Isidro Lucas, former seminarian, 1981[2]

When Hilda Portillo first arrived in Chicago in 1957 as a young Mexican wife, she immediately sought out a Catholic church where she could practice her faith. Portillo found a Spanish-speaking mass at St. Francis of Assisi, known locally as the Mexican Cathedral. She traveled from her home in the western suburb of Oak Park to the city's Near West Side on Sundays and became a devout St. Francis parishioner, volunteering her time and energies there for decades.

Single women like Maria Cerda, who arrived from Puerto Rico in the same years, also wanted a local church where they could worship. The closest parish to Maria's YWCA lodging was Holy Name Cathedral, on the Near North Side, which had begun ministering to the thousands of Puerto Ricans settling in the area. A priest at Holy Name would later introduce her to a Mexican American man who eventually became her husband.

Marta Masó, a young Cuban woman in her late teens, arrived with her brother and his family in 1962, assisted by Catholic Charities, the fiduciary agent that handled Cuban refugee resettlement in Chicago. She immediately enrolled at St. Ignatius High School down the street from their Rogers Park apartment and attended St. Ignatius parish along with many other Cubans who had settled nearby. She soon began volunteering with the Cardinal's Committee for the Spanish Speaking, an archdiocesan initiative with offices in the South Loop that aimed to serve the city's rapidly growing Spanish-speaking population.[3]

These three women reflect the diversity of Latin American migrants to Chicago in these years and the importance of the Catholic Church for many of them. As they settled in the city, the archdiocese and local priests became critical collaborators in helping Latinos express their faith and integrate into the metropolis. For its part, the archdiocese faced the challenge of ministering to three distinct ethnic groups who were often dispersed geographically, as the parishes above and their locations suggest. Older Mexican American residents who had been in the city since the 1920s lived primarily in industrial neighborhoods, but some were scattered as far as the suburbs. More recent Mexican, Mexican American, and Puerto Rican arrivals settled primarily in the city's central neighborhoods. As they searched for employment, housing, and a community, many turned to the church for both material and spiritual aid. While these three women were middle-, if not upper-class, most Latino migrants came from much humbler origins.[4] Cuban exiles stood out as the most economically privileged, bearing the advantage of being classified as refugees, and brandishing the shield of staunch anticommunist politics in the Cold War era.

Yet religion and politics intersected in surprising and unpredictable ways, depending on the encounters that took place between distinct Latinos, the personal inclinations and prejudices of individual priests, and the social movements of the day. The Chicago Archdiocese addressed and worked with these separate Latin American people by responding to their interests, concerns, and priorities, while seeking to cultivate a deeper loyalty to the church. Though some migrants gravitated to Protestant sects, and others spurned religion altogether, with the creation of the Cardinal's Committee for the Spanish Speaking in 1955, the see had the competing tasks of identifying "Spanish-speaking" Catholics as a pan-ethnic religious community while also attending to and respecting their cultural and national idiosyncrasies (such as their unique representations of the Virgin Mary) and their distinct economic needs.[5] The church became an important influence in Latinos' social and political formation as members of civic society just as it became a vehicle through which to practice their activism and volunteerism. It played a prominent role by responding to the labor movements, civil rights campaigns, and local issues of the day. Fortunately, it also left some archival evidence of its policies and practices in ministering to the city's various Spanish-speaking Catholics, which reveals clues about how white Catholic leaders understood Latinos as discrete ethnic groups and as a multiethnic collective.[6]

* * *

The Catholic Church has reigned as a dominant institution over the lives of the colonized people of the Americas for over five centuries. Historically speaking, people in Spanish-speaking countries have had varying degrees of indoctrination, loyalty, and piety toward the Catholic Church; nonetheless, it has played a prominent role in structuring social relations in Latin America. Indeed, the region's independence wars and even the Mexican Revolution and its postwar politics were animated at least in part by dissent against the Catholic Church and its omnipotence. Regardless of one's personal devotion, the church has figured in the lives of Latin Americans both in their countries of origin and in the United States. As the editors of this volume affirm in their introduction, religion has been woefully overlooked in documenting the historical experiences of Latino populations. While Latin Americans have been nominally Catholic historically, due to a lack of churches and priests in the region, clerics encountering them in the United States have seen them as rather "unchurched" people lacking in catechistic training and the fulfillment of sacraments.[7] Cubans and Puerto Ricans, for example, experienced the "paradox of a culture pervaded by Catholic symbols, attitudes, and traditions, but shockingly out of touch with the values and priorities of the institutional Church."[8] When distinct Spanish-speaking migrants began arriving in Chicago in the twentieth century, they brought with them diverse views about religious faith, the clergy, and their obligation to observe the sacraments. Certainly, Spanish-speaking people in the city practiced various other religions besides Catholicism since the 1920s (Baptist, Methodist, Mennonite, and Pentecostal sects, to name just a few),[9] but as the largest religious institution in the city, the Catholic Archdiocese loomed large.

Religious scholars have noted how the integration of Latin American Catholics into the American Catholic Church has been a contentious and fitful process. Indeed, Latinos have brought culturally distinctive liturgical practices, and their "popular religiosity" has not always conformed to the standards or expectations of American clerics. Moreover, as more than one scholar notes, Latinos have not generally brought their own native priests.[10] Thus, Latino incorporation into American parishes, their acceptance by fellow Catholics and clergy, and their sense of belonging have been rather uneven. Other scholars have examined the lived experience of Chicago's Latino Catholics in greater detail than what I present here.[11] In what follows, I describe the church's encounter with Latinos (both newcomers and old-timers) and the complex politics that emerged in the process.

The Chicago Archdiocese: Ministering to Spanish-Speaking Catholics

Like Catholic churches in other cities, Chicago's parishes organized primarily along ethnic lines throughout the nineteenth and early twentieth centuries. As Thomas Kelliher notes,

> Ethnic Catholicism and Chicago Catholicism were inseparable in the 1920's. Germans, Poles, Lithuanians, Italians, Slovaks, and other nationalities divided the archdiocese along ethnic lines. Immigrant groups built their own national parishes. It was not uncommon for a national parish to open within two blocks of another national or English-speaking territorial parish. Ethnic groups identified themselves with their parishes. Consequently, parishes reinforced ethnic rivalries within the archdiocese.[12]

If the parish structure reinforced European nationalism for most immigrants, in "territorial" or non-ethnic-specific parishes, the Irish generally dominated. As a result, ethnic parishes frequently turned Mexican immigrants away, while territorial ones may have accepted them only begrudgingly in the 1920s and 1930s. By 1924, the archdiocese had officially abandoned the "national" model for establishing new parishes, recognizing the limitations of organizing worshippers along strict ethnic lines, and instead promoted "territorial" parishes based on geography.[13]

As the archdiocese faced a growing number of Mexican immigrants after World War I, it paid little attention to them at first, intentionally choosing not to establish Spanish-speaking parishes. Nevertheless, based on their geographic dispersal, most Mexicans concentrated in three enclaves, where they established two parishes—Our Lady of Guadalupe in South Chicago, and Immaculate Heart Vicariate in Back of the Yards—and became the majority at St. Francis of Assisi on the Near West Side. As had been the case since the nineteenth century for Southern and Eastern European immigrants, Mexicans encountered a church dominated by an Irish American—and, to a lesser extent, German American—clerical hierarchy.[14] By the mid-twentieth century, Italian and Polish priests increasingly joined their ranks, but the highest prelates remained overwhelmingly Irish, and occasionally German. At the three "Mexican" parishes, however, Spanish Claretian brothers tended to the flock, such as Father Tort, a Spaniard who had been sent to Mexico as a young priest but then fled during the Mexican Revolution and eventually relocated to Chicago in 1924. Rather than restrict the Claretians to South Chicago's Our Lady of Guadalupe, where they had come to work, Cardinal George Mundelein encouraged them to minister to Mexicans throughout the city, a herculean task, given the enormous need in South Chicago alone. The Cordi-Marian Sisters, another religious order that was exiled by the anticlerical Mexican government in 1926, settled on Chicago's Near West Side, serving the ethnic enclave there. By 1927, five Claretian priests and two brothers "estimated they had to minister to about 50,000 Mexicans" in Chicago.[15]

Decades later, the archdiocese acknowledged its long-standing neglect of Mexicans, stating that they "have been almost exclusively under the care of the Claretian Fathers, who over the years have done yeoman service in providing for the needs of the Mexican people. . . . Because of limited personnel in the parishes, and perhaps a lack of vision at higher levels, the great mass of the Mexican community has never been effectively and truly reached by the church, nor its full religious and cultural potential contributed to the church in Chicago."[16]

As long as Mexican immigrants and their children were concentrated in St. Francis of Assisi, Our Lady of Guadalupe, and Immaculate Heart, the church hierarchy saw little need to assign greater resources to the population or to minister to them separately. Moreover, by World War II, second-generation children of immigrants who had assimilated and dispersed to outlying neighborhoods or even suburbs hardly seemed to require special services or attention.[17] Over the years, when Mexicans did turn to the church for material help, it was often Catholic Charities that responded to their needs.

By World War II, the three oldest churches that had served Mexican immigrants since the 1920s became the primary parishes for newly arriving Mexican immigrants, Mexican Americans, and even some Puerto Ricans. Other parishes soon became important for Latino Catholic life as well, especially as the population diversified and dispersed across the city.[18] The archdiocese found that growing numbers of Spanish-speaking migrants collided with its official policy of discouraging national parishes and encouraging assimilation and Americanization.

The Bishops' Committee for the Spanish Speaking

As Mexican immigrants, state-contracted braceros,[19] Mexican Americans, and Puerto Ricans began migrating throughout the country during and after World War II, the national Catholic hierarchy began to see the need for greater attention to Spanish-speaking Catholics. The National Catholic Welfare Conference (later renamed the National Conference of Catholic Bishops) created a Bishops' Committee for the Spanish Speaking (BCSS) in 1945 to address the needs of Spanish-speaking Catholics in the US Southwest and the growing numbers of Mexican braceros and migrants arriving in rural communities to work in agriculture. Led by San Antonio archbishop Robert E. Lucey, and funded by the American Board for Catholic Missions, the BCSS included diocesan leaders from throughout the Southwest and some even farther afield. Archbishop Samuel A. Stritch of Chicago (1939–1958) served on the committee early on, although the Mexican population in Illinois had declined significantly since the Great Depression and was not nearly as large as that of Texas, California, or other states.[20] Still, the BCSS identified its work with Mexican immigrants, Texas Mexican Americans, and New Mexico

Hispanos under the umbrella term "Spanish-speaking," signaling a collective label for people of Mexican descent regardless of their citizenship, nationality, immigration status, or tenure in the United States.[21] Focused initially on Mexican Americans and migrant populations in the Southwest, clergy soon recognized that a migrant stream of families regularly traveled to north central states for seasonal farm labor. They also felt the threat of Protestant sects and saw the need to shore up their Mexican faithful, the oldest Catholics on the continent.[22]

As the migration of Spanish-speaking Catholics to the United States increased steadily at mid-century, some clerics also saw the newcomers as the key to affirming the church's foothold in Latin America, particularly in the face of evangelical proselytizing, and as the key to the future of the US Catholic Church. In 1945 Monsignor John J. Burke reportedly predicted that "the Mexican might some day be the salvation of the Church in the United States."[23] Ten years later, Father Joseph P. Fitzpatrick, a sociologist who worked with Puerto Ricans in New York City, identified both that ethnic group and Mexicans as the "bridge builders" who would strengthen the US Catholic Church's links to Latin America. Indeed, Fitzpatrick, like other clergy who worked with the Bishops' Committee for the Spanish Speaking, predicted that the church's future would be determined by its northward migrants and the strength of the church south of its borders. He asserted, "If the Spanish-speaking in the United States become a vigorous and well-instructed Catholic people, they will be the very ones who can serve as the cultural and religious link between the two parts of our hemisphere."[24] By the 1960s, advocates noted that the Spanish-speaking made up nearly one-quarter of all Catholics in the United States.

The Bishops' Committee for the Spanish Speaking established a Chicago regional office to complement its San Antonio headquarters in 1958. Although the BCSS initially focused on the needs of Mexican-origin Catholics, it had begun recognizing a diversifying constituency, as Spanish-speaking "problems" were no longer limited to the Southwest but were now national in scope and included other national origin groups. Father John A. Wagner, the committee's executive secretary, noted that Puerto Ricans were going to New York, Cubans to Florida, and Mexicans, Central Americans, and South Americans to various parts of the country.[25] The decision to establish a Chicago office was likely the result of the region's growing significance as a crossroads of migration to both the city and surrounding agricultural areas. Puerto Ricans, Mexican American Tejanos, and Mexican immigrants all descended on the Midwest, many recruited by employers and others simply in search of better wages and working conditions.[26]

Despite the initial focus on Mexican Americans in the Southwest, Father Wagner and Archbishop Lucey described both Mexicans and Puerto Ricans as the neediest Spanish-speaking Catholics. Lucey noted, "Every year a very large number of Mexican nationals and Puerto Ricans enter the United States to become residents here. Practically all of them are baptized Catholics. Strangers in a strange land, impoverished and unlettered, they make their way to every state in the Union. Only the coordinated efforts of all of us can help them to adjust to American life and retain their traditional Catholic faith."[27] The majority of Mexicans and Puerto Ricans came from decidedly humble origins. Wagner described what migrants experienced as "a poverty more devastating than the ordinary poverty of poor Anglos in the US."[28] While these descriptions aimed to elicit compassion and understanding for the newcomers, they characterized them with patronizing language that was not applied to Cuban refugees, who tended to be middle- or upper-class and well educated. It also did not describe the hundreds of middle-class professionals among Mexican and Puerto Rican populations in the United States. These class differences, as well as local and national political considerations, guided the Chicago Archdiocese's very distinct approach to all three populations as they converged in the Second City.

The Catholic Church historically had an uneven record in providing culturally sensitive and specific ministry to "new Americans." In an Irish-dominated institutional hierarchy, local dioceses and clergy responded to (im)migrant groups (Italians, Poles, Puerto Ricans) in varying ways, ranging from hostility, to begrudging acceptance, to sympathy.[29] In New York City, Father Joseph Fitzpatrick championed Puerto Rican rights and welfare. In San Antonio, Texas, Archbishop Robert E. Lucey defended Mexican Americans. In Miami, clergy established a Centro Hispano Católico (Hispanic Catholic Center) when upper-class Cubans began fleeing the Castro revolution and relocating to South Florida.[30] In Chicago, the church split its attention three ways and depended on each group's need for pastoral or welfare work as much as the church's own preconceptions of and assumptions about each Latino population.

While the Chicago Archdiocese had left pastoral work with Mexican immigrants to the Claretians for decades, it began working with Puerto Rican newcomers in 1947, pressured perhaps by middle- and upper-class Puerto Rican students and professionals who were living in the city at this time.[31] The Catholic Youth Organization (CYO) became the primary office that served island migrants. By 1954 the CYO's funding ran out and Catholic Charities took over as the main agency to serve the group.[32] At the parish level, priests at Holy Name Cathedral near the Puerto Rican enclave on the Near North Side, and at Holy Cross parish among those who settled in the Woodlawn neighborhood began working more directly with the growing population. At Holy Cross, Puerto Rican parishioners reportedly approached the recently ordained Father Leo Mahon asking for greater spiritual guidance and religious education. Mahon began working with them in 1953 to create the Spanish Speaking Committee of Woodlawn, later renamed the Woodlawn Latin American Committee. By the following year, the committee had relocated to nearby St. Clara's parish and Mahon looked for help to broaden the group's reach. He enlisted the help of others, including University of Chicago affiliates, such as Lester Hunt, Nicholas Von Hoffman, and Saul Alinsky, who had worked closely with Bishop Shiel. Mahon also received financial support from Cardinal Stritch. By 1955, more than a decade after the first braceros had come to the city and eight years after the first state-sponsored labor migrants had arrived from Puerto Rico, Stritch officially established the Cardinal's Committee for the Spanish Speaking (CCSS) to work primarily with the Puerto Rican community.[33]

The Cardinal's Committee for the Spanish Speaking

The growing hostility against both Puerto Ricans and unauthorized Mexican immigrants and their increasing visibility as "problems" in the city likely prompted the archdiocese's decision to begin addressing their needs more directly. Like the national BCSS, the Cardinal's Committee was also aware that Protestant social settlements like Hull House and others represented a threatening influence on the Spanish-speaking as well.[34] Yet the work with Spanish-speaking newcomers was meant to be only temporary, to help them adjust to their new environment. Eventually, the archdiocese presumed, Puerto Ricans and others would assimilate, learn English, and be integrated into neighborhood parishes as many European immigrants had done, and would rely strictly on parish-specific services. Yet the fact that so many European immigrants and their descendants continued worshipping in their "ethnic" parishes belied this expectation of assimilation. What was more likely was that there were not enough ethnic-specific parishes that had fully embraced the Spanish-speaking and showed interest in helping them get settled.[35]

Cardinal Stritch generally expressed a benevolent attitude toward the Spanish-speaking. In introducing the CCSS in a 1957 publication he stated, "Esta gente buena, son hijos e hijas de la Iglesia; tenemos que ayudarlos a resolver sus propios problemas y que puedan tomar sus puestos en nuestra comunidad de Chicago."[36] He assigned Monsignor Edward M. Burke as chairman of the committee, and two relatively young priests—Father Gilbert A. Carroll as coordinator and Father Leo Mahon as executive assistant to the coordinator. The committee included clergy and nuns from other diocesan agencies and from parishes with significant Spanish-speaking attendance.[37] In 1958 Cardinal Stritch was replaced by Cardinal Samuel B. Meyer (1958–1965), who according to Father Don Headley avidly supported the committee's pastoral work. The committee's leadership was reorganized under Cardinal Meyer's tenure. By 1962, Meyer made Mahon the executive director of the committee, with Carroll serving as chairman.[38]

The CCSS initially approached Saul Alinsky and his Industrial Areas Foundation, upon Mahon's advice, to help it in organizing the Puerto Rican community. This signaled an appreciation for community-based, grassroots civic engagement. Alinsky assigned Nick Hoffman and Lester Hunt to lead the effort in surveying the Near North Side neighborhood where many Puerto Ricans lived under the threat of urban renewal displacement. While Mahon had been working with Puerto Ricans on the South Side, Puerto Rican men and priests at nearby Holy Name Cathedral had begun organizing as well. The Cardinal's Committee soon approved the formation of a fraternal group called Los Caballeros de San Juan (Knights of St. John) after the island's patron saint. The Woodlawn Latin American Committee had established the first Caballeros council and others soon followed suit. By 1958, they counted eight councils

TABLE 2.1. Los Caballeros de San Juan Councils, 1964

Council Number	Parish	Neighborhood
1	St. Clara	Woodlawn
2	Holy Name Cathedral	Near North Side
3	St. Michael	Lincoln Park
4	Our Lady of Sorrows	East Garfield Park
5	St. Jarlath	Near West Side
6	Santa Maria Addolorata	West Town
7	St. Joseph	Waukegan, Illinois
8	St. Mark	West Town (Humboldt Park)
9	no parish	Lincoln Park
10	St. Mel	West Garfield Park
11	Our Lady of Mt. Carmel	Lake View

Adapted from Thomas G. Kelliher Jr., "Hispanic Catholics and the Archdiocese of Chicago, 1923–1970" (PhD diss., University of Notre Dame, 1996), 147.

around the city, and eventually grew to at least eleven (some claim thirteen), including one in the outlying suburb of Waukegan (see table 2.1).[39]

Hardly radical in their politics, priests who sponsored the Caballeros expressed interest in bringing Puerto Rican men closer to the church. They were concerned that men were less devout than their wives and attended church less frequently.[40] Thus, the Caballeros functioned to organize social and religious activities, develop community cohesion, and promote churchgoing among men.[41] The group sponsored sports teams across the archdiocese. They also identified potential lay leaders, men like Juan Sosa, Gabino Moyet, Cesar Rivera, Jesus Rodriguez, the Chevere brothers, and others who became staff members with the committee or worked closely with the brotherhood. Priests who worked with the group maintain that it became the primary vehicle to develop leaders, educate the community, and sponsor festivals in these early years.[42] While the Caballeros effectively organized social events and created a sense of community, the archdiocese eventually began more direct evangelical efforts through the formation of Hermanos en la Familia de Dios (Brothers in the Family of God), a religious society that placed greater emphasis on catechistic instruction and the fulfillment of sacraments.[43] Father Headley recalled that he and Hermanos members would go to local white pastors and encourage them to integrate their Latino congregants into parish life more fully. Some pastors denied having many Spanish-speaking members at all, though the numbers proved otherwise.[44] The Caballeros and Hermanos organized retreats, *cursillos*, and other catechistic training. A separate women's group called Las Hijas de Maria organized Puerto Rican women as well, focusing on similar kinds of religious instruction.[45]

Though the Cardinal's Committee saw an urgent need to focus primarily on newly arriving Puerto Ricans in its first few years, the committee soon began to address its Mexican flock. Mexican migration continued at a brisk pace. But Mexicans also had a longer tenure in the city with better-established community ties, and could count on the political pressure of middle-class, Catholic Mexican American leaders to demand greater attention. They were, after all, the largest Spanish-speaking population in the city. Perhaps because of this, the CCSS's office manager was a Mexican American woman, Carmen Mendoza, who worked closely with the local Mexican Chamber of Commerce and businessmen (members) like Arturo Velasquez. Unlike the emphasis on religious instruction for Puerto Ricans through the Caballeros, Hermanos en la Familia de Dios, or Las Hijas de Maria, however, Mexican Americans who were affiliated with the Cardinal's Committee, especially businessmen, focused primarily on economic development. The Mexican American entrepreneurial class's influence likely prompted the CCSS to partner with the Illinois Federation of Mexican Americans (IFOMA), a coalition of twenty-five separate Mexican ethnic organizations and clubs, with Velasquez as chair and Mendoza as co-chair, as the primary engine for organizing Mexicans, unlike the more explicitly religious societies that it sponsored for Puerto Ricans. The CCSS left pastoral work to the Claretian fathers and catechistic training to religious societies in the predominantly Mexican parishes.[46]

The Cardinal's Committee had several staff assigned to work with each ethnic population. Father Michael Cody oversaw "Mexican work," assisted by lay worker Abbie Toribio, while lay workers Juan Sosa and Gabino Moyet did "Puerto Rican work."[47] As Cuban exiles began arriving in the city, Father Antonio Mañes handled "Cuban work," with lay worker Justa Rodriguez assisting him. Although a shared Catholic faith provided some "cultural adhesive" between all three populations, their cultural idiosyncrasies, distinct histories, and separate migration paths called for specialized efforts.[48] While the church sought to help all three groups in their adjustment, its approach varied based on their clientele's cultural origins, degree of education, and professional or vocational background.

Cubans were not known for being avid churchgoers on the island, but they were understood as nominally Catholic, especially among the middle and upper classes.[49] A pioneering enclave of Cubans created their own religious association in 1960, Asociación Cubana, inviting Cardinal Meyer to attend the inaugural event, perhaps confident that the city's highest prelate would be interested in their activities. As in Miami and other cities, a Cuban Resettlement Committee operated in Chicago with federal funding under Catholic Charities to facilitate Cuban adjustment, help them find professional job placement, identify suitable housing, and enroll children in Catholic schools. Catholic Charities also helped with placing unaccompanied children in foster homes (part of Operation Peter Pan). Altogether, the CCSS noted that it helped resettle 5,828 Cubans in Chicago between June 1961 and July 1966.[50]

Early waves of exiles came from upper- and middle-class backgrounds like the smattering of Central Americans and South Americans who blended into white parishes during these years. Still, Cubans maintained a seemingly unique relationship with the Catholic Church in the United States, especially as the church embraced an anticommunist posture against the atheist Soviet Union. Other factors shaped Cuban exceptionalism as well: they identified as exiles who expected their stay to be temporary; they represented their country's elite; and many had been educated in Catholic schools. As Marta Sayeed (neé Masó) explains, exiles saw themselves as distinct from immigrants because they were not fleeing poverty or deprivation in their home country but rather were forced to leave "because of political reasons." Otherwise, "you had a good life [back home]." Cuban exiles in Miami similarly embraced "a strong exile consciousness infused with religious fervor and a powerful connection to national identity." Chicago Cubans constituted a much smaller exile community and were a much longer distance from the homeland, but they came from a higher social class than most of the recent Spanish-speaking immigrants who surrounded them.[51]

The archdiocese estimated that approximately twenty-six thousand Spanish-speakers attended Catholic churches in the metropolitan area by 1961 (see table 2.2).[52] They worshipped throughout the region, but St. Francis of Assisi remained the main parish, with an estimated five thousand people at mass every week. Our Lady of Guadalupe in South

TABLE 2.2. Estimated Weekly Attendance of Spanish-Speaking People at Mass, 1961

Parishes with Sermon in Spanish		Parishes without Sermons in Spanish	
Holy Name – St. Joseph	1,000	Our Lady of Mt. Carmel	100
Our Lady of Sorrows	1,200	Holy Trinity (Wolcott)	100
Precious Blood	1,000	St. Mary of the Lake	200
St. Boniface	500	St. Mel Holy Ghost	300
St. Charles Borromeo	300	Presentation	200
St. Cyril	300	Providence of God	300
St. Dominic	200	St. Procopius	700
St. Mark	600	St. Vincent de Paul	350
St. Michael	1,500	St. Matthew	200
St. Patrick	300	Notre Dame	400
St. Pius	400		
Our Lady of Guadalupe	2,000		
Immaculate Heart	500		
St. Francis of Assisi	5000		
Chinese Mission	50		
St. Clara	600		
St. Jarlath	600		
*St. Therese – Palatine	250		
*St. Joseph – Waukegan	500		
*St. Casimir – Chicago Heights	600		
St. Francis Cabrini	400		
		Estimated total weekly attendees	20,850
		Approximate attendees at other parishes	5,300
		Total Spanish-speaking attendees	26,150

* Located outside Chicago
Reproduced from Cardinal's Committee, "Report for 1961," 3, Cardinal's Committee for the Spanish Speaking Folder, Albert Cardinal Meyer CBC General Correspondence, Chicago Archdiocese Archives.

Chicago had the second-highest numbers, with about two thousand attendees, followed by St. Michael's on the Near North Side, Our Lady of Sorrows, Holy Name—St. Joseph, and Precious Blood on the Near West Side. Before the Second Vatican Council reforms that allowed mass to be performed in the vernacular, these churches offered mass in Latin with a sermon or homily in Spanish. Altogether, approximately twenty churches in the Chicago area (including the suburbs) offered Spanish sermons at the time. Another ten parishes without Spanish sermons nevertheless saw between one hundred and seven hundred Spanish-speaking worshippers on a weekly basis.[53]

The Cardinal's Committee office at 1300 S. Wabash supplemented the pastoral work of individual parishes by providing job placement assistance and other referrals. Serving distinct Spanish-speaking populations presented challenges, however, and reflected disparities in government policies. Marta Sayeed recalled that staff served each ethnic group in separate sections and that tensions simmered below the surface. She remembered how Cuban refugees received special resources and privileges compared to other more impoverished migrants: "We [Cubans] would get money and household [allowance], you know, would get help to find a place to live. And they [Puerto Ricans and Mexicans] didn't.... Within two weeks, you [Cubans] got $100." Mexican immigrants, Mexican Americans, and Puerto Ricans might receive referrals to factories that were hiring, but they certainly did not immediately qualify for government welfare programs as Cubans did.[54] While Cuban refugees vocally opposed communism, they willingly accepted the largesse of the US welfare state aimed at helping exiles defeat the Castro regime.

Still, despite the different treatment they received, the Cardinal's Committee became an important meeting site where Mexicans and Puerto Ricans frequently gathered.[55] By 1968, the office became the Chicago headquarters for the United Farm Workers consumer boycott efforts in the Midwest, as the movement gained increasing support from Catholic priests and dioceses committed to social justice. Sayeed recalls receiving vocal criticism from fellow Cubans for attending a UFW march in downtown Chicago. While she did not support communism, she credited her parents with raising her to be open-minded enough to appreciate the farmworkers' struggle for labor rights. Indeed, several priests were closely involved with local labor struggles among Latino industrial workers. Still, the church was quite divided in its politics, and not all priests or laypeople endorsed radical, militant, or leftist politics. Some priests could be culturally inclusive or tolerant of Spanish speakers but politically conservative. Father Peter Rodriguez at St. Francis, who defended undocumented immigrants from INS raids, nevertheless had harsh criticisms of Father Headley and Dr. Jorge Prieto (César Chávez's personal physician when he visited Chicago), reportedly accusing them of being communists for their advocacy work.[56] Long-standing tensions simmered between the Cardinal's Committee and the Claretians, for example. One Claretian priest had been accused by a Mexican activist of being a fascist. In 1943 Father Joaquin De Prada allegedly declared, "Long live Spain! Franco's Spain!" at a community meeting at St. Francis. Mexican American leader Frank Paz wrote to Cardinal Stritch denouncing De Prada and explaining that the majority in attendance took offense to the fascist outburst.[57] Decades later, differences persisted between more cautious clergy entrenched in Cold War conservativism and progressives or liberals who embraced the edicts of Vatican II, liberation theology, and the civil rights, anti-war, and social movements of the age. Navigating and negotiating interethnic relations could be uncomfortable, particularly at a moment when some Mexican Americans and Puerto Ricans were shifting to the left politically while Cubans had fled those very politics in their native country.

Clerics also brought their own ethnic stereotypes and assumptions to bear on their ministry. Father John D. Ring, for example, claimed that a Father Gallegos told the Mexican community that Ring preferred Puerto Ricans. As Ring tried to articulate diplomatically, "It is a bit difficult at times to keep all the Cubans, Puerto Ricans, and Mexicans happy. It requires a lot of diplomacy and also it sometimes puts us in positions we do not want to take." But Ring also held much more favorable opinions of Cubans. He revealed, for example, his belief that Mexican and Puerto Rican men were prone to abandon their children and families, a shameful act that he could not fathom Cuban men would ever commit.[58]

After Cardinal John Cody (1965–1982) replaced Cardinal Meyer, the archdiocese took a decidedly conservative turn and became less interested in the kind of organizing work it had accomplished in its early years. Cody had never visited the office that bore his name before the summer of 1967. When he did and was being introduced to the various staff members, a UFW volunteer asked him whether he supported the grape boycott. According to Marta Sayeed, Cody was incensed. After he left the office he informed the executive director that the committee's name would be changed to the Archdiocesan Latin American Committee (ALAC). Cody did not want to be associated with the work of the UFW or with any political activity that might sully his reputation. According to Father Don Headley, Cody was less interested in following the mandates of the Second Vatican Council, which called for Catholics to develop their human potential more fully, than in maintaining good relations with Mayor Richard J. Daley, the city's Irish Catholic Democratic machine boss who ruled the city with an iron first. Daley had forged racial segregation and inequality into the city's built environment, and apart from supporting charitable causes through the Catholic Church, had little interest in social justice or economic equality.[59] Regardless of the organizational channels through which the CCSS worked, the see's ties and cooperation with the conservative Daley administration were readily apparent. Irish American prelates dealt with Spanish-speaking Catholics carefully, so as not to upset the local political order.

During the federal government's War on Poverty, the Archdiocesan Committee turned increasingly to public funding to serve the economically vulnerable. ALAC took advantage of the Manpower Development Training Act to offer vocational training for Latino men, for example. In 1968 it had 145 students enrolled in English classes, another thirty learning machine operation, and fifteen learning welding at the Washburne Trade School, a Chicago Public Schools vocational institute that notoriously excluded African Americans and Latinos through grandfather clauses that required that a family member sponsor trainees. The committee also coordinated with the USWA Local 65 in South Chicago to offer English classes to residents in that neighborhood.[60] Helping men become more capable breadwinners did not upset social relations but rather reinforced traditional gender roles and reduced the need for social welfare programs. While the church had operated as a conduit for connecting blue-collar and unskilled workers to employers for years, by the early seventies corporate recruiters turned to ALAC in search of Latino white-collar employees as well.[61]

* * *

The Catholic hierarchy both in Chicago and nationally did very little to promote the growth of the Latino priesthood in the United States. The archdiocese was reluctant to train Latino priests, encouraging very few to seek vocations or join the priesthood. It also turned away volunteer priests from Latin America who offered to practice locally, feeling that they stymied the assimilation of recent arrivals. This seems rather surprising given that Latin America had a much deeper Catholic colonial heritage than the United States and such priests could better relate to migrants and their cultures. Yet even in Latin America, priests often seemed to come from Spain, reflecting a persistent colonial hierarchy and preference for *peninsulares*[62] rather than homegrown priests. As one former seminarian claimed, "Except in the case of Hispanics, the American church has never been faced with a minority population of Catholics who were without their own native clergy."[63]

In the Southwest, especially under Archbishop Lucey's direction, church leaders had insisted that European American priests working in a Mexican American parish receive Spanish-language training; in Chicago, by contrast, this was not initially common practice. As late as May 1966 the archdiocese noted that it had only four priests "who speak Spanish with minimal fluency." As the Spanish-speaking population continued to grow, the Cardinal's Committee proposed language training for white priests rather than "importing Spanish clergy."[64] The archdiocese began sending Irish American, Italian American, and Polish American priests to Mexico, Puerto Rico, and elsewhere in Latin America for language training and Spanish-immersion experiences rather than developing indigenous talent among Latino Catholics beyond lay leadership.[65]

One of the first and few homegrown Mexican American priests in the city, Father Severíno Lopez, pointed to racial discrimination as early as the 1940s. He related the story that when he and three other young men arrived for their training in a California Claretian seminary, the two darker-colored initiates were sent home, deemed unsuitable for the priesthood. Even decades later, devout St. Francis parishioner Hilda Portillo accused local Chicago area seminaries of discriminating against Hispanics and refusing to admit them until the mid-1970s.[66] European American clergy held a tight grip on the church hierarchy.

Even as late as 1980, only 400 Catholic priests nationwide were US-born Latinos, and only 12 of the 360 Catholic bishops in the United States were Hispanic.[67]

Conclusion

Pope John Paul II's visit to the Mexican barrio of Pilsen during his tour of the United States in 1979 marked the Vatican's recognition of Chicago's Latino Catholics as an important constituency for the church. It also strategically reflected the "preferential treatment for the poor" that Vatican II had demanded, for the pope could simply have welcomed all of the city's Hispanics to a large arena or stadium without bringing particular attention to the impoverished residents of the working-class neighborhood. If Spanish-speaking people, especially the Mexican American community, had for so long been ignored by the church hierarchy, the archdiocese and Rome, as well as other religious sects, were now well aware how critical the city's nearly half a million Latinos were to the future. Nationally by 1980, one in four Catholics in the United States was Latino. At the dawn of the twenty-first century, Latinos represented more than a third of all US Catholics and half of all under the age of twenty-five.[68]

Spanish-speaking migrants throughout the mid-twentieth century turned to the Catholic Church in their times of want, when they needed to consecrate life's milestones, and when they desired spiritual guidance. Chicago's archdiocese responded based on the archbishop's sensitivity to their needs, and priests' willingness to work with newcomers. Some of those Latinos wielded more power and social status than others. And their requests for assistance varied accordingly. Still a former Spanish seminarian offered a critical though not entirely negative assessment of the church's role. Isidro Lucas maintained, "It would be inaccurate to say flatly that the Catholic Church has not assisted in the economic and social progress of Hispanics." The role of some priests in the farmworker struggle, for example, stands out. But Lucas underscored the church's original dilemma dating back to the Roman Empire—"whether the primary allegiance of the established church as a human as well as a spiritual institution is to the poor or to the power structures of the social and political world."[69]

Serving the poor, the exiled, and the displaced certainly proved challenging for Chicago's archdiocese. Yet Marta Sayeed remembered that the Cardinal's Committee tried to forge community among the Spanish-speaking without much success. The committee would hold mass in its chapel on the first floor, and then each ethnic group would take turns preparing a communal meal: "We did a Mexican luncheon, a Puerto Rican luncheon, and a Cuban luncheon. But I don't think it really established [community], you know, because everybody still felt . . . who they were," Sayeed recalled. Though the cultural exchange did not necessarily forge intimate bonds, for a young woman who had been raised to be open-minded to others, the experience made an impression on her. "It was the first time in my life I've ever eaten homemade tortillas," she recalled. And she appreciated the Mexican woman who had volunteered to help prepare the food. Still, Sayeed remembers, "At the end, everybody, when we went upstairs to work, everybody scattered." While the Cardinal's Committee (later the Archdiocesan Committee) could not force unity among people of different class backgrounds, political views, and social interests, perhaps the greatest lesson it imparted on Catholics like Marta Sayeed was solidarity. As Father Don Headley notes in the epigraph, "Spirituality is nothing if it's not solidarity. Solidarity is very special."

NOTES

1. Donald Headley, "Father Donald J. Headley Video Interview and Biography," Digital Collections, Grand Valley State University Library, accessed August 26, 2020, https://digitalcollections.library.gvsu.edu (hereafter cited as Headley interview). Father Don Headley was ordained in 1958 and first assigned to St. Patrick's Church in Chicago, on Adams and DesPlaines Streets, which included Skid Row and a sizable Puerto Rican population.
2. Isidro Lucas, *The Browning of America: The Hispanic Revolution in the American Church* (Chicago: Fides/Claretian Books, 1981).
3. Carolyn Eastwood, *Near West Side Stories: Struggles for Community in Chicago's Maxwell Street Neighborhood* (Chicago: Lake Claremont, 2002), 286–87; Maria Cerda, interview with author, June 25, 2004, Chicago; Marta Sayeed (neé Masó), interview with author via Zoom, January 8, 2021.
4. I use the rather flawed but simplest term "Latino" throughout this essay, as it is also the most historically accurate term for the period I am describing. While more gender-inclusive and nonbinary terms like "Latinx" have become favored by academics at the time of this essay's publishing, it was simply not the term in use at the historical moment that I analyze.

5   See Mario T. García, *Católicos: Resistance and Affirmation in Chicano Catholic History* (Austin: University of Texas Press, 2008). For a comparative treatment of Latino Catholics in four major cities—Chicago, San Antonio, Miami, and New York City—see David A. Badillo, *Latinos and the New Immigrant Church* (Baltimore: Johns Hopkins University Press, 2006). Juan Gonzalez mentions a contemporary account of inter-ethnic conflict over the representation of the Virgin in an East Harlem church. See Juan Gonzalez, *Harvest of Empire: A History of Latinos in America*, first edition (New York: Penguin, 2000), xvi.

6   This essay does not offer an exhaustive history of the Catholic Church and Latinos in Chicago, nor does it address the community's religious history more generally. Numerous other scholars have addressed Latino Catholic history in the United States, such as Badillo, *Latinos and the New Immigrant Church*; Timothy Matovina, *Latino Catholicism: Transformation in America's Largest Church* (Princeton: Princeton University Press, 2011); and Jay P. Dolan et al., eds., *The Notre Dame History of Hispanic Catholics in the US*, 3 vols. (Notre Dame: University of Notre Dame Press, 1994).

On Catholicism and specific Latino ethnic groups, see David Badillo, "Catholicism and the Search for Nationhood in Miami's Cuban Community," *US Catholic Historian* 20, no. 4 (2002): 75–90; García, *Católicos*; Gerald Eugene Poyo, *Cuban Catholics in the United States, 1960–1980: Exile and Integration* (Notre Dame: University of Notre Dame Press, 2007). For an excellent collection of primary sources on Latino Catholicism, see Gerald Eugene Poyo and Timothy M. Matovina, eds., *Presente! US Latino Catholics from Colonial Origins to the Present* (Maryknoll, NY: Orbis, 2000).

7   Lucas, *Browning of America*, 56.

8   Jay P. Dolan and Jaime R. Vidal, eds., *Puerto Rican and Cuban Catholics in the US, 1900–1965* (Notre Dame: University of Notre Dame Press, 1994), 3.

9   See, for example, Anita Jones, cited in Thomas G. Kelliher Jr., "Hispanic Catholics and the Archdiocese of Chicago, 1923–1970" (doctoral thesis, University of Notre Dame, 1996), 121, 123–24; and Malachy Richard McCarthy, "Which Christ Came to Chicago: Catholic and Protestant Programs to Evangelize, Socialize and Americanize the Mexican Immigrant, 1900–1940" (doctoral thesis, Loyola University Chicago, 2002).

10 On the popular religiosity of Mexican Catholics in Chicago, see Deborah Kanter, *Chicago Católico: Making Catholic Parishes Mexican* (Urbana: University of Illinois Press, 2020). On Puerto Ricans, see Dolan and Vidal, *Puerto Rican and Cuban Catholics*, 44.

11 John Flores reminds us that the Cristero Wars and anticlerical sentiment in Mexico during the 1920s elicited diverse responses and attitudes among Mexican revolutionary immigrants or exiles during that decade. John H. Flores, *The Mexican Revolution in Chicago: Immigration Politics from the Early Twentieth Century to the Cold War* (Urbana: University of Illinois Press, 2018). Deborah Kanter contends that Mexicans' integration into the Catholic churches of the Near West

Side and Pilsen in the postwar era was much smoother and amicable than other scholars have argued. See Kanter, *Chicago Católico*.
12 Kelliher, "Hispanic Catholics," 74. On Italian American Catholicism, see, for example, Robert A. Orsi, *The Madonna of 115th Street: Faith and Community in Italian Harlem, 1880–1950* (New Haven: Yale University Press, 2010). On Polish Americans, see John Radzilowski, "A Social History of Polish-American Catholicism," *US Catholic Historian* 27, no. 3 (2009): 21–43. On religion in urban America more generally, see Robert A. Orsi, ed., *Gods of the City: Religion and the American Urban Landscape* (Bloomington: Indiana University Press, 1999).
13 Kelliher, "Hispanic Catholics," 56–57, 109–10; Badillo, *Latinos and the New Immigrant Church*, 84. One of the concerns included that immigrants would not assimilate as easily if they worshipped only with fellow countrymen and -women. On this policy of "integrated parishes" in postwar New York City, for example, see Dolan and Vidal, *Puerto Rican and Cuban Catholics*, 73–79. The problem of residential, especially racial, succession would become a major concern around ethnic parishes by the sixties as well. See, for example, John T. McGreevy, *Parish Boundaries: The Catholic Encounter with Race in the Twentieth-Century Urban North* (Chicago: University of Chicago Press, 1996); and Eileen McMahon, *What Parish Are You From? A Chicago Irish Community and Race Relations* (Lexington: University of Kentucky Press, 1995).
14 James Barrett and David Roediger argue that the American clerical leadership was primarily Irish, although in Chicago there seemed to be a number of Germans as well. On the dominance of Irish clergy and leadership in the American Roman Catholic Church, see James R. Barrett and David R. Roediger, "The Irish and the 'Americanization' of the 'New Immigrants' in the Streets and in the Churches of the Urban United States, 1900–1930," *Journal of American Ethnic History* 24, no. 4 (2005): 4–33; and James R. Barrett, *The Irish Way: Becoming American in the Multiethnic City* (New York: Penguin, 2012), 57–104.
15 On the Spanish Claretians, see McCarthy, "Which Christ Came to Chicago." The turmoil of the Mexican Revolution and the Cristero Wars meant that Mexico itself lost much of its clergy, so some Mexicans rarely had a church or even a priest in their hometowns. Some Spanish and Mexican priests who fled Mexico in these years ended up ministering to Mexicans in the United States, but there is no evidence that many of them made their way to Chicago. Kelliher, "Hispanic Catholics," 16–23, 65, 77, 66; Kanter, *Chicago Católico*, 26. The estimated population is cited in Kelliher, "Hispanic Catholics," 73. This figure was likely an overestimation. On the distinction between Mexican liberals and conservatives or traditionalists who fled the revolution and settled in the Chicago area, see Flores, *Mexican Revolution in Chicago*.
16 Cardinal's Committee for the Spanish Speaking in Chicago, "Report for 1961," Cardinal's Committee for the Spanish Speaking Folder, Albert Cardinal Meyer CBC General Correspondence, Chicago Archdiocese Archives (hereafter CAA).

17 On Mexicans/Mexican Americans in Pilsen's neighborhood parishes, see Kanter, *Chicago Católico*.
18 See Kelliher, "Hispanic Catholics," 63–69.
19 Braceros were state-sponsored contract migrant workers who came to the United States temporarily, primarily for agricultural and railroad work. An extensive literature exists on the subject, including, among others, Kitty Calavita, *Inside the State: The Bracero Program, Immigration, and the INS* (New York: Routledge, 1992); Deborah Cohen, *Braceros: Migrant Citizens and Transnational Subjects in the Postwar United States and Mexico* (Chapel Hill: University of North Carolina Press, 2011); Barbara A. Driscoll, *The Tracks North: The Railroad Bracero Program of World War II* (Austin: Center for Mexican American Studies, 1999); Ernesto Galarza, *Merchants of Labor: The Mexican Bracero Story; An Account of the Managed Migration of Mexican Farm Workers in California, 1942–1960* (Charlotte, CA: McNally and Loftin, 1964); Mireya Loza, *Defiant Braceros: How Migrant Workers Fought for Racial, Sexual, and Political Freedom* (Chapel Hill: University of North Carolina Press, 2016); and Ana E. Rosas, *Abrazando el Espíritu: Bracero Families Confront the US-Mexico Border* (Berkeley: University of California Press, 2014).
20 "Meeting of the Archbishops and Bishops of the Four Southwest Provinces, Oklahoma City," January 1945, Folder 8, Box 20, Bishops' Committee for the Spanish Speaking, CAA. See also CLUC 13/09, BCSS-Oklahoma City Meeting, 1945/01, Robert Emmet Lucey Papers, University of Notre Dame Archives (hereafter UNDA); and "Report of the Regional Conference: The Catholic Council for the Spanish Speaking," 1946, Folder 9, Box 459, George Gilmary Higgins Papers, Special Collections Library, Catholic University of America. For more on Archbishop Lucey and his advocacy for Mexican Americans, see Badillo, *Latinos and the New Immigrant Church*, 69–73. See also "Catholic Council for the Spanish Speaking Seventh Regional Conference," 1955, Folder 19, Box 382, Dr. Hector P. Garcia Papers, Special Collections and Archives, Mary and Jeff Bell Library, Texas A&M University-Corpus Christi. Folder 5, Box 84, Bishops' Committee for the Spanish Speaking, 1960–69, George Gilmary Higgins Papers, Catholic University of America.
21 The label could also have echoed Mexican Americans' desire to distance themselves from the racially maligned term "Mexican," which in fact had been identified as a distinct racial category on the 1930 census. Alternatively, it could have been an intentional recognition of the population by linguistic heritage, although no other ethnic or national group (Italians, Poles, Czechs, etc.) was identified by language. On Mexican American racial politics in Texas in this era, see Thomas A. Guglielmo, "Fighting for Caucasian Rights: Mexicans, Mexican Americans, and the Transnational Struggle for Civil Rights in World War II Texas," *Journal of American History* 92, no. 4 (2006): 1212–37.
22 García, *Católicos*, chap. 4; Matovina, *Latino Catholicism*, 68–69.
23 García, *Católicos*, 129.

24 Joseph P. Fitzpatrick, "Mexicans and Puerto Ricans Build a Bridge," *America*, December 31, 1955, 373–75. Father Wagner made a similar statement in 1963: "The importance of a good national office for the Spanish speaking cannot be overemphasized because the future of the Church in America will depend pretty much on what we do with the faith of the Spanish speaking in the US at this point in history." Father Wagner to Archbishop Lucey, September 9, 1963, Bishops' Committee for the Spanish Speaking, Chicago 1956–1967 Folder, Robert E. Lucey Papers, UNDA.

Two and a half decades later, this concept persisted, as observed by former seminarian Isidro Lucas. Lucas, *Browning of America*, 66.

25 The Chicago regional office was not operating to everyone's satisfaction, however. San Antonio archbishop Lucey complained that the Chicago office's director, Monsignor William J. Quinn, was ineffective and not fully dedicated to the work. As a result, the office was closed in the early summer of 1967 and relocated to Lansing, Michigan later that fall. "Minutes of the Annual Meeting of the Bishops' Committee for the Spanish Speaking, Catholic University of America," November 16, 1960, Bishops' Committee for the Spanish Speaking Folder, Albert Cardinal Meyer CBC General Correspondence, CAA.

26 See Bishops' Committee for the Spanish Speaking, Chicago 1956–1967 Folder, Robert E. Lucey Papers, UNDA.

27 "Minutes of the Annual Meeting," November 16, 1960; Most. Rev. Robert E. Lucey to His Eminence Albert G. Cardinal Meyer, February 25, 1960, Bishops' Committee for the Spanish Speaking Folder, Albert Cardinal Meyer CBC General Correspondence, CAA. Cardinal Meyer did not attend the Bishops' Committee conference that year or the next one in 1962, for unknown reasons.

28 "Minutes of the Annual Meeting of BCSS, Catholic University of America," Washington, DC, November 15, 1961, Bishops' Committee for the Spanish Speaking Folder, Albert Cardinal Meyer CBC General Correspondence, CAA.

In 1960 the BCSS discussed the details of creating a specific Bishops' Committee on Migrant Workers, as Cardinal Samuel Stritch had agreed to do with a headquarters in Chicago. The details on this committee's purview in relation to the BCSS were ambiguous, and BCSS members had to sort this out. After Cardinal Stritch was replaced by Cardinal Meyer, however, Meyer fulfilled Stritch's promise and established the committee. Monsignor William J. Quinn, memorandum to Albert Cardinal Meyer, July 16, 1963, Bishops' Committee for the Spanish Speaking, Chicago 1956–1967 Folder, Robert E. Lucey Papers, UNDA.

29 On Italians and the Catholic Church, see, for example, Rudolph J. Vecoli, "Prelates and Peasants: Italian Immigrants and the Catholic Church," *Journal of Social History* 2, no. 3 (Spring 1969): 217–68; and Orsi, *Madonna of 115th Street*. On Poles, see Radzilowski, "Social History"; Dominic A. Pacyga, "To Live amongst Others: Poles and Their Neighbors in Industrial Chicago, 1865–1930," *Journal of American Ethnic History* 16, no. 1 (1996): 55–73. On Irish dominance in the Catholic Church,

see Barrett, *The Irish Way*, chap. 2. On the Irish, race, and ethnicity in the urban north, see McGreevy, *Parish Boundaries*; and McMahon, *What Parish Are You From?*

30 "Minutes of the Annual Meeting," November 16, 1960. Thomas A. Tweed, "Diasporic Nationalism and Urban Landscape: Cuban Immigrants at a Catholic Shrine in Miami," in Orsi, *Gods of the City*, 131.

In 1960 Miami officially counted only 29,500 Cubans. Between January 1, 1959, and October 22, 1962, however, nearly 250,000 had fled the island, the majority of them settling in Miami. María Cristina García, *Havana USA: Cuban Exiles and Cuban Americans in South Florida, 1959–1994* (Berkeley: University of California Press, 1996), 13.

31 There was a minute Puerto Rican population in Chicago and suburbs at this time, but students from the island, such as Elena Padilla, Milton Pabon, and Muna Muñoz, frequently came to study at local universities. Lilia Fernández, *Brown in the Windy City: Mexican and Puerto Ricans in Postwar Chicago* (Chicago: University of Chicago Press, 2012), 44; Elena Padilla, "Puerto Rican Immigrants in New York and Chicago: A Study in Comparative Assimilation" (MA thesis, University of Chicago, 1947).

32 Badillo, *Latinos and the New Immigrant Church*, 87; Manuel Martínez, *Chicago: Historia de Nuestra Comunidad Puertorriqueña* (Chicago: Reyes and Sons, 1989), 94–97; Kelliher, "Hispanic Catholics," 127–28, 130. On the CYO's sports programs and African Americans, see Timothy B. Neary, *Crossing Parish Boundaries: Race, Sports, and Catholic Youth in Chicago, 1914–1954* (Chicago: University of Chicago Press, 2016).

33 Kelliher suggests that this effort was intended to weaken Bishop Shiel's stronghold on Puerto Rican work through the CYO. There is also no evidence that Stritch expected anyone other than the Claretians to continue working with Mexicans. Kelliher, "Hispanic Catholics," 133–34. See also Headley interview.

34 Cardinal's Committee, "Report for 1961"; "Minutes of the Annual Meeting," November 15, 1961. See also Kanter, *Chicago Católico*, 21–23.

35 See, for example, McGreevy, *Parish Boundaries*; McMahon, *What Parish Are You From?*; and Neary, *Crossing Parish Boundaries*.

36 Author's translation: "These are good people. They are sons and daughters of the church. We have to help them resolve their own problems so they can assume their rightful place in our community of Chicago." "El Comite del Cardenal para los de Habla Hispana en Chicago," *Vida Latina* 6, no. 5 (June 1957): 24. The interethnic youth violence between Italians and Puerto Ricans may have prompted local priests to respond to the newcomers' needs as well. See Catholic Interracial Council, "Dear Friend in Christ," July 30, 1954, Folder 675, Box 49, Near West Side Community Committee Records, Special Collections, Richard J. Daley Library, University of Illinois at Chicago.

37 Cardinal's Committee, "Report for 1961." Badillo covers this story as well; see Badillo, *Latinos and the New Immigrant Church*, 86–87. The committee obtained

its funding through Catholic Charities rather than the vicar general's office or the Chancery, a blessing according to Father Don Headley, since Catholic Charities director Monsignor Vincent Cook was an excellent fundraiser. Headley interview.
38 Cardinal's Committee, "Report for 1961"; Headley interview.
39 Knights of St. John Correspondence, May 1957 to July 1959, Folder 151, Saul Alinsky/Industrial Areas Foundation Collection, Special Collections, Richard J. Daley Library, UIC.
40 According to Dolan and Vidal, the Catholic Church had successfully expanded its efforts on the island in the fifties; thus, migrants were ripe for evangelization when they came to the mainland. Dolan and Vidal, *Puerto Rican and Cuban Catholics*, 43–51.
41 Kelliher, "Hispanic Catholics," 131, 136; Martínez, *Chicago*, 98–99; Badillo, *Latinos and the New Immigrant Church*.
42 Badillo, *Latinos and the New Immigrant Church*, 87; Headley interview.
43 Puerto Ricans, like other rural migrants, frequently practiced only common-law marriages that had not been consecrated by the church. Hence, priests began performing religious ceremonies to have marital unions recognized by God. Dolan and Vidal, *Puerto Rican and Cuban Catholics*, 24, 45–46.
44 Headley interview; Kelliher, "Hispanic Catholics," 139–45.
45 On the *cursillo* movement, see, for example, Dolan and Vidal, *Puerto Rican and Cuban Catholics*, 109–11.
46 Cardinal's Committee, "Report for 1961"; Mike Amezcua, *Making Mexican Chicago: From Postwar Settlement to the Age of Gentrification* (Chicago: University of Chicago Press, 2022), chap. 4; Louise Año Nuevo Kerr, "Mexican Chicago: Chicano Assimilation Aborted, 1939–1954," in *The Ethnic Frontier: Essays in the History of Group Survival in Chicago and the Midwest*, ed. Melvin G. Holli and Peter d'Alroy Jones (Grand Rapids, MI: Eerdmans, 1977), 324. The business elite had formed IFOMA in 1949 under the auspices of the Welfare Council of Metropolitan Chicago, although there are conflicting accounts that establish its origins in 1961.
47 Cardinal's Committee, "Report for 1961."
48 I borrow the term "cultural adhesive" from Eduardo Contreras, *Latinos in the Liberal City: Politics and Protest in San Francisco* (Philadelphia: University of Pennsylvania Press, 2019).
49 Tweed, "Diasporic Nationalism," 136; García, *Havana USA*, 19; Badillo, "Catholicism." Some also practiced the Yoruba tradition of *santería*.
50 Reverend Leo T. Mahon to His Eminence, Albert Cardinal Meyer, November 17, 1961, Cardinal's Committee for the Spanish Speaking Folder, Albert Cardinal Meyer CBC General Correspondence, CAA; García, *Havana USA*, 19–45; Marta Isabel Kollmann de Curutchet, "Localization of the Mexican and Cuban Population" (MA thesis, University of Chicago, 1967), 81.
51 García, *Havana USA*, 19, 15, 20. Badillo suggests that 80 percent of early exiles "identified with the Church." Badillo, "Catholicism," 79. See also Dolan and Vidal,

Puerto Rican and Cuban Catholics, 4; Marta Sayeed, interview with author via Zoom, February 10, 2021; Tweed, "Diasporic Nationalism," 137; and Gerald Poyo, "'Integration without Assimilation': Cuban Catholics in Miami, 1960–1980," *US Catholic Historian* 20, no. 4 (2002): 91, 92.

Cuban clergy who also fled the Castro regime, particularly the 130 priests expelled in 1961, perhaps smoothed the cultural transition for exiles who sought to practice their faith in the United States. Cuban clerics helped promote the exceptionalism and nationalism that set their compatriots apart from other Spanish-speaking migrants. Exiled Cuban bishop Eduardo Boza Masvidal lectured in a 1962 Miami mass that "expatriate Cubans faced [the task] of building exile communities dedicated to denouncing Communism and preparing the return home while at the same time forging a new life in a foreign land without losing their identity." Despite their strong sense of purpose and political consciousness, however, Cubans faced some prejudice in American Catholic churches, particularly Irish American and other white priests' reluctance to incorporate Cuban clergy into their churches.

52 Headley interview; Cardinal's Committee, "Report for 1961."
53 Cardinal's Committee, "Report for 1961."
54 Sayeed interview; Kollmann de Curutchet, "Localization of the Mexican and Cuban Population," 72.
55 Headley interview.
56 Headley interview; Eastwood, *Near West Side*, 298, 306.
57 Año Nuevo Kerr, "Mexican Chicago," 319; Kelliher, "Hispanic Catholics," 104.
58 Rev. John D. Ring to Cardinal John P. Cody, n.d., re: Fathers David Sanchez and David Gallegos, Archdiocesan Latin American Committee Correspondence (1969–1971), John Patrick Cody Records, 1965–1973, CAA; Sayeed interview.
59 Sayeed interview; Archdiocesan Latin American Committee, Correspondence 1967–68 Folder, John Patrick Cody Records, 1965–73 Box, Executive Records-CBC Diocesan Taskforce and Committee Files, CAA; Headley interview. On Richard J. Daley, see Adam Cohen and Elizabeth Taylor, *American Pharaoh: Mayor Richard J. Daley: His Battle for Chicago and the Nation* (Boston: Little Brown, 2000); Leon M. Despres, *Challenging the Daley Machine: A Chicago Alderman's Memoir* (Evanston: Northwestern University Press, 2005); Milton L. Rakove, *Don't Make No Waves, Don't Back No Losers: An Insider's Analysis of the Daley Machine* (Bloomington: Indiana University Press, 1975); Milton Rakove, *We Don't Want Nobody Nobody Sent: An Oral History of the Daley Years* (Bloomington: Indiana University Press, 1979); and Mike Royko, *Boss: Richard J. Daley of Chicago* (New York: Dutton, 1971).
60 Archdiocesan Latin American Committee newsletter, n.d., 1968, Archdiocesan Latin American Committee, Correspondence 1967–68 Folder, John Patrick Cody Records, 1965–73 Box, Executive Records-CBC Diocesan Taskforce and Committee Files, CAA.

61 A manager from Ralston Purina Company wrote to Cardinal Cody asking for assistance in identifying qualified Spanish-speaking salespeople for "attractive, well-paying jobs for which many whites are looking." Cody referred the manager to the Archdiocesan Committee and its "excellent employment program." That the manager characterized the jobs as appealing to whites underscored that these were not low-skilled, low-wage factory jobs but suitable for educated and professionally trained bilingual prospects who could help open up Spanish-speaking markets for the company. Cody's enthusiastic response may also have reflected his preference for advocating on behalf of more respectable, middle-class Spanish-speaking Catholics. J. M. Whealan to Archbishop Cody, June 30, 1972; John D. Ring to John Cardinal Cody, July 17, 1972 memo, Archdiocesan Latin American Committee Correspondence, 1972–73, John Patrick Cody Records 1965–1973, Executive Records-CBC Diocesan Taskforce and Committee Files, CAA.

62 The term referred historically to those born on the Iberian Peninsula rather than in Spain's colonies in the Americas.

63 Lucas, *Browning of America*, 54.

64 Rev. Gilbert A. Carroll and Rev. Donald J. Headley to Archbishop John Cody, May 25, 1966, Office of Urban Affairs (January–May 1966) Folder, John Patrick Cody Records, CAA.

65 On the practice in the Southwest, see García, *Católicos*, 122–23. On Archbishop Spellman's promotion of Spanish training in Puerto Rico for priests serving New York City's Puerto Rican Catholics, see Dolan and Vidal, *Puerto Rican and Cuban Catholics*, 97–98; and Badillo, *Latinos and the New Immigrant Church*, 81–83.

66 Kelliher, "Hispanic Catholics," 75, 88; Eastwood, *Near West Side*, 314, 317.

67 Rev. G. A. Carroll and Rev. D. J. Headley to Most Reverend John P. Cody, March 15, 1966, Bishops' Committee for the Spanish Speaking, Chicago 1956–1967 Folder, Robert E. Lucey Papers; Lucas, *Browning of America*, 39, 40. The only exception to this policy was at the start of the Korean War, when the church collaborated with the Mexican Catholic Church to have Mexican priests come minister to braceros in the United States in rural areas. Quinn, memorandum to Meyer, July 16, 1963.

68 Lucas, *Browning of America*, 3. A May 1980 national meeting of bishops held in Chicago, which included a half-day session on Latinos and a visit to a Latino parish in one of the city's barrios, similarly signaled the church hierarchy's increasing understanding that it needed to cultivate a closer relationship to its Spanish-speaking believers for the sake of preserving the church. Lucas, *Browning of America*, 68, 4; Matovina, *Latino Catholicism*, preface.

69 Lucas, *Browning of America*, 61.

3

Pan-Latino Placemaking and Housing Dynamics

St. Joseph the Worker in Grand Rapids, Michigan, 1956–2000

DELIA FERNÁNDEZ-JONES

"There's a lot of history there," said Hilario Zapata, a Tejano man from Grand Rapids, when referring to St. Joseph the Worker in 2008. The church was in the process of relocating out of the majority-Latino neighborhood into a nearby economically declining suburb, after the Latino population had outgrown the building. The diocese had declined to support constructing a new church on the same site. Hilario and his wife, Katie, joined St. Joseph after leaving the migrant trail in the 1970s. Zapata chose St. Joseph because "being able to come in and listen to the church in Spanish was really what I needed," he remarked. At that time, St. Joseph the Worker was one of the only churches that had multiple Spanish masses in the small but urban center in West Michigan. It was also the only church wherein most of the parishioners were Latinos, including Tejanos, Mexican nationals, and Puerto Ricans, including myself and my family, who have been in the area for decades.[1] In particular, Zapata found, "It was very inspiring to us to come to a church where you were family—where you really felt like someone cared about you."[2] Unbeknownst to Zapata, by the time he arrived in the 1970s, there had already been decades of work to create this community. Since the late 1940s, when a large wave of Latinos arrived in Grand Rapids, they had been working to create a pan-Latino space in this conservative, Protestant city.

The Grandville Avenue corridor in which the parish was located has come to house one of the most densely populated areas of Latinos in the city. After arriving via labor migration in the 1950s, like many other Latinos in the Midwest, Tejanos and Puerto Ricans sought both housing and a place to worship in a segregated landscape.[3] They found that most landlords and homeowners would not rent or sell to Latinos in the Grandville Avenue area at the time. They held mass in small chapels near the cathedral for about twenty years until housing dynamics shifted in the mid-1960s. As white Grand Rapidians left for the suburbs, Latinos as well as African Americans moved into the previously all-white neighborhoods. Mexicans, Puerto Ricans, and Cubans began worshipping at St. Joseph shortly after moving into the area. Together, they formed a pan-Latino church. The parish served as a destination for new waves of Latino immigrants and migrants from across Latin America and has been recognized as one of the community's foundational institutions for over forty years. This chapter chronicles how this pan-Latino community engaged in placemaking that transformed St. Joseph the Worker and the Grandville Avenue corridor into a place where Latinos could meet their everyday religious and secular needs.[4]

Chronicling the transformation of the Grandville Avenue corridor via the history of St. Joseph the Worker engages with various Latino religious and placemaking scholarship. Borrowing social scientists Katia Balassiano and Marta María Maldonado's definition of placemaking as when places are used in the "pursuit of shared socially and culturally specific goals," I recognize how quotidian acts on the part of Mexicans, Puerto Ricans, and Cubans made them agents of change in Grand Rapids.[5] Like Hilario Zapata, in searching for a place to worship in Spanish when they arrived, Latinos helped to transform the local Catholic religious landscape. This is also a story of ethnic succession that is akin to the transformation of previously "ethnic white" churches and neighborhoods like that of Latino spaces in Chicago too, most notably studied by Deborah Kanter.[6] As seen in Lilia Fernández's chapter in this anthology, the diverse Latino population in Grand Rapids mirrors that of Chicago as well. However, whereas Chicago's archdiocese had to contend with various Latino populations in different churches, this work focuses on the development of one shared parish among various Latino ethnic groups. I argue that this pan-Latino church developed in a previously European immigrant parish because the community had a history of forming pan-Latino spaces that preceded their presence at St. Joseph and expanded beyond religious spaces. Persistent placemaking efforts over the course of the 1950s to the 2000s resulted in St. Joseph the Worker becoming a central site for Latino life and an integral part of a vibrant Latino neighborhood in Grand Rapids. This community received limited support from the diocese for its efforts, underscoring how pan-Latino placemaking was an effective tool these immigrants and migrants used to upset the local power dynamic and make a place for themselves.

Documenting Latino Catholics in a mostly white, mostly Calvinist city has been difficult. Grand Rapids has long been known as the epicenter of Reformed Protestantism in the Midwest.[7] These churches dotted almost every neighborhood in Grand Rapids, a city of about 175,000 people in the time period of this study. Ultimately, Latino Catholics were a double demographic minority in this midwestern city.[8] The Diocese of Grand Rapids, admittedly, does not have many documents from St. Joseph the Worker. As a scholar who is from this particular community and who grew up in this parish, I have drawn on my family and community's tradition of oral storytelling to guide this research. In addition to oral history interviews, the parish's sacramental registrars, limited documents from the diocese's sparse Hispanic Apostolate archive, and newspapers were instrumental to reconstructing an important but not well documented history. This work is not only evidence of Latino placemaking in religious settings, but is also an attempt to rescue the history of St. Joseph from certain erasure. This chapter chronologically examines the first pan-religious site Latinos made in the 1940s and 1950s, follows the community's movement to St. Joseph in the late 1950s and 1960s, and details parish life at St. Joseph from the 1970s to the early 2000s.

A History of Pan-Latino Religious Space: The Mexican Apostolate and Our Lady of Guadalupe

To many, Grand Rapids seemed like an unlikely place for Latinos to make a home for themselves. Unlike its Rust Belt counterparts, Grand Rapids was not an auto or steel city. Rather, it had a diversified economy, making it an attractive place for many immigrants and migrants alike. Like many other northern midwestern cities, the city was mostly white, Anglo-Saxon, and Protestant, with a smaller population of African Americans who were segregated into menial labor and limited housing options. However, unlike other locales, in the early 1900s, a small tight-knit community of Dutch Reformed Protestant immigrants and their descendants began to impact the city's culture. In its strictest forms, this denomination prohibited dancing, drinking, and many forms of public entertainment. Instead, members prided themselves on how honest, hardworking, and thrifty they were and fiercely kept to themselves. Their turn inward helped them to resist forms of assimilation that would bring them further away from their religious devotion. For its part, the Catholic diocese had conformed to local conservative mores and did not intervene to help its followers unless prompted.[9] When Mexicans and Puerto Ricans began arriving in this city en masse in the 1940s and 1950s in search of work off of agricultural fields and via railroad work, they settled in a locale with conservative religious values and limited institutional support.

As early as the 1940s and 1950s, the Mexican and Puerto Rican communities began to transform the ethnic and cultural landscape of Catholicism in Grand Rapids. As a key support system for incoming migrants, St. Andrew's Cathedral became the first stop for many of them. Located in downtown Grand Rapids, the cathedral was less than half a mile from the neighborhoods Mexican families occupied on the south side of the city from the 1920s to the 1950s. Two Mexican couples, Daniel and Guadalupe Vargas and Daniel and Consuelo Vásquez, helped to draw the Diocese of Grand Rapids's attention to the small but growing number of Mexican Catholics who were arriving at the cathedral for mass. In turn, the diocese established the Mexican Apostolate in the late 1940s. Vargas and other Mexicans were involved in steering this ministry, which served as the diocese's formal outreach to the Mexican community. Newly settled migrants used the apostolate as part of an organizational base to host Mexican devotional activities. For example, in concert with the Sociedad Guadalupana, a men's religious group formed in the early 1940s, the Mexican Apostolate held celebrations for Our Lady of Guadalupe for the mostly Mexican community. Having this ministry, a men's religious organization, and Mexican religious celebrations helped to welcome the growing network of Mexicans in Grand Rapids.[10]

Mexicans, soon joined by Puerto Ricans, worked diligently for a space of their own to worship. By the 1940s, the Catholic Church had all but ceased to create new ethnic-based parishes, but Mexicans in Grand Rapids made a case for a creation of their own in 1948.[11] The diocese helped them purchase a house near St. Andrew's Cathedral that would serve as a one-room chapel.[12] At first the Mexican community shared it with Latvians, who had come to Grand Rapids as refugees in the late 1940s. There, Titus Narbutas, a Lithuanian priest who arrived in Michigan via Chile, led mass for the Mexican community in the chapel.[13] However, the chapel could hardly contain the growing number of Mexicans and recently arriving Puerto Ricans in the mid- to late 1940s. While the pre–World War II Mexican community numbered just about a hundred people, by 1945 there were five hundred of them. Within five years, Puerto Ricans also began arriving at the chapel for mass. By 1952, the community had raised money and received support from the diocese to purchase another, larger house as their chapel.[14] They worshipped there for four years. By 1956, the growing community again relocated to a chapel that was built alongside the cathedral. The diocese assigned them Father Leo Roselonic, a Polish priest, to give mass in Spanish in the chapel and then named the church the Mexican Chapel, to the chagrin of some of the Puerto Rican minority.[15] Intense discussions occurred among Mexican and Puerto Rican parishioners to find a name that would actually represent their shared pan-Latino chapel. They settled on Our Lady of Guadalupe, who had become the patroness of Latin America by this time.[16] Indeed, Mexicans had been there longer than Puerto Ricans, but the latter group had made contributions to the parish as well. Whether the diocese was unaware that Puerto Ricans were a part of this community or assumed that they were Mexican is unclear. However, contending with the erasure of Puerto Ricans was part of the sometimes-difficult process of pan-Latino placemaking that this group needed to consider. Though there was conflict over naming the chapel, it still served as a space where Mexicans and Puerto Ricans engaged one another and organized pan-Latino religious events.

One liberal bishop was key to ensuring that Latinos would continue to have priests to provide mass in a language they could understand. Bishop Francis Haas was appointed to the Diocese of Grand Rapids in 1943 after a career that centered on social justice, making him a bit of an outlier for this more conservative diocese. After serving as a negotiator for the National Labor Relations Board, becoming a sociologist, and being appointed dean of social action at Catholic University, he became the bishop of the Diocese of Grand Rapids toward the end of his life.

He made one decision that helped to transform Grand Rapids into a welcoming place for Latino Catholics. In 1950 he started sending seminarians to San Antonio, Texas.[17] There they joined a host of other white priests who were sent for pastoral development and religious education as it pertained to Mexican Americans and Latinos.[18] One such priest was Father Ted Kozlowski, a young Polish American man. His studies centered on learning Mexican culture, Spanish, and theology. Upon his return, he was ordained a priest in 1958.[19] Father Ted Kozlowski became Our Lady of Guadalupe's first priest trained in Mexican American culture. Though he still had to learn about Puerto Ricans, his time as the chapel's rector immersed him in a diverse set of Latino cultures. In fact, he was often witness to the continued development of a pan-Latino religious community.

Latinos' choice of godparents for their children baptized at Our Lady of Guadalupe indicates the strength of the bonds these groups maintained. While friendships formed informally among neighbors and coworkers, Catholicism provided a formal way to create a network via *compadrazgo*, or godparentage. Choosing godparents for one's children meant electing someone who would guide them in the Catholic faith. In the event that their parents were unable to care for a child, godparents would theoretically step in to raise the child.[20] Examining the choices for *padrinos* illustrates how the community created cross-ethnic relationships. In many cases, Mexican parents selected Mexican godparents while Puerto Ricans sought Puerto Rican godparents for their children. However, Puerto Ricans also made regular practice of selecting prominent Mexican leaders in the community as godparents for their children. For example, a Puerto Rican couple, Leopoldo and Guadalupe Figueroa, chose Gregorio Chavez, who was Mexican, and Leopoldo's sister, Santa Sánchez, who was also Puerto Rican, as godparents for their son Santiago.[21] Chavez and his family had actually helped Puerto Ricans settle in Grand Rapids, even offering to house the Sánchez family for a time. Choosing the Mexican man as a godfather was a way to formalize the relationship that was forming between these families.

Since Mexican Americans had helped to establish the community and constituted the majority of Our Lady of Guadalupe's parishioners, choosing a Mexican godparent also opened up possibilities for mobility within the Latino community. For instance, Saturnino and Priscilla Ayala, a Puerto Rican couple, chose Daniel Vásquez, one of the Mexican Apostolate's founders, as godfather for their son Carlos. Connecting to some of the most well-known Mexican families was a regular practice, not just for Puerto Ricans, but for Mexicans alike throughout the history of Our Lady of Guadalupe. This phenomenon increased as Mexicans and Puerto Ricans came into more frequent contact with one another at work and in shared neighborhoods. After presiding over so many sacraments at the chapel, Father Ted Kozlowski was transferred by the diocese to St. Joseph the Worker in 1965, a nearby parish situated in an area in which there was a growing presence of Latinos. This had a profound impact on the parishioners at both Our Lady of Guadalupe and St. Joseph the Worker.

From the VanDrunens to the Torreses: White Flight and the Transition of a Parish

St. Joseph the Worker and the area it inhabited underwent both structural and demographic changes since its founding in the 1890s to the 1960s, when Latinos arrived. The site started as an undeveloped rural area. When the bishop of Grand Rapids facilitated the purchase of land to be made into a parish for the Dutch Catholics in the city, the diocese remarked that the area was just a "potato patch on a hill." On Rumsey Street off Grandville Avenue on the southwest side of the city, the would-be Dutch parishioners and Father Henry Frenken, a priest who had just arrived from Holland, helped to construct the church themselves. After they consecrated the site in 1889, the church held bilingual masses in Dutch and English. Frenken remarked that people were "glad to have their own church where they could hear their own language spoken"—something Latino parishioners would say about the space almost one hundred years later.[22] Within ten years of the parish's formation, over six hundred children were baptized at the church, which was within walking distance of its parishioners' homes. Within a few decades, however, the area drastically changed to include a diverse range of European immigrants. Middle- and lower-class Dutch, Polish, and Italian families who found housing in the area surrounding St. Joseph worshipped alongside one another beginning in the 1920s and 1930s. At the same time, a small Mexican community settled alongside the influx of African American participants in the Great Migration just blocks away from what were becoming all-white neighborhoods. Some of the "ethnic white" parishioners of St. Joseph began looking for housing outside the Grandville Avenue area in the late 1940s and early 1950s.

Baptism records reveal that despite their exodus from the neighborhood, a diverse cross section of European-descended families still attended St. Joseph. For example, in 1952 a Dutch couple, Peter and Lois VanDrunen, baptized their daughter Sally at the church though they lived on the northeast side of Grand Rapids, an area generally open only to whites.[23] Peter's family grew up across the street from the church at 416 Grandville Avenue, and it appears that he brought his family back to his childhood parish. Other families did the same. Italians Frank Amado and his wife, Antionette D'Amico, were in a similar situation. Frank had grown up in the neighborhood, but by the time they baptized their daughter Catherine at St. Joseph in 1952, they had already moved out to a newly forming suburb south of Grand Rapids.[24] In another instance, Raymond and Mary Galewski, a Polish couple, baptized their daughter Linda Lu in December 1953 at St. Joseph. They too had moved out of the neighborhood and into the southeast side's newly developing, all-white Garfield Park area. By this time, these European-descended families had shed most of their cultural markers in the public sphere and had access to some of Grand Rapids' exclusively white housing. Their Latino counterparts did not make the same journey.

When Latinos began trying to secure housing on the southwest side, they encountered a neighborhood in flux. Although some white families had moved to the suburbs, many others remained. This was certainly the Alvarez family's experience. In 1952 Robert Lee Alvarez lived with his parents, Santos Alvarez and Natividad Palma, and his grandparents at 731 Grandville Avenue, one block from St. Joseph.[25] Except for the Mexican American man who lived next door, white families occupied the houses to the right and left of them for blocks.[26] Baptism records also evidence this trend. Robert Lee Alvarez, one of the first Spanish-surnamed persons baptized at St. Joseph, was baptized in 1952 and was part of the second generation of Mexican Americans in the area. He was one the few Latinos baptized during this period.[27] Throughout the 1950s, on average there were about thirty baptisms per year, six of which were of Latino children. While there was not an outright ban on Mexicans and Puerto Ricans in the neighborhoods around the church, it was clear that they were not entirely welcomed there.[28]

Indeed, few Latinos had the same housing opportunities as white Grand Rapidians in the 1950s. Even as white families left for the suburbs, they often refused to sell or rent their homes to Mexicans and Puerto Ricans. For example, when Mike Navarro, a migrant from Mercedes, Texas, earned enough money to buy his own home in 1957, the Dutch homeowner refused to sell to him. Navarro had to seek the intercession of his previous employer, also a Dutch man, to help him negotiate the purchase. My paternal grandparent's experience with housing also gives a glimpse into anti-Blackness and housing segregation.[29] My Puerto Rican grandparents, Luísa and Pío Fernandez, and their children reflected Puerto Rico's racial diversity in their skin tones. They quickly became familiar with Grand Rapids' racial segregation after arriving in 1955 from Aguas Buenas, Puerto Rico. Luísa only took her lightest-skinned children with her and her brother—not her darker-skinned husband—to find an apartment. She remarked that if you were "dark-skinned, you couldn't get an apartment" in 1955.[30] Indeed, this was also the case for African Americans attempting to live on the southwest side. By the late 1950s and the early 1960s, however, as more whites left the area, Latino and Black families found more housing opportunities in areas that had rejected them just a few years earlier.

As the area started to transition, the first Latinos who attended St. Joseph the Worker both lived next to the church and sent their children to the parish school. The neighborhood around the church went from all white in the 1940s to a mixed neighborhood with working-class African Americans, Mexicans, Puerto Ricans, and whites all sharing space by the late 1950s and early 1960s. St. Joseph's kindergarten through eighth grade school was representative of the neighborhood. One of the school's earliest Latino families included the Torres children. Robert and Lucia were a part of the first generation of Mexican Americans born in Grand Rapids in the early 1950s. They were baptized at St. Andrew's in 1954 and 1951 respectively. They lived just a block away from St. Joseph and spent their elementary years there.[31] My paternal aunts and uncles joined the Torres children at parish school. After finding a home just a couple of houses away from the Torres family, my Puerto Rican grandparents decided to send their children to St. Joseph. My oldest aunt, Rosalia Espindola, and uncle, Cirilo Fernández, had trouble transitioning to Grand Rapids' public schools from Puerto Rico. St. Joseph's school provided an opportunity for their parents to form close relationships with teachers and staff they trusted as members of the Catholic faith.[32] Thus, in 1961 Rosalia and Cirilo made their First Communion with the Torres children as both families started attending St. Joseph. Mexican and Puerto Rican children at the school and at the parish helped to draw in other newly arriving families.

By the late 1950s and early 1960s, the presence of some Latinos at the church and the neighborhood started to encourage others to seek out the parish. At the time, about twenty Latino families attended St. Joseph; most of them were migrants from Texas and Puerto Rico, and Cuban immigrants who had just settled in Grand Rapids. The church was still mostly white at this time and offered only an English mass, but Latinos started to attend St. Joseph regardless of where they lived. For example, the Cantú family, who lived in Beeville, Texas, before settling in Grand Rapids, was able to purchase a house at 824 Oakland Street, just a five-minute walk to St. Joseph. Their children completed their First Holy Communion in 1961.[33] Other families who came in the late 1950s also quickly found St. Joseph after deciding to stay in the area. On the other hand, the Bérrios family, from Guayama, Puerto Rico, drove from about a mile away to have their son take confirmation classes at St. Joseph in 1963.[34] Lastly, Angelo and Mario Lopez, two Afro-Cuban brothers who were born and baptized in Pennsylvania in 1952, were both confirmed at St. Joseph in the early 1960s.[35] They lived a twenty-minute walk or five-minute car ride from the parish. Many Latinos in the area were accustomed to pan-Latino religious spaces from their experiences at Our Lady of Guadalupe. As St. Joseph began to embody that same characteristic, it attracted more Latinos, especially as their presence in the surrounding neighborhood grew. From the late 1950s to the mid-1960s, St. Joseph existed as a racially and ethnically mixed church. Though Latinos were in the minority, they had a steady but growing presence.

While Our Lady of Guadalupe Chapel was still an option for Latinos, that many people in this community started to transfer to St. Joseph the Worker in the early 1960s shows how Latinos began to feel more comfortable in this space. Though there were only English masses at St. Joseph at this time, there was a school nearby their children could attend, many of them could walk to mass as they started to move into nearby neighborhoods, and even more, there were other Latinos—an indication that they too were welcome. While Our Lady of Guadalupe had Spanish-speaking Father Ted Kozlowski, St. Joseph had a burgeoning Latino neighborhood that attracted another wave of incoming Mexicans, Puerto Ricans, and Tejanos, as well as some newly arrived Cubans, in the mid-1960s. Many Mexican and Tejano families continued to settle off the migrant trail in Grand Rapids, where they had extended family and kinship networks. Some Puerto Ricans came straight from the island, and others relocated from Chicago and New York in search of smaller, safer cities. Though the first wave of Cubans that arrived in the early 1960s were a part of an upper-class, mostly white Cuban migration that settled among white Grand Rapidians, subsequent waves joined the growing working-class Mexican and Puerto Rican community.[36]

"Why New Mexico When There Are So Many Hispanics Here?": Serving a Pan-Latino Religious Community and Making Pan-Latino Places

From the mid-1960s to the early 1980s, the Grandville Avenue corridor had many visible Latino spaces, including St. Joseph the Worker Parish. One of the most obvious signs that the neighborhood welcomed Latinos was the presence of the Latin American Council. In 1968 a pan-Latino group of community pioneers formed this grassroots organization to help Latinos in Grand Rapids. Within a few short years and with the aid of federal anti-poverty funding, the council developed into a full-fledged social service agency and center for cultural programming. It had its own employment services, offered translation at appointments, and a food and clothing pantry, among a variety of services for every member of the family, from babies to the elderly.[37] In addition, it celebrated pan-Latino cultural placemaking. For example, youth group leaders taught area teenagers different Mexican and Puerto Rican folkloric dances and hosted classes so the youth could learn to cook Cuban, Mexican, and Puerto Rican cuisines. The LAC also showed films about Guatemala, Cuba, Mexico, and Puerto Rico in community businesses to try to reach various members of the Latino population. By this time there were a handful of Latino-owned bars, restaurants, and corner stores on or near Grandville Avenue as well.[38] All of these establishments were within walking distance of St. Joseph the Worker. As the area became increasingly more Latino, members of the community worked to transform the space around them to fit their various material, cultural, and religious needs.

One of the most visible signs of community change came when Our Lady of Guadalupe closed in 1965 and the demographics of St. Joseph dramatically changed. Some of the Latino parishioners at Our Lady of Guadalupe recalled that the diocese wanted to "mainstream" them. Miguel Bérrios surmised that the diocese wanted to integrate Latinos with white parishioners at the time, as it had done with European immigrants some forty years earlier.[39] Given the fervor for integration in the 1960s, this was a plausible reason. Father Ted Kozlowski, however, assumed that it was because he was getting transferred to St. Joseph as a part of the regular rotation of priests. Regardless of the intent, within one year of Kozlowski's relocation, the baptismal registers reflected an increasingly Latino church. For example, for ten years between 1952 and 1962, only sixteen Spanish-surnamed babies were baptized at St. Joseph. However, after a shift in the parishioners and the neighborhood, in 1965 nine children with Spanish surnames were baptized in one year alone. Almost as if a switch was turned, after Kozlowski arrived at St. Joseph, a large portion of the white parishioners seemed to disappear from the clerical records. For example, though in 1965 all the children baptized belonged to "ethnic" white families, in 1966 only two of them did. In fact, after 1966, the overwhelming majority of children baptized at St. Joseph came from Latino families: twenty-eight out of thirty in 1966 and twenty-eight out of forty-two in 1967. Every succeeding year, Latino families made up the preponderance of the baptismal rolls. These records and census data point to a pattern of white flight evident in housing dynamics in the 1950s and within the church in the late 1960s. These records also provide evidence of Latino placemaking. St. Joseph the Worker became a visibly Latino church at the same time the surrounding area started to house Latinos, community-owned businesses and grassroots organizations developed, and a Spanish-speaking priest joined St. Joseph.

While some parishioners followed Father Kozlowski to St. Joseph from Our Lady of Guadalupe, many Latinos who joined St. Joseph in the 1960s were newcomers to the area. In fact, church records show that these recent arrivals were very mobile and likely migrant farmworkers. For instance, the Castillo family's oldest son, Daniel, was baptized in Trinidad, Colorado, in 1950, while their second and third sons, Mario and David, were baptized in San Antonio, Texas, in 1958. Lastly, in 1960 their daughter Raquel was baptized in Hart, Michigan, a rural town that was a frequent stop for migrant workers just an hour's drive from Grand Rapids.[40] Other Mexican American youths were born in rural Michigan and their families settled in Grand Rapids before their confirmation. Examples included Rosa Rocha Ramirez, who was baptized at St. Apolonia in Stanton, Michigan, in 1956, and Gloria Rodriguez, who was baptized at St. Francis de Sales in Lakeview, Michigan, in 1957. Both of these young Latinas made their confirmation at St. Joseph in 1968. Gloria's older sister Sara, who was also confirmed alongside the two others, was baptized in a different farming community's parish in nearby Greenville, Michigan. All of those cities were situated in the rural periphery within fifty miles of Grand Rapids. As migrants were looking for neighborhoods and jobs to help them settle in Grand Rapids, St. Joseph the Worker became part of that process. As more and more Latinos joined the church, the pastoral staff and others continued to shape the church into a welcoming place.

Vatican II and the ongoing civil rights movement likely had an influence on the welcoming atmosphere that both Father Ted Kozlowski and Sister Lucia Zapata, a newly professed nun, built at St. Joseph beginning in 1965. As a high school student in Saginaw, Michigan, Lucia Zapata, a Mexican American woman, was inspired by her principal, Father Theodore LaMarre. A civil rights activist in his own right, LaMarre was an inaugural member of Saginaw's Human Relations Commission, a city agency that tried to troubleshoot racial and ethnic issues. He received honors from the American GI Forum for his commitment to Mexican Americans and was a member of the State of Michigan's Civil Rights Commission.[41] Zapata was a secretarial aide for LaMarre as a high school student and helped to type his correspondence with state officials at the capitol in Lansing, Michigan. She was impressed that he was fighting for the "rights of the people—the Hispanics and the Blacks!"

she recalled, enthusiastic about his widespread support for various racial groups. While her family had not been migrant farmworkers themselves, Zapata worked in the fields during her summer breaks to pay for her tuition. Her experiences with migrant farmworkers and her Catholic upbringing inspired her to invest in making changes for poor people, leading her to a life of religious devotion. She started the process of becoming a professed nun in Grand Rapids immediately after graduating from a Catholic high school in Saginaw. She found her new Dominican order to be quite conservative and a bit out of touch with the local community. For example, her superiors were interested in sending her to New Mexico to complete her schooling and to work with the Hispanic population there. Zapata was puzzled at the proposal. She wondered, "Why New Mexico when there are so many Hispanics here?" She was relieved when her order decided to let her stay in Grand Rapids. Zapata was not fully professed when she arrived at St. Joseph the Worker School in 1965 to be a student teacher to a combined class of third and fourth graders. Between teaching during the week and helping to plan and attend mass, she was excited to be immersed in a Latino community and to work alongside Kozlowski. Together the two fostered a parish that would meet Latino needs.

Given the diverse ethnicities of Latino parishioners, St. Joseph offered opportunities for ethnic-specific celebrations, but it also hosted a plethora of community-wide events. Mexicans and Mexican Americans made up the majority of Latinos in Grand Rapids. They also had a long-standing tradition of celebrating the Virgen de Guadalupe's feast day as early as the 1940s in Grand Rapids. Many Puerto Ricans and even some Cubans joined them when they celebrated this event at St. Joseph in the late 1960s. The other groups also observed their own feast days. For example, Sister Lucia helped organize a celebration for La Virgen de Caridad del Cobre for Cubans.[42] The creation of Spanish masses, however, served to further unify these parishioners. Since Vatican II in 1962, mass at St. Joseph had been delivered in English.[43] When Father Ted arrived, he created a Spanish mass alongside an English one.[44] These offerings were representative of the diverse language abilities of Latinos in the late 1960s. A Spanish service was an obvious sign that St. Joseph was welcoming to all Spanish-speaking Latinos, while an English mass was also necessary for the second- and even third-generation Latinos who were bilingual or monolingual English-speaking. The church was where Latinos of varying ethnic identities and language abilities could feel welcomed.

The parish, via Father Ted, Sister Lucia, and other staff, had an active presence in the Latino community outside church. In particular, Kozlowski and Zapata worked to ensure parishioners had access to what they needed. Kozlowski recalled, "In the summer we celebrated Mass on Wednesdays in a [local] shop. We would talk with the youth and the adults after and offer them food and clothing."[45] He also suggested that Sister Lucia Zapata and another Mexican American sister and teacher, Ellen Mary López, carry out home visits to help assess the spiritual, educational, and material needs of the families who attended St. Joseph the Worker School. Together they tried to connect families to resources, many of whom the clerical staff referred to the Latin American Council.[46]

In 1968 Kozlowski took their ministry a step further by creating the St. Joseph Mission Program to help provide activities for the youth who lived near the parish. The program's purpose was to "give children an integrated atmosphere and provide recreation in an area where little is available." The entrenched housing and school segregation in Grand Rapids prevented white youth and their Black and Latino counterparts from spending time with one another. Kozlowski helped to pick two houses that would serve as host to this teen program, both of which were within walking distance of the parish. Young people could attend mass on Mondays at the sites if they cared to, but otherwise all of their activities were secular in nature. Many white volunteers staffed the centers and brought their children with them. One of them, Susan Budzynski, remarked, "It's not run for the purpose of conversions or to preach Catholicism. It's just something to enjoy."[47] The mission program offered dances, pool, picnics, and arts and crafts. While the Latin American Council would soon provide its own youth group and youth spaces in the early 1970s, Kozlowski and St. Joseph helped provide a solution to the glaring lack of resources for Grand Rapids' Latino and Black youth in the southwest and southeast side neighborhoods. This sustained outreach became a cornerstone of the parish's service to its community. Moreover, it was part of a broader effort to create more spaces wherein Latinos would be welcomed.

With St. Joseph and other grassroots organizations in place for Grand Rapids' Latinos, the diocese started to send bilingual priests to other nearby areas that needed Spanish services. Kozlowski, as one of the few Spanish-speaking priests in the diocese, was needed to attend to a growing Mexican American community in nearby Holland, Michigan. Many migrant farmworkers were settling in the area and attending St. Francis de Sales. The diocese also tried to supply Spanish-speaking priests when it could to St. Joseph. In the meantime, one of the first Puerto Ricans to settle in Grand Rapids, Dionicio Bérrios, became a lecturer and cantor in the church in the 1960s. He also translated for any monolingual English-speaking priests the church hosted and was seen as a leader in the parish.[48] In addition, a newly ordained priest, Father Pedro García, served as a temporary substitute priest in the meantime. Born in Texas, he and his family worked a migrant circuit across the Midwest until they settled in Holland, Michigan, in the 1950s. García was only temporarily available to the more permanent population at St. Joseph the Worker due to the growing need to serve the migrant population that spent a large part of their year on western and northern Michigan's fields.

In the 1970s, in a sign that the Latino community at St. Joseph had access to resources within their parish and other avenues, the diocese shifted its attention to the stream of migrants who came to Michigan annually. Along with Fathers Pedro García and Ted Kozlowski, Father Steven Dudek, another white, Spanish-speaking priest, and Sisters Lucia Zapata and Lupe Moreno, another Mexican American nun, formed the Hispanic Apostolate. This was the Diocese of Grand Rapids' response to the migrant workers' urgent and impending need for sacraments and other social services. The members of the Hispanic Apostolate drove to various farms that dotted the lakeshore and northern Michigan, providing much-needed resources. In some cases, this was the only contact migrant workers had with people who spoke Spanish and with non-migrant worker Latinos.[49] While the Latin American Council and St. Joseph provided resources for Latinos in Grand Rapids, migrants could access these resources only if they could get to the city. The demanding farmworking schedule and limited transportation prevented them from doing so regularly. Thus, Hispanic Apostolate members dedicated their time, attention, and resources to those with the greatest need, while parishioners at St. Joseph and organizers served Grand Rapids' Latinos.

"The United Nations of Latino Catholics": Saving a Pan-Latino Religious Site

The Latino population grew in size and diversity in Grand Rapids in the 1970s and 1980s, leading many of them to seek out St. Joseph. Indeed, many people living near the church desperately needed services. The 1980s ushered in two significant changes: the city's disinvestment in the now mostly Latino and Black neighborhood, and increased unemployment during the recession. Of the people living in the same census tract as the church, 12 percent were out of work, compared to about 3 percent of the suburban population.[50] St. Joseph became an additional place that Latinos could go to for help. Under the direction of the all-Latino parish council two white priests helped to supply people with emergency funding during the 1980s when they could.[51] However, when possible, the church tried to direct those in need to the Hispanic Center of West Michigan and Latin American Services. When the Latin American Council closed its doors in 1978, these two organizations formed in its stead. Like their predecessor, they provided cultural programming, but more importantly social services. St. Joseph, the Hispanic Center, and Latin American Services became centers of compassion and resources for this growing pan-Latino community.

As people from across Latin America started to inhabit both the neighborhoods and the church, the Charismatic movement also provided opportunities for people from various Latino ethnic groups to bond with one another and foster a welcoming environment even during trying times.[52] Officially known as Catholic Charismatic Renewal, this phenomenon marked the embracing of expressive religious devotion. Father Pedro García, who became the permanent priest at St. Joseph in 1994, noted that parishioners from various Latino backgrounds flocked to the increasingly more Charismatic mass, which had a Puerto Rican band, because it was "so joyful." Indeed, the mass was filled with people from all over Latin America. By the 1990s and early 2000s, St. Joseph seemed like a microcosm of Latinos in the United States. Father Pedro García jokingly referred to the church as "the United Nations of Catholic Latinos."[53] Though the church had been Mexican, Puerto Rican, and Cuban for decades, by the 1990s there were families from Colombia, Ecuador, the Dominican Republic, and Guatemala. The decades of work that parishioners, priests, and nuns had done to provide a welcoming place for Latino Catholic devotion bore fruit in the form of a diverse, pan-Latino space.

Meanwhile, though, St. Joseph parishioners and its priest were fighting to save their church from closure due to financial constraints. By the time García reached the parish, he was informed that he was there to close St. Joseph. The diocese charged that the church, made up of working-class migrants and immigrants and their descendants, could not support itself. To be sure, the parish was located in one of the poorest census tracts in Grand Rapids. The median family income for households in St. Joseph's neighborhood was $15,966 a year. This was double what segregated African American neighborhoods made, but it was about half of what white working-class families made in a nearby suburb. This amount also paled in comparison to earnings in the highest-income neighborhoods in the lily-white, exclusive nearby city of East Grand Rapids, where families averaged between $62,000 and $77,000 a year.[54] Parishioners would need to give a larger portion of their limited salaries to keep the church afloat. García was able to encourage the parishioners to give more to save their church. He told them, "You have to fight for your church!" Indeed, he succeeded in increasing offerings from "$200 to $400 a week to almost $2,000," preventing the diocese from closing the church.[55] The congregants and García engaged in an active struggle to protect a space for Latinos in a neighborhood that they helped to develop.

While St. Joseph was not closing, the growing congregation posed a problem for the small church. As it was, the church could seat 250 people, but the church had long outgrown that. By the early 2000s, 900 people were attending three masses every weekend. Latinos stood on the stairs outside the packed church trying to hear mass.[56] For comparison, at its peak in the 1970s, over 70 children were baptized at St. Joseph in one year. In the 2000s, the church was baptizing 300 Latino children a year in the same space. Throughout the late 1990s and early 2000s, they had collected $30,000 for a building fund, but it was not enough for the entire remodel necessary to house the growing population.[57] In the early 2000s, the diocese began to look at options outside the Grandville Avenue neighborhood. To leave the neighborhood, however, would be to leave a growing web of institutions and resources to which migrants and immigrants had grown accustomed. For example, just one street over from the church stood Clínica Santa María, a medical clinic run by the city's Catholic hospital system that performed well-baby checks, primary care visits, and a rotating dental clinic, among many other services performed by a bilingual staff. Just one block from the clinic sat Southwest Community Campus. This neighborhood school expanded its building in the early 2000s to have enough space for more students living in the area and started to offer a dual-immersion Spanish-language program. In addition, there were other arts and cultural institutions in the area. Instead of staying and rebuilding on the site, in 2007 the diocese chose to purchase a former Christian Reformed church in the nearby suburb of Wyoming for $423,500 and sold the building that had housed St. Joseph the Worker Parish for over a century.[58]

Though Wyoming had been a white working-class suburb for decades, by the early 2000s it too had begun to change. The General Motors Fisher I plant that occupied one square mile in the suburb since the 1950s had recently closed, drastically decreasing the tax base. Though the presence of Latinos in the area surrounding the church's new location had doubled, from 10 percent of the population to 26.7 percent from 2000 to 2010, the white population in the area was still the majority. These white working-class families that stayed behind had to adjust to the influx of hundreds of Latinos to the area every week. García retired before the move, but he occasionally substituted at St. Joseph in its new location. The shift in space was obvious to him. He remarked, "The neighborhood complains about everything."[59] The mostly white neighbors were not used to vivacious religious experiences held at St. Joseph. This area was unlike the vibrant Latino neighborhood that the parish had left behind.

Decades of placemaking made the Grandville Avenue corridor and St. Joseph the Worker a Latino space that welcomed and housed Latinos from the 1950s to the early 2000s. Surely white flight played a large role in the transition of this area, but for their own part, Latinos actively worked to make this place a home. From the faith-driven choices Mexican, Puerto Rican, and Cuban families made about where and how they would practice their versions of Catholicism to the formation of Latino organizations, a diverse group of Latinos transformed Grand Rapids' southwest side. In addition, Father Ted Kozlowski studied Latino culture, spoke Spanish, and listened to the needs of Latinos and provided for them when he could. With the help of Sister Lucia and other pastoral support staff, church leadership made St. Joseph synonymous with a welcoming, safe place for Latinos in a majority-white city.

In such a conservative, heavily Protestant area, and with limited support from the diocese, their efforts were exhibitions of the power they had as a faith community. Members of the community were sad to see St. Joseph leave the neighborhood, but they recognized how the space facilitated their relationships. Acknowledging that he would miss the building that hosted meaningful occasions for his family, like his son's wedding and his mother's funeral, Hilario Zapata optimistically remarked, "I feel that I will eventually feel comfortable in [the new] building. . . . The community will be the same, so that's going to make it fine."[60] Indeed, in its new location St. Joseph the Worker parishioners attempt to replicate the same tight-knit relationships they had on Grandville Avenue. One way they have done so is to celebrate its pan-Latino identity in the new building. Behind the altar, alongside a statue of St. Joseph the Worker and the Virgin of Guadalupe, the church boasts various statues of the Virgin Mary in her many iterations as the patroness of various Latin American countries. This includes statues of la Virgen de Caridad del Cobre of Cuba, la Virgen de Providencia of Puerto Rico, la Virgen de Altagracia of the Dominican Republic and la Virgen del Rosario of Guatemala, among others. Though the church building is not in the same neighborhood that served as the historical base for this pan-Latino parish, St. Joseph the Worker remains a place where Latinos can meet their spiritual and material needs and build meaningful relationships with one another.

NOTES
1 I mostly use the term "Latino" to refer to the historical actors in this chapter, as it was one of the terms community members used to refer to themselves.
2 Kate Nagengast, "St. Joseph the Worker Parish Carries History to New Site," *Grand Rapids Press*, October 18, 2008.
3 A selected list of Latino Midwest histories includes Gabriela Arredondo, *Mexican Chicago: Race, Identity, and Nation, 1916–1939* (Urbana: University of Illinois Press, 2003); Lilia Fernández, *Brown in the Windy City: Mexicans and Puerto Ricans in Postwar Chicago* (Chicago: University of Chicago Press, 2012); Eileen Findlay, *We Are Left without a Father Here: Masculinity, Domesticity,*

and Migration in Postwar Puerto Rico (Durham: Duke University Press, 2014); Dennis Nodin Valdes, *Al Norte: Agricultural Workers in the Great Lakes Region, 1917–1970* (Austin: University of Texas Press, 1991); Marc Simon Rodriguez, *The Tejano Diaspora: Mexican Americanism and Ethnic Politics in Texas and Wisconsin* (Chapel Hill: University of North Carolina Press, 2011); and Felipe Hinojosa, *Latino Mennonites: Civil Rights, Faith, and Evangelical Culture* (Baltimore: Johns Hopkins University Press, 2014). Relevant work in other disciplines includes Gina M. Pérez, *The Near Northwest Side Story: Migration, Displacement, and Puerto Rican Families* (Berkeley: University of California Press, 2004); and Mérida Rúa, *A Grounded Identidad: Making New Lives in Chicago's Puerto Rican Neighborhoods* (Oxford: Oxford University Press, 2012).

4 Katia Balassiano and Marta Maria Maldonado, "Placemaking in Rural New Gateway Communities," *Community Development Journal* 50, no. 4 (October 2015): 644–60.

5 Balassiano and Maldonado, "Placemaking"; Jesus J. Lara, *Latino Placemaking and Planning: Cultural Resilience and Strategies for Reurbanization* (Tucson: University of Arizona Press, 2018).

6 Deborah E. Kanter, *Chicago Católico: Making Catholic Parishes Mexican* (Urbana: University of Illinois Press, 2020); Kanter, "Faith and Family for Early Mexican Immigrants to Chicago: The Diary of Elidia Barroso," *Diálogo* 16, no. 1 (2013): 21–34; Kanter, "Making Mexican Parishes: Ethnic Succession in Chicago Churches, 1947–1977," *US Catholic Historian* 30, no. 1 (2012): 35–58.

7 James D. Bratt, *Dutch Calvinism in Modern America: A History of a Conservative Subculture* (Grand Rapids, MI: Eerdmans, 1978).

8 By 1917 there were thirty-eight Christian Reformed churches within Grand Rapids' city limits. They housed the three waves of Dutch immigrants that had all arrived in Grand Rapids by 1893. Together, they made up 42 percent of the foreign-born population in Grand Rapids—larger than any other ethnic group in the early 1900s. These turn-of-the-twentieth-century demographic trends have resulted in the prevalence of Calvinism in Grand Rapids into the present. Finding Latinos, who made up 5 to 7 percent of the population between 1960 and 1980, has been a challenge given their status as a demographic minority. In addition, Catholics were also a demographic minority. In 1980, 19 percent of the residents of Kent County, where Grand Rapids is located, reported that they were Catholic. While that is higher than some of the surrounding counties in West Michigan, most of which reported on average 11 percent, it is much lower than Macomb and Wayne Counties (which house Detroit and its suburbs), at 41 percent and 26 percent respectively. Even so, it pales in comparison to the 43 percent of Chicagoans who reported their religion as Catholic that same year.

9 Jeffery Kleiman, "The Great Strike: Religion, Labor, Reform in Grand Rapids, Michigan, 1890-1916" (PhD diss., Michigan State University, 1985).

10 Delia Fernández, "Becoming Latino: Mexican and Puerto Rican Community Formation in Grand Rapids, Michigan, 1926–1964," *Michigan Historical Review* 39, no. 1 (2013): 71–100.

11 Sergio M. González, "Interethnic Catholicism and Transnational Religious Connections: Milwaukee's Mexican Mission Chapel of Our Lady of Guadalupe, 1924–1929," *Journal of American Ethnic History* 36, no. 1 (2016): 5; Brett C. Hoover, *The Shared Parish: Latinos, Anglos, and the Future of US Catholicism* (New York: New York University Press, 2014); Kanter, *Chicago Católico*; Timothy M. Matovina, *Latino Catholicism: Transformation in America's Largest Church* (Princeton: Princeton University Press, 2012).
12 Zulema Moret, "A Life of Self-Surrender," *Diocese of Grand Rapids*, n.d., https://grdiocese.org, accessed November 2, 2020.
13 María Aguilar, interview with author, Grand Rapids, MI, 2012.
14 "Obtain House for Chapel, Catholics Plan Mexican, Latvian Services," *Grand Rapids Press*, February 14, 1952.
15 Baptism Records, 1952–1957, St. Andrew's Cathedral, Diocese of Grand Rapids, Grand Rapids, MI; Rosalia Espindola Fernández, interview with author, Grand Rapids, MI, 2013.
16 Miguel Bérrios, interview with author, Grand Rapids, MI, 2011; Mary E. Odem, "Our Lady of Guadalupe in the New South: Latino Immigrants and the Politics of Integration in the Catholic Church," *Journal of American Ethnic History* 24, no. 1 (2004): 55.
17 "Diocesan Plan for Hispanic Ministry," Diocese of Grand Rapids, September 21, 2019, https://grdiocese.org.
18 This was becoming a more common phenomenon in dioceses across the country. For more on the Mexican American Cultural Center, see Socorro Castañeda, "Mexican American Cultural Center and the Politics of Spiritual Empowerment," in *Latino Religions and Civic Activism in the United States*, ed. Gastón Espinosa, Virgilio P. Elizondo, and Jesse Miranda (Oxford: Oxford University Press, 2005).
19 Moret, "Life of Self-Surrender."
20 Helen Rose Ebaugh and Mary Curry, "Fictive Kin as Social Capital in New Immigrant Communities," *Sociological Perspectives* 43, no. 2 (Summer 2000): 195.
21 Santiago Figueroa, Baptism Records, St. Andrew's Cathedral, Diocese of Grand Rapids, Grand Rapids, MI.
22 Henry Franken, "St. Joseph Catholic Church, 1889–1989: A History of the Founding of the Parish as Told by Father Henry Frenken, Pastor from 1887 to 1907," Folder 8, Box 4, Collection 299x, St. Joseph Catholic Church (Grand Rapids), Early Parish History, Eduard Adam Skendzel Polonian Historical Collection, Grand Rapids Public Library (GRPL).
23 Sally VanDrunen, Baptismal Register, August 31, 1952–August 15, 1982, St. Joseph the Worker Parish, 1.
24 Catherine D'Amico, Baptismal Register, August 31, 1952–August 15, 1982, St. Joseph the Worker Parish, 5.
25 Santos Alvarez, Polk Grand Rapids City Directory, 1952.
26 An analysis of the homeowners in the 1952 Grand Rapids City Directory living in the 600 block of Grandville Avenue to the 800 block of Grandville Avenue

revealed Anglo surnames and other European-descended families, given their Polish or Italian last names, for example. Staunch segregation in the area also indicates that not many African Americans lived in this area until the 1960s.

27 Robert Lee Alvarez, Baptismal Register, August 31, 1952–August 15, 1982, St. Joseph the Worker Parish, 2.
28 For further discussion on Latinos' proximity to and the construction of whiteness in the United States, see Ian Haney López, *White by Law: The Legal Construction of Race* (New York: New York University Press, 2006), 104; Neil Foley, *The White Scourge: Mexicans, Blacks, and Poor Whites in Texas Cotton Culture* (Los Angeles: University of California Press, 1999), 22; Natalia Molina, *How Race Is Made in America: Immigration, Citizenship, and the Historical Power of Racial Scripts* (Los Angeles: University of California Press, 2014), 25–26; Mae Ngai, *Impossible Subjects: Illegal Aliens and the Making of Modern America* (Princeton: Princeton University Press, 2004), 24–25; and Thomas A. Guglielmo, *White on Arrival: Italians, Race, Color, and Power in Chicago, 1890–1945* (Oxford: Oxford University Press, 2004).
29 Santos Alvarez, Polk Grand Rapids City Directory, 1951.
30 Luisa Fernández, interview by Kate Schramm, Grand Rapids, MI, 2001, Box 2, Folder 1, Collection 292, Hispanic Oral History Collection, GRPL.
31 Lucia Torres, Baptism Records, 1952–1957, St. Andrew's Cathedral, Diocese of Grand Rapids, Grand Rapids, MI; Robert Torres, Baptism Records, 1952–1957, St. Andrew's Cathedral, Diocese of Grand Rapids, Grand Rapids, MI.
32 Rosalia Espindola, interview with author and John Fernández, Grand Rapids, MI, 2020.
33 Cantu Family, First Holy Communion Records, May 14, 1961, May 12, 1963, May 10, 1964, St. Joseph the Worker.
34 Jorge Bérrios, First Holy Communion Records, May 12, 1963, St. Joseph the Worker.
35 Angelo and Mario López, First Holy Communion Records, May 12, 1963, St. Joseph the Worker.
36 For more on waves of Cuban immigration, see María Cristina García, *Havana USA: Cuban Exiles and Cuban Americans in South Florida, 1959–1994* (Berkeley: University of California Press, 1997).
37 See my forthcoming work, *Latinos against the Grain: Mexican and Puerto Rican Placemaking in Grand Rapids, Michigan* (Urbana: University of Illinois Press).
38 Jim Mencarelli, "A Special Bond: Most Mexicans Share a Special Experience," *Grand Rapids Press*, July 28, 1986, A1.
39 Bérrios, interview. See also David A. Badillo, *Latinos and the New Immigrant Church* (Baltimore: Johns Hopkins University Press, 2006).
40 Daniel, David, Mario, and Raquel Castillo, March 24, 1968, Confirmation Records, St. Joseph the Worker.
41 Rev. Fr. Theodore LaMarre, obituary, *Saginaw News*, June 16, 2009, https://obits.mlive.com.

42 Sister Lucia Zapata, O.P., interview with author, Lansing, MI, 2020.
43 Espindola, interview, 2020.
44 For more on Spanish-language mass in the US Catholic Church, see Kanter, *Chicago Católico*. On a lack of Spanish-speaking priests in midwestern dioceses, see Zaragosa Vargas, *Proletarians of the North: A History of Mexican Industrial Workers in Detroit and the Midwest, 1917–1933* (Berkeley: University of California Press, 1999), 143.
45 Moret, "Life of Self-Surrender."
46 Zapata, interview.
47 Hank Bornheimer, "Recreation Program Livens Inner City," *Grand Rapids Press*, September 16, 1968.
48 Espindola, interview, 2020.
49 Moret, "Life of Self-Surrender"; "1995 Inaugurates the Diocesan Hispanic Ministry Team," *Catholic Connector*, January 1995, 1.
50 US Census Bureau, "Persons 16 Years and Older: Unemployed," 1980 Census, Census Tract 26, Kent County, MI.
51 Juanita Lucio Campos, interview with author, Lansing, MI, 2020.
52 For more on the Catholic Charismatic Renewal, see Susan A. Maurer, *The Spirit of Enthusiasm: A History of the Catholic Charismatic Renewal, 1967–2000* (Lanham, MD: University Press of America, 2010); Ashley Palmer-Boyes, "The Latino Catholic Parish as a Specialist Organization: Distinguishing Characteristics," *Review of Religious Research* 51, no. 3 (2010): 302–23; Richard J. Bord and Joseph E. Faulkner, *The Catholic Charismatics: The Anatomy of a Modern Religious Movement* (University Park: Pennsylvania State University Press, 1983); and Allan Figueroa Deck, "The Challenge of Evangelical/Pentecostal Christianity to Hispanic Catholicism," in *Hispanic Catholic Culture in the US: Issues and Concerns*, ed. J. Dolan and A. Deck (Notre Dame, IN: University of Notre Dame Press, 1994).
53 Rev. Fr. Pedro García, interview with author, Lansing, MI, 2020.
54 US Census Bureau, Household Family Income in 1989 Dollars, 1990.
55 García, interview.
56 Michelle Jokisch Polo, "Rumsey Street: Leaving Behind a History of Sacred Space," *Rapid Growth Media*, October 19, 2017, www.rapidgrowthmedia.com; Nagengast, "St. Joseph the Worker Parish."
57 García, interview; Matt Vande Bunte, "Diocese Helps Bulging Hispanic Catholic Church," *Grand Rapids Press*, December 1, 2007, C2.
58 Nagengast, "St. Joseph the Worker Parish."
59 García, interview.
60 Nagengast, "St. Joseph the Worker Parish."

4

Latina/o Mormons

Spanish-Speaking Saints Negotiating Identity in the Deseret

SUJEY VEGA

There is a double standard now—one for Sunday and one for Monday through Saturday. . . . We want to write to the prophet to say the feelings of brotherhood have to be followed all the time.
—Alfredo Gallegos, resident of Sandy, Utah

Mormon missionaries increasingly are confronted by prospective converts who believe the church is anti-immigrant and some Latinos don't even feel welcome in their own LDS congregations because of anti-immigrant rhetoric.
—Tony Yapias, Proyecto Latino de Utah

Shortly after Arizona's infamous SB 1070, a bill that intended to criminalize undocumented immigrants, penalize anyone "trespassing, harboring and transporting" them, and sanction local law enforcement to stop and detain anyone they viewed with "reasonable suspicion" for being unlawfully present, was signed into law in 2010, *Salt Lake Tribune* reporter Kristen Moulton sought the perspective of Latino Latter-day Saints (LDS) in Utah.[1] She interviewed Tony Yapias and Alfredo Gallegos, who, as illuminated in the above epigraphs, voiced an ongoing rift within the LDS Church. Like much of the nation, Utah was embroiled in its own political debates, influenced by Arizona's draconian "show me your papers" law. These two states, Utah and Arizona, shared more than a conservative anti-immigrant turn in politics. Unlike other areas with state-based legislation against undocumented immigrants, Arizona and Utah also shared a critical role in Mormon history. As Alyshia Gálvez describes, religiosity provides Latino populations the space to "contextualize, signify, and actively redefine their place in the United States."² Gallegos and Yapias were directly confronting the "double standard" of a faith that on the one hand prides itself on transnational missioning efforts while on the other supports conservative politicians who demonize those very populations. Beyond advocating for the material needs of the community, immigrant activists like Gallegos, Yapias, and others also spoke back to the actual history and theology of the LDS Church, centered on tales of migration and movement.

From the outset, the Book of Mormon establishes the history of migration, warfare, and spiritual salvation of the Jeredites and Nephites, or lost tribes of Israel, who fled to the Americas. According to the Book of Mormon, while the Jaredites traversed across the earth, they "did also carry with them Deseret, which, by interpretation, is a honey bee; and thus they did carry with them swarms of bees" (Esther 2:1–3). As a result of this doctrinal claim, all members of the LDS community consider themselves part of this "deseret." In addition to the doctrine, the deseret diaspora also includes the nineteenth-century history of expulsion and resettlement. Exiled out of their original settlements in New York, Ohio, Missouri, and Illinois, the Saints' trek to Utah provides an epic history of migration that frames the ethos of Mormon identity. The migratory beginnings entrenched in LDS ideology and history are central to the experiences of Latina/o Saints who wanted their church to publicly defend them as part and parcel of the Mormon deseret. Latina/os formed an integral part of the LDS Church, and individuals like Gallegos simply asked their church to stand behind its gospel and come to the defense of generations of migrants who "did carry with them" the right to exist without fear of deportation or family separation. Echoing what Catholic Father Luis Olivares proclaimed decades earlier, "God is not neutral on injustice," these activists felt that their faith, too, should stand up against unjust anti-immigrant legislation.³

Mormon Tablitas

The immigration politics of 2010 and subsequent LDS activism that followed took place in what I am calling the Mormon Intermountain West Corridor, or Mormon Corridor for short. This includes the states of Utah, Idaho, and Arizona, and even expands into northern Mexico. The Mormon Corridor has multiple layers that we must unpack in order to understand the contemporary importance of this treason to Latina/o Saints. The span of Mormon history from 1875 to 2010 may seem too unwieldy of a trajectory to follow; however, these palimpsests illustrate the layered epistemic relation to history seared onto the Mormon mindset. Anyone familiar with the LDS Church knows that Mormons have, as part of their doctrine, a proclivity toward documenting their past. History, and knowing where one comes from, is built into the church's genealogy efforts. Knowing the names of one's ancestors is important for the practice of baptism by proxy. The ability to baptize deceased ancestors into the LDS Church is unique to Mormons and assures them that the souls of those departed can come to know the LDS gospel so that all family members can be together forever in the afterlife. Thus, genealogy, keeping records, and attention to history matter to LDS members. As an ethnographer interested in present-day experiences of Latina/o members, I place this attention to history at the forefront of my analysis.

As with a tablita toy, or Jacob's ladder, often found in Mexican gift shops and markets, I find it necessary to metaphorically flick my wrist between past and present to reveal ribbons linking Latina/o Saints across generations. These Mormon tablitas reveal how Latina/o Saints came to assert their belonging and navigate the pressures of assimilating in this Utah-based church. The transition back and forth across the twentieth and twenty-first centuries provides an incredibly rich context for understanding how race, ethnicity, belonging, and theology manifest for the experience of Latina/o Saints in the LDS Church. I ask the reader to embrace this interdisciplinary trek across archives, interviews, and contemporary reflections to appreciate the heretofore understudied experience of Latina/o Mormons. My hope is that this dance between past and present reveals the complex nature and doctrinal positioning that present-day Latina/o Saints find themselves in and continue to redefine for themselves.

The first tablita, or block, in this arrangement would be marked by the arrival of Mormons in what was then Alta California. The Mormon Corridor began with the 1847 border crossing of Mormons into what was then Mexico. Later known as Utah, this was the area where Brigham Young decided to set down roots and form an oasis of religious freedom, free of the murderous mobs that Mormons had encountered in Illinois and Missouri.[4] Though they continuously encountered antagonism in the United States, Mormons signed up to fight on the American side of the Mexican-American War. Rather than join the country in which they had just settled, their collective possessive investment in Whiteness[5] led Mormons to strategically place themselves on the side of the very nation whose citizens had pushed them out of their homes in New York, Ohio, Missouri, and Illinois. When the war was over, Mormons found themselves in what became known as Utah Territory. Though they established a political stronghold in Utah, national negative attention continued to influence a Mormon migratory drive to seek possibilities elsewhere.[6]

Veterans from the Mexican-American War returned to Utah describing lands in Arizona and Mexico where they could grow the deseret. By 1875, Mormons formed their first expedition into Mexico and traversed Arizona along the way. They were in search of both a place to mission and an environment to establish colonies that might serve as refuge from increasing anti-polygamy sentiment in the United States.[7] As the leader of the expedition to Arizona, Daniel Webster Jones was given a choice of which families to bring with him to settle Arizona. When asked by Brigham Young himself, "Who would you like to go with you?," Jones responded, "Give me men with large families and small means so that when we get there they will be too poor to come back, and we will have to stay."[8] Thus, from the outset Arizona's LDS settlements were built by those searching for promise and financial opportunities through faith-based social networks.

Jones initiated relationships with Pima, Tohono-O'odham, and Yaquis in the area. His command of Spanish also helped significantly with those who only a few years prior had been considered Mexican citizens. Keenly aware of the difficulties of thriving in an arid and hot desert landscape, Jones took it upon himself to develop an agreement of shared resources with the preexisting communities and even baptized a few Native members into the LDS Church.[9] Disagreements with Jones's inclusive policies arose among colonists who preferred to distance themselves from Native and Mexican populations. Even as Jones was open to working with and incorporating the surrounding populations in the Mormon settlement, other colonists grew incensed by his cordial dealings. Despite their own poverty, a growing number of LDS settlers were intolerant of working as equals alongside Indian populations. That Jones successfully baptized several Indian converts upset their colonial privilege and placed them on equal footing with each other. Jones, for his part, imagined a potential symbiotic relationship where otherwise impoverished LDS colonists would learn from and work with Native communities who were very knowledgeable about the area. Jones's "rising tide will lift all boats" approach met opposition with settlers so invested in a system of White supremacy that they would risk their actual survival in the desert over working with and accepting communities of color.

Over a century after White Mormons left Utah to settle in the Salt River Valley, these same divisions remained. This time, the questions surrounding belonging, acceptance, and fellowship centered on Latina/o residents in the area. Continuing the century-long disputes regarding who belonged to and could claim legitimacy in the LDS Church, fissures within the deseret diaspora grew once again. The hive, as it were, was in danger of imploding from the pressures of immigration politics in the twenty-first century.

Drawing parallels from the past provides a glimpse into the racist residue that continues to inform contemporary LDS encounters with belonging. Jones's Arizona colony followed familiar settler colonial models of missioning while simultaneously displacing Indigenous inhabitants.[10] While Jones did baptize Native members to the LDS Church, the plan was to expand, displace, and claim ties to Arizona. Thus, the relationship between White Mormons, Native, and Latina/o communities in Arizona is tangled by attempts at conversion and moments of tension. This was especially the case in Mesa, with its complicated history of reluctant symbiosis, purposeful ministering, and more recently the denial of legal/political belonging.

Toward an LDS Politics of Belonging

The next tablita moves us into the twentieth century and the continued growth of Mesa's Mormon diaspora. Not only were more members from Utah settling in Arizona, but the persecution of polygamous families in the United States drew many to the Mexican colonies just south of the border. In addition, Brigham Young continued his plan "to grow the gospel to Lehi's millions of Mexican descendants."[11] By the beginnings of the Mexican Revolution (1910–1920), Mormon missionaries were just starting to baptize enough converts to form small branches throughout Mexico.[12] Due to the instability of the revolution, White Mormon missionaries were ordered to flee Mexico in 1913, but a small number of Mexican Saints continued to share their gospel and "branch membership soon increased tenfold."[13] Meanwhile, exiled missionaries refocused their efforts on Latina/os north of the border. Branches began springing up in Colorado, Texas, Arizona, New Mexico, and California.[14] This tablita, from roughly 1910 to 1940, depicts the initial growth of Spanish-speaking membership both in Latin America and the United States.[15] As a result, Arizona became a bridge between Mexico and Salt Lake, and Mesa was designated as a viable site for Arizona's only temple in 1919 (Mesa remained the only temple in Arizona until 2002).

Temples for the LDS Church are sacred sites where only active members in good standing enter and perform rites and ceremonies related to the faith. Marriage rites, baptisms for the dead, and preparing oneself for the afterlife all happen in this Mormon-exclusive site. Prior to Arizona's temple, members had to travel to Utah if they wanted to have their marriage blessed or conduct other rituals. The Mesa Arizona Temple was the first temple built outside Utah in the continental United States since Mormons had fled persecution in the Midwest. Also important was its unofficial naming as the "Lamanite Temple"—or a temple built to serve those identified by the LDS Church as Lamanites, primarily Native and Latina/o members. Not long after its dedication in 1927, the Mesa Temple also became the first to offer services in a language other than English. These Spanish translations of temple rites occurred in 1945, and signaled a critical moment in addressing the needs of growing Spanish-speaking members throughout the United States and Latin America.

The location of the Mesa Temple signals the importance of Mesa in the Mormon Intermountain West and Arizona specifically as a destination for Latina/o LDS members who had nowhere else to go for rituals critical to the faith. Indeed, oral histories with Latina/os trace Mesa as the site of regional meetings where Spanish-speaking families from throughout the Southwest and Mexico convened during religious excursions from 1945 to the 1980s. Some members remembered meeting their spouses at church-sponsored dances during these conferences; others recalled driving from Utah to meet their Mexican grandmothers at the Mesa Temple. For roughly forty years, Mesa became the center point for Latina/o Saints to conduct temple rites in Spanish and simultaneously schedule transnational and transregional family reunions. The growth was noticeable in the area. When the temple was first dedicated, there was only one chapel/meetinghouse designated for Spanish-speaking Mormons in Phoenix in the 1930s.[16]

Moving forward a few tablitas, by the twenty-first century there were thirty wards dedicated to Spanish speakers in the area.[17] The growth was not always welcomed. Generations after settling in Arizona, some descendants of early Mormon inhabitants presumed authority over who could and should claim belonging. Mesa went from welcoming Spanish-speaking Saints to supporting a legislator who made it his mission to seed division and animosity against Latina/o residents of Arizona. In 2008 Mesa elected Russell Pearce to the Arizona State Senate. Two years later he made a national name for himself by introducing SB 1070. By this point, Latina/o Saints had multiple options for conducting temple rites in Spanish, including temples in Latin America itself. Though pilgrimages to Mesa stopped, living within Pearce's district and the state of Arizona meant daily encounters that made Spanish-speaking members feel unwelcomed. LDS members who attended sacrament meetings together often stood on opposite sides of the political debate. In Mesa, the political vitriol was heavy in the air. One local resident recalled an encounter outside the public library where an older retired man literally pushed a woman who dared voice disagreement with Pearce. Police were called and the library had to maintain a security presence for weeks to follow. Wards were divided by the immigration debate. Politics were supposed to be off the table during sacrament meetings, but one could feel the tension. As Josefina, a bishop's wife, mentioned, "My husband knew he shouldn't, but he snuck in the importance of getting along and acceptance during one of the sacrament meetings."

Pearce's actions also threatened the national image of the LDS Church as a mainstream religion open to all, an image it had been battling to retrieve since its involvement with California's Proposition 8 campaign, which denied same-sex couples the right to marry in 2008. As a Mormon himself, Pearce repeated Mormon dictates about following the law in his rhetoric. By the time I started conducting research in

2014, White and Latina/o LDS members still recalled the "anger" and "despair" caused by "ese Pearce y Arpaio." Elder Ted, an older White LDS member who had worked with Spanish-speaking members since his mission in Mexico some forty years earlier, lamented, "We lost a lot of leadership then. It was a huge blow to our community. People left, they fled in fear for their families." In years of gathering narratives among LDS Saints, I have heard from many White LDS members who disagreed with nationalist persecution of undocumented immigrants. On a few occasions (four that I can recall), White LDS members spoke to me in hushed tones, lamenting the legal system that kept so many Latina/os in limbo. These few members also quietly disagreed with vocal politicians like Pearce and Donald Trump. This surface-level, hushed support meant that when it came down to fighting systems of oppression and the politics of belonging, Latina/o Saints could not count on their White brethren to actively confront politicians and church leadership.

Church headquarters in Utah fielded questions from the media and their Spanish-speaking brethren. As Gallegos and Yapias illustrated earlier, individuals questioned whether the LDS Church would defend a community it so actively courted in missioning efforts. In response, a coalition of Latina/os and non-Latina/os created the Utah Compact, which called for more humane, compassionate recognition of the undocumented as people and suggested resolving the broken immigration system ahead of criminalizing families. In addition, Latinos gathered over a hundred signatures to send to the Mexican authorities asking them to deny visas to LDS missionaries.[18] Given that publicly questioning church authority is a major taboo in Mormonism and could lead to excommunication, that they gathered a hundred signatures of Latinos in Salt Lake City, Utah, and willingly asked the Mexican government for consequences against their own church was significant. They argued that a church unwilling to stand up on this issue should not be allowed to proselytize in a country whose citizens are targeted by such cruel legislators. Caught between staunch conservative members like Pearce and its efforts to welcome Spanish-speaking converts, the Church of Latter-day Saints finally released an official statement in June 2011, a full year after SB 1070 was passed. The statement utilized the LDS' own history with persecution to draw parallels with undocumented families:

> The history of mass expulsion or mistreatment of individuals or families is cause for concern especially where race, culture, or religion are involved. This should give pause to any policy that contemplates targeting any one group, particularly if that group comes mostly from one heritage.

This church statement, the Utah Compact that preceded it, and the countless efforts of Latina/o and non-Latina/o members to promote a more compassionate approach toward immigration all provided an alternative narrative to that of Pearce and his allies. In Arizona, a coalition of Mormons and non-Mormons organized a recall campaign that successfully led to the ouster of Pearce from office in November 2011. Though the progeny of earlier settlers to Mesa similarly attempted to deny Mormons of color a seat in the temple, this time, their White supremacy was met with fierce objections by local and regional actors in the Mormon Corridor.[19]

Establishing Ethnic Lineage

Though my tablitas metaphor follows the history of the Mormon Corridor from roughly 1847 to 2010, the LDS Church would likely start its tablitas some 2,500 years ago. The Book of Mormon begins with an account of Lehi's family. Considered to be part of the lost tribes of Israel, the family fled to the Americas after the father, Lehi, received a message from God. They are perceived as the progenitors of modern-day Native populations of the Americas. Though unsubstantiated by DNA evidence establishing such a connection, this "Jewish Indian Theory" once popular in the seventeenth century continues to hold a dominant place in LDS doctrine.

Once Lehi's family reached the Western Hemisphere, one of Lehi's younger sons, Nephi, also received a message from God directing him to lead his family on its spiritual journey. Lehi's older sons, Laman and Lemuel, resisted the divine authority of their younger brother. They questioned, defied, and plotted to kill Nephi. They did not succeed, but the family split up and became the progenitors of modern-day Indigenous populations in the Americas. Those who respected the leadership of Nephi became successful farmers and built magnificent structures. Laman's descendants, the Lamanites, fell away from Christ and turned to violence, idol worship, and mayhem. After centuries of warring, the Nephites died off, leaving only the Lamanites to survive. Later, these descendants of Laman would receive a holy visit from Jesus. This visit to the Americas marks a distinct aspect of the LDS faith in that it speaks to a moment prior to Ascension wherein Jesus Christ appeared to the descendants of Lehi to relay the teachings of the one true church and fulfill the covenant to all of Abraham's progeny, including those lost tribes that ended up in the Americas.

This account positions Latina/os, and other Indigenous populations in the Americas, as descendants of Lehi through his son Laman, and as such preordained to receive the blessings of Christ if they return to their earlier knowledge of the faith. The Book of Mormon foretells that if Lamanites accept the teachings of the LDS Church, the descendants of Laman could return to being "pure and delightsome" and restore the "knowledge of their Fathers" (Nephi 30:5). Importantly, the line in the Book of Mormon initially read "white and delightsome"; in 1981 this was changed to "pure and delightsome."

This Lamanite narrative informed how Mormons justified Latin American missioning and formed the basis for Latina/o conversion. However, in interviews LDS Latina/os expressed a complex relationship with this Lamanite identity. When I asked two LDS Latinas in their eighties about a Lamanite connection, they responded with outright laughter, "Remember when they used to call us Lamanites?" These senior LDS Latinas giggled in a way that revealed some discomfort. Later in the interview they recalled gleefully the memories of Lamanite conferences and taking advantage of Lamanite scholarships to BYU, and one of the women tearfully recalled the importance of her father's Yaqui Indian roots. Indeed, many interviewees remembered annual "Lamanite conferences" held at the Mesa Temple, where Latina/os would come from throughout the Southwest and convene in Mesa, Arizona, for a weekend filled with prayer, temple work, and recreational activities like dances. These conferences gathered Latina/o Saints from California, Utah, Colorado, and Texas to join Saints in Arizona from roughly 1945 to the 1970s.[20] In the later years, Latina/o Saints from Mexico and Central America joined and had their own dedicated weekends where they too could participate in temple work and come together as one united community. The LDS Church even built them a dormitory to house the hundreds who visited the temple grounds. This convening of Latina/o Saints from throughout the Southwest in Arizona signals the momentous importance of Mesa's history to this experience. Still, the awkwardness of scriptural ties to Laman as the wayward son lingered in conversations with present-day Latina/o Saints who explained to me, a non-member, how the church enacted a kind of tiered system of belonging that marked Latina/o Saints as always already separate and apart from White members.

Other members had more positive affinity for their Lamanite inheritance and asserted that "it is us, our story, our people," and "it's meaningful, it's our history." Interestingly, this theology provides unique parallels with other stories of religious conversion. For instance, the Virgin of Guadalupe has been credited with the conversion of Indigenous Mexicans to Catholicism. The Virgin of Guadalupe (with her darker skin and symbols that echoed pre-Hispanic goddesses) marked Mexicans (and specifically Indo-Mexicans, or mestizos) as a chosen people, those whom the Virgin Mary herself chose to deliver the message of love to otherwise arrogant Spanish European church leaders. This tie as Guadalupanos congealed a collective Catholic sense of identity that united a people across borders and through political economic strife.[21] According to Roberto Treviño, "Ethno-Catholicism played a pivotal role in sustaining generations of Mexicans and Mexican Americans by giving them a sense of cultural identity and independence, community integrity and hope in the face of adversity."[22] I suggest that the ethnic tie to the Book of Mormon similarly created a sense of collective ethno-religious identity.

Because they lacked centuries of religious indoctrination tying faith and culture, as Catholicism had, the Mormon ethnic lineage began with this tie to a Lamanite past and was nurtured by the role of periodicals to unite a people across geography and imagine a collective ethno-religious community.[23] Now known as the LDS Church's international periodical, the *Liohona* began as a Spanish newsletter that united members across borders and throughout the Spanish-speaking missioning efforts throughout the Americas (including the United States). Though the *Liohona* has provided Spanish speakers with a collective sense of community from 1945 to the present, the magazine began as *In Yaotlapixqui: El Atalaya de Mexico* in January 1937. Sold for "cinco centavos" or "cincuenta centavos por el año" (five cents an issue or fifty cents for a yearly subscription), the magazine was tied to missionary efforts and similar magazines in El Paso (*Tonatiuh Itzacual*), Brazil (*El Brasileño*), and Argentina (*El Mensajero*). *In Yaotlapixqui* served to communicate major church teachings and Spanish hymns, provide advice for converts, explain Mormon terms, make announcements about local events in the mission, and even provide a cartoon lampooning the "aventuras de un nuevo misionero" (the adventures of a new missionary). The magazine ran from 1937 to 1944 as a Mexican-specific and Mexican-inclusive periodical space to establish community and connect with members who may otherwise have been a small minority in their towns.

In 1945, however, the magazine was consolidated with other international Mormon periodicals into the *Liahona* magazine. From the first *Liohona* Spanish edition, it seems that the intent was to conform the international readership into one Utah-specific message. This was evident in an article in the first issue titled "América, un País Escogido," which was an address given in Salt Lake City that boasted about the ideals of the "great nation" (read the United States) and had drawings of the Statue of Liberty and pilgrims landing to further the romance of the United States as a chosen land for the renewed gospel. Whereas the previous magazines had utilized Indigenous languages for their titles and included more specific narratives by locals (either missionaries or converts) in Mexico, the *Liohona* marked a significant change that relied on translated messages and speeches that came primarily out of Utah. Still, the *Liohona* would open with images of new missionaries assigned to Mexico and provide updates and briefs from Spanish-speaking branches. Even as it transitioned to include more Utah-specific content, the magazine was still used as a means of communicating for Spanish speakers in the church. Indeed, members I've spoken with in the twenty-first century recall receiving their *Liohona* and immediately flipping through the pages to get caught up with friends and family throughout the deseret diaspora. In a time before the Internet, they used the *Liohona* "in their quest to belong in the religious landscapes" throughout Latin America and the United States.[24]

Though the *Liohona* provided images and teachings from Utah, at the time it was one of the only church periodicals that featured Mormons of color. Additionally, a few front covers featured Native Indigenous iconography to signal the importance of Lamanite heritage and identity to gospel. As Lamanites, Latina/os were part of the lost tribes of Israel, and as such they were predestined or chosen for celestial glory if they converted. This automatic empowerment in the faith, the knowledge that you were predestined to partake in the glory because you were descendants of Lehi, exalted Latina/o LDS by sheer virtue of their Indigenous inheritance. This tie to Laman was heavily discussed during a Salt Lake City convening held in 1978 to discuss Latina/o Saints and their role in the church. Then LDS bishop and University of Utah professor Dr. Orlando Rivera utilized this Lamanite narrative and tied it to Chicano nationalism:

> We are ourselves Chicanos, and all Chicanos think of themselves as having an Indo-Hispanic background, of having ancestral roots native to America as well as to Europe. Thus you considering us Lamanites is in no way offensive, but rather acceptable to our people. We are proud of our Native American progenitors.[25]

For Rivera, one should highlight claims to a Lamanite past when speaking to a Chicano community that recognized Indigenous heritage as a positive thing. It should be noted that Rivera was not necessarily toeing the line here or overly praising the church; he was directly informed by a politics of identity shaped by Chicano nationalism. Thus, Rivera depicts the second tablita that engages how the next generation of Spanish-speaking Saints, the sons and daughters of parents who joined in the 1950s and 1960s, melded their religious upbringing with Chicano nationalism. In his book *Católicos*, Mario García explored the role of faith in Chicano identity and described how Chicanismo was "the ideological grab bag that was rooted in what the movement referred to as cultural nationalism. This stressed a renewed sense of pride in being Chicano and rediscovering the historical roots of the Chicano, especially the pre-European Indigenous background."[26] This merging of Mormonism with Chicanismo presented a place from which to demand rights and acknowledge the attributes of a people otherwise dismissed in the national imaginary of the United States. For Rivera, that Chicanos, vis-à-vis their Indigenous ancestors, played a prominent role in the Book of Mormon meant that they should be recognized both in the LDS Church and in the United States in general as forebearers of salvation. Rivera wanted to see Latina/o Saints no longer demoted or perceived in paternalistic tones; he wanted them to lead the church and be appreciated for what they brought to the faith, not just what services they needed.

As further proof of his weaving of Mormonism with Chicano nationalism, Rivera went on to inform his Mormon audience about the "internal colonialism" model and explained the exploitive relationship between Anglos and Latina/os in the United States. He suggested that Mormons could begin the process of healing, but in order to do so they must be cognizant of "the barriers that inhibit such a bridging."[27] Rivera critiqued the expectations by White Mormons who assumed that their Latino brethren would assimilate into Anglo American culture. He also lamented the closing of Spanish-speaking wards toward that aim. Following his clear framing within Chicano nationalism, Rivera asserted the need for self-determination among the growing Latina/o LDS communities: "We must have an opportunity to plan for and administer and do things in our own way, for our own selves, completely independently."[28] For Rivera, pride in Indigenous Lamanite heritage meant also claiming autonomous agency from English-dominant LDS leadership. This identity politics made sense for the kind of Chicano nationalism Rivera himself was engaging with in the 1970s, for it reified both a celebration of indigeneity and a sense of autonomy necessary for progress. As Arlene Sánchez-Walsh would observe years later, the focus of some Protestants with Latino ministries has centered around "social services . . . without the addition of political advocacy for systemic changes."[29] Rivera attempted to push LDS leadership toward recognizing the systemic changes that were needed as a result of internal colonialism and simultaneously providing more avenues for autonomy wherein Latina/o Saints did not need to seek the approval of White membership for their religious or secular activities.

In more contemporary encounters with church identity politics, millennial Latina/os revealed in interviews with me a more complicated relationship with the Lamanite narrative. Like Rivera, some millennials recognized how the church provided an opportunity to reclaim and retrace the indigeneity long supplanted by the Catholic Church. Angel recalled how his grandmother, a convert, came into her identity as an "India realizada" who was proud of her Totonaco heritage. Another millennial, Inez, recalled her transcendental connection when participating in a New Mexican sweat lodge: "I felt like the sages and everything, prayers and ceremonies that were done . . . in Albuquerque, like I felt like that was missing for the longest time, . . . like something that our ancestors did, you know?" Inez felt an unexplained sense of familiarity, "like when you go to your mom's house . . . that feeling of home." All of a sudden, the stories she heard in church and the possibility of a pan-Indian spirituality that tied Native populations together started to make sense. Still, even Inez felt conflicted given the underlying White supremacy in the scriptures. She felt that the implicit segregation within the church directly fed into a Lamanite versus Nephi juxtaposition that positioned descendants of Laman as subordinate.[30] In this kind of genealogical schema, the descendants of Laman (Indigenous) hailed from a "blackness" bequeathed onto the Lamanites because they "hardened their hearts" toward Christ (2 Nephi 5:21).[31] Thus, some LDS Latina/os were uncomfortable with the way the scriptures cast their Indigenous ancestors as devoid of morality until Mormon exposure.

Critically, ties to particular doctrinal populations become a defining marker in the church. All LDS members become identified as relating to one House or doctrinal tribal community or another in what is called a patriarchal blessing. Like genetic ancestral testing, this religious moment becomes a way to trace one's lineage to a particular doctrinal community and place individuals in direct line with faith-aligned progenitors. These proto-Indigenous ties to Lehi, vis-à-vis Laman, actually revealed deeper problematic connections to a fallen son. As descendants of Laman, some Latina/o Saints felt subconsciously viewed through a history of violence, rebellion, or worse—as novices to the faith. Rosa felt that White members of the church were condescending toward Spanish-speaking members: "We have like this scripture about the Lamanites flourishing in the desert, I used to treat it like these cute pets that are going to get better. . . . I don't want [my children] to grow up with that in mind." This view echoed the references to microaggressions that positioned Latina/o LDS members on a scale of worthiness depending on how much they assimilated into White Mormon culture. It is as if the descendants of little brother Nephi are still holding something over the descendants of Laman and additionally asserting a neocolonial responsibility, or burden, to control or pity them.

Indigeneity and Latinidad should have been celebrated, as it was for Bishop Rivera; however, in practice a top-down savior mentality infiltrated the way White and light-skinned upper-middle-class members interacted with darker-skinned and/or working-class members. The resulting exaltation of a Utah-centered middle-class Whiteness created leadership gaps where Latinos themselves served as bishops of their wards but maintained a subsidiary role in other church-related hierarchies. Similarly, research on global Mormon communities reveals the discrepancies of thriving global Saints still led by or controlled through a Utah-centric ideal.[32]

Sanctuary in Spanish

Following Rivera's advocacy of autonomy for Latino congregations within the church, a common threat for Latina/o Saints in the United States has centered around language and whether they would be able to continue worshiping in Spanish. For over a century, the Church of Jesus Christ of Latter-day Saints designated space for Spanish-speaking members in the United States to worship, sing, and connect in language-specific wards, or congregations. These Spanish wards, or *barrios*, evoked both linguistic and cultural connections for Latin American Saints. Spanish barrios offered a reprieve from microaggressions and overt slights experienced in White English-dominant wards. Still, though safe heavens, barrios were stigmatized for some. As Ignacio García explained in the 1990s to Jessie L. Embry, "Ethnic wards are not minor-league teams that prepare people to go to major leagues. These wards are for people who have a different culture, different style."[33] García wanted to reconcile his Mormon faith with his Chicano identity and, in the words of Felipe Hinojosa, he enacted a kind of Latino religious identity politics for Chicano communities wherein Mormonism could be "relevant and responsive to their needs."[34]

García came of age during the rise of Chicano nationalism, and though he didn't meet Rivera, he, too, was proud of his linguistic and ethnic heritage. Indeed, while García was a graduate student at the University of Arizona, he would go on to write what later became a quintessential book in Chicano studies, *Chicanismo: The Forging of a Militant Ethos* (1997). As García continued to navigate his faith with his Chicano identity, he was eventually called to be bishop of a ward in Tucson, Arizona.[35] García then represents the next tablita, which includes continued assimilation pressures, resentment by some White members of the church, and resistance by Chicano/Latino members, now in positions of leadership, who asserted the right to practice in Spanish. This assertion of the right to practice in Spanish was aided by increases in immigrant arrivals from Latin America from the mid-1990s to the early 2000s.[36] This tablita relates to the previous one in as much as García's generation came of age during the civil rights era and took that knowledge to advocate on behalf of their wards.

García's efforts and leadership led to the creation of the type of religious community in Tucson that Latina/o investigators wanted to join. Meanwhile, in wards in California there was pushback to Latina/o growth. Between the 1980s and 1990s there was mixed response toward Spanish-speaking members. Jessie Embry collected the voices of Latina/o Saints who detailed what it was like to be part of the church in the United States and still feel marginalized by decisions that dismissed their ethnic and linguistic autonomy. Latina/o Saints revealed feeling unappreciated, ignored, and dismissed when they were forced to attend English wards. Martha Zavela noticed right away a difference between social interactions: "They are just drier as opposed to Latins who are just warm and very affectionate and expressive."[37] Others related going "inactive" because there simply wasn't the same sense of community and callings that were in place in Latin American and Spanish wards. One member begged, "Please don't make me go to the English Ward."[38] Embry drew on archives and oral histories collected starting in 1984. This marked a period in Mormon history just after Spanish-serving wards were suspended and members told to worship in English-only congregations. Much like the issues of representation plaguing Mexican Saints in the early twentieth century, this decision to dissolve existing Spanish wards was an autocratic directive without input from Latina/o Saints themselves. Moreover, those who ordered this change did so without consideration for the detrimental impact it would have on Latina/o Saints.

García disagreed with attempts to enforce an English-only approach in LDS wards. Working with stake leaders, García worked on co-constructed joint programs that recognized the leadership potential of Spanish speakers. Regrettably, the willingness to view Spanish wards on par with English wards ebbed and flowed depending on local leadership or national trends in immigration politics. During García's time and before, there was always a threat that Spanish barrios would be disbanded, and members sent to their English-dominant wards. The problem, of course, was that the push to disband Spanish congregations was not simply linguistic but saturated with cultural, ethnic, and racial implications. I have interviewed Latina Mormons in their seventies, eighties, and even nineties who lovingly related their early experiences worshiping together and forming *hermandad* decades prior to being disbanded by White LDS leadership.[39] Even after these Spanish-speaking Mormons were directed to attend their geographic English wards and dissolve the Spanish wards in 1972, women joyfully recalled still getting together in each other's homes to worship, sing, and enjoy fellowship in Spanish among Latina/o friendly faces.[40] Indeed, by 1978 the church rescinded its policy in Arizona because a previously thriving and growing Latina/o membership had dwindled. Even a decade later, when García was bishop in Tucson, Arizona, the church reverted to asserting power and dominance once García made the decision to leave his ward for a career move to Texas.[41] It only took a few years to make Latina/o members attend their English-dominant geographical wards. What remained of the Spanish ward was to be used only by newly arrived immigrants; anyone else who knew basic English was forced to attend English wards. At the surface this issue of disbanding and forcing Latina/os to English may seem simply a battle for linguistic accommodations. The actions in Tucson could be read as justified if the only difference is language, and then once someone learned English they could simply "move up to the majors," as García phrased it. However, as an interview with his sister revealed, "all members of the Spanish-speaking ward who could speak English had been asked to go to the geographical ward. The ward was only for those who could not communicate in English."[42]

The threat of closure, or rather reorganization, still hovers over congregations in the twenty-first century. Spanish-speaking wards are often reshuffled or reorganized into new wards when growth or decline occurs. In practice, this means that one could worship among certain families for years and then be told to move wards abruptly. This constant shift, or threat of change, breeds uncertainty and derails the emotional ethnic faith-based cohesion that comes with worshiping *en comunidad*. Religious studies scholars have well documented the critical importance of ethnic faith-based community interactions.[43] Perhaps because in the past this ethnic unity resulted in political coordination and demands for autonomy among Spanish-speaking Mexicans, the contemporary LDS Church has chosen to maintain wards in flux.[44] This decision, however, can create unintended consequences for the way barrios come together and find solace in each other through faith and belonging.

An entry in the 2014 *LDS Living*, a bimonthly magazine akin to *Southern Living*, was written by Nelda McCalister, who wrote in "My Story as an LDS Latina," about the ways she melded culture with faith and resented the way Spanish-speaking Saints were positioned by the dominant church. McCalister made specific references to the differences between English-dominant and Spanish-speaking or "Hispanic Saints." She referenced behaviors like personable hugs and overall markers of friendliness that differentiate English-dominant wards from what she terms "the Mormon Raza." McCalister's narrative clearly aimed to promote appreciation for the particularities of Latina/o members to the general readership of *LDS Living*, most of whom were White Mormon women; still, there was a moment in her narrative in which McCalister deeply laments the loss of her culture and identity. She admitted fears she had of losing her heritage or "forgetting what it means to be Hispanic." I have heard this similar concern with the women I have interviewed in Mesa, Arizona. They are concerned, not for themselves but for their grandchildren: Are they losing who they are? Do they see the richness in their heritage? In states like Utah and Arizona where conservative White Mormons freely voice dangerous anti-immigrant rhetoric to garner votes, the pressures to assimilate or even deemphasize one's ethnic identity remain strong. Whereas some LDS families proudly emphasize bilingual attributes as a way to better prepare oneself for eventual mission work, Latina/o teens in the church still feel a certain pressure to worship and enact Whiteness through their sense of self. Indeed, mixed marriages have produced mixed-race progeny who may not associate with their Latina/o heritage at all. This was precisely what McCalister and others with whom I have spoken fear. In the LDS Church's push toward a particular cultural and linguistic center, the resulting hegemonic identity crisis usurps the potential possible when ethnic wards do thrive through community placemaking tied to their cultural heritage.

Conclusion: The Law and Faith

By 2000, church statisticians were already predicting that Spanish-speaking Mormons would outnumber English-speaking members by 2020.[45] Based on previous decades of growth and trends of Spanish speakers joining the LDS Church, this increase in membership did not occur overnight. Moreover, I suggest that generations of earlier Latina/o Saints laid the foundation for bringing in record numbers of Spanish speakers to the fold. The centrality of the LDS Church as geographically and historically bound to the United States generates a unique politics of belonging. Humans assert borders demarcating who belongs and who is suspect through religiously informed identity politics. Regardless of religious denomination, nationalist immigration politics can become embedded in faith communities and create a complicated belonging based on race and nationalism. The LDS Church is not exempt from this phenomenon of exalting White male privilege in its history and leadership. One need only look at the exclusion of Black men from the priesthood until 1978 for proof. A brief introduction to LDS theology can also situate how LDS doctrine propagated a system of White supremacy toward Latina/o members as well.

Returning to the opening epigraphs, Gallegos and Yapias illustrate how LDS Latina/os coalesced into a shared cultural and linguistic religious identity to combat the historical, doctrinal, and contemporary *rechazos* of being ethnic in a predominantly White-controlled church. This investment in one's ethnic community was, in part, a result of having spaces of faithful practice specifically designated for Spanish speakers. In these Spanish wards, Latina/o members worshiped together, their children grew up together, and they celebrated events together. Mormons in general consider themselves as "set apart" as "peculiar people" for being Latter-day Saints, but Latina/o Saints were simultaneously set apart from their non-LDS ethnic group and within their predominantly White church.

As other scholars of Latina/o religious experience have explored throughout this volume, I posit that it is important for Latina/o religious communities to create safe spaces where their ethnicity and multiplied identities are free to flourish and their transnational religious ethnic belonging is recognized. For Latina/o Saints, this means that their unique experience in Mormonism should be celebrated and unhampered by the pressures to replicate Utah-centered Mormonism.[46] Exploring the way Latina/o Saints navigated their religious identities through their ethnic identities, this chapter unearthed a long-ignored history of active nationalist Spanish-speaking Saints who asserted a claim to their own unique presence in the faith and in the United States. Whether asserting the right to belong in twenty-first-century immigration debates or placing Chicano nationalism within their genealogical connections to the Mormon doctrine, Latina/o Saints demand to be seen and acknowledged as equal members of the kingdoms of glory. Their Latina/o religious politics informs how they confront the barriers for acceptance both in the faith and in the nation. Do they assimilate and risk the deep nostalgia for a Latino connection that Nelda McCalister grieves? Do they adopt and highlight the Lamanite proto-indigenous narrative that Bishop Rivera and Angel recognized? Do they form separate autonomous successful Latina/o wards that celebrate ethnic identity rather than supplant it, as Bishop García did in Tucson? Or do they stand up and demand action from elders in the church to combat politically divisive rhetoric? As sociopolitical moments continue to impact Latina/o LDS families in very real, material ways, the role of their faith and the recognition of their historical experience in the church can alleviate or exacerbate their situation.

NOTES

1 Members of the Church of Jesus Christ of Latter-day Saints call themselves Latter-day Saints. In colloquial conversations I have had, both Latina/o and non-Latina/o members refer to the community as Latino Saints. Additionally, I will use "Latina/o" to refer to the population in general. Though I include members of the LGBTQ community, these individuals identified with he/she pronouns and therefore fell under the framing of Latina/o.
2 Alyshia Gálvez, *Guadalupe in New York: Devotion and the Struggle for Citizenship Rights Among Mexican Immigrants* (New York: New York University Press, 2010), 5.
3 Mario T. García, *Católicos: Resistance and Affirmation in Chicano Catholic History* (Austin: University of Texas Press, 2008), 225.

4   Though Joseph Smith was lynched in Illinois, it was the state of Missouri that officially had an "extermination order" in place against Mormons.
5   George Lipsitz describes the possessive investment in Whiteness as, among other things, the "prefiguring, presenting, and preserving political coalitions based on identification with the fiction of 'whiteness.'" I suggest that this preserving of Whiteness among Mormons led them to side with the United States rather than Mexico in the Mexican-American War. See George Lipsitz, *The Possessive Investment in Whiteness: How White People Profit from Identity Politics* (Philadelphia: Temple University Press, 2005), 370.
6   For a history of Mormons in Utah politics, see Jo Ann B. Shipps, *The Mormons in Politics: The First Hundred Years* (Ann Arbor: ProQuest Dissertations Publishing, 1965).
7   F. LaMond Tullis, "Early Mormon Exploration and Missionary Activities in Mexico," *BYU Studies Quarterly* 22, no. 3 (1982): 289–310.
8   D. L. Turner, "Forgotten City of the Saints: Mormons, Native Americans, and the Founding of Lehi," *Journal of Arizona History* 47, no. 1 (2006), 61.
9   See Turner, "Forgotten City of the Saints"; and Daniel Webster Jones, *Forty Years among the Indians: A True yet Thrilling Narrative of the Author's Experiences among the Natives* (Salt Lake City: Bookcraft, 1960) for more on these early Arizona Mormon settlements.
10 Elise Boxer, "'The Lamanites Shall Blossom as the Rose': The Indian Student Placement Program, Mormon Whiteness, and Indigenous Identity," *Journal of Mormon History* 41, no. 4 (2015): 132–76; Margaret D. Jacobs, "Entangled Histories: The Mormon Church and Indigenous Child Removal from 1850 to 2000," *Journal of Mormon History* 42, no. 2 (2016): 27–60.
11 F. LaMond Tullis, *Mormons in Mexico: The Dynamics of Faith and Culture* (Logan, UT: Utah State University Press, 1987), 13.
12 A "branch" is a small emerging LDS community. If the community is big enough (approximately three hundred members), a "ward" is established. Wards are then governed by a "stake," which consist of five to twelve wards/branches. Every level of congregation has a governing body (president or bishop and counselors). The stake president presides as leader over the presidents/bishops of the branches/wards in a stake.
13 Gerry R. Flake, "Mormons in Mexico: The First 96 Years," *Ensign*, September 1972, https://abn.churchofjesuschrist.org.
14 For more on this history of US Latino Saints, see F. LaMond Tullis, *Mormonism: A Faith for All Cultures* (Provo: Brigham Young University Press, 1978); and Jessie L. Embry, *In His Own Language: Mormon Spanish Speaking Congregations in the United States* (Salt Lake City: Signature Books, 1997).
15 White missionaries were banned from Mexico until 1940; in the interim they focused Spanish missioning efforts in the US Southwest and began work in Argentina (1925) and Brazil (1928); see Tullis, *Mormonism*.

16 A chapel differs from a Temple in so far as a chapel is a meetinghouse for weekly Sunday services where members and non-members can attend. The Temple is much more restrictive and requires a "temple recommend" from one's bishop to enter. A chapel is also a smaller, more intimate worship community of a few families; this is otherwise known as a "branch."
17 Wards are significantly larger than branches and can contain anywhere from 150 to 500 members.
18 David Montero, "Latino Activist Urges Mexico to Halt LDS Missionary Visas," *Salt Lake Tribune*, February 13, 2011, https://archive.sltrib.com.
19 According to my genealogical research on the LDS-sponsored website Family Search, Russell Pearce is the great-grandson of a Utah settler who made his way to Arizona and founded the city of Taylor a year after Jones's expedition arrived in the Mesa area. Also of note, Pearce's great-grandparents' first home was a "dug out cave on the side of a hill." FamilySearch.com Life Sketch of James Pearce, KWCN-RJ4.
20 For more on these Lamanite events in Mesa, see Eduardo Balderas, "Northward to Mesa," *Ensign*, September 1972, https://abn.churchofjesuschrist.org.
21 Mario T. García, *Católicos*; Deborah Kanter, *Chicago Católico: Making Catholic Parishes Mexican* (Urbana: University of Illinois Press, 2020); Luis D. León, *La Llorona's Children: Religion, Life, and Death in the US-Mexican Borderlands* (Berkeley: University of California Press, 2004); Lara Medina, *Las Hermanas: Chicana/Latina Religious-Political Activism in the US Catholic Church* (Philadelphia: Temple University Press, 2004); Roberto R. Treviño, *The Church in the Barrio: Mexican American Ethno-Catholicism in Houston* (Chapel Hill: University of North Carolina Press, 2004); Sujey Vega, *Latino Heartland: Of Borders and Belonging in the Midwest* (New York: New York University Press, 2015).
22 Treviño, *Church in the Barrio*, 42.
23 Benedict Anderson, *Imagined Communities: Reflections on the Origin and Spread of Nationalism* (New York: Verso Books, 1983).
24 Felipe Hinojosa, *Latino Mennonites: Civil Rights, Faith, and Evangelical Culture* (Baltimore: Johns Hopkins University Press, 2014), xiii.
25 Orlando Rivera, "Mormonism and the Chicano," in *Mormonism: A Faith for All Cultures*, ed. F. LaMond Tullis (Provo, UT: Brigham Young University Press, 1978), 116.
26 García, *Católicos*, 13.
27 Rivera, "Mormonism and the Chicano," 121.
28 Rivera, "Mormonism and the Chicano," 124.
29 Arlene M. Sánchez-Walsh, *Latino Pentecostal Identity: Evangelical Faith, Self, and Society* (New York: Columbia University Press, 2003), 30.
30 Thomas W. Murphy, "From Racist Stereotype to Ethnic Identity: Instrumental Uses of Mormon Racial Doctrine," *Ethnohistory* 46, no. 3 (1999): 451–80.
31 For more on this form of Whiteness and the LDS Church, see Hokulani K. Aikau, *A Chosen People, a Promised Land: Mormonism and Race in Hawai'i*

(Minneapolis: University of Minnesota Press, 2012); and Gina Colvin and Joanna Brooks, eds., *Decolonizing Mormonism: Approaching a Postcolonial Zion* (Salt Lake City: University of Utah Press, 2018).

32 Colvin and Brooks, *Decolonizing Mormonism*; M. W. Inouye, "The Oak and the Banyan: The 'Glocalization' of Mormon Studies," *Mormon Studies Review* 1 (2014): 70–79.
33 Embry, *In His Own Language*, 46.
34 Hinojosa, *Latino Mennonites*, 176.
35 Ignacio M. García, *Chicano While Mormon: Activism, War, and Keeping the Faith* (Madison, NJ: Fairleigh Dickinson University Press, 2015).
36 Jeffrey S. Passel and Roberto Suro, "Rise, Peak and Decline: Trends in U.S. Immigration, 1992–2004," Pew Hispanic Center, September 27, 2005, www.pewresearch.org.
37 Embry, *In His Own Language*, 83.
38 Embry, *In His Own Language*, 86.
39 Vega, *Latino Heartland*.
40 Embry, *In His Own Language*.
41 Ignacio M. García, *Chicano While Mormon*.
42 Embry, *In His Own Language*, 47.
43 Mario T. García, *Católicos*; Kanter, *Chicago Católico*; Martínez, *PADRES*; Medina, *Las Hermanas*; Treviño, *Church in the Barrio*.
44 Gomez, *Las Hermanas*; Ignacio M. García, *Chicano While Mormon*; Embry, *In His Own Language*.
45 Jay M. Todd, "Historic Milestone Achieved: More Non-English-Speaking Members Now Than English-Speaking," *Ensign*, September 2000, www.churchofjesuschrist.org.
46 See, for instance, David A. Badillo, *Latinos and the New Immigrant Church* (Baltimore: Johns Hopkins University Press, 2006); Gastón Espinosa, Virgilio Elizondo, and Jesse Miranda, eds., *Latino Religions and Civic Activism in the United States* (Oxford: Oxford University Press, 2005); Mario T. García, *Católicos*; Hinojosa, *Latino Mennonites*; and Treviño, *Church in the Barrio*.

PART II

Freedom Movements

5

Pentecostalism's Instrumental Faith and Alternative Power

César Chávez and Reies López Tijerina among Pentecostal Farmworkers, 1954–1956

LLOYD D. BARBA

In that little Madera church, I observed everything going on about me that could [be] useful in organizing. Although there were no more than twelve men and women, there was more spirit there than when I went to mass where there were two hundred. Everybody was happy. They all were singing. These people were really committed in their beliefs and this made them sing and clap and participate. I liked that. I think that's where I got the idea of singing at the meetings. That was one of the first things we did when I started the Union.
—César Chávez

I read in the Bible that mercy and truth met, and justice and peace hugged. . . . It was the religious life for the satisfaction of the yearning of my heart for justice. This is what I got from religious life.
—Reies López Tijerina

In 1954 César Chávez found himself at a Pentecostal church service in the home of pastor Mariano Marín. Chávez had originally visited the pastor to assist him and his family with an immigration issue; with the deportation orders of Operation Wetback sweeping across Mexican American communities that year, vulnerable Mexicans throughout the United States could waste no time arranging their legal paperwork. But during the course of the meeting and the breaking of bread, the pastor had to dismiss himself. Unbeknownst to Chávez at that moment, the pastor headed to the living room to conduct a church service, and Chávez later followed him to the living room. This small church in the agricultural town of Madera, located deep in the heart of California's Central Valley, introduced Chávez to a new sacred environment. Chávez, unfamiliar with the ways of Pentecostal worship, would have observed all around him the farmworker faithful elevating their hands heavenward and lifting up their voices as they spoke in unknown tongues and sang.[1] During the worship service, Chávez would have encountered singing from the vast collection of upbeat Mexican Pentecostal hymns and *corridos*, a sonic environment that can best be described as one that redeemed the *fiesta* of Mexican culture.[2] Such effervescence bubbled over in that home-church that Chávez remarked how there was "more spirit" in that service with about as many disciples as Jesus had than in a mass with multitudes. Chávez stepped into a religious sensory realm unlike anything he had ever witnessed firsthand before. If the combination of exalted hands, elevated voices, bursts of glossolalia (speaking in tongues), and lachrymose prayers ranging from still contrition to shouts of joyful redemption did not leave an impression on Chávez, then surely irony of sacred music sung in the secular genres (*corrido, bolero, canción romántica*, and so on) would have captured the attention of the young community organizer.[3] As he attests, this fortuitous encounter inspired him to incorporate music into the farm labor union meetings and rallies that he would lead a decade later. Marín's church, in turn, was also inspired by Chávez's vision as a community organizer and the whole church joined Madera's newly formed chapter of the Community Service Organization. They drew inspiration from one another.

What Chávez experienced in that church service that day was just another ordinary high-energy Pentecostal worship environment. The Mexican Pentecostals (Apostólicos, as they called themselves) of the quiet agricultural town could hardly escape the *aleluya* epithet aptly applied to them by detractors all across the country for their remarkably noisy church services.[4] Chávez's encounter at that little church in Madera was much more than that of chance, for in dealing with farmworkers in California's agricultural towns in the mid-twentieth century, crossing paths with the Pentecostal proletariat was a predictable eventuality. In fact, he was not the only nascent Chicano movement leader to happen upon and politically mobilize Pentecostals in the 1950s.[5] Two years later and on the other side of the state's golden hills, we come across more Pentecostal activism underway in Salinas, once again, suffused with "more spirit."

While Chávez arrived in Madera intent on helping Mexicans claim their right to stay where the pastor had established a church, another major figure of the Chicano movement, Reies López Tijerina, arrived two years later in Salinas claiming that Mexicans needed to flee. Tijerina, a longtime farmworker and an exiled Assemblies of God minister, arrived to preach a two-week revival. During his time in Salinas, Tijerina enjoined a group of farmworkers at the church to follow him from Salinas to El Valle de Paz (Valley of Peace), a utopian community he established in the Sonoran Desert of Arizona. Disillusioned with the political and religious systems of the world, Tijerina believed that the only way to survive and carry out his divinely mandated mission was to form a separatist community of God-fearing believers. For Tijerina, the politics and discrimination toward Mexicans boiled over; his hope, unlike that of Chávez, did not lie in reform, but in a refuge made with his own hands.

Chávez secured his place in the pantheon of Chicano movement political and civil rights leaders through his efforts to reform the labor conditions for farmworkers, and his is a well-regarded name beyond academic literature and activist communities today. Until recently, however, the role of religion in Chávez's activism remained an overlooked (or perhaps worse, distorted) aspect of his work and legacy.[6] Tijerina, lesser-known to the general public but not unfamiliar to those in Chicanx history, is mostly remembered for leading land grant protests in New Mexico. In 1966 he first led a demonstration at Echo Amphitheatre, property of the US National Parks, which he believed legally belonged to Mexican descendants who were able to furnish land grant claims. But Tijerina's more recognized protest came the following year, when he led an armed takeover of the Tierra Amarilla Courthouse. These daring demonstrations indelibly inscribed Tijerina into the annals of Chicanx history. His lesser-known struggle at El Valle de Paz is often overlooked; scholars have contended that this glossing over likely owes to his efforts being passed off as religious zealotry. Such activism provides little to no usable history that fits into the typical narrative of Chicano civil rights protests.[7]

This chapter makes a case for understanding marquee moments in the lives of Chávez and Tijerina through the lens of Pentecostal affect and dispositions. In short, the two utilized instrumental aspects of the Mexican Pentecostal faith to pursue alternative modes of power. In both Chávez and Tijerina we see significant religious experiences in the 1950s that would help shape their political activism later. In both cases, religion shaped their own tenets of love, charity, and justice. These ideas remained with them even as they moved away into more explicitly political efforts in the 1960s. Nevertheless, in the decade before the heyday of the Chicano civil rights movement we find Chávez and Tijerina in places where we might not think to find them, much less fancy that they drew any meaningful inspiration from them. A pericope of the biography of César Chávez in his days as neophyte in the Community Service Organization in 1954 and another of the life of Reies López Tijerina in his role as an itinerant preacher in 1956, together offer historians moments to assay the limits of religious inspiration of each leader in unexpected places. Before Chávez and Tijerina garnered national attention in the 1960s, both utilized their faith in instrumental ways by working with alternative power. From these two stories, situated two years and just over a hundred miles apart in the thick of California's industrial agricultural lands, we learn that religion inspired resistance in those moments and later in the lives of the Chicano leaders.

The seeds of unrest germinated under the pressure and heat of labor exploitation in the borderlands. Chávez and Tijerina proved to be masterful husbandmen. Apostólicos merely comprised a small but growing religious movement in the borderlands, but by the time that Chávez and Tijerina garnered national attention in the mid-1960s, Apostólico farmworkers had already left indelible imprints on their respective movements. These episodes in the lives of Chávez and Tijerina among Mexican Pentecostals ought to caution historians against assuming that Pentecostals have historically bowed out of political engagement. In fact, it appears to be the case that a template of early white Pentecostal abstinence from politics has all along been applied to Pentecostals from Black and Latinx contexts who actually activated their religion to address various kinds of discrimination.[8] We can gather from these two small episodes alone that the enthusiastic, dynamic, and grassroots nature of Mexican Pentecostal beliefs and practices informed the developmental stages of the charismatic Chicano leaders' activism. Their encounters with Pentecostals teach us about the imbrication of faith and power.

Chávez in Madera, 1954

By the early 1950s, Chávez had already been acquainted with the exploitation endemic to migrant farm labor in the Southwest. In 1939 his family had lost a farm after an agreement with an underhanded Anglo landowner in Arizona's Gila Valley. Landless, the family worked on the migrant farm labor circuit in California, moving from one valley to the next. In the early 1940s the Chávez family settled in San Jose, in the Mexican quarters of the city known as "Sal Si Puedes" (Get Out If You Can). Residents of this area knew all too well poverty stemming from unfair wages and lack of protections for agricultural laborers. Chávez served in the then-segregated Navy from 1946 to 1948, returning to civilian life with a resolve to ameliorate the conditions of his fellow Mexicans trapped in cycles of exploitation. In the early 1950s he became acquainted with Father Donald McDonnell, an activist priest in San Jose. Under McDonnell, Chávez learned the tenets of Catholic social doctrine, providing for him a theological and scriptural basis to carry out his vision of civil and labor rights reform. At that time, he also came under the tutelage of Fred Ross, a community organizer with the Community Service Organization (CSO), in part supported by the more nationally known Industrial Areas Foundation. During this period the doctrines of the Catholic Church and the Marxist teaching of the CSO and others coalesced for Chávez. In 1952 Chávez hit the road as a faith-inspired community organizer intent on mobilizing Mexican voters and defending them from the state's capricious immigration system.[9]

Accordingly, then, in 1954 we find Chávez regularly traveling up and down northern California, stopping in towns off the beaten path to organize Mexican American communities. Chávez originally arrived in the agricultural area of Fresno and Madera to investigate allegations that the precinct election board discouraged certain voters by requiring older Mexicans to take literacy tests. But in the end Chávez wound up having to deal with larger problems, including unfavorable immigration laws. This found him in the home-church of Mariano Marín. Chávez soon encountered a thicket of discrimination around more voting violations and immigration concerns, so in the summer of 1954 he relocated his family to Madera to launch a CSO chapter.[10]

Chávez learned in his time with Father McDonnell that Mexican congregations proved to be a particularly promising site for organizing. The pragmatic advantage was that the people were already gathered under one roof, obviating the need for a separate meeting time and site. And furthermore, those gathered in their respective churches had already held some beliefs in common. The shared experience of labor exploitation would ideally put those in the pews on the same page when it came to organizing. But unlike in San Jose, where Chávez enjoyed the support of activist priests, in Madera the Catholic priest Father Dominic Albertelli sided with the farm operators and managers who red-baited Chávez, making him out to be a communist, a blasphemous offense to many in McCarthy-era America. But even prior to the more overt red-baiting, Albertelli criticized Chávez for having too many Protestants in the CSO, though Chávez refused to submit to criticisms about religious representation on the board. Protestants quickly joined and did not express the same misgivings that Albertelli did. Lacking the support of Albertelli, Chávez turned to Protestant clergy for assistance with convening Mexicans under one roof. From there Chávez effectively organized a CSO chapter board that for many years was comprised of a Protestant majority. Chávez's regular interactions with Protestants brought him into community with the Apostólicos. In the fuller quote cited in the epigraph, we can better capture the texture of that account:

> I didn't know it then, but I was in for a special education in Madera.... When I went to their home, which was very, very humble, we talked and ate. Then he excused himself to conduct services. "I'll be back in about an hour," he said." "Can you wait for me?" He went into a little room—it hadn't occurred to me that it was a church—I thought it was just a living room.... After they started service I asked if I could join them.... *So in that little Madera church, I observed everything going on about me that could [be] useful in organizing.* Although there were no more than twelve men and women, there was more spirit there than when I went to mass where there were two hundred. Everybody was happy. They all were singing. These people were really committed in their beliefs and this made them sing and clap and participate. I liked that. I think that's where I got

the idea of singing at the meetings. That was one of the first things we did when I started the Union. And it was hard for me because I couldn't carry a tune.[11]

This unlikely episode unfolded in the home of Apostólico pastor Mariano Marín, where Chávez convinced all those in the congregation to join the CSO. The issues facing Mexican Americans overwhelmed many in the area, making for ripe conditions to organize the working-class community. While we may never recover what exactly Chávez said to the Mexican Pentecostals to convince them to join, the fact that the whole church signed on with the CSO stood out to Chávez. In time, Marín's family would assume leadership roles, with his daughter Sallie Torres (Marín) serving as the first corresponding secretary of the Madera CSO chapter and her husband, Jerry Torres, on the executive board.[12] Chávez held the Madera chapter in high esteem. He later commented about the chapter, "I radicalized that chapter more than any other chapter, I guess, in that short period of time. They weren't afraid to take on the police or the immigration service. They weren't afraid to fight for their rights."[13] Chávez's descriptions offer a rare perspective from an outsider who enters a Pentecostal context and intervenes with no particular motivation. His encounter is evidence to the contrary with respect to those who maintain that a religious anodyne inured Pentecostals from the motivating pain to organize for their earthly rights.[14]

Mexican Pentecostalism's demonstrative worship as witnessed by Chávez lent him an effective tool for community organization. The participatory elements of the worship service in which the secular genres of *corridos* bound together the band of twelve stood out. Moreover, the liveliness of the music would have carried a vastly different sound compared to the sacred music in both Catholic and mainline Protestant services familiar to Chávez. Consider the differentiation of music in social contexts, where sacred sounds usually connoted Catholic ones. No doubt that Apostólico soundscapes operated as sacred sonic stimuli that in some ways compensated for the heavily visual world of pre-Vatican II Catholic spaces.[15] In contrast to Catholic visual religious stimuli, Pentecostals wielded the power of the sonic, to such a degree that a group of twelve could exhibit "more spirit" than two hundred in mass. A larger set of demonstrative sensory experiences in the church service would have surfaced, the same ones that even mainline Protestant clergy often denounced. The accompaniments to the singing also would have distinguished it from contemporaneous sacred soundscapes: heavy repetition of choruses, "Spirit-led" individual dancing, collective and/or individual shouting, and, more distinctly, bursts of glossolalia. The presence or types of instruments in the service Chávez attended remain unknown, but the most likely would have been guitar, some percussion, and perhaps a smaller piano in the living room. All this movement and instrumentation would have accompanied the hearty singing of hymns. Fashioned in vernacular genres, these Apostólico soundscapes appealed to the everyday laborers and resonated with the working-class Chávez. So deep was the impression on Chávez's mind that he would recall that moment decades later.

Apostólico music at the time drew from genres more closely associated with secular music of the time, including *corridos*.[16] Even a cursory examination of the music employed by the Chávez-led United Farm Workers reveals the effective incorporation of the kind of music he would have heard at the church in Madera. *Corridos* especially found resonance in the movement's repertoire throughout the 1960s. (Today, most remember the farmworkers movement's iconography, bodily self-sacrifice, pageantry, marches, and robust musical repertoire.) Eight years after the service in Marín's home, music would once again be a source of inspiration at a house meeting in Madera on September 25, 1962. On this day Rosa Gloria penned the first *corrido* of the farmworker movement: "El Campesino."

The melody of "El Campesino" followed that of a popular Mexican folk ballad titled "El Corrido de Cananea" (The Ballad of Cananea), also popularly known as "La Carcel de Cananea" (The Cananea Jail). This *ranchera*, written in three-four time, was music of the common folk.[17] "El Campesino" harkens back to the twilight of Porfirio Díaz's regime, when Mexican workers in the copper mines of Cananea in Sonora, Mexico, launched a strike over the higher wages paid to American workers for the same work. The ensuing strike resulted in casualties on both sides, but the massacre stood as a protest of the working class and as a harbinger of the impending Mexican Revolution. The myth of the strike was immortalized in the 1917 song "La Carcel de Cananea." Gloria's song, written nearly half a century later in Madera, demonstrates the sorts of music that traveled with farmworkers on their migrant journeys in the borderlands and its melody invoked the song that highlighted the legacy of American injustice and the oppression of working-class Mexicans. Gloria's rendition, embedded in the religious and cultural milieu of the Central Valley, struck a powerful, yet religiously modulated, chord.

We find, then, that when Chávez brought to fruition his 1954 inspiration of using music to rally union support, religious overtones maintained an important place, imbuing the farmworkers' struggle with a sense of sacrality. This is not to suggest, however, that all or even most of the music produced by or for the National Farm Workers Association or the United Farm Workers bore religious significance. But we do find that sacred music, or music that invoked sacred stories, proved effective. The parallels to biblical narratives, for example, would have resonated with the farmworkers of California, a majority of whom came from religious backgrounds.[18]

In a 1963 interview Chávez discussed the efficacy of music in rallying together support. Once again, the inspiration came from a Pentecostal church. He recalled,

> A couple of years ago, I was driving home from Los Angeles. I passed a Pentecostal church at night and it was full of people and I thought to myself, why do all the people come there so much. It must be because they like to praise God—and to sing.[19]

Chávez felt comfortable adopting ideas and symbols from religious groups. Since his time with the CSO, he straddled a delicate line between Protestant and Catholic churches, claiming that he was one of the few Catholics in San Jose who would set foot inside Protestant churches.[20]

When he later launched the grape strike and boycott from 1965 to 1970, the religious imagery often took center stage. In the wake of massive walkouts late in 1965 and in the days leading up to Easter in 1966, Chávez coordinated a twenty-five-day, 250-mile journey on foot from Delano to Sacramento. While many referred to the event as a "march," consistent with the lexicon of protest movements, Chávez unequivocally understood the demonstration as a *peregrinación* (pilgrimage). He clearly likened the *peregrinación* to a religious pilgrimage. Chávez required that participants fill out a registration form in order to participate in the pilgrimage. The terms on the top of the second page of the registration form read "*Peregrinación, Penitencia, Revolución.*"[21] The multivalent meanings of the pilgrimage resonated with a larger audience beyond Catholics. The absence of Marian language in the call appealed to Protestants; the very notion of public marching and revolutionary rhetoric appealed to college students.[22] Even though Chávez specifically stated on the registration form that "this is a religious march" and registration was mandated for participation in the march, nonbelievers joined the ranks.[23]

While the registration form had been shorn of language that favored too strongly any particular religious tradition, the pilgrimage itself assumed strong Catholic overtones while retaining trace elements of Pentecostal fiesta in the singing and celebration. The overwhelming Catholic aura of the pilgrimage, however, disturbed some of the nonreligious participants. Furthermore, to the chagrin of Protestants, Marian icons held prominent positions in the *peregrinación*, and Protestants disagreed with the need for strikers to pay penance. As disputes arose over the Catholic iconography, National Farm Workers Association cofounder Dolores Huerta recalled, "the question was brought up at a special meeting. We put the Virgin to a motion, and virginity won."[24] The salience and binding power of Guadalupe was manifested clearly in "El Plan de Delano," which identified her as "the patroness of the Mexican people." The *peregrinos* held a rally every night, most of which were religious (even Pentecostal) in nature.[25] As the pilgrims made their way through towns, newspapers tracked their movement, capturing both the solemnity and the collective effervescence of these meetings. In the end, the pilgrimage's overwhelming Catholic aura proved unpalatable for a significant portion of tongue-talking Pentecostal participants, who, historian Alan Watt notes, "bolted from the union altogether."[26] The movement had gained so much support by this point that few seemed to notice their departure.

The pilgrimage proved to be a massive success in the sense that it garnered national support for the farmworkers' strike and mobilized the international boycott on certain brands of grapes. Beyond the throngs of sympathizers who marched with Chávez, the accompanying music and artistic productions put on by El Teatro Campesino (The Farmworker Theatre) boosted the pilgrimage and larger movement. Because of that

1954 church service in Madera, music would serve as a necessary accompaniment to the movement. Unbeknownst to Apostólicos, their music and enthusiastic style of worship inspired the identity and solidarity of the farmworker movement.

While Chávez made great strides in California working toward reforms for farmworkers and was able to masterfully implement music to build up the movement's esprit de corps, Tijerina's activism in New Mexico took on a more confrontational approach. Chávez's and Tijerina's approaches and goals have been compared to those of Martin Luther King Jr. and Malcom X, respectively. Chicano movement leaders thrust their prophet Chávez to center stage for a highly publicized takedown against growers. As the preeminent hero of the Chicano movement, Chávez had a large base of supporters in his corner ranging from Indian and Yemeni to Filipino farmworkers. He also entered the arena with the mentoring of influential whites, including Saul Alinsky and Robert Kennedy. In keeping with King's model of civil rights, he crossed religious lines (from Chicano Catholicism to multiracial Protestantism). Meanwhile, the more violent elements of the Chicano Power movement manifested themselves in the person, following, and beliefs of Tijerina. His call to action stemmed from the belief that tracts of land throughout the Southwest legally belonged to Mexican families cheated by officials who did not honor the Treaty of Guadalupe Hidalgo (1848). The revelation emboldened him and his followers to reclaim the land by settling on it, sometimes resorting to armed force. Tijerina's opponents—local, state, and federal officials—proved to be much more formidable than the growers Chávez brought to their knees. Even though the fulfillments of his promises were short-lived and in some cases did not come to fruition, Tijerina has been extolled in Chicano literature as the fiercest and most violent of the four horsemen of the "Chicano Apocalypse."[27] Chávez, the better-known of the four horsemen, on the other hand, epitomized the principles of nonviolence. While Chávez's pacifist approach was heavily influenced by King, Tijerina's own militant strategy and rhetoric are comparable to those of Malcolm X. But before Tijerina engaged in armed confrontations, his activism assumed unmistakable prophetic and separatist dimensions. And like Chávez in the mid-1950s, Tijerina found himself among Apostólicos.

Tijerina's Influences on Apostólicos

By the middle of the century, the Salinas Valley became home to major growers and a few Apostólico congregations. The Spreckels Sugar Company attracted thousands of farmworkers to work the sugar beet fields of Salinas. The growth of Apostólico churches in places like Madera and Salinas attests to the phenomenon of churches largely following and flourishing alongside labor-intensive crops. The Apostólico congregation in Salinas in 1956 thrived but lost its founding pastor that same year to the church in San Jose. In this transition the young Manuel Pérez stepped in.[28]

But little did Pérez know that he had inherited a thriving congregation on the precipice of a schism. While he may have been prepared for the basic duties of pastoring a church (preaching, teaching, prayer, etc.), no one foresaw (or could have been prepared for) the larger-than-life personality of Tijerina stopping by for a multi-week revival, wherein he enticed believers to leave the Salinas Valley for El Valle de Paz.[29] In the Salinas church, Tijerina's powerful charisma burrowed deep into the dynamic interpretation of dreams, the Bible, and eschatology. At this time of his ministerial career, as explained by Ramón Gutiérrez, Pentecostal services were

> exuberant gatherings full of singing and clapping, sobbing and shouting, with fits of anger and punching motions into the air to banish evil and Satan from their midst and guttural, other-worldly, seemingly ghostly speaking in tongues. Tijerina constantly announced that the living God would soon arrive and that it was time to repent and be saved.[30]

Much of Tijerina's life experiences had led up to his spiritual activism. He grew up in Texas in a family of farmworkers experiencing the very worst of Depression-era America. Subject to the vicissitudes of life on the migrant farmworker trail, little sustained the Tijerinas other than their faith. Over the years, Tijerina developed three core features that sustained the kind of confrontational and prophetic activism he carried out in his life: a divinely inspired sense of mission, an intensely charismatic, autocratic religiosity, and a theology that critiqued an inherently unjust US society.[31] His critiques of the United States at the time of the founding of El Valle de Paz reflected his objections to nuclear proliferation and the sense of doom in the Cold War era.

But to understand Tijerina's activism and sense of mission, we must briefly turn to his upbringing. Mainline Protestants and Pentecostals heavily proselytized south Texas, working in competition against one another. Tijerina's father claimed to have converted to Protestantism in order to escape the even worse treatment of Catholics. As a youth Tijerina began to tell of his "Super Dreams." He recounted uncanny dreams of heaven, divine protection, and unnatural phenomena. His childhood and teenage years spent in poverty and on the migrant trail likely influenced the nature of his dreams. The constant swindling of wages and intimidation at the hands of growers and klansmen impelled Tijerina to leave Texas to look for jobs in the Midwest's booming automobile industry. While picking sugar beets in Michigan, he had his own conversion experience. A Baptist missionary came into the fields to speak with Tijerina about the gospel. The fifteen-year-old Tijerina listened intently, was baptized in a nearby river, and encountered a text that provided the language to articulate his dreams: the Bible.[32]

Tijerina also found in the Bible the words that articulated his later political and religious protests. He became enamored with the text. He recalled, "I read in the Bible that mercy and truth met, and justice and peace hugged." This passage from Psalm 85 summed up the interplay between religion and justice. He described how "then it was the religious life for the satisfaction of the yearning of my heart for justice [a]nd [of] my idols [beginning] with Moses on [to the others]. This is what I got from religious life. I gathered up the strengths and liberties of justice out of the lives of those Biblical men of old."[33] From this point forward, Tijerina pursued justice through the mechanism of religion. In his pursuit of justice, he took issue with the United States' illegitimate land grabs. He became a man of the Book, figuratively speaking, in his literal interpretation of scripture, an interpretation shaped by mid-century Pentecostal hermeneutics.

The Bible became the focus of Tijerina's religious formation. In 1944 he found great company for this hermeneutical adventure when he matriculated into the Instituto Bíblico Latino Americano, a ministerial training institute affiliated with the Assemblies of God Latin American District in Saspamco, Texas. He sought out a biblical education alongside prospective Mexican American evangelists being groomed to minister to the booming immigrant population. Here, Tijerina learned a Pentecostal style of charismatic preaching that fueled his speeches throughout his political career and short-lived ministry as a licensed preacher with the Assemblies of God (1946–1950).[34] As an unaffiliated preacher, in the 1950s he established his own itinerant ministry. This allowed him to navigate through various denominations and eventually find himself among Apostólicos in Salinas. Tijerina recalls how he spent his time "teaching, talking to people, . . . farmworkers in the town going from one church to another where I was invited."[35] But by the end of 1955, he gave up on institutional Christianity and began to recruit members, called Los Heraldos de la Paz (The Heralds of Peace), for his utopian desert community.

In contrast to the intense church building and expansion carried out by numerous religious leaders in the postwar Sun Belt, Tijerina turned inward, spurning organized religion and the rife corruption in the United States.[36] The establishment of El Valle de Paz (The Valley of Peace) in 1956 marked the only Chicano utopian community up to that point, symbolized the zenith of Chicano religious zealotry, and demonstrated the extent to which Tijerina would exhibit his interpretive predilections to be a "man of the book." The Heralds of Peace purchased 160 acres for $1,400 in the Sonoran Desert between Eloy and Coolidge, about six miles from Casa Grande. Tijerina sought out a location isolated enough so that they would not disturb anyone or have anyone disturb them. Tijerina understood this pursuit as a biblical commandment:

> We had abandoned a form and a style of life that we considered evil and opposed to the road to justice that had been indicated to us by the Man from the Holy Land.[37]

As noted earlier, by 1955 Tijerina had renounced organized religion and so, too, did his followers. Like other religious utopian communities, the purpose of El Valle de Paz was to withdraw from the system of a corrupted church world and society. In keeping with his Pentecostal hermeneutic, Tijerina took the events recorded in the Book of the Acts of the Apostles as scriptural mandates. He read how after the pouring out of the Holy Spirit on the Day of Pentecost described in the second chapter of the Acts of the Apostles, the believers "held all things common, and they sold their possessions and goods and distributed them to all, as any had any need." Tijerina understood this as a scriptural mandate in the same literalist hermeneutical style that led Pentecostals to believe that the Spirit could be poured out upon believers, who would then in turn speak in tongues as described throughout the Acts of the Apostles. But Tijerina was no ordinary literalist. He also took the latter half of that chapter as scriptural precedent for the establishment of a shared living community. Writing twenty years after the fact, Tijerina praised his followers, calling them *los valientes* (the brave ones). The number of *valientes* differs in the several biographies, but in his autobiography he listed seven heads of households: Rodolfo Márez, Juan Reyna, Francisco Flores, Simón Serna, Luis Moreno, Vicente Martínez, and Manuel Mata.[38] The final four listed here at some point joined the ranks of Apostólicos in California's valleys; the last three hailed from Manuel Pérez's flock in Salinas.[39] Apostólicos comprised over half of the male leadership in the valley and perhaps even the majority of the residents of El Valle de Paz. Tijerina successfully recruited in Salinas as well as in Visalia, another farm town in northern California.[40]

Doctrinal nuances aside, mid-century Apostólicos had many common characteristics with other Pentecostals when it came to matters of revivalism and dress codes. Manuel Pérez, the pastor of the Salinas church when Tijerina arrived in 1956, shared with me in a 2015 interview that he invited Tijerina to preach a multi-week revival. Generally, ministers and visiting congregants arrived at churches with letters of recommendation from a pastor. In lieu of a letter of recommendation, the neophyte pastor Pérez welcomed Tijerina at the insistence of a mutual friend, Vicente Martínez, a layman in Pérez's church. Much of what Tijerina imparted to Pérez's flock aligned with the worldview of Apostólicos and he conformed to the culture of the local assembly (he even wore a necktie, which he very reluctantly donned). But it was precisely Tijerina's doctrines on dress and appearance that troubled Pérez. As he recalls it, Tijerina was "suave," "smooth," and "tactical" in his pulpit homiletics. Through his charismatic sermon delivery, Tijerina introduced radical egalitarian ideas of apparel. He espoused that men and women ought to don plain tunics because Jesus had done so and also contended that men should let their beards grow out because Jesus had done so, as evidenced by the fact that they plucked his beard when he was crucified.[41] (Once in El Valle de Paz, women indeed wore long dresses that reached the floor and also covered their heads. Some later reflected on how they felt embarrassed for the way they stuck out when buying groceries.[42]) Of all of Tijerina's preaching, the "tactical" consistent references to dress codes are what Pérez remembered most clearly. Mexican Pentecostals already adhered to strict dress codes, most distinguished by the way the women dressed. The principle of modesty was lived out by a rejection of jewelry, makeup, and short hair. Women generally wore only dresses or skirts well below the knee and shirts that covered their arms and had high necklines. But Tijerina espoused an even more radical rejection of the world, so much so that his teachings on modesty even alarmed the rather conservative Apostólicos. Ultimately, his teachings alarmed Pérez, but convinced some of the congregants. Behind the pulpit, he only modestly referenced some ideas he tenaciously defended in private. While raising suspicion for some in attendance, such interpretations harmonized with strict literalist readings of scripture; nor were such bold proclamations unknown to Mexican Pentecostalism.[43] Rather than any one particular idea, the accumulation of divisive teaching drove Pérez to dismiss Tijerina from his church and to halt the revival.[44]

During this time, Pérez also learned that Tijerina had met with the Martínez clan privately. Included in the larger clan were the Moreno and Mata families. Again, Martínez was Pérez's personal friend and the one who had invited Tijerina to preach. This invitation coincided with the time when Tijerina would have already finalized (or at least have been close to finalizing) the purchase of 160 acres. Pérez recalled this purchase and commented how when the families left Salinas, they went directly "to the Arizona desert to live in caves." The Martínez family from Salinas comprised almost half of the leadership of the new utopian community. Why the Martínez family did not simply venture out on its own without Tijerina's visit is not clear, but the fact that Vicente Martínez invited Tijerina to preach a multi-week revival in Salinas may suggest that Martínez saw the folks of the Salinas church as prospects for the utopian community. He likely also viewed Tijerina as a charismatic and "suave" evangelist, a fresh voice with power to sway farmworkers of a hyper bible-centric worldview. Owning land, living communally (as suggested in Acts, in a prominent passage for Pentecostals), dressing modestly (another major Pentecostal tenet), and imitating the appearance of Jesus (Oneness Pentecostals especially employed a Christocentric hermeneutic) would have appealed to impoverished Bible-centric farmworkers.[45] The mere digressions about clothes, modesty, and biblical restoration likely had a larger appeal with staying power. Pérez estimates that of the one-hundred-member church, about fifteen left. This rupture left the church devastated, and the young Pérez found little help within the denomination's leadership to deal with the defection. Such schisms, after all, were not altogether uncommon in Pentecostal churches, where claims of a new revelation or a call from God provided the foundation of legitimacy to leave and establish new churches.[46]

Once in El Valle de Paz, Tijerina, now with the help of like-minded *valientes* from the Apostólico tradition, set out to establish communal living in the end of days. They lived under trees until they were able to gather enough scrap materials from nearby Eloy to build subterranean homes. Though sunken deep into their own turf and lifestyle, they could not avoid the surrounding Cold War politics and Pentecostalism's heightened sense of the end of days. Tijerina and the Heralds of Peace tenaciously defended the significance of the Book of Revelation concerning world events. In all, the short-lived Valle de Paz stands out as a marquee moment in Tijerina's activism up to that point. The utopian community dissolved in February 1957 due to numerous reasons. The physical demise came with its social dissolution. Heavy rainstorms and flash floods destroyed Tijerina's home, and youths on horseback tromped on the subterranean homes. Moreover, charges of theft compromised the leadership, but the final death knell sounded when the state of Arizona cracked down on the commune for not sending the children to school or providing suitable educational facilities.[47] The end of El Valle de Paz, however, did not spell out the terminus for Tijerina's followers' convictions to engender the kingdom of God on earth.

In the years following El Valle de Paz, *los valientes* slowly went their own ways, with some following Tijerina to New Mexico once they had to disband in Arizona. But several Pentecostal followers maintained a divine sense of mission. One former *valiente*, Simón Serna, took up an epistolary correspondence with Tijerina in the early 1960s, seeking ways of selling the land in order to purchase a new lot where they could once again build up their holy experiment. By 1967 Serna changed tone and excoriated Tijerina for aligning with churches, calling him a "hypocrite, son of the devil, enemy of justice of God" who "shouldn't pervert the righteous paths of God."[48] By that point, Tijerina had gained national notoriety and, perhaps worse in the eyes of Serna, had become Catholic. In time, Serna joined the ranks of the sectarian Mexico-based Pentecostal denomination known as La Luz del Mundo. The vast colony impressed Serna, who confessed to Tijerina that El Valle de Paz was not the kingdom of God on earth. Rather, La Luz del Mundo's rapidly growing and bustling colony in Guadalajara, La Hermosa Provincia, was the kingdom that *los valientes* had pursued.[49]

Maria Moreno took a different route with her Pentecostal faith, inspired by Tijerina in the mid-1950s. Moreno, the daughter of Vicente Martínez (the man who persuaded Pérez to invite Tijerina to preach), kept alive a vision of reform. By the end of the decade, Moreno became a labor union organizer and played a major role in the Agricultural Workers Organizing Committee (AWOC), which later joined forces with Chávez's National Farm Workers Association and formed the United Farm Workers in 1965. After a falling-out with male organizers and leaders, she returned to the desert to find her calling in life. Then in answer to the call, she spent her days as an itinerant Pentecostal preacher in the US and Mexico borderlands.[50]

Following the experiment at El Valle de Paz, Tijerina entered his "fugitive years," from 1957 to 1963, wherein he set out to undertake a study of land grant violations perpetuated by the United States against Mexicans in the Southwest after the signing of the Treaty of Guadalupe Hidalgo. Tijerina read the documents of Spanish land grants with as strong of a literalist conviction as he read scripture, and he pursued the reclaiming of land grants with the same sense of conviction that he exhibited in his preaching. At least one *valiente*, Rodolfo Márez, continued on with Tijerina in these pursuits. By the mid-1960s, Tijerina had reached national acclaim for his confrontational political activism. In these various ways we see how faith proved to be an instrument for Tijerina and the former *valientes* to harness alternative power.

Conclusion

In the decade following their encounters with Apostólicos in the rural agricultural towns of northern California, Chávez and Tijerina would establish themselves more concretely as leaders of the burgeoning Chicano civil rights movement. They continued to find religious tactics, imagery, and symbols useful, although for many years Chicanx historians have glossed over these important details of their lives. Some scholars, for example, have attributed the lack of attention to César Chávez's religious dimensions to the seemingly incompatible Marxist teachings prominent among Mexican American scholars. Many of them early on maintained the facile notion that religion (the "opiate of society") had no role in the real-life issues of labor, land, and citizenship. Furthermore, Marxist and socialist agendas of radicals in the 1960s and 1970s treated religion as an anti-intellectual avenue of study. While many have held up Chávez as an example of the relegation of the role of religion in scholarship, Tijerina's case is similar. Rudy Busto took Chicanx studies to task for such oversights. And, while the Chicano movement produced a critical mass of Chicanx academics, the focus on the first cohort and the genealogies that they produced suggest the ways that this intellectual frame had more staying power than it otherwise might have. Texts on the Chicano movement for the majority of the field's history have treated religion as non-essential to ethnic empowerment.[51]

An examination of Chávez's and Tijerina's own words and recollections offers us a much different result and new way of recovering Latino religious politics as engagements with systems of political power. Beyond finding that both involved themselves with religious folks and had a heightened sense of divine purpose for the work they carried out, we find them at moments engaging with individuals we might not necessarily expect. Pentecostals certainly are not known today as players in the Chicano civil rights movement, but in their own ways they had a direct influence upon the key leaders of the movement in the decade before their nationally recognized activism. Tijerina's Pentecostal interactions might be not entirely unexpected, given his time as a student at Bible college. Nevertheless, the way Tijerina mobilized Pentecostals is much more surprising. The salience of this formative political endeavor at

El Valle de Paz did not elude Tijerina years later when he penned his autobiography. In fact, Tijerina's autobiography began with the work at El Valle de Paz, yet his biographers missed this important facet of his life and thinking. This appears to be a glaring omission, given that Tijerina and others staked a territorial claim in El Valle de Paz that set into motion his longer fight against the government for land rights of *Hispanos*.

Chávez, on the other hand, had little to say about Mexican Pentecostals. In this case, lack of frequency does not mean lack of significance, as Chávez credited the Pentecostals in Madera as the source of inspiration to integrate music into his massively popular protests. In his autobiography, Chávez made his religious motivation quite clear. He expressed his conception of social protests as Christ-centered: "[With] the teachings of Christ, . . . I think you need very little else to make things work."[52] Reinforcing this point, Chávez said, "I was convinced that [my ideology was] very Christian. . . . I don't think it was so much political or economic."[53] In these ways, Chávez himself corrected those who assumed that he based his actions solely on secular ideology. In hindsight, he stated,

> Today I don't think I could base my will to struggle on cold economics or some political doctrine. I don't think there would be enough to sustain me. For me the base must be faith.[54]

That faith is easily read as Vatican II Catholicism—with ecumenical gestures—but it ought to push students of Latinx history to better understand the deep theological currents that carried Chávez's activism throughout the decades.

At the end of each story taken up in this chapter, Chávez and Tijerina left Madera and Salinas, respectively, with a clearer vision of what protest might look like and with a larger base of supporters: the entire Apostólico church joined Chávez's CSO, and several families split from the church to follow Tijerina to his utopian community. The settings of Chávez's and Tijerina's experiences were all too similar, yet the contexts do not cohere to the usual narratives of each leader. Historians must have the ears to hear the Apostólico music that moved Chávez to implement a remarkable element of his successful movement and the preaching that drove Tijerina and his followers to establish El Valle de Paz.

Both leaders emerged from these episodes with a new vision of religious politics, believing that God sided with those who suffered and struggled. In each case discussed above, the faith of the community sublimated into the visionary leader's alternative methods to mobilize power.

NOTES

1 Pentecostals emphasize the infilling and working of the Holy Spirit, fashioning their distinctive doctrines and practices after the events on the Day of Pentecost in the Acts of the Apostles and New Testament teachings regarding the charismata (gifts of the Spirit). The Pentecostal movement arose in the early twentieth century. See Arlene Sánchez-Walsh, *Pentecostals in America* (New York: Columbia University Press, 2018). On Latino Pentecostalism, see Arlene Sánchez-Walsh, *Latino Pentecostal Identity: Evangelical Faith, Self, and Society* (New York: Columbia University Press, 2003); Gastón Espinosa, *Latino Pentecostals in America* (Cambridge: Harvard University Press, 2013); and Daniel Ramírez, *Migrating Faith: Pentecostalism in the United States and Mexico in the Twentieth Century* (Chapel Hill: University of North Carolina Press, 2015). For a synthesis of Latino Pentecostalism, see Lloyd Barba, "Latino Pentecostalism," in *Oxford Handbook on Latinx/a/o Christianity in the US*, ed. Kristy Nabhan-Warren (New York: Oxford University Press, forthcoming).
2 Ramírez, *Migrating Faith*, 218.
3 On the kinds of music in Mexican Pentecostal sacred spaces, see ibid., 220–21.
4 "Apostólico" is the preferred term used by members of the Asamblea Apostólica de la Fe en Cristo Jesús (Apostolic Assembly of the Faith in Christ Jesus), a Oneness Pentecostal denomination whose formation dates to the 1920s and whose most significant doctrinal heterodoxy includes a rejection of the trinitarian nature of God and an insistence that legitimate baptisms are performed in the "name of Jesus," rather than "Father, Son, and Holy Spirit." Ramírez, *Migrating Faith*.
5 In keeping with the scholarship on the topics, this chapter uses the term "Latino" or "Chicano" as the modifier for the Chicano movement, Chicano civil rights, and Pentecostalism. However, I employ the terms "Latinx" or "Chicanx" as gender-neutral terms when describing these respective groups more generally.
6 Stephen R. Lloyd-Moffett, "The Mysticism and Social Action of César Chávez," in *Latino Religions and Civic Activism in the United States*, ed. Gastón Espinosa, Virgilio Elizondo, and Jesse Miranda (New York: Oxford University Press, 2005), 35–52; Luis León, "César Chávez and American Civil Religions," in Espinosa, Elizondo, and Miranda, *Latino Religions and Civic Activism*, 51–64.
7 Rudy Busto, *King Tiger: The Religious Vision of Reies López Tijerina* (Albuquerque: University of New Mexico Press, 2005), 35–46; Lorena Oropeza, *The King of Adobe: Reies López Tijerina, Last Prophet of the Chicano Movement* (Chapel Hill: University of North Carolina Press, 2019); Ramón A. Gutiérrez, "The Religious Origins of Reies López Tijerina's Land Grant Activism in the Southwest," in *A*

New Insurgency: The Port Huron Statement and Its Times, ed. Howard Brick and Gregory Parker (Ann Arbor: University of Michigan Publishing Services, 2015).

8 Jonathan Chism, *Saints in the Struggle: Church of God in Christ Activists in the Memphis Civil Rights Struggle, 1954–1968* (Lanham, MD: Lexington, 2019); Espinosa, Elizondo, and Miranda, *Latino Religions and Civic Activism*.

9 Jacques E. Levy, *Cesar Chavez: Autobiography of La Causa* (Minneapolis: University of Minnesota Press, 2007), 116–20. On Chávez's religious background, see Roberto Chao Romero, *Brown Church: Five Centuries of Latina/o Social Justice, Theology, and Identity* (Downers Grove, IL: Intervarsity Press, 2020), 120–41; Mario T. García, *The Gospel of César Chávez: My Faith in Action* (Lanham: Sheed and Ward, 2007); Frederick John Dalton, *The Moral Vision of César Chávez* (Maryknoll: Orbis, 2003); Luis D. León, *The Political Spirituality of César Chávez* (Berkeley: University of California Press, 2015); Alan J. Watt, *Farm Workers and the Churches: The Movement in California and Texas* (College Station: Texas A&M University Press, 2010).

10 César Chávez, "Reports of César Chávez," July 16, 1954, box 1, folder 2, Fred Ross Sr. Collection, Walter P. Reuther Library of Labor and Urban Affairs, Wayne State University, Detroit.

11 Levy, *Cesar Chavez*, 115–16.

12 Levy, *Cesar Chavez*, 116; Sallie Marín to César Chávez, correspondence, undated (ca. 1954 or early 1955), part 1, box 2, folder 6, United Farmworkers Office of the President Collection (hereafter UFWOPC), Walter P. Reuther Library of Labor and Urban Affairs, Wayne State University, Detroit; Madera Executive Board to Cesar Chavez, "Thank You" card, October 12, 1954, part 1, box 2, folder 5, UFWOPC.

13 Levy, *Cesar Chavez*, 120.

14 The litany of charges against Pentecostal disengagement with real-world issues is discussed in Ramírez, *Migrating Faith*, 10–11.

15 Keith F. Pecklers, "The Evolution of Liturgical Music in the United States of America, 1850–1962," in *Renewal and Resistance: Catholic Church Music from the 1850s to Vatican II*, ed. Paul Collins (New York: Peter Lang, 2011), 166–70. On how Protestant music compensated for limited visual context, see Edwin David Aponte, "Music and the US Latina and Latino Religious Experience," in *Introduction to the US Latina and Latino Religious Experience*, ed. Hector Avalos (Boston: Brill, 2004), 242–60.

16 Ramírez, *Migrating Faith*, 220–21.

17 Ibid.; César Chávez, interview with Wendy Goepel, 1963, https://libraries.ucsd.edu, accessed November 6, 2017. Goepel's later publications list her name as Wendy Goepel Brooks.

18 On the religious contours of this *corrido*, see Lloyd Barba, "More Spirit in the Little Madera Church: Cesar Chavez and Religious Landscapes, 1954–1962," *California History* 94, no. 1 (Spring 2017): 26–42.

19 Chávez, interview with Goepel, 1963.

20 Levy, *Cesar Chavez*, 115.
21 César Chávez, Registration for Peregrinación, series I, box 48, folder 4, UFWOPC.
22 Watt, *Farm Workers and the Churches*, 74–78.
23 Chavez, Registration for Peregrinación.
24 Watt, *Farm Workers and the Churches*, 79.
25 Levy, *Cesar Chavez*, 206–14.
26 Watt, *Farm Workers and the Churches*, 79.
27 This term is borrowed from the characterization of César Chávez, Reies López Tijerina, Rodolfo "Corky" Gonzalez, and José Angel Gutiérrez in Matt Meier and Feliciano Rivera, *The Chicanos: A History of Mexican Americans* (New York: Hill and Wang, 1994). On the King and X comparisons, see Espinosa, Elizondo, and Miranda, *Latino Religions and Civic Activism*, 9.
28 Lloyd Barba, "Farmworker Frames: Apostólico Counter Narratives in California's Valleys," *Journal of the American Academy of Religion* 86, no. 3 (September 2018): 691–723; Manuel Pérez, interview with author, March 2015, Coral Gables, FL.
29 Pérez, interview.
30 Gutiérrez, "Religious Origins."
31 Oropeza, *King of Adobe*, 14–15.
32 Busto, *King Tiger*, 35–46; Oropeza, *King of Adobe*; Gutiérrez, "Religious Origins."
33 Quoted in Busto, *King Tiger*, 39.
34 Ibid., 39–41.
35 Michael Jenkinson, *Tijerina: Land Grant Conflict in New Mexico* (Albuquerque: Paisano Press, 1968), 21.
36 On the growth of evangelical Christianity in the Sun Belt, see Darren Dochuk, *Bible Belt to Sun Belt: Plain-Folk Religion, Grassroots Politics, and the Rise of Evangelical Conservatism* (New York: Norton, 2011).
37 Reies López Tijerina, *They Called Me King Tiger: My Struggle for the Land and Our Rights*, trans. José Ángel Gutiérrez (Houston: Arte Público, 2000), 1. Tijerina opens his memoir with this story and exposition; Oropeza, *King of Adobe*, 47–48.
38 Tijerina, *They Called Me King Tiger*, 1.
39 Pérez, interview.
40 Oropeza, *King of Adobe*, 45–46.
41 Tijerina and his members eventually grew out beards and wore long tunics once at El Valle de Paz. Gutiérrez, "Religious Origins," 47–48.
42 Oropeza, *King of Adobe*, 51–52.
43 Influential self-proclaimed prophets arose in the Mexican Apostólico ranks during the movement's formative years. In Monterey, Torreón, and Guadalajara, these "prophets" and founders of churches and denominations assumed biblical names, believed that they received visions, and taught new doctrines such as the growing out of beards and the removal of shoes before entering a temple. For more information on the sectarian branches within the Apostolic movement, see Kenneth D. Gill, *Toward a Contextualized Theology for the Third World: The Emergence and*

Development of Jesus' Name Pentecostalism in Mexico (Frankfurt, Germany: Peter Lang, 1994), 47–57.
44   Pérez, interview.
45   On the Christo-centric elements of Oneness Pentecostalism, see David Reed, *"In Jesus' Name": The History and Beliefs of Oneness Pentecostals* (Blandford Forum, UK: Deo, 2008), 32–43.
46   A short while after Tijerina's schism, Pérez also left the congregation. Pérez, interview.
47   Busto, *King Tiger*, 130–32; Oropeza, *King of Adobe*, 49–51.
48   Simón Serna to Reies Tijerina, 1967 (no month/date), box 48, folder 2, Reies Tijerina Papers, Center for Southwest Research, University of New Mexico, Albuquerque.
49   Simón Serna to Reies Tijerina, correspondence, "19 May 1982," "6 June 1982," "19 September 1982," "15 November 1982," box 48, folder 2, Reies Tijerina Papers.
50   Oropeza, *King of Adobe*, 63.
51   Espinosa, Elizondo, and Miranda, *Latino Religions and Civic Activism*, 3–16; Felipe Hinojosa, "Latina/o Religious Studies since the 1970s," in *The Oxford Handbook of Latino Studies*, ed. Ilan Stavans (New York: Oxford University Press, 2020); Chao Romero, *Brown Church*, 1–19; Busto, *King Tiger*. For revised historical accounts that investigate Chávez's involvement with the alternative religion Synanon, see Matt Garcia, *From the Jaws of Victory: The Triumph and Tragedy of Cesar Chavez and the Farm Workers Movement* (Berkeley: University of California Press, 2012); Frank Bardacke, *Trampling Out the Vintage: Cesar Chavez and the Two Souls of the United Farm Workers* (New York: Verso, 2011); Miriam Pawel, *The Union of Their Dreams: Power, Hope, and Struggle in Cesar Chavez's Farm Worker Movement* (New York: Bloomsbury, 2009); and Miriam Pawel, *The Crusades of Cesar Chavez: A Biography* (New York: Bloomsbury, 2014).
52   César Chávez as quoted in Lloyd-Moffett, "Mysticism and Social Action," 43.
53   Ibid., 44.
54   Ibid. Also see Dalton, *Moral Vision*.

6

Lived Religion in East Harlem

The New York Young Lords Occupy First Spanish—The People's Church

JORGE JUAN RODRÍGUEZ V

God is not dead.
God is bread.
The bread is rising!
Bread means revolution.
Organize for a new world.
Make the church a people's church.
Wash off your brother's blood.
The streets belong to the people.
And the church belongs to the streets.
In the midst of occupied territory,
The liberated zone is here.
—Celebration for a People's Church[1]

In December 1969 dozens of residents of East Harlem alongside the newly minted New York Chapter of the Young Lords Organization shared this celebration at the First Spanish United Methodist Church.[2] Yet this church, located in the center of El Barrio at the corner of Lexington Avenue and 111th Street, was no longer a Methodist church beholden to denominational politics. This church was now "La Iglesia de la Gente, The People's Church," as the banner that hung from the building's second floor declared.[3] For eleven days this "liberated zone" hosted breakfast for children, a clothing drive, lead-poisoning and tuberculosis testing, classes on Puerto Rican history, poetry slams, theatrical productions, and cultural events. Through these programs the Young Lords shared a glimpse of what society could be—one where cost of treatment was not a barrier to health care, where children woke up to a hot meal, where the culture of those on the underside of empire was celebrated. This vision was echoed in the "Celebration for the People's Church," where Young Lords and their sympathizers advanced a theological claim about God's presence in the world, manifest in "the people"—a diverse collective, "demanding material and epistemological liberation"—who could usher in a more just society.[4]

This story of the First People's Church Offensive is often retold with a particular narrative arc: after months of failed negotiation with church leadership over use of their mostly idle church building, the Young Lords occupied the First Spanish Church for eleven days to establish community programming that served thousands in El Barrio. The church in this narrative is often presented as a one-dimensional foil to the Young Lords, and questions of religion are often subsumed under broader analyses of "politics." Yet when one sits with Young Lords and church members present during the occupation, one realizes that the history of the congregation and questions of religion were central to the story. Church youth grew sympathetic to the Young Lords, who they believed were advocating for the justice Jesus proclaimed; church leaders found the militancy of the Young Lords disrespectful to the church's history; and Young Lords engaged this church with religious language in an attempt to respect what congregants held dear. Young Lords were aware that this church was not an English-speaking, White-dominant church, as was the case in similar church occupations across the country. This was the church of their aunts, uncles, and grandmothers.

What follows, then, is a reexamination of the Young Lords' First People's Church Offensive that takes seriously the history of the occupied church and the role of religion within the occupation. This reexamination begins with a discussion of lived religion—the idea that religion is not merely professed beliefs but embodied practices, idioms, and places that people make/understand as sacred. Lived religion helps us analyze the history of the First Spanish Church and contextualize its leadership's unwillingness to negotiate with the Young Lords in 1969. As we will see, the church's objections were situated in a nearly fifty-year history of seeking space for their religious life in the Methodist denomination and the United States diaspora. Starting here allows us to reexamine the story of the First People's Church Offensive as an intra-Latinx struggle in 1960s New York City arbitrated through religious embodiment, language, and institutions.[5]

Such an analysis builds on New York Young Lords scholarship by asserting that fully telling the story of the First People's Church Offensive requires (1) substantively engaging religion, and (2) contextualizing the story within the history of the occupied First Spanish Church. Darrel Wanzer-Serrano and Johanna Fernández have written beautifully on the Offensive from the perspective of rhetoric and the New Left, respectively. Yet neither scholar contextualizes the Young Lords within church history and religious studies. Elías Ortega-Aponte engages the latter by analyzing the occupation in relation to Latin American humanism, but his study remains focused on the Young Lords rather than the First Spanish Church. The same is true for Felipe Hinojosa, who situates the Young Lords in connection to other church occupations at the time. While this chapter builds on these scholars, I contend that centering religion and beginning the story with the church provide greater clarity about what was at stake for each group and how they built their arguments, and forces us to sit with the complexity of Latinxs trying to make meaning in a nation that has historically sought our denigration and exploitation. I want us to grapple with the multiple, competing, and sometimes contradictory ways Latinxs have sought stability and progress. I believe that sitting in that murkiness yields lessons for our own pursuits of justice.[6]

Lived Religion and the First Spanish Church

Religion is often imagined as disembodied articulations of belief that use Enlightenment language to make "logical" and "rational" statements that distinguish faith traditions. Thus, we distinguish Protestants, Catholics, and Muslims based on what they claim to believe and whom they claim to worship. Aside from the colonial tendencies of this understanding, the contention of lived religion as an analytic lens is that limiting religion to well-crafted articulations of belief does not account for everyday life. As historian Robert Orsi writes, "'Religion' is best approached . . . [by moving] toward a study of how particular people, in particular places and times, live in, with, through, and against the religious idioms available to them in culture."[7] Meredith

McGuire puts it this way: "Religion . . . is about how people make sense of their world—the 'stories' out of which they live, . . . not merely the packages of religious narratives supplied by institutions but . . . *the myriad ways by which ordinary people remember, share, enact, adapt, create and combine the 'stories' out of which they live*."[8] Physical spaces often center these everyday practices, which leads Edwin Aponte to suggest that "particular locales come to be recognized as sacred because of the stories told about them."[9] It could be said that *in space* people make meaning through ritual and idiom and it is that meaning making that allows communities to understand sites as sacred. This lens illuminates the history of the First Spanish Church and its rupture with the Young Lords in 1969.

The First Spanish Church traces its history to a Spanish-speaking Methodist gathering in lower Manhattan, formed on May 28, 1922. Within a few years this gathering merged with other Spanish-speaking Methodist groups, came under the leadership of the Reverend Ferdinand Aparicio, moved uptown, and was co-located with East Harlem's English-speaking Church of the Saviour on 111th Street and Lexington Avenue.[10] Under Aparicio's leadership, Spanish ministries at Church of the Saviour established Sunday schools and ladies' aid societies and held public worship. They also established economic relief programs, ministries to visit the sick, and youth mentorship programs. As welfare programs expanded in the 1930s, the Spanish Church became an intermediary between public and private officials and migrants who reported social needs. Aparicio built coalitions with leaders from at least eight denominations to facilitate this work.[11] By the late 1920s, over three hundred people joined the Spanish Church as membership swelled through the mid-1930s. Yet as Spanish ministries grew, so did tensions with Church of the Saviour.

In 1929 the New York District superintendent of the New York Methodist Conference, Hough Houston, praised Aparicio while noting tensions with the Church of the Saviour:

> The Spanish speaking people come together in great numbers. They meet in the Church of the Saviour in such times and places as can be spared by this busy church. There is more or less embarrassment on the part of both churches because of lack of time and space.[12]

The Spanish Church began unsuccessfully seeking its own space as the situation became increasingly untenable. Retelling this history, the First Spanish Church wrote that "En el lapso de seis años, por una u otra razón, las dos congregaciones no podían convivir bajo el mismo techo" (In the lapse of six years, for one reason or another, the two congregations could not live under the same roof).[13] In 1938 the Reverend Diego Flores—who assumed leadership after Aparicio withdrew from ministry in 1935—provided greater texture to this event, stating that the Spanish Church had "experienced diverse vicissitudes, [having been] at various times victims of skullduggery and malice" during its time at Church of the Saviour.[14]

By 1934, First Spanish left Church of the Saviour and began what it described as a "peregrinación," a period of wandering mirroring the Exodus narrative of Israel wandering in the wilderness, searching for the promised land. Over the next decade, in the context of the Great Depression and increased financial strain, the First Spanish Church faced declining membership and decreased capacity for community services, all while moving its church across four different locations in the course of ten years.

Instability forced First Spanish to become co-located with Church of the Saviour a second time in 1946, precisely as New York City underwent one of its most significant demographic shifts in the twentieth century.[15] From 1950 to 1970 New York City's African American population grew from 9.5 percent (~748,000) to 21 percent (~1,668,000), while the Puerto Rican population grew from 3.1 percent (~246,000) to 10.7 percent (~846,700) with over 250,000 Puerto Ricans arriving in New York City between 1949 and 1953 alone. This occurred as "White flight" pushed 1,698,200 White people out of New York City to growing suburbs between 1940 and 1960.[16] Methodist leadership—who through their City Societies owned church properties throughout New York City—was overwhelmed by the demographic shifts. Even though many of the Puerto Ricans were Protestant, having "nearly a half-century of American tradition" due to US colonialism and Protestant missions on the island, they remained foreign to the White-majority Methodist leaders.[17] In 1953 Leland P. Cary, executive secretary of the New York Methodist City Society, visited the First Spanish Church and reflected that throughout the service they had not "the slightest idea of what was said," feeling the "handicap of language."[18] Cary's remarks reveal the Methodist investment in Puerto Rican newcomers, and a lack of understanding about who the newcomers were.[19]

Following demographic trends, Church of the Saviour lost significant membership to White flight precisely as First Spanish grew and reestablished ministries and social service programs. This created an opening for First Spanish to advocate for itself. On April 9, 1954, First Spanish Church sent a petition to Leland Cary asking that Church of the Saviour's building at 111th Street and Lexington Avenue be given to them. They wrote, "We have been preaching the Gospel of Jesus Christ for the past 32 years and in spite of all our efforts to obtain a Church building from the New York City Society has been in vain. . . . We are asking a Church building for our own use in order to serve the community and God more efficiently."[20] They argued, "The present Church of the Saviour does not support itself because we see in the weekly bulletins what they collect every week, and yet the New York City Society is support[ing] a non-Spanish Church in a Spanish community."[21] In 1956, without much reference in denominational documents about First Spanish's advocacy, Church of the Saviour dissolved and 111th Street and Lexington Avenue became the First Spanish Methodist Church.

This was more than a transfer of property. First Spanish sought a building to center its religious life after years of strife and wandering, one that would allow it to host the revival services, women's and children's ministries, and food drives that were central to its faith.[22] The building was more than a building, it was a site where religious life manifest through community service could be centralized, as churches have often functioned in Latinx communities.[23] As a result, 111th Street and Lexington Avenue became sacred for the First Spanish Church because it was storied by strife, wandering, and petition.

Over the next few years, the storied significance of this church increased after a fire erupted on July 5, 1964 that engulfed the building. Community members looked on at falling ashes as over 60 percent of the building burned to the ground.[24] Amidst destruction, in recollecting this time the First Spanish Church interpreted the fire as a "purification" of the church building, a way for God to cleanse the discord staining its walls and create opportunity for something greater.[25]

Over the next three years, the congregation worked with the City Society to rebuild the church, a process that reflected a shift in the socioeconomic and political realities of the congregation. Extant documents suggest that before the fire, membership, ministries, and community engagement in and by the church decreased as the congregation underwent changes in leadership and focused on fundraising for church remodeling.[26] At this time, several congregants moved out of East Harlem, became business owners, and entered the middle class.[27] Class mobility was reflected by the fact that alongside insurance payments and funding from the New York Methodist Conference, the rebuilding of the church was funded by nearly $70,000 the congregation raised in "fondos Pro-Templo" (funds for the building) as well as additional mortgages negotiated by members of the church board.[28] After the church was rebuilt by 1968 with brand-new appliances, a fully functional basement, large classrooms, and a large fellowship hall, a new pastor came to lead this flock: the Reverend Dr. Humberto Carrazana.

Carrazana had led one of the first Spanish-speaking Methodist congregations for Cuban "refugees"—as he called them—in Miami after he left Cuba following the Revolution of 1959. Before moving north, Carrazana spent years with this Cuban population that, according to him, were generally conservative; he described them as tempered pietists who abstained from tobacco, alcohol, and other substances. He noted that "liberation theology [that engaged Marxist analysis and argued that God was on the side of the poor] [was] not well received [by this population].... [They were] traumatized by their political experiences in Cuba and Central America."[29]

Carrazana brought these experiences in Miami to his 1968 appointment at First Spanish, a church that had a vacancy after their previous pastor—a progressive Puerto Rican—resigned after barely three years in the position. Johanna Fernández cites church youth from this time who argued that Carrazana's predecessor was "'chased out of the church' by its high officials for his progressive and Puerto Rican nationalist leanings," reflecting a growing conservativism within the congregation.[30] Carrazana better fit the sensibilities of this church that, after decades of strife, wanted to protect the storied space it petitioned for and purchased. It is no surprise, then, that within a year the Young Lords would have a historic clash with the First Spanish Church.

The Young Lords Organization

As the civil rights movement developed, the Vietnam War and the Cold War raged, and relations between the United States and Cuba became tenser, more militant activists emerged in the United States, calling for the creation of a new society. The urgency of these activists—among them the Black Panthers and American Indian Movement—was further fueled by the effects of deindustrialization, largely in northern cities, that created a permanent underclass of unemployed young adults, many of whom just arrived from war only to face police brutality, unemployment, and subpar housing at home.[31]

In this context, a street gang in Chicago transformed into the Young Lords Organization (YLO). Led by José "Cha Cha" Jiménez, the YLO worked with Puerto Ricans and Latinxs in Chicago, built coalition with Black Panthers and a group of working-class Whites called the Young Patriots, and called for the liberation of Third World peoples and creation of a socialist society. Attracted to the YLO's activism—which included occupying a Chicago Methodist church in early 1969 to establish breakfast programs and clothing drives—a group of Puerto Rican and Black activists from New York City met with Cha Cha in hopes of becoming a chapter of the YLO. Their wish was granted in the summer of 1969.

After a successful summer forcing the city of New York to improve trash cleanup in El Barrio, the New York Young Lords continued searching for ways to serve. Seeking hosts for what they called "serve the people programs," Lords partnered with churches in El Barrio because these institutions were often respected by community members and had access to many resources. Precisely because the building was large, had brand-new facilities, and was in such an ideal location, in the fall of 1969 the New York Young Lords reached out to Pastor Carrazana at the First Spanish Church. But as we have just examined, the Lords entered negotiations with the church at a time when the congregation had just solidified its place in East Harlem and the Methodist denomination, was increasingly conservative, and had just come under new leadership.

The People's Church

In a letter dated October 22, 1969, Young Lords petitioned the First Spanish Church for space for a breakfast program for children. Noting the church's inactivity during the week, they also suggested that the church "could be used as a provisional shelter for the needy, a daycare for working mothers, or a recreational facility for neighborhood youth."[32] The church's board denied the Lords' request, citing the vast political differences between the church and the organization.[33]

Their main opposition came from Carrazana and the church board, so Young Lords began appealing to parishioners directly, believing that they, especially those who lived in the community, would be more sympathetic. Young Lords began attending Sunday services, arriving early to pass out leaflets stating their desire for space and staying late to speak directly with parishioners. While some congregants grew sympathetic to the Lords, church leaders felt that their presence was a hindrance to worship and an affront to the church's right to control its own space.[34]

Tensions increased, coming to a breaking point on Sunday, December 7, 1969, when Young Lords chairman Felipe Luciano went to the podium during a time of *testimonios* to address the congregation. When he stood, the organist, Benita Rodríguez, attempted to drown him out by leading the congregation in singing "Onward Christian Soldiers." In response, a Lord unplugged the organ, resulting in a heated argument between the Lords and parishioners. Things escalated when plainclothes officers, with the consent of Pastor Carrazana, asked the Lords to leave. Upon their refusal, the officers beat and arrested the Young Lords inside the church. Thirteen Young Lords, eight men and five women, were arrested, suffering injuries ranging from broken arms to lacerations. In response, 150 Lords and community members held a march that night, culminating in a rally at the church, where they restated their demands for space.[35]

Following this chaos, a group of congregants within the church expressed concern over Carrazana and the church board's response to the situation. This group urged the pastor to reach out to youth who were inactive in the church. Perhaps these youth could provide nuance to the conflict. On Sunday, December 14, these youth attended the service alongside over five hundred Young Lords and community members. When the service ended, "sympathizers [of the Lords] remained in their pews during [a] three-hour meeting that followed among" Young Lords, church leadership, and church youth.[36] Carmen Pietri was among the youth who struggled with both sides of the argument. On the one hand, she and others felt that the Young Lords lacked tact as they wore military-style outfits, Afros, and berets—"looking like the children of Che Guevarra"—to a meeting with a conservative church led by a Cuban exile.[37] Yet Pietri and others were also struck by how board members denigrated Puerto Ricans in the community, portraying them as poor, lazy, and drunk. Such portrayals stood in contrast to Lords who spoke eloquently about systemic oppression, cited history, politics, and theology, while providing radical alternatives. Though questioning their tactics, church youth were compelled by the message of the Lords and asked board members to consider implementing certain community programs. Church leadership denied this request and accused the church youth of sympathizing with the Lords, going as far as to brand them "Judases."[38] After this, the Lords arrived at the church one more Sunday in a futile attempt to negotiate. And on December 28 they decided that new tactics were needed.

On that last Sunday of 1969, Young Lords and dozens of community members packed the pews of the First Spanish Church. Service was held as any other Sunday: scripture was read, hymns sung, a sermon preached, prayers offered. Unlike other Sundays, though, as soon as the service ended, Young Lords swiftly moved to each exit and bolted the doors shut with railroad spikes they had hidden in violin cases. Lords had spent days studying the floor plan of the church, allowing them to barricade the entire building within minutes. Micky Meléndez recounts:

> Bedlam quickly erupted among some in the congregation. [Young Lord] Pablo ["Yoruba" Guzmán] informed them that they would be free to leave within a few minutes. The excitement subsided then, and we proceeded to escort out those who wanted to leave. Only about thirty people left—

men, women, and children. Over two hundred people remained seated. Among those leaving was Reverend Carrazana, who seemed to be in shock.[39]

Congregants who left sang hymns as they exited the building and stood outside watching what ensued in their church—reminiscent of how they watched fire ravage the building half a decade earlier. Inside the successfully secured church, community members waited patiently until chairman Felipe Luciano provided instructions to complete the occupation. A banner was hung from the second floor renaming the building "The People's Church," Christian and US American flags that sat on the church stage were removed and replaced with the flag of Puerto Rico's Independence Party, and a press conference was set up in front of the building, where Young Lords declared that the First Spanish Church had been "liberated" to serve the people.[40]

Over the next eleven days, community members were escorted in and out of the church for daily programs by Young Lords wearing their iconic purple berets.[41] Children received hot breakfast before attending Liberation School, where they learned math, Spanish, and Puerto Rican history. Community members were tested for lead poisoning and tuberculosis. A clothing drive and day care center in the basement operated during the day, and in the evening, community dinners were served, followed by entertainment, including poetry readings and music. Church youth led a service on Sunday, January 4, which some sympathetic First Spanish Church members attended.[42] During this service the People's Church was honored, people sang, and a version of the "Celebration for the People's Church," shared at the beginning of this work, was recited as part of the liturgy.[43]

In light of these services it is no surprise that after police arrested 105 Young Lords and supporters on January 7, 1970, ending the occupation, membership in the organization swelled and the group gained national prominence. Many joined the organization that over eleven days provided programming for an estimated ten thousand people, served hot breakfast to about seventy-five children each morning, and treated dozens for lead poisoning and tuberculosis.[44] In particular, female membership grew. As Iris Morales recalls, "The *People's Church* had women occupying a central role."[45] Elsewhere, Morales reflects,

"Young women were drawn by the radical political ideas but also because they saw women in charge speaking on bullhorns, running programs, and getting arrested."[46] With increased female membership, the women of the Young Lords successfully underwent a "revolution within the revolution" in the months following the People's Church Offensive that restructured the organization, placed women in central leadership, and opened space for a Gay and Lesbian caucus within the organization that even developed connections with STAR (Street Transvestite Action Revolutionaries) that formed after the Stonewall riots.[47]

The People's Church Offensive also restructured the First Spanish Church. Some church members joined the Young Lords and others left the church entirely. But many congregants felt that the occupation was a disrespectful imposition into a sacred space that they had fought hard to acquire. After the occupation, the congregation underwent a moment of prayerful reflection internally while Carrazana and the legal team of the Methodist denomination went to court with the Young Lords. Many Young Lords faced charges, including trespassing. Herman Badillo, a prominent Puerto Rican politician, defended the Young Lords and negotiated with Carrazana and the denomination. Charges against the Lords were dropped and other church spaces in El Barrio were offered to the Lords for community programming. Shortly after, a Puerto Rican minister took over for Carrazana as pastor of the First Spanish Church. On March 20, 1972, after two years of planning following the occupation, the First Spanish Church established a day care center with the help of the New York Methodist City Society and New York City Department of Social Services—fulfilling a promise made by the church immediately after the occupation.[48]

Gods in El Barrio

First Spanish Church members always used religious language to describe their experiences in Manhattan, calling themselves "peregrinos," invoking the Biblical image of Israel searching for a promised land epitomized by a church they owned and controlled. For them, the wilderness was the New York diaspora and the Methodist denomination that should have been a refuge but often was not. By 1969, what made the building at 111th and Lexington Avenue sacred for the First Spanish

Church was that the building represented their steadfast faithfulness to God as expressed through their advocacy in the denomination, hard work, and economic sacrifice. This sensibility coincided with middle-class aspirations of property ownership and upward mobility, the proverbial American Dream. The best way to honor God's faithfulness was to protect the building that God had purified by fire.

But in 1969 First Spanish encountered a group of youths who also used religion to make meaning of/in the church at 111th and Lexington Avenue. Like other militant groups of the period, the Young Lords critiqued Christianity's oppression of "Third World peoples." As chairman Felipe Luciano said on December 21, 1969, in front of the First Spanish Church, speaking about First Spanish while making a broader claim about Christianity, "[The church] is a symbol of the oppression that our people are going through. A symbol of the narrow-mindedness that doesn't allow them to look out on the fresh air and see faces."[49] Yet instead of denouncing the church by arguing that the institution and Christianity therein were morally bankrupt, the Lords argued that the reason First Spanish and those like it were morally bankrupt was *that they were not being church!* In the same speech, Luciano stated that because the Lords sought to serve the people, what they were doing was "much more Christian, much more brotherly, than anything that any church—not only this church—but any church in this country [was] doing."[50] This sentiment was repeated and expanded throughout the organization.

In an interview with the National Council of Churches, an ecumenical body founded in 1950 to build coalition among various Christian denominations, the Young Lords minister of information, Yoruba, was asked whether the Lords considered Christ a revolutionary. Yoruba responded by saying, "We believe that [if Christ was alive today, he would have been a Young Lord]. We also believe that if Christ came back today, they'd crucify him again."[51] He continues,

> The Bible is used as an instrument of oppression in the hands of imperialists. They teach only the parts of the Bible that will nullify the people.... They don't show you the parts like when things were going bad in the temple, Christ went in and threw them out and he wasn't non-violent—he was a pretty violent cat when he had to be.... And that's why we've got Christ right up there next to Mao [Zedong]—he was a heavy cat.[52]

According to Yoruba, because Christ was a "heavy cat," those who follow Christ—that is, the church—need also be "heavy" and challenge ideologies of docility perpetuated by imperialists.

Young Lords spread a similar message in leaflets in the weeks leading up to, and during, the offensive. One leaflet read,

> The first responsibility of the church is to the people. The church is supposed to serve the people, help them and work with them. This is what it means to be Christian.[53]

In another, they wrote,

> The wrong interpretation of Christianity leads people to forget the teachings of the Bible. They use the Bible to excuse themselves from facing the realities of life, which are made very clear in the following verses from the Bible: / (Matthew 25: 31–40) / "Come receive the kingdom which has been ready and waiting for you ever since the world was made. I was hungry and you fed me; I was thirsty and you gave me something to drink; When I was a stranger you took me in, and when I had no clothes you gave me something to wear." / The Young Lords will continue to go to church to make these realities clear to the church. ALL POWER TO THE PEOPLE![54]

In each example—from Luciano, to Yoruba, to the flyers distributed by Young Lords—the Lords advanced a theological argument that the church "is *supposed* to serve the people," and the First Spanish Church was not.

In the weeks leading up to the occupation, they embodied this theology in the quotidian tasks of speaking to parishioners, passing out pamphlets, and attending Sunday services. During the occupation they further embodied this theological claim by changing the physical symbols within the institution in order to maintain its recognizable character as a church—something that was important to the community—while reinterpreting what "church" meant. As a result, the Puerto Rican Independence flag hung behind the podium, the fellowship hall hosted breakfast for children, and a banner declared the "liberation" of the People's Church. Young Lords embodied a lived religion, using religious language from and in their context to make a claim upon a physical institution. And many observing the situation read this religious claim clearly.

In a 1970 issue of the *Christian Century*, Dean Kelley of the National Council of Churches argued that while the Young Lords

> haven't claimed to be Christian; they just want the *church* to be! With below-zero weather and families without heat in nearby tenements, the church has made no effort to provide emergency shelter. . . . Since the church can't seem to [bestir] itself from its huddle [of] inactivity, the Young Lords have resolved to shake it loose for the sake of "the people."[55]

A colleague of Kelley, Robert Chapman, shared the sentiment when they wrote that "Yes, a good thing can, a good thing has, come out of Nazareth—the Young Lords."[56]

From leaders to cadres, the Young Lords argued that church is to serve the people and because First Spanish was *not* serving the people, it was not being church. They framed their position not only in relation to "community control" and "the people," but in relation to theology—making a Christological claim on the person of Jesus (as a Young Lord) and, by association, an ecclesiological claim about how the institution that follows him ought to be in the world.[57] When the Lords occupied the church, bolted its doors, renamed it the People's Church, and declared it a "liberated zone," the Lords *lived the ecclesia* they theologized: a theology palpable enough for even those outside the organization to articulate.

Many of First Spanish's congregation also interpreted the occupation religiously, but they did so within the nearly fifty-year narrative of their religious life. For them, the church had historically served the community and because of their faithfulness amidst discrimination, God guided them to acquire a building to center their religious life. How would they respond when young people from within their community in the wilderness of Manhattan told them that their religious vision misunderstood the purpose of the church, Jesus, and ultimately the community they identified with? That their desire for the American Dream and social mobility ignored the American Nightmare their people daily lived? Was their steadfastness in vain?

Abuela's Kitchen Table

Fifty years after the occupation, on December 7, 2019, Young Lords returned to the building at 111th Street and Lexington Avenue, which had recently been renamed FSUMC—The People's Church. In a panel moderated by Pastor Dorlimar Lebrón Malavé, Young Lord Gilbert Colón reflected on his experiences in that very space. Immediately after the occupation, Gilbert visited his grandmother, María Colón, who was a member of First Spanish in 1969. María looked at Gilbert as only a grandmother can and asked, "What were you people doing [at the church], because that was disrespectful." Gilbert responded to his abuela, explaining that the Young Lords were doing "God's work," caring for the poor, caring for the needy, caring for the sick. As Gilbert spoke, he says, his grandmother's look softened. She responded simply, "Está bien, mijo" (It's all right, my child). Fifty years later, Gilbert further reflected:

> This [church] right here, this is a sacred space . . . and the older I get the more I understand that the actual takeover, the first takeover, might have been very offensive to some people. . . . It must have felt as a violation of their personal sacred space. But I hope, sincerely, and I think a lot of people realize now, that our intent was to do what people of every faith tradition aspire to do, which is to take care of the least of these.[58]

Gilbert Colón's reflection forces us to sit with an image some of us have had the privilege to experience: a young adult sitting with their grandmother, discussing their most sacred values. His reflection raises a pivotal reality about the First People's Church Offensive that may apply to other examples of Latinx religious politics: what happens when you occupy your abuela's church?

The occupation of the First Spanish Church was an intra-Latinx struggle arbitrated through religious language, embodiment, and space. In each expression of meaning making within this story we get a glimpse into the realities of Puerto Ricans and Latinxs in twentieth-century New York City: some who understood themselves as "peregrinos" seeking God's faithfulness as manifest through property, some identifying with Jesus the "heavy cat" who stood up to authorities seeking to murder him. Raising both stories helps us understand the full breadth and depth of a community with competing religio-political visions of stability, justice, and empowerment. It eschews simple monolithic readings of minoritized peoples while forcing us to wrestle with the ways lived religion is constitutive of Latinx activism and resistance.

Put differently, we miss something when we don't tell the story of the church and of religion. The Young Lords didn't occupy a White-dominant, English-speaking church. They occupied a church in their community made up of people who looked and sounded like—or in some instances were—their grandmothers and grandfathers. They pushed the church using language "of church" in part because the Lords, too, made meaning through that religious lexicon. But the problem with telling the story in this way is that it's messy. From the perspective of each group, the church *did* "belong to the people" and was a "liberated zone," but who constituted the people and what liberation meant were vastly different. But unless we are willing to sit in the nuances of that difference—to sit on the street corner watching a church burn as the falling ashes declare purification, as well as in a church pew waiting to bolt doors shut and reclaim space for the Jesus of the streets—unless we are willing to sit with the complexity of *the people*, we will never fully understand *the people*. And in turn, we'll never fully understand our communities, our ancestors, and even ourselves.

What I leave you with, then, is not an easy answer of one side being right or wrong. What I leave you with is the image of Gilbert and María Colón—grandson and grandmother—sitting in an apartment, in their different yet deeply connected experiences of the world, trying to make meaning in religious language about sacred space. In many respects, it is this complex struggle, arbitrated through religion, that guides this chapter and every other chapter in this volume. From Lloyd Barba's exploration of Pentecostals in the farmworker movement to Lara Medina's analysis of Las Hermanas and their struggle for women's and immigrant rights, Latinx religious politics has always been about making meaning in community as people wrestle with the sacred.

Perhaps in examining that wrestling, we can find lessons for engaging an earth that is on fire, an economic system that continues breeding inequality, and a white supremacist and patriarchal world that still considers some lives more valuable than others. Perhaps God is not dead. Perhaps God is bread, and the people have risen. May we seek to understand how, learn from their wrestling, and rise once more . . .

NOTES

1 Robert L. Wilson, *The First Spanish United Methodist Church and the Young Lords, 1970* (New York: Department of Research and Survey, National Division of the Board of Missions, United Methodist Church, 1970), 15.
2 "First Spanish United Methodist Church" gained this name after 1968, when the Methodist Church merged with the Evangelical United Brethren Church. Before then, this congregation was referred to as "Spanish Ministries," "the Spanish Congregation," "Iglesia Episcopal San Juan," and "First Spanish Methodist Church." I use "First Spanish Church" for ease.
3 Iris Morales, "The Young Lords' Early Years, 1969–1971: An Overview," in *Through the Eyes of Rebel Women: The Young Lords, 1969–1976*, ed. Iris Morales (New York: Red Sugarcane, 2016), 21.
4 Darrel Wanzer-Serrano, *The New York Young Lords and the Struggle for Liberation* (Philadelphia: Temple University Press, 2015), 146.
5 I use the term "Latinx" throughout this chapter in reference to peoples of Latin American origin or descent who now reside in the United States. It should be noted that this modern, gender-inclusive term was not used by the actors depicted in this history, who either described themselves based on their country of origin (e.g., "Puerto Rican") or by the term "Spanish." The term "Latinx," however, is part of the linguistic lineage of how peoples of Latin American origin or descent were racialized and came to identify racially. Put differently, we can trace a historical through line from "Spanish" to "Hispanic" to "Latino/Latina" to "Latinx" (an argument that is outside the scope of this present work). Thus, for ease of analysis, I read this term back into the history at various points in this chapter.
6 Wanzer-Serrano, *New York Young Lords*; Johanna Fernández, *The Young Lords: A Radical History* (Chapel Hill: University of North Carolina Press, 2020); Elías Ortega-Aponte, "Raised Fists in the Church! Afro-Latino/a Practice among the Young Lords Party: A Humanistic Spirituality Model for Radical Latino/a Religious Ethics" (PhD diss., Princeton Theological Seminary, 2011); Felipe Hinojosa, *Apostles of Change: Latino Radical Politics, Church Occupations, and the Fight to Save the Barrio* (Austin: University of Texas Press, 2021).
7 Robert Orsi, "Everyday Miracles: The Study of Lived Religion," in *Lived Religion in America: Toward a History of Practice*, ed. David D. Hall (Princeton: Princeton University Press, 1997), 7.
8 Meredith McGuire, "Embodied Practices: Negotiation and Resistance," in *Everyday Religion: Observing Modern Religious Lives*, ed. Nancy T. Ammerman (New York: Oxford University Press, 2007), 187.
9 Edwin David Aponte, *¡Santo! Varieties of Latino/a Spirituality* (Maryknoll, NY: Orbis, 2012), Kindle ed., loc. 2140.

10 Lorrin Thomas, *Puerto Rican Citizen: History and Political Identity in Twentieth-Century New York City* (Chicago: University of Chicago Press, 2014), 2–3, 24.
11 "Letter from Ferdinand Aparicio, February 25th, 1934. Obra Hispana Bilingue en la Conferencia Annual de Nueva York," New York City Society, Unorganized.
12 New York Annual Conference Journal (henceforth NYCJ), 1929, 48.
13 Primera Iglesia Metodista Unida, "Cincuentenario de la Primera Iglesia Metodista Unida, New York: 28 de Mayo 1922–1972" (New York: Primera Iglesia Metodista Unida, 1972).
14 "The History of the Church, Written and Translated by Brother Flores, May 19, 1938," New York City Society, Unorganized.
15 NYCJ, 1946, 290.
16 Sonia Song-Ha Lee, *Building a Latino Civil Rights Movement: Puerto Ricans, African Americans, and the Pursuit of Racial Justice in New York City* (Chapel Hill: University of North Carolina Press, 2016), 25–26, 39.
17 NYCJ, 1950, 118–20.
18 NYCJ, 1953, 107–8.
19 NYCJ, 1954, 127.
20 "Letter to Dr. Leland P. Cary on the Church Building for First Spanish, April 9, 1954," New York City Society, Unorganized.
21 "Letter to Dr. Leland P. Cary."
22 Some Young Lords have noted during informal conversations with me that their families would go to the First Spanish Church in the holiday season throughout the 1950s to get donated groceries. Reports in the New York Annual Conference Journal (NYCJ, 1951, 96) and the church's own petition corroborate this testimony.
23 See, for example, Felipe Hinojosa, *Latino Mennonites: Civil Rights, Faith, and Evangelical Culture* (Baltimore: Johns Hopkins University Press, 2014).
24 "Report from the City of New York on Requirements for Burned Building, July 9, 1964," New York City Society, Unorganized.
25 Primera Iglesia Metodista Unida, "Cincuentenario."
26 "Letter to Clair M. Jones from Henry Whyman, October 22, 1963," Box 2574-2-1: 24, Records of the National Division of the General Board of Global Ministries, General Commission on Archives and History, Drew University, Madison, NJ.
27 Benita Rodriguez, oral history, interview by Jorge Juan Rodríguez V and Johanna Fernández, October 9, 2019.
28 NYCJ, 1966, 1151; Primera Iglesia Metodista Unida, "Cincuentenario."
29 Humberto Carrazana, "The Southeastern Jurisdiction," in *Each in Our Own Tongue: A History of Hispanics in United Methodism*, ed. Justo L. González (Nashville: Abingdon, 1991), 103–4.
30 Fernández, *Young Lords*, 159.
31 Johanna Fernández, "The Young Lords and the Social and Structural Roots of Late Sixties Urban Radicalism," in *Civil Rights in New York City: From World War II to the Giuliani Era*, ed. Clarence Taylor (New York: Fordham University Press, 2011), 152.

32 Johanna L. del C. Fernández, "Radicals in the Late 1960s: A History of the Young Lords Party in New York City, 1969–1974" (PhD diss., Columbia University, 2004), 118.
33 Dean M. Kelley, "The Young Lords and the Spanish Congregation," *Christian Century*, February 18, 1970, 208.
34 Wilson, *First Spanish United Methodist Church*, 31.
35 Michael T. Kaufman, "8 Hurt, 14 Seized in a Church Clash," *New York Times*, December 8, 1969.
36 Fernández, *Young Lords*, 168.
37 Fernández, *Young Lords*, 168.
38 Fernández, *Young Lords*, 169.
39 Miguel Meléndez, *We Took the Streets: Fighting for Latino Rights with the Young Lords* (New Brunswick: Rutgers University Press, 2005), 117.
40 Henry C. Whyman, "First Spanish United Methodist Church and the Young Lords" (New York, NY, January 9, 1970), 24, National Council of the Churches of Christ in the United States of America, Communication Center.
41 Frances Negrón-Muntaner, "The Look of Sovereignty: Style and Politics in the Young Lords," *Centro Journal* 27, no. 1 (2015): 4–33.
42 Fernández, *Young Lords*, 186; Wilson, *First Spanish United Methodist Church*, 15–16.
43 Wilson, *First Spanish United Methodist Church*, 15.
44 Fernández, "Radicals in the Late 1960s," 124.
45 Ortega-Aponte, "Raised Fists in the Church!," 198.
46 Morales, "Young Lords' Early Years," 22.
47 Fernández, *Young Lords*, 185, 250–69; Wanzer-Serrano, *New York Young Lords*, 117–18.
48 "Letter from Rev. Pedro Pirón to Nicanor Quiñones, President of the Board of Directors of the FSUMC Day Care Center, Inc., September 7, 1972," New York City Society, Unorganized.
49 Graciela Smith, "Speech by Felipe Luciano, New York State Chrmn., Young Lords Organization, at the First Spanish Methodist Church in El Barrio (111th St. & Lexington) on Sunday December 21, 1969," tape transcription (New York, December 24, 1969), 3–4, National Council of the Churches of Christ in the United States of America, Communication Center.
50 Smith, "Speech by Felipe Luciano," 3.
51 Graciela M. Smith, "Interview with Yoruba, Minister of Information, Young Lords Organization Regarding Confrontations at the First Spanish Methodist Church in El Barrio (Spanish Harlem)," tape transcription (New York, December 19, 1969), 30, National Council of the Churches of Christ in the United States of America, Communication Center.
52 Smith, "Interview with Yoruba," 30.
53 "Young Lords Defy Take-Over Order," *New York Times*, January 3, 1970.
54 Wanzer-Serrano, *New York Young Lords*, 153.

55 Kelley, "Young Lords," 210.
56 Robert Chapman, "Article by Rev. Robert Chapman, Dir. Racial Justice, NCC" (New York, January 2, 1970), 2, National Council of the Churches of Christ in the United States of America, Communication Center.
57 Wanzer-Serrano, *New York Young Lords*; Fernández, *Young Lords*.
58 "They Joined with Their Hearts: A Conversation with the Cadre of the New York Lords" (First Spanish United Methodist Church, December 7, 2019), Facebook, www.facebook.com.

7

From the Fields to the Cities

The Rise of Latina/o Religious Politics in the Civil Rights Era

FELIPE HINOJOSA

The day was not as dramatic or chaotic as some had made it out to be. Yes, James Forman did read parts of his bold and controversial "Black Manifesto" to a room full of mostly white Presbyterians at the 181st General Assembly of the United Presbyterian Church in the USA (UPCUSA) on May 15, 1969. People were genuinely nervous about that. I mean, how could they not be? The manifesto was demanding half a billion dollars in reparations from white Christian churches and few denominations were as wealthy, or wealthier, than UPCUSA.[1] Add to that the fact that in the weeks prior, the former SNCC leader had made big news when he took over a meeting of the National Black Economic Development Conference in Detroit and disrupted a worship service at the elegant Riverside Church in New York City. In both incidents, Forman read his Manifesto out loud to a stunned crowd. But this day in San Antonio was different. What the writers at *Christianity Today* called the "San Antonio Shakedown," with drama as rich as the moment when "nearly 200 frontiersmen [fought] against the armies of the Mexican 'Napoleon' Santa Anna," was actually quite undramatic. Those who heard Forman speak described his speech as "witty, knowledgeable, . . . couched in much milder language than the Black Manifesto."[2] Forman had charmed the Presbyterians.

If there was any drama on that day, it happened inside the heart and mind of the Mexican American minister Roger Granados. For much of the 1960s, Reverend Granados served as a staff member for the Board of National Missions; served on the UPCUSA Commission on Religion and Race; led multiple consultations to the US/Mexico border; served on the San Joaquin Migrant Ministry board; and helped facilitate the Consulta

Internacional Fronteriza.³ Granados was in San Antonio to hear Forman speak, but also to support the small cadre of Latino activists there that day.⁴ Obed López, a Mexican American organizer from Chicago, was there to make demands on behalf of the Young Lords (a predominantly Puerto Rican group of organizers), who just days prior had occupied the Stone Building of the McCormick Theological Seminary (affiliated with the Presbyterian Church in the USA) in Chicago's Lincoln Park neighborhood. Eliezer Risco, a leader in the Chicano movement in Los Angeles, and Tomás Chávez Jr. of the Spanish-American Outreach in Detroit, were also there to provide support and present their own "Brown Manifesto."⁵ As speaker after speaker took the podium, Granados sat silently, barely keeping up with the flood of emotions he was feeling inside:

> strange feeling sitting in front of you—realize I don't quite feel a part of you. The UPUSA Ch[urch] born and raised. A sense of strangement [sic] . . . language, culture, lands deliberately denied . . . many of our churchmen perplexed— We've tried to assimilate them. They now demand their own churches. . . . Many people trying to define Raza. For me = an assertion: A new race neither Spanish nor Indian. Detroit, Milwaukee, Puertorriqueño, Hispano, Mexicano, español . . . Church programs humiliated and bound us. . . . We were objects of someone else's mission. . . . The greatest majority of our people not interested in church . . . among us [Latinos] no common denominator of details. No consensus on anything. Common cause to be free.⁶

No drama, no shakedown, and no Alamo myth. Granados's words were from the heart. As far as I know, he never shared these words publicly. They were simply written down, amidst pages of notes that Granados had taken that day. Here was a Mexican American minister coming to terms with his identity, his faith, and the failures of his church. His words are as poetic as they are historic. And in his political and faith commitments, Granados was not alone.⁷

The late 1960s signaled a new era for many Latina/o religious leaders whose fight on behalf of farmworkers in the Southwest had come face to face with the crisis in the American city. Conferences with titles like "La Iglesia y La Raza Unida" became commonplace as Latina/o religious leaders started to pay close attention to the changing political attitudes in the city as they worried about where the church might fit within this new militancy.[8] Against the backdrop of an urban crisis and pressure from multiethnic neighborhood organizations, Latina/o radicals and religious leaders engaged the politics of the city.[9] From the fields of central California to the streets of East Harlem, Chicana/o and Puerto Rican radicals breathed life into religious movements that had otherwise remained irrelevant or tied to local and regional dynamics. Even as Granados sat with his thoughts about a Latino identity with "no common denominator," it was clear that by the late 1960s activism in the fields and cities had come to define Latina/o religious politics.

Postwar Politics: The California Migrant Ministry

Progressive religious movements have a long history in the United States. In the latter part of the nineteenth century, religious reformers envisioned a Christianity that concerned itself with the poor and marginalized of society. The "Social Gospel" urged Christians to work against poverty and discrimination in all forms as the work of salvation became as much about building a more just society as it was about a heavenly afterlife.[10] The use of Christian theology to critique national and political structures, what theologians call "theopolitics," accelerated during the middle part of the twentieth century as the war against fascism overseas and the fight for civil rights at home elevated once again the role of religion in American politics.[11] In the midst of this evangelical and Social Gospel spirit, African American Christians played a monumental role in the fight to end Jim Crow segregation as leaders saw their cause not simply as a civic duty, but as a way to redeem the nation's soul through a moral and spiritual awakening that some call a "religious revival."[12] That spirit spread throughout the country as both Catholic and Protestant leaders began to pay closer attention to the growing number of Latina/o immigrants in the urban North and out West. In the Catholic Church, for example, the Spanish-speaking councils that organized in the 1950s—from the Southwest to the Midwest—investigated and organized responses to health care concerns, housing needs, and the high infant mortality rates among Mexican Americans and other Latina/os. In Brooklyn, Encarnación Padilla de Armas organized to get the

Catholic Church to provide more services for the newly arrived Puerto Rican migrants settling in East Harlem and in other boroughs across the city. In the early 1950s, Padilla de Armas organized the Spanish Catholic Action and would later go on to chair the planning committee for the Primer Encuentro Hispano de Pastoral (First Hispanic Pastoral Encounter) in 1972.[13] And in California, a small and mostly forgotten organization, the California Migrant Ministry, started making moves that in the 1960s would profoundly transform Latina/o religious politics.[14]

The ecumenical and Protestant-led California Migrant Ministry (CMM) started in the 1930s, at the height of the Great Depression, as a ministry to migrant farmworkers. In the years that followed, it established ministries in the San Joaquin and Imperial Valleys of California with camps for migrant children, English classes, personal hygiene classes, and boys and girls clubs.[15] From the 1930s to the 1950s the CMM's work focused on distributing clothes and Bibles, providing food and shelter when needed, and meeting the spiritual needs of the farmworkers. It had long been admired by pastors and growers in central and southern California. It was, as Miriam Pawel described it, a "milk-and-cookies approach" to advocacy that steered clear of conflict and relieved wealthy donors of any responsibility for the meager wages and horrendous working conditions of farmworkers.[16]

But by the late 1950s Doug Still, the CMM's director, had grown increasingly frustrated by the CMM's limited approach and in 1957 he registered his staff to be trained by organizers from the Community Service Organization (CSO). The training allowed staff to join either Fred Ross (who helped start the CSO) or César Chávez, a new organizer at the time and one of Ross's students, for six to eight weeks as they went about their organizing work. That partnership proved fruitful several years later with the arrival of a young Presbyterian minister, the Reverend Chris Hartmire, who took over as director for the CMM in 1961. When Hartmire arrived in California, it was the young CSO organizer César Chávez whom he first sought out. At one of their first lunch meetings in East Los Angeles, Chávez shared his vision and desire to organize farmworkers, something the CSO was reluctant to do.[17] Farmworkers earned pitiful wages and lacked access to clean drinking water, housing, health care, restroom facilities, lunch, or rest breaks. To make matters worse, farmworkers and domestic workers were not protected under minimum wage laws or eligible for unemployment insurance. Organizing farmworkers would be a herculean task.

Regardless, Hartmire was hooked. His relationship with Chávez grew strong in the coming years, with the CMM providing the necessary resources for Chávez's upstart union. It provided him with a mimeograph machine, car rides whenever Chávez needed them, and use of the CMM credit card for any expenses related to union work. In 1965, when the National Farm Worker Association (NFWA) joined Filipino farmworkers to strike in Delano, Hartmire had become one of Chávez's closest allies in the movement. In fact, it was Hartmire whom Chávez first called on for advice and support as he considered joining the strike.[18] By 1967, less than ten years after being nearly forgotten, the CMM had taken its place as one of the most important organizations in the farm labor strike and boycott that by this time had spread across the country.

But increased visibility and presence in the farmworker movement also came with deep criticism from the churches the CMM represented. In 1966, only a year after the strike began, the CMM lost a large portion of its support from churches in the Fresno area. Out of the fifty-seven churches that supported the CMM before the strike, only twelve churches remained a year after the CMM stood behind striking farmworkers. The First Presbyterian Church in Fresno demanded that none of its donations go to the striking workers, and the Delano Ministerial Association condemned the strike, issuing a statement asserting that "the Association does not encourage any ecclesiastical demonstration of interference in the farm labor situation and it looks with disfavor upon any non-resident church or clergy making such expression."[19]

Even so, the CMM carried a legitimacy that Chávez and Dolores Huerta needed in order to build a broad base of support and gain the trust of religious leaders and their institutions. No organization had the voice, the reach, and the ear of mainline Protestants and Catholic leaders more than the CMM. In the weeks after the strike began, major religious periodicals, including *Christianity and Crisis*, *National Catholic Reporter*, and *Presbyterian Life*, each made appeals asking for funds to be sent to the CMM. Hartmire wrote of support he received from Jews and Christians who "reject the heresy that churches and synagogues are to be concerned only with so-called spiritual matters."[20] Support also came in from the Student Nonviolent Coordinating Committee (SNCC), Congress of Racial Equity (CORE), the Diocese of California, the Cardinal's Committee for the Spanish Speaking in Chicago, the Knights of St John (a Puerto Rican organization in Chicago), the San Francisco Presbytery, the Texas Council of Churches, and Homeland Ministries of the United Church of Christ (UCC); a group of fifteen pastors from the mostly conservative San Joaquin Valley area wrote a letter to their fellow clergy urging them to aid Hartmire and the Migrant Ministry.

In Texas, the Rio Grande Annual Conference (Methodist) passed several resolutions supporting the farmworkers in their fight for collective bargaining, fair wages, and decent working conditions. Prominent clergy from the Annual Conference—Joel Martínez, Leo Nieto, Isabel Gómez, and Arturo Fernández—all joined in and made public statements voicing their support for farmworkers.[21] The Reverend Pablo Jimenez of the Mexican Baptist church in Fresno served as a representative for the CMM and the Reverend Pedro Torres helped extend the CMM's reach by starting two chapters, first in Minnesota and later in Sacramento. This growing cohort of supporters came to include countless other clergy volunteers who remain unidentified, listed simply as "Spanish pastors" in CMM newsletters in the 1960s.[22] It's important to remember that all these moves took place against the backdrop of a Catholic Church in the midst of a dramatic shift. The Second Vatican Council did more than shift the church away from some of its strictures. It ushered in a new theological framework that endorsed a preferential option for the poor and created an atmosphere, a "spirit," that slowly started to move the Catholic Church in a new and bold direction.

By 1968 the majority of the CMM's resources went to farmworkers involved in the strike. This included organizational support inside and outside the fields—counseling, religious services, educational programs.[23] Part of the appeal of the CMM, and one of the reasons why Latina/o religious leadership stood up confidently to support it, was that the CMM could not be labeled "as Johnny-come-lately's or as opportunists" in its work with farmworkers. No other religious organization had that kind of power and legitimacy.[24] This made the transition to politics much easier for Latina/o clergy. But this movement also hit close to home. In striking farmworkers, Latina/o religious leaders saw themselves and their congregants as migrant workers who yearly made the trek north to pick cherries in Michigan or tomatoes in Ohio. The workers striking for better wages and better working conditions looked like them, in many cases worshiped in the same churches, and in all cases held on to a faith rooted in the knowledge that God's protection followed them in their travels.

That familiarity gave Latina/o religious leaders the courage to, for the first time, question the theology and politics of white Protestants and Catholics and, in some cases, actually move contrary to the mandates of the church. That point cannot be stressed enough. Supporting farmworkers and seeing the morality of their cause, against the apathy and ignorance of white religious leaders, were significant steps for Latina/o faith leaders. The struggles that the Reverend Roger Granados articulated in the opening paragraphs of this essay are rooted in the dramatic turn toward religious politics inspired by striking farmworkers. Religious leaders like the Reverend Lydia Hernandez, whose family had worked for migrant ministry programs in the late 1950s and early 1960s, maintained a close relationship with César Chávez, even hosting him in her home when he visited Florida.[25]

Joining this movement also put the historically antagonistic Latina/o Catholics and Protestants side by side as allies for the first time. "We were not supposed to associate with Roman Catholics because they were pagans," remembered Presbyterian Reverend Ruben Armendáriz, "and the Catholics thought we were crazy, they'd call us 'Protestantes' or 'Aleluyas' and then they would clap their hands and say that we sang loud and rolled around on the floor."[26] These new interactions, while still relegated to the leadership primarily, did at least start to chip away at the misconceptions that both groups had about each other. Politics, and specifically political engagement via the farmworker movement, brought Latina/o Catholics and Protestants together in ways that, at least momentarily, pushed aside denominational differences in pursuit of a common cause.

And yet even as Latino Protestants and Catholics made strong proclamations in support of farmworkers, the needs in the barrio remained overlooked. The urban crisis that had crippled American cities, some literally being burned to the ground, was seen as a Black and white struggle, with the Black freedom movement receiving much of the attention from liberal white Protestants. In 1970 a report of the Board of Christian

Social Concerns stated what many already knew, that churches across the conference and the Southwest had overlooked the issues faced by Mexican Americans and other Latina/os in American cities.[27]

One of the early Latino leaders to investigate the issues of the city was the Presbyterian pastor Jorge Lara-Braud. In 1966 Lara-Braud helped start the Hispanic American Institute (HAI) at Austin Presbyterian Theological Seminary in Austin, Texas. The HAI served as an ecumenical center for research and religious training for ministry in Mexican American and Latina/o communities across Texas and the nation. As director of the institute, Lara-Braud challenged white church leaders to understand Latina/os not as a population in need of Americanization, but as a group with important faith traditions and family values, one that continued to struggle under the sting of institutional racism.[28] Part of what made Lara-Braud unique, and what helped sharpen his vision for urban ministry, was his belief that church leaders should work with community leaders outside the church: activists, labor leaders, and community organizers.

In a 1967 report to the Programing Committee of the Presbyterian Church US Synod of Texas, Lara-Braud stressed the importance of the church partnering with "civil and political groups, including LULAC, the GI Forum, MAPA, PASO, but also MAYO, the UFW, and La Raza Unida."[29] At the time this was actually a pretty radical position. But it confirmed the directions of Latina/o religious leaders who fashioned their own movements after Chicana/o movement organizations. In California and Arizona, for example, Mexican American Methodists organized the Latin American Methodist Action group in 1968 as a way to address discrimination and racism in the church.[30] In New Mexico, two Latino Presbyterians, Tomás Atencio and Facundo Valdéz, founded the Academia de la Nueva Raza as a way to conduct research on the needs of the community. In the Catholic Church, a group of Chicano priests who called themselves PADRES (Padres Asociados para Derechos Religiosos, Educativos, y Sociales) organized in February 1970, and shortly thereafter a group of Latina nuns organized as Las Hermanas.[31]

Each of these groups sought to elevate the voices of Mexican Americans and Latina/os in the church, especially around the lack of representation and the church's relationship to the civil rights movement. Aside from Las Hermanas, which was a pan-Latina and transnational organization, most of these religious movements remained regional, and some, like PADRES, practiced a strident nationalism that maintained that only Chicano priests could join the group. The moves that Latina/os made within their respective Protestant denominations and Catholic parishes in the late 1960s all grew out of a desire to have a voice in the rooms where the action was happening, where decisions on church leadership and politics were being made. And for all these groups, the farmworker movement was the cause they latched on to. Church folks did not come with sermons, or membership cards; they came as negotiators, ready to join the fight and help where needed, whether that meant providing food and money or pressuring DiGiorgio Corporation or Perelli Minnetti Vineyards to hold union representation elections. But if the farmworker movement was where things started, the urban movements would ultimately propel Latina/o religious politics into a larger conversation on race, poverty, and the future of the church in America.[32] That moment in San Antonio, at the 181st General Assembly of the United Presbyterian Church USA, where Granados sat, lost in his own thoughts, was the place where it had become abundantly clear that the struggles and movements of Latina/os in the city had now taken center stage.

Religion in the City: From Church Occupations to Faith-Based Organizations

On May 14, 1969, just minutes before midnight and with the help of seminary students, the Puerto Rican Young Lords Organization (YLO) took over and occupied the Stone Academic Administration Building at McCormick Theological Seminary in Chicago's Lincoln Park neighborhood. The initial group that occupied the building that night numbered around eighty, with a good mix of mothers, fathers, Black Panthers, YLO, and clergy and religious leaders from the Northside Cooperative Ministry (NSCM). They quickly renamed the building the Manuel Ramos Memorial Building in memory of their good friend and brother killed by an off-duty police officer just a few days earlier. This was an occupation led by the YLO, but with the support of the Poor People's Coalition (PPC), seminary students, Black Active and Determined (BAD), Black Panthers, Students for a Democratic Society, Concerned

Citizens of Lincoln Park, Welfare and Working Mothers of Wicker Park, and the Latin American Defense Organization (LADO).[33]

A few days after the occupation, Obed López, one of the coalition's most articulate leaders, presented a list of demands to Presbyterian leaders at their annual General Assembly in San Antonio. The demands included funding for low-income housing in Lincoln Park (a neighborhood that in 1969 was on the brink of being overrun by urban renewal), facilities for a day care center, and space for a Puerto Rican cultural center.[34] López's opening words at the General Assembly were direct and succinct: "Last night, the poor community of Lincoln Park, under the leadership of the Young Lords Organization, a Latin American community—a political action group—took under its control the McCormick Theological Seminary of Chicago." Yet, for many Presbyterians at the General Assembly, López's words sounded "like far off thunder," coming from an activist whose grievances as a Mexican immigrant, as a Latino, were "only just beginning to come to the surface."[35] In fact, many participants at the UPCUSA General Assembly that day had still not heard of the occupation of McCormick Seminary, and hardly anyone knew who the Young Lords were.

But that would change in the weeks and months that followed as Latina/o activists from across the country—from New York to Houston to Chicago—occupied church spaces to protest urban renewal, poverty, and police brutality. In 1969 and 1970, just as César Chávez, Dolores Huerta, and the farmworker movement brought the agricultural industry to its knees, urban Latina/o activists captured the attention, and ire, of mainline Protestant and Catholic churches. Seven months after the McCormick occupation, the New York Young Lords occupied the First Spanish Methodist Church in East Harlem, the Mexican American group Católicos por La Raza disrupted Christmas Eve mass at St. Basil's Catholic Church in Los Angeles, and a few months after that, activists from the Mexican American Youth Organization (MAYO) occupied the Juan Marcos Presbyterian Church in Houston, Texas.[36] In almost rapid succession, these takeovers and disruptions—sensational, dramatic, and short—tipped the scales in favor of neighborhood activists whose actions forced religious leadership to finally take seriously the crisis of displacement and poverty in Latina/o communities. These short but fertile political moments, and the politics that emanated from them, also managed to shine a light on the quiet activism of Latina/o Protestants and Catholics. While Latina/o religious leaders already had a long and active history of engaging their white religious leadership—starting most forcefully in the fields of central California and south Texas—the occupations and disruptions in 1969 and 1970 moved them from the margins to the centers of religious power in Protestant and Catholic churches. Latino pastors, from the Presbyterian Latin American Council to the Catholic group PADRES, owe their political rise to these short but dramatic bursts of political power. They were game changers. In the late 1960s Latina/o religious leaders, buoyed by the dramatic occupations, became central players in the political drama of race, theology, poverty, and the fight to provide refuge for millions of Central Americans fleeing the wars and atrocities of their home countries.[37]

In the following decades, groups such as PADRES and Las Hermanas emerged as forceful and legitimate voices that supported farmworkers and Chicana/o militants in the barrios, advocated for more Latina/os in church leadership, published a joint newsletter for three years, and formed part of the sanctuary movement.[38] For their part, Protestant denominations appointed more Latina/os to church leadership positions as they were pushed by Latina/os such as the Reverend Jorge Lara-Braud to be "inclusive of all ethnic groups in the membership as well as in policy and decision-making bodies."[39] The shift marked a new era in Latina/o religious politics as leadership came to value their ethno-racial identity as much as their religious identity.[40] In the 1970s Latina/o religious leaders established culturally relevant educational programs in theological schools, published religious materials in Spanish, and saw its leadership numbers grow. These new developments prompted religious schools and seminaries to adjust their curriculum accordingly and increase their offerings in Mexican American and Latina/o theological studies. The Hispanic American Institute (Austin, 1966), the Mexican American Cultural Center (San Antonio, 1972), and the Mexican American Program at the Perkins School of Theology (Dallas, 1974) were among the most visible of these programs.

But this new focus on identity included more than diversifying church boards, creating Spanish-language church curricula, or establishing Latina/o theological studies; it was also about creating and participating in mutual aid organizations—what later became identified as faith-based organizations—that focused on the much-neglected needs of urban Latina/os. In fact, since the 1970s, participation in faith-based community organizations has become the centerpiece of Latina/o religious politics. Organizations such as Communities Organized for Public Service (COPS) in San Antonio, the United Neighborhood Organization (UNO) in Los Angeles, and Acción Cívica Evangélica in New York City emerged as civic voices grounded in the fights that first began in the fields and the barrios.

In 1974 Catholic leadership in San Antonio's westside partnered with the Industrial Arts Foundation (IAF) and organizer Ernie Cortés to found COPS. Started as a way to address the flooding problem on the westside that for years had plagued the mostly Mexican American community, COPS quickly became a force in San Antonio. It filled city council meetings with residents ready and willing to share their stories of flooding in their neighborhoods, and in a matter of months the city approved a total of fifteen new drainage projects. In subsequent years COPS helped bring in more than $1 billion in improvements for barrio residents that included sidewalks, drainage channels, parks, and adult literacy programs.[41] Much of the early success of COPS was due to the brilliant organizing of Ernie Cortés, who first secured the support of Catholic clergy and then organized house and church meetings to explain the work that needed to be done. Cortés identified leaders, trained them to be organizers, and advised them to choose winnable causes that would directly benefit the community. In 1976 auxiliary bishop Juan Arzube, the first Latino bishop of the Los Angeles archdiocese, visited San Antonio and was so impressed by COPS and the organizers he met—many of them families and working people—that he brought the idea back to Los Angeles. Not long after that he helped start the United Neighborhood Organization (UNO) in Los Angeles. With help from the IAF and Ernie Cortés, UNO started working with parishes in the heavily Mexican American neighborhoods of Boyle Heights, Lincoln Heights, and El Sereno.

UNO and COPS were both faith-based organizations that used the Alinsky model of organizing, which followed the golden rule of organizing: "Listen to the people that you are trying to organize."[42] Sticking to this mantra, UNO tackled everything from redlining and faulty street signs to the need for new traffic lights and the high auto insurance rates that people in these neighborhoods paid. At the first formal convention for UNO in 1979, members elected Gloria Chavez as president, Lydia López as vice president, and Sister Jo'ann DeQuattro as secretary-treasurer for the organization.[43] Two years later, in 1981, López, a Protestant, was elected president of the largely Catholic UNO. She won a majority of the delegate vote with help from her good friend Father Luis Olivares.[44] Her first action as president was to grant $5,000 to SCOP (South Central Organizing Project) as a way to build a coalition between African Americans and Latinos in the city, adding that politicians can no longer "play the Black community off the Brown community."[45] López was, by her own admission, a "pushy broad" in those days with a keen sense of humor and a no-nonsense approach to her work. One of her strengths was making sure that she controlled the narrative. For example, when Governor Jerry Brown met with UNO in East Los Angeles in the early 1980s, he made it a point to say that he made history by meeting with them there. López quickly reminded him, "No, we made history by getting you here."[46]

With López's leadership as vice president and then president, UNO pressured major insurance companies to lower their rates to residents on the eastside, persuaded the Safeway grocery store chain to modernize its stores in the barrios and even build a new one, and convinced the sheriff's department to increase patrols in high-crime areas. Rooted in the church and the community, and with a strict adherence to the Alinsky method, UNO became a living manifestation for the visions of political activists and religious leaders in 1970s Los Angeles.[47]

Across the country, in New York City, another faith-based movement emerged in 1974. Acción Cívica Evangélica brought together forty Protestant denominations totaling more than five hundred Latino, mostly Puerto Rican, congregations and organized nutrition programs, youth employment opportunities, continuing education for pastors, and centers for the elderly. Acción Cívica Evangélica emerged as the most important Latino faith-based organization in the city. Co-founded by Dr. José Caraballo, an Assemblies of God minister and dean of Hispanic studies at New York Theological Seminary, Acción Cívica was the first major and widely recognized organization of Latino religious leaders made up of mainline Protestant and Pentecostal churches. The historian

Elizabeth Ríos noted that the "organization was able to have representatives from every major Pentecostal council in New York City . . . [and] some of New York's best and brightest youth ended up working for [Acción Cívica Evangélica] and going on to become scholars and voices in the city for a different generation."[48] Between 1974 and 1976, the group raised more than $3 million from federal, state, and city resources. It channeled those funds to social welfare programs, including an additional $2 million in federally sponsored breakfast and lunch programs for approximately forty thousand children across the city.

The move to establish Acción Cívica Evangélica grew out of a deep "concern that some of the younger ministers had for the social implications of the Gospel."[49] The impact that Acción made was seen most directly when in October 1976 three Latino churches were set on fire, some left with obscenities written on the walls, and in each case pastors receiving threatening phone calls from the arsonists. With the good will that the organization had built within the city, pastors were able to bring attention to the fires by increasing police presence in Latino churches across the city.[50] The work of Acción Cívica Evangélica gained its political power in a city more accustomed to Pentecostal preachers working with drug addicts and gang leaders than working with city leaders.[51] And yet through it all, the group managed to maintain, as the Reverend Raymond Rivera noted, its "evangelical fervor and still remain socially involved."[52] Groups like COPS, UNO, and Acción Cívica Evangélica raised the political consciousness of their communities in the 1970s and offered a new vision for faith-based work in America's cities. These were organizations in barrios, organized around their churches, that thrived in local and regional contexts and that in the 1980s built strong networks of support for Central Americans seeking refuge in the United States.[53]

By the 1990s, a new push emerged to establish a nationwide network of Latina/o leaders and churches. In 1992 the Pentecostal minister and professor Dr. Jesse Miranda founded the Alianza Ministerial Evangélicos Nacionales, also known as AMEN (National Alliance of Evangelical Ministers), as a way to provide a national organization, unite Latino churches, and have a voice in national politics. With leadership from across North America and the Caribbean, AMEN soon became the nation's leading Latino Protestant advocacy group, continuing in the tradition of Acción Cívica Evangélica's mix of evangelical and social concern.[54] AMEN also gave rise to what today is considered one of the most conservative voices in Latina/o religious politics, the Reverend Samuel Rodriguez. In 2001 Rodriguez started the National Hispanic Christian Leadership Conference (NHCLC), which five years later merged with AMEN to become the largest and most influential Latina/o religious organization in the country. Rodriguez, a Puerto Rican Assemblies of God minister from New York City, became a staunch advocate for immigration reform in the early 2000s, working with both the Bush and the Obama administrations.

But Rodriguez has also been a new kind of Latino religious leader in that he has been much more willing to align with conservative and largely evangelical politics, especially with regard to the pro-life movement and in his opposition to gay marriage. His work pushing for immigration reform continued under the administration of Donald Trump, but he has also come under fire from Latino activists for not distancing himself from Trump's largely anti-immigrant and family separation policies.[55] A rival of sorts to Rodriguez's conservative politics with the NHCLC is the National Latino Evangelical Coalition (NaLEC), led by the Reverend Gabriel Salguero. NaLEC has historically taken a much more progressive stance on issues regarding poverty, immigration, and even the death penalty, noting, "We're pro-life: womb to the tomb."[56] But however different, and whatever distinctions might exist in their political leanings, both Rodriguez and Salguero are yet another iteration in a long tradition of movements that defy easy categorization. This is a tradition whose origins are grounded in the radical politics of the 1960s and 1970s, but who today cannot simply be pinned as part of the religious left or right. It's not that Latina/o religious politics have become centrist since the 1990s, or that they lack any political will; the shift has more to do with the rise of Pentecostalism, whose theopolitics are far more conservative than the historic mainline Protestants and Catholics who were active in the civil rights era.[57] This is why current political pundits often mischaracterize Latina/o religious politics when they assume a liberal or conservative bent. In fact, they are both. As the Reverend Raymond Rivera from Acción Cívica Evangélica in New York City argued, these are political movements that carry an "evangelical fervor and still remain socially involved."[58]

Conclusion

In a *New York Times* article on Latino evangelical support for Donald Trump in the 2020 election, Pastor Jose Rivera of the Church of God of Prophecy in Arizona labeled himself "politically homeless." Troubled by some of the policies pushed by Democrats, but feeling betrayed by the antagonistic rhetoric of Republicans, Rivera summed up the place of Latina/o religious communities.[59] The numbers from the 2020 election reveal the chasm that has become the new normal for an increasingly conservative religious group. According to the Public Religion Research Institute (PRRI), 57 percent of Latino evangelicals approved of President Trump, while only 27 percent of Latino Catholics did and only 16 percent of religiously unaffiliated Latinos. The PRRI went on to note that "religion is the largest demographic divider among Hispanic Americans, excepting only partisanship."[60] These numbers reveal a chasm that has always existed and will not soon go away.

But given these trends, it is significant to think and write about the radical tradition of Latina/o religious politics that first began in the fields and eventually moved to the cities, where faith-based organizations became powerful agents for change. Throughout much of this history, we see how different people and multiple organizations helped Latina/o religious politics become a recognizable force of ideas and movements. This began with the careful and deliberate work of the Reverend Chris Hartmire and the California Migrant Ministry. They laid the groundwork and provided the legitimacy that helped capture the support of Latina/o Protestants and Catholics. And yet, even as religious leaders joined in their support for farmworkers, it would be Latina/o radicals in the streets of New York and Chicago who would breathe new life into the movement and bring much-needed awareness to the issues Latina/os faced in America's cities. The church occupations and disruptions of 1969 and 1970 caught the attention of religious leaders across the country as they shined a light on the issues of displacement, poverty, and underemployment faced by Latina/o communities. In the 1970s Latina/o religious leaders became central players in the fight against racism and poverty even as they forged ahead to develop Latina/o theology and contextually specific theological studies. Moreover, the rise of faith-based organizations such as COPS (San Antonio), UNO (Los Angeles), and

Acción Cívica Evangélica (New York) helped establish an infrastructure of support across neighborhoods and churches that would help sustain and support the necessary networks to provide refuge for thousands of Central American refugees in the 1980s, which my colleagues will take up in subsequent chapters. This history should remind us that Latina/o religious politics have evolved and changed over time, that they are not static, and that even today's more conservative politics are tied to this history. This is why studying Latina/o religious politics today is so important. It forces us to cross political and disciplinary borders, it challenges us to pay attention to the ordinary as much as to the extraordinary, and it means taking into consideration social movements that at first glance might seem void of any religious involvement.

When we examine the many expressions of Latina/o religious politics—from the fields to the cities—we begin to see that these movements are not simply about religious leadership, reforming church denominations, or the kind of theology one practices. They are also about labor organizing, grassroots community movements, and the significant roles that religious outsiders have played in defining the political edge of Latina/o religiosity and politics. From these movements we learn about the multiethnic coalitions formed in the fields of central California with organizations like the California Migrant Ministry and in the barrios like Lincoln Park where a Black, Brown, and white coalition first occupied McCormick Theological Seminary. We learn that Latina/o religious politics have presented themselves in different forms, that they brought Catholics and Protestants together, and that there has always existed a back-and-forth struggle between reformist and revolutionary politics. And perhaps most importantly, it means that to understand Latina/o religious politics means moving beyond the walls of the church and examining the ruptures and coming together of religious insiders and outsiders.

From the fields of central California and south Texas to the barrios across America, you can hear the faithful praying, see them marching, and feel their sense of hope and possibility. We see clergy raising religious symbols and offering prayers and we see prophets in the fields and in the streets reminding the church to be the church. And through it all, we can hear more clearly the words of the Reverend Roger Granados, who, in 1969, wrote about the betrayals of the church and the complexities of Latina/o identity, and about the differences and conflicts, and yet reminded himself (and all of us today) to remember that our "Common cause [is] to be free."[61]

NOTES
1 Jerry K. Frye, "The 'Black Manifesto' and the Tactic of Objectification," *Journal of Black Studies* 5, no. 1 (September 1974): 66.
2 "Challenge and Response," *Presbyterian Life*, June 15, 1969, Pitts Theological Library, Emory University.
3 "Challenge and Response."
4 I use "Latina/o" when discussing the community as a whole and use "Latina" and "Latino" when addressing gendered experiences specifically.
5 Chávez and Risco were in attendance to present the "Brown Revolution Manifesto," which called for $500,000 for church programs in Latino communities and disinvestment in Latin America, and included a statement of solidarity and support for people of the "third world" and the Black Manifesto. Designed as an equivalent to the Black Manifesto, the Brown Revolution Manifesto was designed to build on the momentum built by Forman and to forge solidarity between Black and Brown activists and clergy. "Brown Revolution Manifesto," presented to the 181st General Assembly of the United Presbyterian Church USA, San Antonio, TX, May 15, 1969, Box F093, File: UPUSA General Assembly 1969, Hispanic American Institute, Austin, TX (hereafter HAI); Roger Granados, "Notes from the UPUSA General Assembly," May 15, 1969, p. 7, Box F093, File: UPUSA General Assembly 1969, HAI.
6 Granados, "Notes from the UPUSA General Assembly," 2.
7 For more on the Reverend Granados's activism during the Chicano movement, see Eduardo Contreras, *Latinos and the Liberal City: Politics and Protest in San Francisco* (Philadelphia: University of Pennsylvania Press, 2019).
8 The seminar "La Iglesia y La Raza Unida" was held at Primera Iglesia Metodista Unida in Arlington, TX, on September 6, 1969. Both Protestant and Catholic Latina/os were invited to attend and workshops were led by the Reverends Jorge Lara-Braud and Leo Nieto. "La Iglesia y La Raza Unida," Box F068, File: Chicano Caucuses, HAI. The emergence of a Latina/o religious movement in the late 1960s mirrored the broader movement that witnessed the rise of pan-ethnic alliances that crossed regional and cultural borders and brought, at least initially, Puerto Ricans and Mexican Americans together. Benjamin Francis-Fallon, *The Rise of the Latino Vote: A History* (Cambridge: Harvard University Press, 2019), 6.
9 A. K. Sandoval-Strausz argues that the urban crisis resulted from federal policies that transformed the city and subsidized the suburbs, resulting in "population loss, economic decline, fiscal crisis, rising crime, and the racialization of all of the above." See A. K. Sandoval-Strausz, *Barrio America: How Latinos Saved the American City* (New York: Basic Books, 2019), 8, 103. For more on the urban crisis, see

also Thomas J. Sugrue, *The Origins of the Urban Crisis: Race and Inequality in Postwar Detroit* (Princeton: Princeton University Press, 1996).

10 The theologian Walter Rauschenbusch first coined the term "social gospel." See Hugh T. Kerr, ed., *Readings in Christian Thought*, 2nd ed. (Nashville: Abingdon, 1990).

11 This growth of Latina/o populations has forced historians to move beyond simplistic and one-dimensional characterizations of religious communities to ones that reveal the transnational cultures, migrant streams, and activist politics spurred on first by Catholic activism that emerged out of a series of social encyclicals by Pope Leo XIII (*Rerum Novarum*) in 1891 and later Pius IX (*Quadragesimo Anno*) in 1930. Teachings on social engagement emerged at critical moments of the Industrial Revolution and as the country sank into an economic depression. Both of these encyclicals aligned the church to the mostly ethnic white labor movement and solidified the Catholic Church "as one of labor's major allies." See Moises Sandoval, *Fronteras: A History of the Latin American Church in the USA since 1513* (Austin: Mexican American Cultural Center, 1983); Leo D. Nieto, "The Chicano Movement and the Gospel," in *Hidden Stories: Unveiling the History of the Latino Church*, ed. David Cortés-Fuentes and Daniel R. Rodríguez-Díaz (Decatur, GA: AETH, 1994); Paul Barton, "*Ya Basta!* Latino Protestant Activism in the Chicano/a Farm Workers Movement," in *Latino Religions and Civic Activism in the United States*, ed. Gastón Espinosa, Virgilio Elizondo, and Jesse Miranda (New York: Oxford University Press, 2005); Richard Martínez, *PADRES: The National Chicano Priest Movement* (Austin: University of Texas Press, 2005); Lara Medina, *Las Hermanas: Chicana/Latina Religious-Political Activism in the US Catholic Church* (Philadelphia: Temple University Press, 2005); Alan J. Watt, *Farm Workers and the Churches: The Movement in California and Texas* (College Station: Texas A&M University Press, 2010); Luis D. León, *The Political Spirituality of César Chávez: Crossing Religious Borders* (Berkeley: University of California Press, 2014); Felipe Hinojosa, *Latino Mennonites: Civil Rights, Faith, and Evangelical Culture* (Baltimore: Johns Hopkins University Press, 2014); Arlene M. Sánchez-Walsh, "Emma Tenayuca, Religious Elites, and the 1938 Pecan-Shellers' Strike," in *The Pew and the Picket Line: Christianity and the American Working-Class*, ed. Christopher D. Cantwell, Heath W. Carter, and Janine Giordano-Drake (Urbana: University of Illinois Press, 2016); Mario T. García, *Father Luis Olivares, a Biography: Faith Politics and the Origins of the Sanctuary Movement in Los Angeles* (Chapel Hill: University of North Carolina Press, 2018).

12 But this renewed commitment to interracial justice, migrant ministries, and educational programs was matched by an equally powerful revivalist fervor that gave rise to large and well-funded missionary organizations. Darren Dochuk, *From Bible-Belt to Sunbelt: Plain-Folk Religion, Grassroots Politics, and the Rise of Evangelical Conservatism* (New York: Norton, 2012); David L. Chappell, *A Stone of Hope: Prophetic Religion and the Death of Jim Crow* (Chapel Hill: University of North Carolina Press, 2004), 87.

13 Timothy Matovina, *Latino Catholicism: Transformation in America's Largest Church* (Princeton: Princeton University Press, 2012), 49–50; Joseph P. Fitzpatrick, *The Stranger Is Our Own: Reflections on the Journey of Puerto Rican Migrants* (Kansas City: Sheed and Ward, 1976), 8–9.
14 Miriam Pawel, *The Union of Their Dreams: Power, Hope, and Struggle in Cesar Chavez's Farm Worker Movement* (New York: Bloomsbury, 2009), 11.
15 Ronald A. Wells, "Cesar Chavez's Protestant Allies: The California Migrant Ministry and the Farm Workers," *Journal of Presbyterian History* 86 (Spring/Summer 2009): 11.
16 Pawel, *Union of Their Dreams*, 12.
17 Pawel, *Union of Their Dreams*, 11.
18 Chris Hartmire, interview with author, digital recording, Claremont, CA, February 12, 2014; "The Delano Grape Strike," *California Harvester*, Fall 1965, Box 1, File 6, Collection: National Farm Worker Ministry, Walter P. Reuther Archives, Detroit, MI (hereafter WPR Archives). For more on Chávez's spirituality, see León, *Political Spirituality of César Chávez*; Mario T. García, *The Gospel of César Chávez: My Faith in Action* (New York: Sheed and Ward, 2007); and Nora O. Lozano, "Faithful in the Struggle: A Historical Perspective on Hispanic Protestant Women in the United States," in *Los Evangélicos: Portraits of Hispanic Protestantism*, ed. Juan Martínez and Lindy Scott (Eugene, OR: Wipf and Stock, 2009).
19 Wayne C. Hartmire, "The Church and the Emerging Farm Worker Movement: A Case Study," July 22, 1967, Box 10, File 13, p. 34, Collection: National Farm Worker Ministry, WPR Archives; Rev. J. R. Jennings, "Letter from First Presbyterian Church," January 26, 1966, Box 11, File 3, Collection: National Farm Worker Ministry, WPR Archives; "Statement of the Delano Ministerial Association," October 1965, Box 11, File 3, Collection: National Farm Worker Ministry, WPR Archives.
20 Hartmire, "Church and the Emerging Farm Worker Movement."
21 Hartmire, "Church and the Emerging Farm Worker Movement"; "To the Clergy of the San Joaquin Valley," March 15, 1966, Box 11, File 7, Collection: National Farm Worker Ministry, WPR Archives; Barton, "*Ya Basta!* Latino Protestant Activism," 128.
22 "Some Tentative Thoughts about the Present and Future," May 20–21, 1966, Box 2, File 4; "Summer Program Capsules," *California Harvester*, Fall 1962, Box 1, File 6, Collection: National Farm Worker Ministry, WPR Archives; Virgilio Elizondo, "A Theological Interpretation of the Mexican American Experience," Box F068, File: Comite Sesion de CHE 1974, San Antonio, TX, HAI.
23 "Servanthood to the Movement," *California Migrant Ministry Newsletter* 1, no. 1 (June 1968), Box 1, File 7, Collection: National Farm Worker Ministry, WPR Archives.
24 Hartmire, "Church and the Emerging Farm Worker Movement," 26.
25 Barton, "*Ya Basta!* Latino Protestant Activism," 131.
26 Ruben Armendáriz, oral history interview with R. Douglas Brackenridge, April 19, 1975, Austin, TX, Tape 509, Presbyterian Historical Society, Philadelphia.

27 Barton, "*Ya Basta!* Latino Protestant Activism," 134.
28 The institute emerged out of a partnership between the Presbyterian Church US and the Presbyterian Church USA. Jorge Lara-Braud, "Our Spanish-American Neighbors," *Christian Century* 85 (1968): 43–45.
29 "The Church's Partnership with Mexican Americans," in the Reports of the 114th Session (May 20–22, 1969), 61, Synod of Texas (PCUS) Collection, 1851–1972, 1995–1998, Austin Presbyterian Theological Seminary. See also Brice Alfred Bongiovanni, "Mainline Protestants, *La Raza* Protestors: Jorge Lara-Braud and the Hispanic-American Institute, 1965–1969" (MA thesis, University of Texas at Austin, 2018).
30 Félix Gutiérrez, "The Western Jurisdiction," in *Each Their Own Tongue*, ed. Justo González (Nashville: Abingdon, 1991), 82.
31 Martínez, *PADRES*; Medina, *Las Hermanas*.
32 This was something that I suspect even Hartmire understood. In his notes and writings, Hartmire often entertained the idea that the urban crises and anti-war sentiment might finally awaken larger numbers of religious leaders. Wayne C. Hartmire, "Goals for California Migrant Ministry, Priorities," Box 2, File 11, Collection: National Farm Worker Ministry; "Director's Report to the Commission on the California Migrant Ministry," September 29–30, 1967, Box 2, File 4, Collection: National Farm Worker Ministry, WPR Archives.
33 "Community Seizes McCormick Building," *FRED: The Socialist Press Service* 1, no. 14 (May 19, 1969): 2, private archive, Prof. Ken Sawyer, McCormick Theological Seminary, Chicago.
34 A month after occupying McCormick Seminary, the Young Lords took over the Armitage Methodist Church.
35 "Challenge and Response."
36 For more on these occupations and disruptions, see Felipe Hinojosa, *Apostles of Change: Latino Radical Politics, Church Occupations, and the Fight to Save the Barrio* (Austin: University of Texas Press, 2021).
37 Hinojosa, *Apostles of Change*, 5.
38 Medina, *Las Hermanas*, 102.
39 Jorge Lara-Braud, "A Hispanic-American Speaks to the National Council of Churches," National Council Churches, Triennial Assembly, Detroit, December 2, 1969, HAI, Box F098, Austin Presbyterian Theological Seminary, Austin, TX.
40 Barton, "¡*Ya Basta!* Latino Protestant Activism," 128.
41 García, *Father Luis Olivares*, 184.
42 García, *Father Luis Olivares*, 197.
43 García, *Father Luis Olivares*, 205.
44 Lydia López, interview with author, Alhambra, CA, July 4, 2018.
45 "Lydia López to Lead UNO," *Eastside Los Angeles Tribune*, April 8, 1981.
46 Robert Knowles, "East LA Group Takes RTD Chief for a Ride—with Mixed Results," *Los Angeles Herald Examiner*, November 13, 1983; "Lydia López to Lead UNO."

47. Frank del Olmo, "Latino Activists from UNO Turn Backs on Ballot Box," *Los Angeles Times*, July 27, 1980.
48. Elizabeth Ríos, "The Ladies Are Warriors: Latina Pentecostalism and Faith-Based Activism in New York City," in Espinosa, Elizondo, and Miranda, *Latino Religions and Civic Activism*, 208–9.
49. David Vidal, "Hispanic Protestant Church Group Forges New Role," *New York Times*, August 2, 1976.
50. George Dugan, "Lower East Side Churches Mobilize against Vandalism and Fires," *New York Times*, October 31, 1976.
51. Vidal, "Hispanic Protestant Church Group."
52. Vidal, "Hispanic Protestant Church Group."
53. UNO and COPS especially remained on the forefront of what would come to be known as the sanctuary movement. For more on this, see García, *Father Luis Olivares*.
54. Gastón Espinosa, *Latino Pentecostals in America: Faith and Politics in Action* (Cambridge: Harvard University Press, 2014), 343.
55. Gastón Espinosa, "'Today We Act, Tomorrow We Vote': Latino Religions, Politics, and Activism in Contemporary US Civil Society," *ANNALS of the American Academy of Political and Social Science* 612, no. 1 (July 2007): 152–171.
56. David R. Swartz, "Global Encounters and the Evangelical Left," in *The Religious Left in Modern America: Doorkeepers of a Radical Faith*, ed. Leilah Danielson et al. (London: Palgrave Macmillan, 2018), 288.
57. For more on the rise of Pentecostalism since the 1980s, see Arlene M. Sánchez-Walsh, *Latino Pentecostal Identity: Evangelical Faith, Self, and Society* (New York: Columbia University Press, 2003); Espinosa, *Latino Pentecostals*; and Tony Tian-Ren Lin, *Prosperity Gospel Latinos and Their American Dream* (Chapel Hill: University of North Carolina Press, 2020).
58. Vidal, "Hispanic Protestant Church Group."
59. Jennifer Medina, "Latino, Evangelical and Politically Homeless," *New York Times*, October 11, 2020.
60. Natalie Jackson, "Religion Divides Hispanic Opinion in the US," Public Religion Research Institute (PRRI), November 17, 2020, www.prri.org.
61. Granados, "Notes from the UPUSA General Assembly."

8

The Legacy of Las Hermanas for Latina/o Religious Politics in the Twenty-First Century

LARA MEDINA

> I saw in many of us that the word power caused fear . . . because we have always associated it with oppression, violence and absolute control . . . that many of us have experienced since we were little. But with Las Hermanas, we learned that power is something very good in us if we know how to use it. . . . We also saw that we use our power without even knowing it.[1]

These words, spoken by a participant at the 1989 Las Hermanas conference, reveal the impact that the organization had on the agency and self-empowerment of grassroots Latinas. This conference, taking place eighteen years after the formation of the organization, brought together many women who were away from their families for the first time. Sharing stories of abuse due to the actions of priests, bosses, husbands, children, and the government shaped the discourse of the conference as the women examined their understanding of power. But as Sister Rosa Martha Zárate pointed out, "These women also shared experiences of resistance, of struggle, of liberation. This was an assembly of hope!"[2] Another participant remarked, "Together we have the ability to plan and act—therefore WE HAVE POWER."[3] This process of consciousness-raising through self-reflection and dialogue that began in 1971 when Las Hermanas first organized continued to facilitate a transformative process for its members, leading them into the political struggles of their time.

Las Hermanas, a national organization of religious and laity active for forty-five years (1971–2016), offers us a legacy of Latina spiritual political activism that bridged their Catholic Christian faith, justice, and social change. In their words, "Living one's faith, means living one's politics." From its inception in 1971, when fifty religious women gathered in Houston, Texas, to discuss and pray about the implications of the Chicano movement for the Catholic Church, they agreed to act as agents of change in their respective religious congregations and to transform religious life to be intimately connected to the secular struggles of their ethnic communities. Through their subsequent direct involvement in the farm labor movement and in the Chicano movement, including the emergence of Chicana feminism, Las Hermanas expanded their ministerial role in the US Roman Catholic Church as they bridged the movement for civil rights with the spiritual needs and concerns of grassroots Mexican American and Latina/o communities. While the co-founders and majority of the members identified as Mexican American and Chicana, they were quickly joined by Puerto Rican, Cuban American, and South American sisters and eventually laywomen.

Las Hermanas organized during a time of intense social upheaval in the church and in the world. Ethnic movements for civil rights in the United States, feminist movements, anti–Vietnam War protests, gay and lesbian activism, the modernization of the Catholic Church mandated by Vatican II, and the emergence of Latin American liberation theology contributed to a milieu of social unrest and radical transformation. To fully engage with the legacy of Las Hermanas today, I believe that as a historian I must consider their historical context with particular attention to Vatican II, Latin American theology, and the Chicano movement. After a brief discussion of these three arenas of great change and influence on Las Hermanas, this chapter will link the historical context with the context of the church and social issues impacting the lives of Latinos and Latinas today as a way to discern what Las Hermanas can teach us about the potential of religious political action today.

Vatican II

The modernization of the Roman Catholic Church under Vatican II, convening in Rome from 1962 to 1965, provided the institutional context and gave "permission" to religious leaders to engage with the concerns of the world. The cries for self-determination among colonized peoples, protests for workers' economic rights, and the struggle for women's equality were singled out as significant pressures requiring attention.[4]

The papal mandate for the church to respond to the "signs of the times" encouraged an unprecedented involvement of religious leaders, both men and women, in social and political affairs. The council's emphasis on culture as a mode of divine presence opened the door to culturally specific ministries, including the use of vernacular languages for liturgical use.

The council produced sixteen documents providing direction to religious leaders and laity, endorsing collegiality among clerics and laity, ecumenism, regional and local diversity, scriptural reflection by the laity, and a recommitment to the social mission of the church.[5] The longest document, *Gaudium et spes: The Church in the Modern World*, declared social justice activity a primary way of fulfilling the mission of the church. As a synthesis of Catholic social teaching, the document declared that the church could no longer remain indifferent to the world and its changes. Such a profound shift in the agenda of the institutional church required a radical adjustment of perspective and behavior between the Catholic faithful and their ministers.[6] According to Las Hermanas member Sister Theresa Basso,

> We questioned our vows. What did obedience, poverty, and chastity mean? Poverty was not just a style of living, but what were we doing to critically look around us at the middle class [life] we lived. We were challenged to look at the real poverty in the world. We were attempting something different.[7]

And Sister Yolanda Tarango adds, "It was an exciting time as it was the beginning of designing what religious life was to be.... There was much social and religious upheaval."[8]

Divisions among the 2,700 ethnically diverse bishops present at the council reflected the ideological differences among its leaders. Conservatives maintained that the weakening of ecclesial authority stemmed from increased secularization, a decrease in faith, and a lessening of respect for clerical authority. Progressives were committed to reform "because the Church was too hierarchical, too impersonal, and too detached from modernity. Service to all humankind should be the church's first priority."[9] Such divergent positions appeared in the final document, *Gaudium et spes*. For example, article 9 emphasizes the mission of the church to accompany humanity as it seeks "to establish a political, social, and economic order . . . which will help individuals as well as groups to affirm and develop the dignity proper to them."[10] In sharp contrast, article 42 states that the church has "no proper mission in the political, economic, or social order. The purpose which Christ set before [the church] is a religious one."[11] Such inconsistencies would serve to support politically divergent interpretations in the years ahead.

Latin American Liberation Theology

The Vatican Council's call for religious leaders to critically examine their ministries in the world challenged bishops of Latin America to examine the role of the church in their specific social contexts. For many of them, the church could no longer maintain close ties with military dictatorships or governments enriched by capitalist greed. The Western European and North American worldview of the council envisioned capitalist development as the solution to economic injustices in "underdeveloped" countries. It failed to discuss institutionalized capitalist systems of oppression that keep the majority of the world's population living in extreme poverty.[12] Three years after the close of Vatican II, Latin American bishops convened in Medellín, Colombia, to further discern the role of the church in the midst of the brutal reality of poverty for the rural and urban masses, and the growing military-backed dictatorships. Documents produced at this historic meeting of the Latin American Conference of Bishops (CELAM—Congreso Episcopal Latinoamericano) called for structural change of oppressive social institutions and a new consciousness of liberation. Liberation meant the poor acting as agents of social transformation or subjects of their own history. Justice would prevail only as a result of the liberation struggle of the people themselves. The faces of the poor became the face of God. A faithful Christian life now required "critical reflective action" resulting in solidarity with the poor in seeking justice.[13] A second CELAM conference was convened in 1979 in Puebla, Mexico, to champion and affirm further the theology expressed at Medellín and to "affirm the need for conversion on the part of the whole church to a preferential option for the poor, an option aimed at their integral liberation."[14]

This momentum for such radical change in the Latin American church had begun at least a decade prior to Vatican II with the National Council of Brazilian Bishops (CNBB—Conferenci a Nacional Episcopal Brazileño), formed in 1952 under the leadership of Archbishop Dom Helder Cámara. The CNBB supported the Movement for Grassroots Education (MEB—Movimiento para Educación de Base) in the development of literacy circles that brought the poor together to analyze the region's poverty and illiteracy. Literacy tools included the Bible and Paulo Freire's consciousness-raising techniques, a process by which people become aware of their rights and responsibilities.[15] These literacy circles became the seeds of the movement for Christian base communities or *comunidades eclesiales de base*.[16] Thus, the presence of a broad disposition to change in Latin American Catholicism predated the encyclicals of Vatican II.[17]

Although Latin American liberation theology was later critiqued by many scholars for its silence about women and gender oppression, this theology had a tremendous impact on Christian theology and Christian praxis worldwide. The 1960s witnessed twenty thousand American sisters alone training and working in Latin America.[18] Members of Las Hermanas were among those studying with Latin American theologians and ministering among the poor. According to Las Hermanas member Sister Carmelita Espinoza,

> We chose [to study] in Quito, Ecuador, because they were training ministers at the Pastoral Institute of Latin America. We had been in white institutions for so long that we really wanted a different exposure. It was clear that the laity had to be empowered and that Western theology was so limiting.[19]

And Sister María de Jesús Ybarra adds, "One of the things I learned [in Latin America] was that the church is not the end but the means to help our people."[20] For Sister Ada María Isasi-Díaz, her experience of working and studying among the poor in Peru in the 1960s and her collaboration with Las Hermanas in the 1970s became the source of her theology later articulated in the United States as mujerista theology, a theology privileging the daily lived experiences of Latinas, "lo cotidiano," as they struggle to survive.[21]

The Chicano Movement

The third arena of influence, the Chicano movement for civil rights, provided the momentum for Mexican American sisters to come into their own political consciousness as Chicana religious women. Spurred by the Black civil rights movement, the farm labor movement led by César Chávez and Dolores Huerta, Chicano student mobilization in the Southwest, national anti–Vietnam War protests, and the challenges of Chicana feminism, members of Las Hermanas were compelled to quickly focus their energies on self-reflection and calling the church to accountability. Chávez's open criticism of the church for its lack of involvement in the farm labor movement conveyed the alienation and anger toward the church that many Chicana/o activists felt.[22] As students strove for self-determination and educational equity, they openly rebelled against the church's lack of financial and political support and its discriminatory practices toward Mexican Americans.[23] Despite the estranged relationship, Chávez, a devout Catholic, understood the power of the church and challenged Chicana/o activists not to ignore it. In 1968 he stated at the Second Annual Mexican-American Conference in Sacramento,

> THERE IS TREMENDOUS SPIRITUAL AND ECONOMIC POWER IN THE CHURCH.... I am calling for Mexican American groups to stop ignoring this source of power. It is not just our right to appeal to the Church to use its power effectively for the poor, it is our duty to do so. It should be as natural as appealing to the government.[24]

Chávez's plea not only challenged the hierarchy of the church but also served to inspire new directions of ministry for Chicana sisters and Chicano priests previously denied the opportunity to work within their ethnic communities. As for many Chicano youth of the 1960s and 1970s, the farmworkers' struggle provided the impetus "for their first experiences of militancy."[25]

Gaining support for boycotts within religious communities was not an easy task for Chicana sisters, as most often their white peers were the daughters of the farm owners. Sister Irene Muñoz shares, "When it came time to boycott lettuce, the sisters said to us, 'Why are you creating so much ruckus, who do you think you are?' It was painful. We were part of the community but not really part of it."[26]

Student activism in Texas involving "walkouts" was the catalyst for two Chicana sisters to join forces and mobilize Mexican American sisters across the nation. Ministering in Abilene, West Texas, Sister Gregoria Ortega experienced the harsh realities of what she described as "Bible Belt country.... They had a real hatred for Mexicans and Catholics. Mexicans had been lynched there."[27] During the several months of her support for the walkouts of Chicano students at Abilene High in protest of blatant discriminatory practices, Ortega's life was threatened by townspeople and she was ultimately expelled from the diocese. Refused a hearing with the bishop and demeaned in the pulpit by the local priest, Ortega felt she "was put on trial, found guilty, and I was not even present!"[28] Following a respite in New Mexico, where she took summer classes in Mexican American studies at the University of New Mexico, Ortega returned to Texas, but this time to San Antonio. There she conferred with an old friend and co-organizer of PADRES, Father Edmundo Rodriguez, who supported her idea to organize Chicana sisters. He encouraged her to meet Sister Gloria Gallardo, a community organizer in Houston. Gallardo responded enthusiastically to the idea and asked, "How can we work together?" Over the next several months, while living on Gallardo's meager salary and participating in more school walkouts and community actions in Houston, Ortega and Gallardo developed their vision for an organization of Mexican American sisters transforming the church to become supportive of Chicanos.

Their initial efforts involved contacting bishops throughout the country asking for the names of Mexican American sisters. Most of the bishops refused to cooperate, reflecting an institutional disregard for the concerns of Mexican American Catholics. Subsequently, they contacted the mother superiors in charge of various religious communities, which resulted in the gathering of fifty religious women representing eight states and twenty religious congregations. Among the women were Mexican American, Chicana, Puerto Rican, Mexican, and Euroamerican sisters, the latter of whom had been working in Spanish-speaking communities. Meeting for three days in Houston in April 1971 proved to be, according to Gloria Gallardo, "a rebirth for all of us!" After two days of sharing their experiences of pain and exclusion as brown women in religious life, they witnessed how the personal is political *and* communal, a central characteristic of Chicana feminist thought. Understanding their potential to effect change by belonging to religious communities that were power bases, they quickly identified their individual and collective purpose: "to enable each other to work more effectively with the Spanish-speaking people of God in bringing about social justice and a truly Christian peace."[29]

Critical self-reflection as Chicanas/Latinas was their first step. How could their bicultural identities empower their work in the church? Their initial hierarchical model of leadership with a president, vice-president, and treasurer soon gave way to a model of a shared leadership team with regional coordinators. This decision enabled the organization to do widespread outreach and attract more members early on. Within six months of this outreach, membership grew to nine hundred, with two hundred sisters attending the second gathering eight months following the first meeting. They united under the motto "Unidas en Acción y Oración!" and chose the organizational name Las Hermanas, a "term . . . which demands a certain identity with, and sharing of the total self with the whole of humanity."[30] Four goals focused their energies for the challenges ahead: (1) activate leadership among themselves and the Spanish-speaking laity; (2) effect social change; (3) contribute to the cultural renaissance of La Raza; and (4) educate Anglo-dominant congregations on the needs of Spanish-speaking communities. Coordinators organized state conferences in California, Texas, and Colorado extending the outreach, and Gallardo addressed the national Conference of Major Superiors of Women Religious, who offered their support.

A deep concern for self-examination as "Chicana religious women" permeates the documents from this early period of the organization. As stated at their second conference in late 1971, "The Church must be made aware of and helped to understand the Chicano movement. It is about time they listened and began to be tutored by the few they have educated."[31] Furthermore, "The mission of the Church is to not only perceive the truth, but to do the truth. . . . How is our role in the Church to be lived out? We must consider our own fields of competence, our cultural heritage. . . . In other words, we must decide where we could best serve as Chicana religious women."[32] Lacking leadership skills did not stop their momentum to hold the church accountable to engage with the issues of social injustice. "We didn't have all the skills but we covered every meeting we could, voiced every position, shared with each other where we should be. . . . We learned as we went."[33]

Despite their decision to remain financially independent from the church and "operating on a shoestring," Las Hermanas became central to the struggle along with PADRES for the appointment of the first three Chicano bishops and the establishment of a national Secretariat of the Spanish Speaking based in Washington, DC. They co-founded the first national pastoral training center for ministry to the Spanish-speaking, the Mexican American Cultural Center in San Antonio, Texas, where they designed and taught the first courses on cultural sensitivity and Spanish language acquisition to white seminarians. Between 1972 and 1974, Las Hermanas targeted the issue of the lack of Latina/o leadership in the church. In 1972 the national coordinators of Las Hermanas initiated Proyecto Mexico, a two-year project challenging exploitative employment practices against Mexican sisters in the United States by church-related institutions. Finding out that sisters from Mexico were providing domestic work in seminaries and rectories heightened their resolve to make the church accountable to its ministerial responsibilities. Las Hermanas began fundraising for scholarships to help the domestic-bound sisters. Some of the sisters from Mexico had already been trained as nurses or teachers but were relegated to service work in the United States in order to help support their congregations. Ultimately, Proyecto Mexico assisted only four sisters, yet in the process Las Hermanas educated their own religious congregations on racism, women, and justice in the church. The project also initiated Las Hermanas' long-term commitment to raise scholarship funds for Latinas in need of assistance for education, with laywomen receiving the majority of aid well into the 1980s.

In 1974 they conducted a parish national survey by borrowing vehicles and driving cross-country to assess the deplorable lack of ministry programs for Spanish-speaking Catholics. Their findings revealed a general ignorance about Latino Catholics on the part of bishops nationwide. In 1972 and 1977 Las Hermanas joined forces with PADRES and convened the first two national Hispanic Pastoral Encuentros, marking the first time ever that Latino laity met to discern and articulate their needs to the hierarchy of the US Catholic Church. These encuentros resulted in the US Catholic Conference of Bishops approving a 1983 pastoral letter, *The Hispanic Presence: Challenge and Commitment*, and calling for a third encuentro and the writing of a national pastoral plan for Latino ministry.[34]

As Las Hermanas worked for reform in the church, they refused to be the subordinate members of a movement for change. From the beginning, their emphasis on shared power in the pulpit, around the conference table, and in community centers, along with their commitment to the empowerment of grassroots Latinas, resulted in confronting the same obstacles and challenges faced by secular Chicana feminists. Unfortunately, by 1973, relations with PADRES were seriously strained and by 1979, Las Hermanas had been officially removed from the board of MACC, an organization they helped to establish. Furthermore, individual sisters faced harassment in their ministries from church officials as their popularity and accomplishments in community service often exceeded those of local priests and bishops. Sister Rosa Martha Zárate in the Diocese of San Bernardino and Sister Sara Murrieta in the Diocese of San Diego offer two harsh examples.[35] Both women had used the principles of liberation theology in their community organizing. Thus, by 1985, Las Hermanas believed that their interests would be served best by focusing primarily on the needs of grassroots Latinas facing issues of domestic violence; being single heads of households; dealing with unequal wages, restrictive reproductive rights, and subordinate roles in the church; and lacking in self-confidence and self-determination. A renewed agenda involved confronting "the patriarchy par excellence" at the 1985 US Catholic Conference of Bishops in Washington, DC, during public hearings on the status of women in the church. Las Hermanas understood that it would take women to continually pressure the church to transform its unjust doctrines and patriarchal structure. Las Hermanas representatives confronted a committee of six bishops and eight women consultants by beginning with a quote from Monsignor Oscar Romero: "I am the voice of the voiceless." Each representative then took a turn describing the realities of Latinas, including single motherhood, the alienation of divorced women in the church, domestic violence, lack of sexual education, loss of children to drugs, and overall lack of pastoral counseling. They assured the bishops that Latinas would not be silenced.[36] When asked "Why are you in the church?," they replied, "We stay to fight!" Over the next several months, Catholic women across the country criticized the bishops, who ultimately abandoned their intent to write a pastoral letter about and for women.[37]

That same year, the bishops convened the III Encuentro. Las Hermanas opposed the meeting, as the recommendations from the first two encuentros had yet to be implemented, and some members criticized an encuentro "under the watchful eyes of dozens of US bishops"[38] that would diminish the voices of grassroots communities. Rather than boycott the encuentro, Las Hermanas decided to mobilize grassroots Latinas who would participate in the encuentro. At regional meetings prior to the encuentro, Las Hermanas solicited the opinions of Latina Catholics across the United States on issues impacting their lives: domestic violence, dual wage systems, sexual abuse, poverty, and exclusion from the priesthood. By the time of the encuentro, Latina laity were prepared to give voice to their concrete realities at the III Hispanic National Encuentro that would set the agenda for Latina/o Catholics in the twenty-first century. Most unfortunately, their efforts proved tremendously disappointing when a majority vote approved by hundreds of encuentro participants from across the country supporting women at all levels of ministry in the church was silenced by encuentro facilitators.[39] This rejection of support for even the possibility of women's ordination deepened Las Hermanas' resolve to focus on the empowerment of Latinas. Following the III Encuentro, regional groups flourished, as did involvement with international women's organizations. By 1986, the organization petitioned the US Catholic Conference of Bishops for a commitment of resources for educational programs on sexuality and sociopolitical realities. They challenged the bishops to denounce domestic violence from the pulpit and to instruct priests "to stop advising women to suffer silently all types of abuse and infidelity ... for the good of their children."[40]

In 1989 a revision to their constitution validated their decision to further advocate specifically for the rights of Latinas. After fifteen years of pushing for institutional reform, they faced the painful reality of "the indifference of the Church towards women." They committed to organizing biennial conferences for Latinas, many of whom had never been away from their domestic roles. Conference themes focused on issues not discussed in the church, such as sexuality, reproductive rights, domestic violence, and power. Women-centered rituals held at the conferences provided a counter-discourse and counter-experience to the male-centered liturgies of the church. By 1987, a theology emerged from Las Hermanas, later named mujerista theology, with its central focus being a God who emerges from the daily lived experiences of Latinas, rather than from the studies of male clergy at elite theological institutions.[41] Mujerista theology has impacted the theology of hundreds of Latina/o theologians and feminist theologies today.

In 1990 Las Hermanas articulated a "spirituality of transformative struggle" whereby embracing struggle in a transformative manner rather than in a passive victim mode is life-giving. As Yolanda Tarango stated,

> The transformation of [struggle] is critical for the liberation of Hispanic women . . . for assuming control over ones' life. . . . *La vida es la lucha*, implies the struggle we must embrace and learn to love in order to survive in the present and envision life with dignity in the future.[42]

A deep faith in a divine presence that desires justice for women and *el pueblo* supported their transformative spirituality.

In 1998 the organization was determined to move into the future with a younger generation leading the way. Several conferences were held, but by 2015 it became apparent that the critical mass of younger Latina Catholics willing to take up the banner of pushing and transcending the patriarchal boundaries of the church would not happen. A conference held in 2015 at the University of the Incarnate Word brought together leaders of the organization, scholars, and community members with the idea of reinvigorating the organization. Speakers addressed issues ranging from immigration reform to religious-political activism, moral agency, sex trafficking, sexual abuse, and climate change. Presenters honored the history and legacy of the tremendous work accomplished and the need for the next phase of growth with a new generation. Unfortunately, the next generation of Las Hermanas did not emerge. The time, resources, and staffing to continue biennial conferences and regional meetings could not be met without the leadership of a younger generation. Yet the legacy of Las Hermanas lives on and is well documented to inspire and teach those religious activists organizing today.[43] Across the board, the lives of women who participated in Las Hermanas were radically changed.

In reflecting on what this legacy can teach religious political movements today, I am struck by the current era of change in the church begun in 2013 under the papacy of Pope Francis. As Allan Figueroa Deck, SJ, writes in the introduction to his book *Francis, Bishop of Rome: The Gospel for the Third Millennium*,

> In a remarkably short time, his [Francis's] words, gestures, and executive actions have set in motion a transformation of both the papacy itself as well as the world wide Roman Catholic Church.... and he gives evidence of maintaining, if not accelerating, the pace of what some analysts have called his radical reforms.... Pope Francis is wrestling with nothing less than "epochal change."... Papa Bergoglio means business and, as many Catholics have intuitively observed, the Holy Spirit is behind this surprising springtime, the stunning renewal of and recommitment to the spirit of the Second Vatican Council.[44]

This spirited enthusiasm would be supported by Pope Francis's consistent pastoral approach and concern for the poor, his initial choices to shun ostentation in his personal housing and in papal ceremonies, his early statements supporting the dignity of nonbinary persons, and importantly, his own early formation and participation in the production and application of Latin American theology in his home country, Argentina.[45] Seven years into his papacy further demonstrates his efforts to reform the church and renew the meaning of a Christian life. As stated in his first Apostolic Exhortation, *Evangelii Gaudium* (The Joy of the Gospel, 2013),

> None of us can think we are exempt from concern for the poor and for social justice: "Spiritual conversion, the intensity of the love of God and neighbor, zeal for justice and peace, the Gospel meaning of the poor and of poverty, are required of everyone." (#201)

Further on in the document,

> It is essential to draw near to new forms of poverty and vulnerability, in which we are called to recognize the suffering Christ, even if this appears to bring us no tangible and immediate benefits. I think of the

homeless, the addicted, refugees, indigenous peoples, the elderly who are increasingly isolated and abandoned, and many others. Migrants present a particular challenge for me, since I am a pastor of a Church without frontiers, a Church which considers herself mother to all. For this reason, I exhort all countries to a generous openness. (#210)

And later in the 2019 exhortation, *Christus vivit*, directed to young Catholics, he offers an invitation for the youth of the church to advise church leaders on matters of social concern and become involved in the world as a requirement of their faith. And in November 2019, the request of the Synod of Bishops for the Amazon that the church define "ecological sin as an act of commission or omission against God, against one's neighbor, the community and the environment" resulted in the pope strongly considering adding "ecological sin" to the Catechism of the Catholic Church.[46]

Unfortunately, these signs of change are greatly diminished by the pope's disappointingly measured efforts to cleanse the church of sexual abuse by clergy,[47] and his refusal to consider the topic of women's ordination.[48] However, in April 2015, two years after his election in 2013, he did put an end to the surveillance of the Leadership Conference of Women Religious (LCRW) begun under Pope Benedict XVI in April 2012.[49] Originally, the investigation of LCRW was given up to a five-year period.[50] However, his most recent dismissal of the proposal from Amazonian bishops to approve women as deacons and ordain married Indigenous Amazonian men in order to address the shortage of priests in the Amazon show that Pope Francis is pulling back on his pastoral vision of drawing near to the Indigenous and the marginalized. Although he seems to have bent to ultra-conservative forces in the hierarchy, which is of grave concern to forward-thinking Catholics, it is predicted, or at least hoped for by Latin American theologian Rafael Luciani of Venezuela, that specific language in his 2020 exhortation, *Querida Amazonia*, indicates the pope's ongoing openness to a regional ecclesial body "among the local churches of various South American countries in the Amazon basin" and that "the journey continues" to be guided by the capacity of the local churches to continue to raise these issues based on their regional needs, including the issue of a diaconate of women. Luciani states, "This is now in the hands of local bishops and the Latin

American regional church, whose task it is now to take a prophetic and creative step in this regard. . . . *Querida Amazonia* must be read from the new hermeneutic (of a local ecclesiology) and in the light of the new dawn in the Latin American Church."[51] I hear in Luciani's statements a calling forth of the role that the Latin American church took during the height of Latin American liberation theology, in ushering forth a return of Christianity to its radical roots of solidarity with the poor, and perhaps this time with women.

Nonetheless, I argue that Las Hermanas organized during a similar, yet admittedly a more dramatic time of change in the church, as well as a time of essential political protest in secular society. I believe that religious political movements today can seize on that spirit of openness to change in the church, although at times incredibly slow, as they take on local and global issues and challenge the institutional church to apply its symbolic and moral authority to the issues of injustice today, such as disastrous climate change, immigrant rights, LGBTQI rights, femicide, reproductive rights, homelessness, poverty, sex trafficking . . . the list goes on. The draconian decisions made under President Donald Trump provide the context for increased levels of political activism. According to Kathy O'Leary, regional coordinator of Pax Christi New Jersey, who has been an immigrant rights activist for twenty years and who is involved in current Catholic activist coalitions, "The groundswell of grassroots support for immigration reform wasn't around a few years ago. But everything changed after the election of Donald Trump."[52]

Catholic activists today, such as the Latinx Catholic Leadership Coalition, consisting of scholars, theologians, ministers, and community organizers, joined forces in October 2019 with the DC Catholic Coalition to protest the separation of immigrant families and detention of children at the border. The protest was held at the US-Mexico border in El Paso, Texas, and brought together various groups of Catholic activists previously protesting in their separate regions. According to Eli McCarthy, professor and director of justice and peace for the Conference of Major Superiors of Men, the coming together "created a space where they could feel more connected and share the work they were doing."[53] At the action, "ten Catholic leaders from various coalitions accompanied fifteen Mexican asylum seekers as they presented themselves for asylum."[54] Coalitions such as these carry on the courageous and collaborative spirit of Las Hermanas, and likewise are challenged by the lack of action on the part of the US Catholic Conference of Bishops. But as the legacy of Las Hermanas shows, the activism can and must continue without the support of the institutional church.

When I recently asked Sister Yolanda Tarango, a core organizer of Las Hermanas, what she believed their legacy could teach us today, her responses targeted the necessity "to stay close to the people." She stated,

> Know the issues first-hand and advocate for them. Las Hermanas gave voice to the realities we were witnessing. Being immersed in the reality strengthened our passion and courage to speak and act for change. The prophet is not the one who predicts the future, but the one who listens and finds words for what others see. The window Pope Francis opened in his early papacy let in a breeze of hope but the fresh air was short-lived. . . . However, Las Hermanas usually acted from the sidelines of the Church while also calling it to accountability.[55]

Historian Timothy Matovina, who has also written about Las Hermanas, notes their practical sense of politics.[56] "Las Hermanas had a broad vision for change in the Church yet they had the ability to organize around specific goals and objectives."[57] For example, they addressed the "use" of Mexican women religious for ecclesial-related domestic duties; they changed Eurocentric structures of clerical formation at the Mexican American Cultural Center and for sisters in their own religious orders; they achieved the appointment of Latina sisters to work among their own ethnic communities in need of ministers; they broke down the divide between religious women and laywomen; and they addressed issues vital to the lives of grassroots Latinas.

Theresa Basso, a Las Hermanas core member, also stressed the importance of focusing on local issues by asking those in need, "What do you think needs to be done?" Basso feels that their choice of a team leadership was a distinct characteristic and was instrumental in their success. "The collaborative sense of power that we held and that we were all equal members whether a sister or a laywoman, gave us a lot of strength. We reflected on our role as bicultural Chicanas and our role as women in the church."[58] The arenas of activism that Las Hermanas chose to be involved in dissolved the constructed divide between the sacred and the secular and brought the Chicano movement into the church and the church into the Chicano movement.

The group solidarity of Las Hermanas formed around the methodology of liberation theology, "see, judge, act," or critical, self-reflective action. This theological method offered members a value system different from the individualism found in the Western way of living. For Las Hermanas member Rosa Martha Zárate,

> With Las Hermanas my self-understanding as belonging to a pueblo, a people, became very clear. I understood that el pueblo is the church, not the institution. I learned how to fight for our rights as a pueblo. We began organizing in the barrios, we made a commitment to the barrios and we formed small Christian base communities as in Latin America. We utilized the faith of the people to help them and us analyze their/our social situations. In my work in the inland empire of southern California I organized eighty CEBs. They were very intergenerational, with children, youth, adults and the elderly all attending and discussing. That way the generations heard each other and analyzed their social needs together. Then we would ask, "What does God say, what does scripture say? Then what does the US Constitution say? What does our baptismal commitment say? And finally, what does the history of our people tell us? What did our ancestors do when they faced injustices? If these documents and our history tell us that we have the right to fight for justice, what are we going to do?" From there in small groups each generation would develop a plan of action. This is how we implemented the methodology of see, judge, act. The activism today must be intergenerational. We need cells of people to analyze their local situation and then the larger issues.[59]

Zárate also feels strongly that celebration must be included in community organizing. Her *nueva canción* songs frequently energized the communities gathered as the songs emphasized the challenges being faced and the ability to construct a new reality based on justice.

Las Hermanas' conferences not only included political and personal consciousness raising but also provided members with the opportunity to celebrate their lives and their solidarity. Mujerista liturgies, woman-centered communal rituals held at every biennial conference and regional meetings, provided the "opportunity for as many women as possible to have an active role in sacred rituals in order to counter their exclusion from approaching the altar during worship in their churches."[60] Mujerista liturgies express most visibly Latinas' religious agency as they take control over expressing and symbolizing their own religious understandings through the language, symbols, and ritual actions chosen. This religious agency reflects the cultural, political, and feminist sensibilities of the women. The liturgy created "a counter discourse in response to the words, rituals, and symbols that emanate from the Vatican."[61] For example, an opening prayer mentions "the power of changing oppressive situations, . . . the power of not giving up, . . . the power that is ours because we are women." For songwriter and singer Rosa Martha Zárate, "Song or *canto* is an essential element in any social movement, as song offers a tool to ask: what is the song talking about? *Canto* will enable a *pueblo* to hear its own *palabra*. Song must accompany a *pueblo luchando*."[62]

Las Hermanas offer us a legacy of challenging ecclesial institutions to accompany *el pueblo* in *las luchas por justicia*. Having a broad vision for justice, yet focusing on specific local issues with intergenerational participation, extending collaborative teamwork into regional, national, then global issues while maintaining a spirituality of transformative struggle celebrated through communal ritual and song, are specific lessons we can learn from Las Hermanas, a forty-year-old national organization. As Rosa Martha Zárate states, "We pounded on the doors as they were not opened for us. What we have now is from our struggle. We were very smart women."[63]

NOTES

1 Conference participant Teresa Barajas, "Reflexiones desde San Antonio," *Informes*, December 1989, 2. Author's translation.
2 Rosa Martha Zárate, "Encuentro Nacional de Las Hermanas," *Informes*, December 1989, 3. Author's translation.
3 María Inez Martínez, IHM, "Empowerment, Enablement, Hope," *Informes*, December 1989, 1.
4 Timothy McCarthy, *The Catholic Tradition: Before and after Vatican Council II, 1878–1993* (Chicago: Loyola University Press, 1994), 62–64.
5 McCarthy, *Catholic Tradition*, 67.
6 John O'Malley, *Tradition and Transition: Historical Perspectives on Vatican Council II* (Wilmington: Michael Glazier, 1989), 17.

7   Theresa Basso, interview with author, March 7, 1997. Basso left religious life in the 1980s after twenty-eight years of service.
8   Yolanda Tarango, interview with author, July 1990, San Antonio, TX.
9   McCarthy, *Catholic Tradition*, 67.
10 Walter M. Abbot, SJ, ed., *The Documents of Vatican Council II* (New York: Guild Press, 1966), 206.
11 Abbot, *Documents of Vatican Council II*, 241.
12 Gregory Baum, "Faith and Liberation: Development since Vatican Council II," in *Vatican Council II: Open Questions and New Horizons*, ed. Gerald M. Fagin, SJ (Wilmington: Michael Glazier, 1984), 85–88.
13 Gregory Baum, "Class Struggle and the Magisterium: A New Note," *Theological Studies* 45, no. 4 (1984): 690–92.
14 "Evangelization in Latin America's Present and Future," in *Liberation Theology: A Documentary History*, ed. Alfred T. Hennelly (Maryknoll, NY: Orbis, 1990), 254.
15 Penny Lernoux, *People of God: The Struggle for World Catholicism* (New York: Penguin, 1989), 122–23.
16 Lernoux, *People of God*, 116–21.
17 Daniel Levine, *Popular Voices in Latin American Catholicism* (Princeton: Princeton University Press, 1992).
18 Mary Jo Weaver, *New Catholic Women: A Contemporary Challenge to Traditional Religious Authority* (San Francisco: Harper and Row, 1985), 83.
19 Carmelita Espinoza, telephone interview with author, October 16, 1996.
20 María de Jesús Ybarra, OP, interview with author, April 10, 1997.
21 Ada María Isasi-Díaz, *En la Lucha/In the Struggle: A Hispanic Women's Liberation Theology* (New York: Orbis, 1993); Isasi-Díaz, *Mujerista Theology: A Theology for the Twenty-First Century* (New York: Orbis, 1996). These are just two of Isasi-Díaz's prolific writings.
22 César Chávez, "The Mexican American and the Church," *Quinto Sol Publications* 1, no. 4 (Summer 1968): 9–12.
23 See Mario T. García, *Chicano Liberation Theology: The Writings and Documents of Richard Cruz and Católicos por la Raza* (Dubuque, IA: Kendall Hunt, 2009).
24 Chávez, "The Mexican American," 11–12.
25 Arturo Rosales, *CHICANO! The History of the Mexican American Civil Rights Movement* (Houston: Arte Público, 1996), 147.
26 Irene Muñoz, SHM, interview with author, July 15, 1997.
27 Gregoria Ortega, interview with author, April 21, 1997.
28 Ortega, interview.
29 Gloria Gallardo, SHG, to Leadership Conference of Women Religious, November 17, 1971, Las Hermanas Collection, Box 4, Mexican American Studies Department, Our Lady of the Lake University, San Antonio, TX (hereafter LHC).
30 Carmelita Espinoza and María de Jesús Ybarra, *La Historia de Las Hermanas* (n.p.: privately printed, 1978), 9.

31 Mario Barron, SJC, "Equipos de Concientización," proposal delivered on November 24, 1971, 3, LHC, Box 6.
32 Anonymous, LHC, Box 6.
33 María Iglesias, interview with author, March 2, 1997.
34 National Catholic Conference of Bishops, *The Hispanic Presence: Challenge and Commitment* (Washington, DC: USCC Office of Publishing and Promotion Services, 1983).
35 *Las Hermanas Informes*, January 1986, 4; and May 1986, 2. For a fuller treatment of the harassment experienced by Zárate and Murrieta, see Lara Medina, *Las Hermanas: Chicana/Latina Religious Political Activism in the US Catholic Church* (Philadelphia: Temple University Press, 2004), 110–17.
36 For a fuller description of this meeting, see Medina, *Las Hermanas*, 102–4.
37 "Catholics Speak Out, Reject the Pastoral on Women's Concerns," *National Catholic Reporter*, November 20, 1992, 13; "Why the Pastoral Was Defeated," *National Catholic Reporter*, December 4, 1992, 2–5.
38 "At Encuentro, Vision, Debate Mold Future," *National Catholic Reporter*, August 30, 1985, 1.
39 Medina, *Las Hermanas*, 104–10.
40 "Las Hermanas DE NUEVA YORK," *Informes*, May 1986, 6.
41 Yolanda Tarango and Ada María Isasi-Díaz, *Hispanic Women: Prophetic Voice in the Church* (San Francisco: Harper and Row, 1988).
42 Yolanda Tarango, "La Vida Es la Lucha," *Texas Journal of Ideas, History and Culture* 2 (1990): 11.
43 The history of Las Hermanas is well documented in my book. I attended several of their conferences and interviewed forty of their members and four male clergy who had collaborated with them early on. I witnessed the energy, passion, and commitment to change that I had read about in their primary documents, now archived at the University of the Incarnate Word, San Antonio, TX.
44 Allan Figueroa Deck, SJ, *Francis, Bishop of Rome* (New York: Paulist, 2016), 1–4.
45 See Deck, *Francis*, particularly chaps. 3 and 4.
46 Francis X. Rocca, "Pope Francis Weighs Adding 'Ecological Sin' to Church Teachings," *Wall Street Journal*, November 15, 2019.
47 Emma Greene, "Why Does the Catholic Church Keep Failing on Sexual Abuse?" *Atlantic*, February 14, 2019; "Pope Ends 'Secrecy' Rule on Child Sexual Abuse in Catholic Church," *Guardian*, December 17, 2019.
48 Joshua J. McElwee, "Pope Francis Confirms Finality of Ban on Ordaining Women Priests," *National Catholic Reporter*, November 1, 2016.
49 Joshua J. McElwee, "Vatican Ends Controversial Three-Year Oversight of US Sisters' Leaders," *National Catholic Reporter*, April 16, 2015.
50 Joshua J. McElwee, "Vatican Orders LCRW to Revise, Appoints Archbishop to Oversee Group," *National Catholic Reporter*, April 18, 2012.
51 Rafael Luciani, "Synod Theologian: Francis' Amazon Exhortation Creates a New Moment for Latin America," *National Catholic Reporter*, February 18, 2020.

52 Sarah Salvadore, "Immigration Activists Step Up in Battle against Trump Policies," *National Catholic Reporter*, February 21–March 5, 2020, 10.
53 Salvadore, "Immigration Activists."
54 Salvadore, "Immigration Activists."
55 Sister Yolanda Tarango, email communication with author, February 22, 2020.
56 Timothy M. Matovina, "Representation and the Reconstruction of Power: The Rise of PADRES and LAS HERMANAS," in *What's Left? Liberal American Catholics*, ed. Mary Jo Weaver and R. Scott Appleby (Bloomington: Indiana University Press, 1999), 220–37.
57 Timothy Matovina, email communication with author, January 2020.
58 Theresa Basso, interview with author, February 1, 2020.
59 Rosa Martha Zárate, telephone interview with author, February 26, 2020.
60 Isasi-Díaz, *Mujerista Theology*, 168.
61 Mary Fainsod Katzenstein, "Discursive Politics and Feminist Activism in the Catholic Church," in *Feminist Organizations: Harvest of the New Women's Movement*, ed. Myra Marx Ferree and Patricia Yancey Martin (Philadelphia: Temple University Press, 1995), 48.
62 Zárate, telephone interview.
63 Zárate, telephone interview.

PART III

Immigrant Transformations

9

Political Fellowship and the Sanctuary Movement

Central American Refugees and Practices of Religiopolitical Accompaniment, 1982-1990

SERGIO M. GONZÁLEZ

The Sanctuary Movement is profoundly religious but inevitably political.
—Chicago Religious Task Force on Central America, "Statement of Faith," 1984[1]

On March 24, 1984, the Excot family completed a seven-thousand-mile journey that had begun in the Guatemalan highlands and ended at the Weston Priory Monastery in the Green Mountains of Vermont. Accompanied by a twenty-eight-car caravan of "conductors," Felipe, Elena, and their five children disembarked from a self-styled "freedom train" in the cold northeastern winter and were met by clanging bells, expectant Benedictine monks, and over five hundred supporters. That day the family entered into sanctuary, making the monastery the one hundredth congregation to join the growing transnational faith-based movement in support of Central American asylees.[2]

The Excots, Mam Indians and Catholics, were fleeing persecution in their home country. Felipe, a catechist, had made the trying decision to leave Guatemala after seventeen of his religious coworkers had been assassinated by government forces for the crime of spreading literacy among their countrymen. The family had first made contact with the movement in Guatemala, where a US Maryknoll priest sent the family northward. The priest placed the Excots in the care of church workers in Mexico, who helped transport the family into the waiting arms of border activists in Arizona. With access to political asylum restricted by the US government, the Excots entered the country as undocumented migrants.[3]

The family clandestinely made their way from the borderlands to Chicago. The Windy City became the launching point for what the Chicago Religious Task Force on Central America (CRTF), the coordinating body of the budding sanctuary movement, referred to as the "Romero Refugee Express." Named in honor of the slain Salvadoran archbishop Oscar Romero, who had given his life fighting for his country's poor and disenfranchised, the caravan sped across the country. At each of the eight cities in which the convoy stopped, the Excots and their companions met with members of the local and national media and church supporters. The asylees and their supporters sought to raise the national consciousness of North Americans as well as shine light on the United States' complicity in Central America's violent wars. One "conductor," explaining his coreligionists' obligation to "walk with" the Excots as they sought safe harbor in the United States, told newspaper reporters, "Let this be the first of thousands of confessions. We have willingly and knowingly conspired and confederated to protect refugees from deportation back to their war-torn homelands."[4]

Each of the Excots, except for seven-month-old baby Inez, disembarked from the caravan with their faces shielded by bandanas. As the monks led a ceremony of song and prayer into a repurposed barn large enough to hold the assembled crowd, the family sat at the center of a semicircle, where they recounted in Spanish the atrocities they had suffered at the hands of the Guatemalan government.[5] In opening their monastery to the Excots, the Benedictine monks at Weston believed that they were making a religious and moral declaration. Five monks from the order had visited refugee camps in Mexico the previous year, where they met with Guatemalan refugees.[6] In a prepared statement issued a few days before the Excots' arrival, the brothers proclaimed that they had been inspired by the "Biblical injunction to 'shelter the oppressed and the homeless.'" Before voting to open their doors to the Excots, order leadership had posed the question to their members: "What are we, as Christians and as monks, called to do as our sisters and our brothers are hunted down and deported to certain torture and possible death?"[7]

Throughout the 1980s, hundreds of North American churches and synagogues posed this same question to their congregants. Motivated by a centuries-long tradition of offering safe harbor to those in need, Christian and Jewish communities of faith joined the sanctuary movement in support of the hundreds of thousands of Salvadorans and Guatemalans fleeing repression and death in their home countries. Launched in the US-Mexico borderlands in 1982, the sanctuary movement grew to include hundreds of congregations and thousands of supporters throughout the decade. Central American asylees like the Excots served as the movement's principal agents, risking detention and deportation by sharing their wrenching experiences of violent repression and excruciating migration. Congregations across the country responded to Central Americans' personal stories not only by offering immediate relief of safe harbor but also by mobilizing alongside asylees to shift their country's domestic and foreign policies.

But why would US church members—many of them middle-class, white, and with little previous knowledge of the violence in Central America—align themselves so determinedly, even in the face of legal sanction, with Salvadoran and Guatemalan asylees? In the 1980s a growing segment of Americans began to understand the plight of Latin American migrants like the Excots as fundamentally connected to their faith traditions' histories as people on the move and in search of refuge. Influenced by scriptural exhortations as well as historical precedent to offer safe harbor to those fleeing persecution, sanctuary members transformed the biblical tenet of accompaniment into a form of spiritual fellowship and political camaraderie. Activists, both Central American and US-born, developed a practice that I refer to as *religiopolitical accompaniment* as a mode of understanding and developing solidarity and movement building across borders, be they national, denominational, ethnic, or otherwise. Often citing the Spanish poet Antonio Machado, who wrote, "caminante, no hay camino, se hace camino al andar" ("traveler, there is no path, you make your own path as you walk"), movement members envisioned themselves as partners "walking together" in the suffering of asylees and their development of strategies to alleviate circumstances causing their distress.[8] Their actions grew into a form of politically engaged religiosity, one in which sanctuary members understood their faith, and their process of accompaniment, as a corrective against the state's inability to care for the needs of refugees. By engaging in an ethic of mutuality through sanctuary, Central American and North American movement members worked to confront asylees' suffering and transform it, as theologian Roberto Goizueta notes, into a source "not of despair but of strength."[9] Sanctuary activists' practice of religiopolitical accompaniment thus converted fellowship into a politically radical act, one that had the potential to reshape US foreign, immigration, and domestic policy.

The history of the sanctuary movement offers an important vantage point from which to assess the intersections between Latino faith, political activism, and transnational solidarity. Throughout the 1980s, the movement invited a collision between church and state, especially with elected officials and church leaders who professed to be so deeply Christian yet supported unwelcoming and politically motivated refugee policies. While many members of the sanctuary movement may have not considered themselves politically liberal, they did understand their mobilization as a direct rebuke to the influence of the ardently conservative Moral Majority, which had captured the imagination and power of those affiliated with the administration of Ronald Reagan. Sanctuary activists challenged the government's refugee and foreign policies and affirmed the country's obligation to protect Central American migrants, doing so by centering Jewish and Christian traditions of "welcoming the stranger." The movement ultimately sought to provide a counter-hegemonic ideological force to the religious right's support within the Reagan administration. Its work went beyond merely injecting a sense of morality into the debate on Central America; in the words of the CRTF, sanctuary's practitioners sought to deny the US government the "moral high ground" it desired as camouflage for its actions in the region.[10]

Through the practice of religiopolitical accompaniment, sanctuary activists developed a resilient movement that stretched national borders. While US sanctuary activists might not have been directly physically affected by the wars in Central America, they believed that they had a *moral obligation* to learn more about their country's complicity in the destruction of the region and thus work alongside Salvadorans and Guatemalans to shift US foreign policy and ensure that the United States lived up to the promises it had made in its refugee laws. These activists were predecessors to religious progressives of the twenty-first century, those who, as Jane Juffer notes, offer a "radical critique" of the "underlying causes of immigration as well as the injustices many migrants encounter in the United States."[11] Faith-based activists continue to practice accompaniment in the renewed sanctuary movement of the twenty-first century, drawing upon, as their predecessors did in the 1980s, the biblical call to "welcome the stranger among us," regardless of documentation status, ethnicity, or denomination.

Central American Wars, Asylum Denied, and the Need for Sanctuary

The transnational sanctuary movement that developed in the 1980s grew out of a confluence of armed conflict in Central America, concurrent mass displacement, and growing anger among Americans concerning their country's intervention in the region. Revolutions in Guatemala (1960–1996) and El Salvador (1979–1992) resulted in the deaths of more than a quarter million people. In the context of Cold War prerogatives, President Ronald Reagan's State Department sought to stem leftist influence in these countries by overtly and covertly supporting repressive right-wing dictatorships, doing so via military spending and training for paramilitary forces. These wars subsequently led to the dislocation of more than two million people, half of whom eventually settled in the United States. In the first half of the 1980s alone, more than half a million Guatemalans and Salvadorans entered the country.[12]

Despite seeking political asylum at the US-Mexico border, Central Americans faced increasingly restricted access to the safe harbor offered via national refugee law. Presenting themselves to Border Patrol agents or immigration officials, potential asylees applied for protected status via the Refugee Act of 1980. The recently passed law had purportedly signaled a change in American asylum practices, which had for decades, under Cold War preoccupations, offered preference for those fleeing countries with communist regimes. The 1980 law instead emphasized individual assessment, affording safe harbor to anyone who could demonstrate a "well-founded fear of persecution on account of race, religion, nationality, membership in a particular social group, or political opinion."[13] Despite these legal shifts, the Reagan administration continued to prioritize asylum requests from those departing countries with leftist governments, such as Cuba and the USSR, while largely denying applications from people fleeing countries receiving US military aid. The results for Central American arrivals were profound. From 1983 to 1990, while the overall approval rate of asylum applications for refugees from across the world stood at 24 percent, US immigration officials approved only 2.6 percent of Salvadoran and 1.8 percent of Guatemalan claims.[14]

Federal officials responsible for screening potential asylees were either unconvinced or unmoved by Central Americans' applications for refuge. Ricardo Ernades, a Salvadoran trade unionist, reached California in the early 1980s, promptly applying for political asylum. Branded an agitator by the state, Ernades had fled his home after dodging multiple murder attempts by government agents, who had already killed his cousin in a case of mistaken identity. Despite Ernades's fears of retaliation, the immigration judge reviewing his petition declared that the Salvadoran had failed to provide "concrete proof" of persecution, subsequently denying him refugee status. Facing deportation, Ernades told a *Los Angeles Times* reporter that he might yet one day provide the physical evidence the magistrate found lacking: "[The judge] can see the concrete proof by my death when I go home."[15]

Ernades's case was illustrative of larger efforts by government officials to deny Central Americans safe entry into the United States. Immigration officers accused arriving Guatemalans and Salvadorans of being migrants in search of work, trying to cheat the country's generous refugee system, rather than asylees with rightful claims of political persecution. Officials at the State Department and Immigration and Naturalization Service (INS) instead categorized Central American arrivals as "economic migrants" who were unlawfully present in the country, and thus subject to removal. Peter Larabee, director of the INS detention facility in El Centro, California, believed that Salvadorans failed to meet the legal category's standard of proof and were merely "just peasants who are coming to the US for a welfare card and a Cadillac." The director of the El Paso detention center, Dan McDonald, similarly remarked that arriving Central Americans were only "looking for jobs, and the only reason they fear going back is because jobs are hard to find down there."[16] In questioning the credibility of asylees' claims, immigration officials parroted the Reagan administration's public stance toward Salvadoran and Guatemalan arrivals. This policy regarded these entrants as economic migrants and thus, without sanctioned refugee status, as being illegally present in the country. The denial of claims had concrete consequences for thousands of Central Americans; beyond denying them asylum, INS on average deported one thousand Salvadorans and Guatemalans every month throughout the decade.[17]

By the early 1980s, faith communities along the US-Mexico border tracked with alarm the mounting violence in Central America as well as the US government's treatment of arriving asylees. The murder of clerical and lay leaders in El Salvador in 1980, including the assassination of outspoken advocate for the poor, San Salvador archbishop Oscar Romero, and the brutal killing of four American missionaries, further drew public attention to the region. Contending that the federal government was purposefully misclassifying Central Americans and their applications for asylum in order to conceal the United States' military involvement in Central America, coalitions of churches and synagogues in Tucson, Arizona, and San Francisco, California, announced in March 1982 that they would house undocumented Guatemalans and Salvadorans within the confines of their places of worship. Aware that harboring unauthorized asylees could be a violation of federal law, these faith communities turned to the biblical practice of sanctuary to justify the opening of their congregational doors.[18]

The call for sanctuary issued in the borderlands spread across the country over the next decade. Border congregations, which offered legal assistance, physical shelter, and humanitarian aid to asylees crossing into the United States, coordinated with the politically active solidarity organization known as the Chicago Religious Task Force on Central America (CRTF) to find refugees safe harbor in hundreds of Protestant, Catholic, and Jewish communities in nearly every state. At the height of the sanctuary movement in the mid-1980s, an estimated thirty thousand people of faith belonging to nearly five hundred churches and synagogues offered physical sanctuary or support to Central Americans.[19]

Movement members across the United States understood the concept of "sanctuary" as holding dual meanings. The physical space of sanctuary is often most colloquially understood as a site where a community of faith gathers for prayer. Activists emphasized, however, that for thousands of years sanctuary had also carried deeply religiopolitical significance. In the Old Testament, temples as well as "cities of refuge" were places where persons guilty of manslaughter were given protection from unjust retaliation. This same tradition was later recognized in Roman law, medieval canon law, and English common law, as churches stood in as locations of safe harbor and delayed due process for accused criminals. Places of worship had also served as sites of safe harbor for enslaved Black Americans fleeing bondage in the nineteenth century through the Underground Railroad, as well as conscientious objectors and draft resisters during the Vietnam War. Because of its long history, practitioners of sanctuary engaged in what they referred to as "a living tradition" of emphasizing both aspects of the term.[20] Participants brought these two definitions of sanctuary into one, reconstructing churches as houses of worship that could also serve as sites of protection for Central American asylees.

Religiopolitical Accompaniment and Practices of Political Fellowship

Through accompaniment, movement members sought and developed connections between Latin American and North American religious communities, working to create an incarnational model of "walking together." Central American and US sanctuary members believed that the practice of accompaniment, one based at the intersection of faith and action, might facilitate a reconciliation to mend the wounds caused by the destruction wrought by US intervention in the region. This movement practice was a way of enacting the concept of mutuality, whereupon the lives and suffering of Central Americans were intimately connected with North Americans. Accompaniment thus had the potential to be a transformative experience, one that could cultivate political fellowship and an ethic of solidarity, or, as Barbara Tomlinson and George Lipsitz have noted, "a disposition, a sensibility, and a pattern of behavior."[21]

Sanctuary members emphasized that their activism, just like their faith, was transnational and multidirectional. The movement served as a critical vector by which to understand how both religiosity and social movements based in faith can stretch across national borders, and even question the very power and authority of these boundaries. Activists, both Central American transplanted and US-born, were greatly influenced by the work of Latin American liberation theologians. Developed in light of significant changes following the Second Vatican Council and the bishops' meeting in Medellín in 1968, this fusion of Christian theology and socioeconomic analysis arose as a response to the ramifications of centuries of European and US colonialism and extraction capitalism.

Identifying the social and economic injustice in the region as a form of sin, practitioners emphasized the obligation of the church to prioritize concern for society's dispossessed and organize for the political liberation of oppressed people. Theologians such as Gustavo Gutiérrez, Jon Sobrino, Leonardo Boff, Juan Luis Segundo, and others wrote of a "preferential option for the poor," a doctrine that stressed the church's obligation to, through word, prayer, and action, demonstrate solidarity with, and compassion for, society's most vulnerable and marginalized members.[22]

While some North American sanctuary activists were well versed in liberation theology, many more were deeply influenced by the incarnate example set by clergy and missionaries who had been killed in Latin America working to put word into deed. No clerical leader stood out more in this regard than El Salvador's Oscar Romero. The archbishop's practice of pastoral accompaniment called on Salvadorans to walk alongside society's dispossessed, a clear enactment of liberation theology's exhortation for a "preferential option for the poor." Romero, who himself had experienced a conversion from liberation theology skeptic to outspoken supporter of the disenfranchised, famously noted, "You should be there next to the campesinos. Accompany them. Take the same risks they do."[23] From his vaunted post as head cleric of San Salvador, the archbishop had pleaded with the United States government to refrain from sending military equipment and advisors to his nation. In calling for the cessation of US involvement in Central America, Romero believed that he was fulfilling, as he noted, his "obligation to ensure that faith and justice prevail" for all Salvadorans, especially those without a political platform from which to speak.[24] It was an obligation that he championed until his final days. In one of the last sermons the archbishop delivered before his assassination in March 1980, Romero exhorted Christians of all social and economic classes to "put themselves alongside the poor."[25] According to the archbishop, then, accompaniment meant not just meeting the immediate needs of those asking for help but supporting the agency of those who had been most disempowered and oppressed. This form of companionship entailed not only empathizing with the poor and aggrieved, but also taking on the risks they faced on a daily basis.[26]

The sanctuary movement served as the most critical space where North and Central American clergy and laypeople could enact the guiding tenets of liberation theology. Drawing from refugees' experiences, missionary interactions, and the nascent theology of the region, they did so by developing the practice of religiopolitical accompaniment. Activists within the CRTF described accompaniment as a way of "walking with" the displaced people of El Salvador and Guatemala, sharing with them, as the CRTF described, their "suffering and hope, their death and resurrection."[27] Put into practice as a political action, however, accompaniment was envisioned by sanctuary activists as more than just sympathy or a way to bear witness to Central Americans' misery. As a political project, the movement deployed the social, economic, and political capital of North American church members on behalf of larger anti-interventionist and pro-asylee objectives.

While adherents of liberation theology hoped that their analysis and call for action might push Latin American churches toward spiritual renewal, military dictatorships throughout the region saw in these doctrines a Trojan horse for Marxist subversion. Catholic and Protestant clergy and laypeople who aligned themselves with this form of Christianity, anyone from the most local of parish priests to archbishops of major Central American cities, could find themselves in their government's crosshairs and face harassment, torture, and even murder for denouncing economic injustice and authoritarian government leaders. Paramilitary and National Guard forces in Central America singled out catechists like Felipe Excot, those they deemed potential subversive elements, for emphasizing *campesino* literacy campaigns and discussion groups that stressed the history of the church as a champion for the downtrodden. These governments also used violent ends to disrupt Christian base communities (*comunidades eclesiales de base*, or CEBs). Established originally to supplement a limited pastoral presence in rural areas, CEBs became spaces where liberation theology could be discussed, sharpened, and implemented among local parishes. In these communities, Catholics learned how colonialism and capitalism had created systems of poverty and oppression within which the clear majority of the region's population lived, and they discussed how to faithfully live a Christian life that could combat these social, economic, and political oppressions.[28]

Asylees weren't the only movement members who sought liberation in the struggle, however; North American compatriots, in confronting their country's militaristic escapades in the region, also looked to free themselves and their countrymen from these sins. Mission trips also served to connect Americans' understanding of the refugee experience across the Americas, and sharpened movement participants' criticism of US Central American foreign policy. US missionaries who visited the region in the second half of the twentieth century came in contact with this rapidly developing and marked turn toward a pastoral preoccupation with the traditionally underserved. Clergy and laity who visited countries like El Salvador and Guatemala had grown frustrated with US churches that remained disengaged from the needs of their congregants or—in their eyes, even worse—those religious institutions and leadership that had entangled themselves with morally compromised politicians. Throughout the decade, faith-based organizations organized solidarity trips to Central America. These excursions served both educational and spiritual ends. National ecumenical networks such as the Salvadoran Humanitarian Aid, Relief, and Education Foundation (SHARE), founded in the San Francisco Bay Area in 1981, as well as groups like Witness for Peace, the Pledge of Resistance, and the Interfaith Office on Accompaniment, aided displaced persons living in United Nations–sponsored camps in Honduras seeking to return to their home villages. Ecumenical delegations from North America witnessed the violence of destruction of local communities and sought to "walk" with Salvadorans, Nicaraguans, and Guatemalans in their suffering. Newly politically mobilized, these activists would then return home to share their stories in an act of "witness" with their home congregations and wider city communities. Along with their re-placement efforts, members of SHARE conducted what they referred to as "fact-finding missions" to the region. They brought back what they saw to the United States, speaking with local congregations as well as testifying to elected officials, as they did before the US House of Representatives Western Hemispheric Affairs Sub-Committee in 1986.[29]

US-based religious orders with significant missionary presence in Central America knew firsthand the effects of the war on local communities. Members of the Jesuits and Maryknolls, as well as other religious communities, who combined literacy campaigns with their evangelization efforts in Nicaragua, Guatemala, and El Salvador, often fell in the crosshairs of paramilitary squads. Forced to flee back to the United

States, clergy and mission workers associated with these orders spread word about the atrocities they'd witnessed firsthand through teach-ins, public speaking tours, and direct lobbying to their elected representatives, and even published numerous books, as Maryknoll sisters did through their publishing house, Orbis Books. Sister Darlene Nicgorski, a native of Milwaukee, Wisconsin, and a member of the School Sisters of Saint Francis, experienced what she referred to as a conversion experience during her time as a missionary in Guatemala. She was inspired by the spirituality and tenacity of her congregants, what she came to understood as "a feeling of peace, aliveness, wholeness, holiness, goodness," and the devotion of laity and clergy alike in spreading a message of the Gospel centered on teaching "the people to work towards their own liberation."[30] The *true* church in the eyes of North American converts like Nicgorski, who upon her return to the United States would become a central "conductor" helping asylees travel from the borderlands to sanctuary congregations across the country, was the one in Latin America, as it was engaged in an active struggle to live out the Gospel.

These lived experiences, as well as liberation theologians' explicit call to serve the disenfranchised, appealed to US church members as they made connections between their religiosity and social justice initiatives. Contact with oppressed communities in El Salvador and Guatemala taught US missionaries to emphasize theology in action, referred to as *praxis* by liberation theologians, over a passive faith experience in order to create a more just society for all. Nicgorski described this work as a form of accompaniment. It was, as she described it, a new form of "spiritual exercise," one that rejected withdrawal into an inner life of prayer for, instead, engagement with the corporal one. Having been exposed to atrocities abroad and now understanding her country's role in facilitating the deaths of thousands, Nicgorski believed that lay and clergy had an obligation to open their country's "eyes to all in order to find the cause of systemic evil."[31] This reconceptualized understanding of faith stimulated a sense of responsibility and solidarity with the poor and disenfranchised, one that, according to anthropologist Hilary Cunningham, "transcended national cultures, identities, [and] obligations."[32]

Nicgorski and other North American church members did not draw these linkages merely to equate their time-limited missionary experiences with the lived realities of fleeing asylees, or even to say that they themselves could ever truly embody living through the terror of violence and displacement that marked many Central Americans' daily lives. Rather, North Americans saw it as their obligation to better understand what was happening in Guatemala and El Salvador through observation and conversation, and then return to their home country as catechists and share these experiences with their countrymen. Accompaniment as practiced in the movement as a form of praxis, or what liberation theologian Gustavo Gutiérrez referred to as an "active presence in history," thus required a recognition of an explicitly politicized ministry.[33] Through this practice, former missionaries saw as their responsibility the need to spread the word of their country's role in destabilizing Latin America, and perhaps more importantly, of American church people's obligation to do something about it. Missionaries-turned-sanctuary activists believed that they carried with them this responsibility to educate Americans, organize them, and eventually activate them to initiate political change.

Through accompaniment, refugees could also assume a position as partners in the movement and thus as central agents in their own liberation. As Héctor Perla Jr. has shown, Central American activists served as key organizers in solidarity coalitions of the late 1970s and early 1980s. Drawing from their own organizing experiences developed in home countries prior to migration, asylees resisted any form of paternalism that either proffered charity or placed them on pedestals as objects to be admired or mourned.[34] Instead, a central objective of the movement was to create a megaphone from which those who had been silenced by the federal government could speak. Offering *testimonio*, or testimony, was one way that refugees themselves might do just that. Standing before a religious congregation, at times with faces concealed beneath bandanas and sunglasses to protect their identity, Central Americans would share their stories of persecution in their home countries and their hazardous passage into the United States. Sanctuary residents would share their histories with congregation after congregation in their receiving community, seeking to cultivate an awareness of and obligation toward those suffering in countries just south of the US border. Linda, living in sanctuary in Tabernacle United Church in Philadelphia in 1985, professed that she employed her *testimonio* as a movement organizer because "it is the way that I can contribute to the cause of the struggle of Salvadoran people that permits us a life of DIGNITY and MAKES OF EL SALVADOR our own SANCTUARY AND HOME."[35] By retelling her personal history to US congregations, Linda, along with thousands of other sanctuary residents who toured the country, sought to educate parishioners and activate them for political action.

Instead of reciting political analysis or statistics about the number of those displaced or dead, personal story via *testimonio* engendered an emotive and potentially more impactful response from North American congregants. Refugees explicitly connected US intervention via military aid in their home countries with their sojourn stories. Amos, a law student from Guatemala living in sanctuary in Madison, Wisconsin, detailed in his *testimonio* the history of US imperialism in Latin America, and centralized it as a precipitating factor for the asylee crisis. Noting that it was not "the lives of human beings that are important (to the Reagan administration), but rather maintaining power and domination over Third World Countries," he called upon Americans to demand that their government end monetary support to repressive governments in the region.[36] Through *testimonio*, Central Americans seized what the movement referred to as a "prophetic platform" and could cease being merely objects of someone else's action, and instead, as Roberto Goizueta notes, "become historical subjects in their own right."[37]

Some of the most active sanctuary residents argued that their participation and leadership in the movement, especially through *testimonios*, buttressed accusations that they were passive pawns being used by activist organizations. Opponents of sanctuary—both federal government officials and church leaders who demurred at the movement's tactics—accused North American church members and solidarity organizations of manipulating asylees for their own political and ideological ends. Instead, Central American members contended that, through accompaniment, asylees assumed the responsibility of bringing their politically infused faith, one guided by the tenets of liberation theology, to the United States. As Felipe Excot, living in sanctuary in Vermont, noted, through their work with Central Americans, North American churches engaged in the movement had now "discovered in the Bible their obligation as Christians and human beings." Excot believed that as "a basic requirement of Christian faith," accompaniment should be a joint undertaking for churched people across the Americas. It was an obligation that was "fed by that hope according to which, LIFE is more important than the laws of death." Drawing from 2 Corinthians, Excot explained that while "the written law [gave] death," it was "the Spirit of God [that gave] LIFE."[38] Excot's remarks were meant to spur reticent Christians in the United States to understand that their salvation would be found not just in heaven, but in the way they approached the life-and-death ramifications of detention and deportation. By resisting the government's summary removal of Central Americans to their countries of origin, accompaniment offered Salvadorans and Guatemalans a chance to survive—literally, to remain alive—and continue to fight for their compatriots back home. According to sanctuary members, compassion through accompaniment, when practiced in conjunction with refugees and not just for them, could, and should, manifest as political resistance against state power.

By referring to asylees as either pliable vessels for North American activists' whims or hapless recipients of charity, opponents of the movement obscured not only the primary objectives of the movement—solidarity and fellowship—but also the lived experiences of the Central American asylees who led sanctuary efforts. As Gustavo Gutiérrez notes, those engaged in accompaniment interpret solidarity not as something done *for* an abstract group of people ("the poor," or in this case, "the Central Americans"), but instead as an interactive custom accomplished "with human beings of flesh and bone."[39] Accompaniment in the sanctuary movement was then not about *giving* a "voice to the voiceless"—an overused idiom too often applied to allyship projects between those with considerable economic and political capital and those without—but instead recognizing that asylees had plenty to say and most importantly sought a platform from which to say it.

Movement members transformed *testimonio* into both a spiritual and political discourse, one that blurred the boundaries between the sacred and the profane. By explicitly introducing political conversations into the physical sanctuary of the church, asylees argued that if immigration officials refused to believe their stories of persecution, religious congregants would. By clearing space for refugees to speak for themselves, *testimonio* transformed the practice of accompaniment into a practice of political empowerment and not just one merely for humanitarian aid, or worse, charity. Dan Dale, organizer for the

CRTF, argued that asylees engaged in a "mission of teaching" when they shared their *testimonios* with North American congregations. The grueling ordeal of laying bare the violence their families had faced in their home countries transformed Salvadoran and Guatemalan activists into the movement's "real evangelists."[40] This was a sentiment shared by asylees, who took on the heavy emotional work of educating North American congregations. Felipe Excot believed that "compassion" amounted to merely "giving money to feed a hungry person." Solidarity, however, practiced through accompaniment, required allied North American church members to go "along sharing the pain of the journey."[41] Movement members were thus able to transform a religious ritual familiar to Christians into a movement strategy. To borrow from religious ethicist Melissa Snarr, this allowed sanctuary participants to ritualize "moral agency" and helped foster a "collective identity" between North and Central Americans.[42]

Efforts from sanctuary activists to foster this spirit of solidarity, both within church spaces and outside them, led to significant victories for Central American asylees, but only after a decade of organizing, petitioning, and demonstrating. A movement that had begun in 1982 in congregations along the US-Mexico border, initiated by the simple act of offering safe harbor to those fleeing persecution, had, through the continued practice of accompaniment, became a transnational effort to both end US military support for murderous regimes in Central America and force the American government to live up to its obligations to migrants arriving at its border. Pushed by lobbying from religious groups and solidarity organizations, federal legislators included provisions in the Immigration Act of 1990 that offered Salvadorans eighteen-month protections through the newly created category of temporary protected status (TPS). A coalition of more than eighty religious and refugee agencies pushed the federal government even further when they sued the executive branch for failing to meet its obligations to Central Americans under the 1980 Refugee Act. Known as the ABC Agreement, the resulting out-of-court settlement permitted Salvadorans who had been present in the United States since September 1, 1990, and Guatemalans who had resided in the country since October 1, 1990, to petition again for asylum.[43] These judicial and legislative victories at the federal level, combined with a decline in Central American migration with the opening of peace accords in Guatemala and El Salvador in the early 1990s, heralded the end of the sanctuary movement.

Accompaniment and Sanctuary Movements Today

Sanctuary activism, dormant for much of the 1990s, came to life again in religious spaces in the early twenty-first century as a counter to an increasingly aggressive and callous immigration enforcement system. Beginning in the early 2000s, both the Bush and Obama administrations built and expanded the parameters by which undocumented communities could find themselves in the crosshairs of Border Patrol and Immigration and Customs Enforcement, including through expanded family detention policies, accelerated immigration raids in workplaces across the country, and partnerships between federal, state, and local law enforcement like Secure Communities and 287(g) agreements. The New Sanctuary Movement, a loose national coalition of congregations and religious organizations committed to immigrant justice, developed in the mid-2000s in response. Its charge was a broader one than that of its predecessor, which focused primarily on Central American asylees arriving at the US border. The renewed movement instead turned to assisting undocumented individuals and families who had lived in the United States for an extended period of time and who faced increasing pressures from a runaway deportation system. Beginning January 2017, the Trump administration intensified enforcement measures at a dizzying pace, threatening to build a wall between the United States and Mexico, increasing border enforcement, ramping up deportations, and even, at the end of 2017, ending temporary protected status for thousands of Central Americans.[44]

In response to the 2016 election, the number of congregations committed to offering sanctuary to undocumented immigrants across the country grew from 400 to more than 1,100 in just a number of months.[45] Supported by Church World Service, a cooperative ministry of thirty-seven Christian denominations, these faith communities continued the practice of accompaniment as physical presence through a variety of movement practices.[46] Laying claim to a historical lineage of connecting religious belief to political engagement, one movement organizing "toolkit" noted that faith communities had been engaged in solidarity with asylum seekers, refugees, and migrants for decades. The document's creators noted that the commitment throughout this history remained the same, "to welcome our neighbors and love them as ourselves, especially those who are made vulnerable or marginalized by violence or policies in their home countries." Like its predecessors, the New Sanctuary Movement defined accompaniment as "the work of walking alongside" an asylum seeker as they navigated the legal process of seeking asylum. The goal of the accompaniment work, according to movement members, was to ensure not only that asylum seekers won their cases and modified their legal status, but also that they secure employment and "begin to have a stable life wherein they can support themselves, their families, and participate in the life of their community." In the spirit of self-determination and empowerment beyond charity, the organization emphasized a ministry of accompaniment focused on the "goal of self-sufficiency and independence."[47]

Members of the New Sanctuary Movement put these physical practices of accompaniment into action through a variety of avenues. Allies, for example, served witness by attending immigration check-ins and court hearings with those facing detention and deportation. In New York City, a rotating cohort of more than three thousand volunteers accompanied more than two hundred immigrants and asylees in legal sessions that could often be emotionally draining, and, for those facing imminent deportation, life-altering.[48] Along with courtroom visitations, sanctuary coalitions across the country also organized Jericho Walks, a form of active prayer modeled after the biblical book of Joshua, where God commanded the Israelites to walk seven times around the opposing city of Jericho in order to bring its walls crashing down. In seeking to bring down the walls that divide citizens from noncitizens, activists marched in silence around immigration centers and courthouses while praying in solidarity with individuals and families who have been caught in an unjust immigration system. As historian Rachel Buff has noted, this form of accompaniment "brings visibility to the ever-present threat of deportation." It's a movement strategy that has proven effective; the physical presence and vocal statements of solidarity from community members, who arrive at court hearings and deportation proceedings in support of undocumented immigrants, have swayed immigration judges, who are empowered through prosecutorial discretion to elect whether or not an individual is separated from their families and community in the United States.[49]

Throughout the late twentieth and early twenty-first centuries, sanctuary activists have continually rejected a separation between their faith and their political engagements. Instead, they have argued that their religious traditions require them to develop fellowship and movements for structural change with their immigrant sisters and brothers, especially those living in the United States who have been pushed into the country's legal shadows by draconian federal policies. They have shown that accompaniment, as theologian Roberto Goizueta notes, is "not an abstraction, or a merely 'spiritual' reality." It instead requires a "mutual bodily presence" from all participants who have agreed to work in this partnership.[50] It is a form of religiopolitical fellowship, one that is born in churches, but which participants believe must be taken into the secular world. Sanctuary activists committed to the practice of accompaniment thus sought and continue to seek to create faith spaces and local communities welcoming to all, regardless of documentation status, in order to, borrowing from the Spanish poet Antonio Machado as 1980s sanctuary activists did, make the path forward together.

NOTES

1 Chicago Religious Task Force on Central America, "Statement of Faith," December 1984, Box 2, Folder 15, Darlene Nicgorski Papers on the Sanctuary Movement, Special Collections, Honnold/Mudd Library, Claremont University Consortium (hereafter Nicgorski Papers).

2 March 24, 1984 also marked the two-year anniversary of the first sanctuary declaration in Tucson, Arizona. Renny Golden and Michael McConnell, "Sanctuary," *International Review of Mission* 73, no. 292 (October 1984): 486–90; "Weston Priory-Site 100th Sanctuary," *Basta! National Newsletter of the Chicago Religious Task Force on Central America*, February 1984, Chicago Religious Task Force on Central American Records, 1982–1992, Wisconsin Historical Society (hereafter CRTF Records).

3 Golden and McConnell, "Sanctuary."

4 Gregory P. Leffel, *Faith Seeking Action: Mission, Social Movements, and the Church in Motion* (Lanham, MD: Scarecrow Press, 2007), 126–27.

5 "Guatemalan Family Reaches Refugee," *New York Times*, March 25, 1984. See also Sarah Wilson, "Monks Join Network Harboring Refugees," *United Press International*, March 24, 1985.

6 Dudley Clenddinen, "Monastery Awaiting 5 Refugees," *New York Times*, March 19, 1984.

7 Rod Clarke, "Refugee Family Finds Refuge," *United Press International*, March 20, 1984. For more on the arrival of the Excots in Vermont, see Golden and McConnell, "Sanctuary."
8 Renny Golden and Michael McConnell, *Sanctuary: The New Underground Railroad* (Maryknoll, NY: Orbis, 1986), 54.
9 Roberto S. Goizueta, *Caminemos con Jesús: Toward a Hispanic Theology of Accompaniment* (Maryknoll, NY: Orbis, 1999), 68.
10 "State of the Movement," January 1987, Box 1, Folder 1, CRTF Records.
11 Jane Juffer, "'They Cling to Guns or Religion': Pennsylvania Towns Put Faith in Anti-Immigrant Ordinances," in *Latin American Migrations to the US Heartland*, ed. Linda Allegro and Andrew Grant Wood (Urbana: University of Illinois Press, 2013), 251.
12 María Cristina García, *Seeking Refuge: Central American Migration to Mexico, the United States, and Canada* (Berkeley: University of California Press, 2006), 13–43.
13 Public Law 96–212 ("Refugee Act of 1980"), 8 USC § 1521 (1980).
14 García, *Seeking Refuge*, 90.
15 Renny Golden and Michael McConnell, "Sanctuary: Choosing Sides," *Christianity and Crisis*, February 21, 1983, Box 3, Folder 54, CRTF Records.
16 National Sanctuary Defense Fund, "Sanctuary Media Packet: Jack Elder and Stacey Lynn Merket—Two Sanctuary Workers Arrested in 1984," n.d., Box 2, Folder 1, Nicgorski Papers; Golden and McConnell, "Sanctuary: Choosing Sides."
17 García, *Seeking Refuge*, 90.
18 Five churches in Berkeley, California, publicly joined the Tucson church in declaring their support for undocumented asylees that spring. See Van Gosse, "'The North American Front': Central American Solidarity in the Reagan Era," in *Reshaping the US Left: Popular Struggles in the 1980s*, ed. Mike Davis and Michael Sprinker (New York: Verso, 1988), 27–28.
19 Ignatius Bau, *The Ground Is Holy: Church Sanctuary and Central American Refugees* (Mahwah, NJ: Paulist Press, 1985), 75–123.
20 National Conference on Catholic Charities, "Committee on Legislation for Social Justice," November 29, 1984, Box 227, Folder 19, Catholic Charities USA, Catholic University Archives.
21 Barbara Tomlinson and George Lipsitz, "American Studies as Accompaniment," *American Quarterly* 65, no. 1 (March 2013): 9.
22 For more on liberation theology, see Gustavo Gutiérrez, *A Theology of Liberation: History, Politics, and Salvation*, 15th anniversary ed. (Maryknoll, NY: Orbis, 1988); Juan Luis Segundo, *The Liberation of Theology* (Maryknoll, NY: Orbis, 1976); and Leonardo Boff and Clodovis Boff, *Introducing Liberation Theology* (Maryknoll, NY: Orbis, 1987).
23 María López Vigil, *Monseñor Romero: Memories in Mosaic* (Maryknoll, NY: Orbis, 2013), 175.
24 Ibid., 265.

25 Oscar Romero, "Louvain Address: The Political Dimension of the Faith from the Perspective of the Option of the Poor," in *Voice of the Voiceless: The Four Pastoral Letters and Other Statements* (Maryknoll, NY: Orbis, 1985), 187.
26 Phillip Berryman, *The Religious Roots of Rebellion: Christians in Central America* (Eugene, OR: Wipf and Stock, 1984), 340; Phillip Berryman, *Stubborn Hope: Religion, Politics, and Revolution in Central America* (New York: New Press, 1995), 173.
27 "December 2, 1986: *Acompañamiento*—the Journey to Liberation," *Central America Report: Bimonthly Journal of the Religious Task Force on Central America*, September/October 1986, Box 4, Folder 65, CRTF Records.
28 Sharon Erickson Nepstad, *Convictions of the Soul: Religion, Culture, and Agency in the Central American Solidarity Movement* (New York: Oxford University Press, 2004), vii-viii.
29 Héctor Perla Jr., "Si Nicaragua Venció, El Salvador Vencerá: Central American Agency in the Creation of the US-Central American Peace Movement," *Latin American Research Review* 43, no. 2 (2008): 136–58; Christian Smith, *Resisting Reagan: The US Central America Peace Movement* (Chicago: University of Chicago Press, 1996), 59–86.
30 Julia Lieblich, *Sisters: Lives of Devotion and Defiance* (New York: Ballantine, 1992), 220.
31 Darlene Nicgorski, "*Acompañamiento*: Where You Go, We Will Go," *Central America Report: Bimonthly Journal of the Religious Task Force on Central America*, September/October 1986, Box 7, Folder 12, Nicgorski Papers.
32 Hilary Cunningham, "The Ethnography of Transnational Social Activism: Understanding the Global as Local Practice," *American Ethnologist* 26, no. 3 (August 1999): 592.
33 Gutiérrez, *Theology of Liberation*, 6.
34 Perla, "Si Nicaragua Venció," 140–42.
35 "Refugees Speak Out about Direction of the Sanctuary Movement," *Basta!*, January 1985, CRTF Records.
36 "Salvador Refugees Find Sanctuary," *Wisconsin State Journal*, May 24, 1983.
37 Goizueta, *Caminemos con Jesús*, 87.
38 Excot referenced 2 Corinthians 3:6, which reads, "He has made us competent as ministers of a new covenant—not of the letter but of the Spirit; for the letter kills, but the Spirit gives new life." "Mayan Indian in Weston Priory Sanctuary Responds," *Basta!*, July 1984, CRTF Records.
39 Gustavo Gutiérrez, "Conversion: A Requirement for Solidarity," in *In the Company of the Poor: Conversations with Dr. Paul Farmer and Fr. Gustavo Gutiérrez*, ed. Michael Griffin and Jennie Weiss Block (Maryknoll, NY: Orbis, 2013), 81.
40 Ignatius Bau, "Strangers and Sojourners Together," *New Catholic World* 228, no. 1365 (April 1985), Box 2, Folder 50, Nicgorski Papers.
41 "Basta Ya! A Call for an Action and Caravan of Resistance and Conscience," *Basta!*, July 1984, CRTF Records.

42 Melissa Snar, *All That Labor: Religion and Ethics in the Living Wage Movement* (New York: New York University Press, 2011), 123–32.
43 The settlement in *American Baptist Churches et al. v. Thornburgh* forced the federal government to reprocess nearly 150,000 asylum requests and allowed more than 350,000 migrants who hadn't previously applied for asylum to seek hearings. Susan Bibler Coutin, "From Refugees to Immigrants: The Legalization Strategies of Salvadoran Immigrants and Activists," *International Migration Review* 32, no. 4 (Winter 1998): 901–25.
44 Beginning in 2017, immigration courts began to deny asylum applications to Central Americans as well as migrants from across Latin America, the Caribbean, and Africa at record-high rates. A variety of changes, including increased bond rates and the creation of the "Remain in Mexico" program, made it harder for migrants to apply for and prepare asylum cases, all while the Trump administration lowered the annual cap on the number of refugees the United States would resettle in the country. Trump also made "sanctuary" jurisdictions—local and state municipalities that refuse to cooperate with federal immigration enforcement—a significant target of his ire. See A. Naomi Paik, *Bans, Walls, Raids, Sanctuary: Understanding US Immigration for the Twenty-First Century* (Berkeley: University of California Press, 2020); Miranda Cady Hallett and Leisy J. Abrego, "Seeking a Permanent Protected Status," *NACLA Report on the Americas*, November 16, 2017, https://nacla.org.
45 Myrna Orozco and Reverend Noel Anderson, "Sanctuary in the Age of Trump: The Rise of the Movement a Year into the Trump Administration," Church World Service, January 2018, www.sanctuarynotdeportation.org.
46 For example, members of the Matthew 25 Movement, a broad coalition of Christian national faith-based groups, clergy associations, and grassroots activists dedicated to immigrant justice, reiterated the importance of accompaniment during a 2018 conference held in Los Angeles. Lloyd Barba and Tatyana Castillo-Ramos, "Sacred Resistance: The Sanctuary Movement from Reagan to Trump," *Perspectivas: Journal for the Hispanic Theological Initiative* 16 (2019): 31; Grace Yukich, *One Family under God: Immigration Politics and Progressive Religion in America* (Oxford: Oxford University Press, 2013), 82–87.
47 National Sanctuary Movement, "Toolkit for Faith Communities to Accompany People Seeking Asylum," n.d., www.sanctuarynotdeportation.org.
48 National Sanctuary Movement, "Resources," n.d., www.sanctuarynotdeportation.org.
49 Rachel Ida Buff, "Sanctuary Everywhere: Some Key Words, 1945–Present," *Radical History Review* 135, no. 1 (October 2019): 31.
50 Goizueta, *Caminemos con Jesús*, 9.

10

"The Needs of Migrant People"

Catholics and Immigrants' Rights in the Twentieth Century

ELADIO B. BOBADILLA

On November 6, 1986, President Ronald Reagan signed into law the Immigration Reform and Control Act (IRCA) to a great deal of fanfare. It was, after all, a momentous occasion. Lazarus, as observers had called the bill, was back from the dead.[1] It was also a major political victory for Reagan, who had previously opposed the bill on the grounds that it was too generous to immigrants, but who now, in typical Reagan fashion, showered it with idealistic language, saying he hoped that the bill would "improve the lives of a class of individuals who now must hide in the shadows, without access to many of the benefits of a free and open society."[2] From this moment on, Reagan's name would be inextricably linked to IRCA. But the law was the product of a much longer and contested history than he was willing to give the appearance of. For one thing, the "Reagan amnesty," and more generally, the policies that IRCA birthed, were conceived several years earlier, during the administration of Jimmy Carter. And it was not the White House—Carter's or Reagan's—that most tangibly and meaningfully shaped the law. Rather, it was Father Theodore "Ted" Hesburgh, whose namesake commission provided the foundation for the law, who was most responsible for the immigration reform legislation that finally passed during Reagan's presidency. And it was no coincidence that the Catholic priest and scholar was behind this landmark piece of legislation—the largest overhaul of immigration law since the 1965 Immigration and Nationality Act (commonly called "Hart-Celler" after its main sponsors, Michigan senator Philip Hart and New York representative Emanuel Celler). After all, throughout the twentieth century, Catholic clergy and laity—particularly in the Southwest and especially in California—had been critical participants in the immigration debate: as activists, critics, policymakers, and intermediaries—and Hesburgh's leadership on the production of immigration reform legislation was the culmination of decades of Catholic involvement in these debates.

Of course, not just on immigration but on every major issue, socially conscious Catholics had been active political agents in the United States since the country's inception (and in many of the regions that would become the United States well before that). Often, however, they were victims rather than activists. From the anti-Catholic hysteria of the Know-Nothings and their nativist successors in the late nineteenth and early twentieth centuries to the 1960 election of John F. Kennedy, Catholics had historically dealt with discrimination and distrust from the larger Protestant population.[3] Even so, when Catholics did emerge as political activists, they could be as conservative as their Protestant counterparts and critics. One need only consider the Catholic mainstream's defense of slavery as a "natural condition that could be explained as part of a symbiotic relationship between those who were inherently unequal" or the hateful Depression-era broadcasts of Father Charles Coughlin, the anti-Semitic and proto-fascist radio personality who was among the first to use mass media to spread reactionary politics.[4]

By the 1960s, however, American Catholics were experiencing a profound transformation. Writing in the early 1970s about the shifts that took place in the decade prior, the historian Philip Gleason characterized the changes happening within Catholic circles as nothing less than a "massive upheaval" and a "religious earthquake" worthy of being called a "revolution."[5] If Gleason's language appears overblown, and if his assessment was far from lasting, his exaggeration at the time did not appear as such. Catholic reform—spurred, shaped, and influenced by the Second Vatican Council (1962–1965), with its focus on, and concern for, "social justice, equity, the dignity of the human person, as well as social and international peace"—coincided with massive global protest movements and progressive struggles in the United States. As the church became more democratic, many of its adherents and leadership often found in it a protest vehicle as well, at least for a time before social issues—especially abortion—and Nixon's political maneuverings broke apart the progressive Catholic movement's momentum.[6]

One of the issues that became critical to Catholic activists during this time was immigration, a matter of growing importance in the United States during this period and one of particular significance to Catholic adherents, who had long been targeted by restrictive immigration policies dating back to the Know Nothing movement. Although immigration has always been a central facet of American political life, Mexican immigration only became a major concern for large segments of the population during and immediately after the "decade of the wetback," roughly from 1949 to 1954, when the number of immigrants in the country rose by an astounding 6,000 percent.[7] The phenomenon of illegal immigration was a parallel development to the Bracero Program. Instituted in 1942 to alleviate a labor shortage resulting from the Second World War, it brought nearly five million Mexican men to work on farms, railroads, and other industries. It continued well past the end of the war, actually peaking in 1959.[8] The Bracero Program, which Catholics largely opposed, even as they sought to minister to its participants, spurred illegal immigration as many braceros returned without documentation after their contracts ended or simply deserted their assignments and took other jobs elsewhere during the program.[9]

Braceros and immigrants suffered greatly in the United States, working long hours, under difficult and dangerous conditions, and risking their lives just to find work north of the Rio Grande. Mexican laborers, mostly poor, uneducated, and of rural origins, quickly became important figures in the American social landscape and political debates. To growers, they represented cheap labor and the prospect of unprecedented profits. To nativists, they served as scapegoats for social and economic ills. To policymakers, they posed a problem to be solved. To Mexican Americans, they were unneeded competition and an obstacle to labor organizing, even if they were also co-ethnics and more often than not, fellow Catholics, as these affinities would only be stressed decades later when activists articulated a way out of zero-sum economic assumptions.[10]

During this time, many Catholics in the United States began to pay attention to the plight of migrants and immigrants, seeing in them their own history of oppression and discrimination and recognizing historical linkages found in the stories of their ancestors. In these migrants, growing numbers of socially conscious Catholics also saw a challenge to enact the social justice promise of the Second Vatican Council and the movement within the church to reckon with the modern world that led to it. A 1951 feature in the liberal Catholic magazine *Commonweal* described with great compassion, even admiration, the plight of braceros and the undocumented in the United States. While sympathetic to the troubles they represented for Mexican Americans, the feature suggested that their stories "paralleled in determination the sagas of our heroic 49ers." It was not unusual, its authors noted, "to meet a man who has walked a thousand miles, often over treacherous terrain."[11]

As the church brought its gospel to laborers, through campaigns such as the "Manual for Braceros" and the "Bracero Hour" on national radio, many Catholic activists went further. Together with other groups, they regularly denounced the working and living conditions of immigrant workers, at times even invoking the horrors of the Holocaust.[12] In 1951, for example, one group of activists that included members of the American Committee for the Protection of the Foreign Born and Catholic clergy called the series of camps that housed immigrants "concentration camps."[13] Obviously, comparing the conditions of immigrants and braceros—detestable though they were—to the wholesale massacre and extermination of Jewish people in Europe was bombastic at the least. But this rhetoric did signal the seriousness with which activists sought to tackle the problems facing immigrants in the Southwest. Still, through this period, the ACPFB's denunciation was the exception rather than the rule, as Catholics largely remained more measured in their rhetoric and approach.

This began to change later in the decade. There were several reasons for this. First, reformist sentiment following Vatican II ignited a new passion for social justice in Catholic communities, one that invoked and recalled Pope Leo XIII's *Rerum novarum*, the 1891 encyclical that called for the church to take on an active role in addressing the needs, rights, and struggles of the working classes of the world. Second, the campaign and election of John F. Kennedy, the first Catholic president in the history of the republic, convinced both the country's non-Catholic majority and Catholics themselves that adherents could and should be a part of the nation's political life. Third, the changes within the church coincided with the radicalism outside it, as the civil rights and anti-war movements gained momentum and attention.

Like most other groups, Catholics were largely divided on these issues, at least initially. One could no more find a "Catholic" position on the Vietnam War or on the black civil rights struggle than one could find a "Methodist" or a "Presbyterian" one.[14] But as with those other groups, progressive elements within the church felt compelled to live out their faith in the politics and social movements of the day.

A plurality of Catholics supported the war in its early stages, largely as a result of long-standing hostility toward communism and a desire to support the Vietnamese regime, led by a Catholic—Ngo Dinh Diem—in a largely Buddhist nation.[15] Opinion began to turn only after the escalation of the conflict in the late 1960s produced atrocities like the My Lai massacre and led to the deaths of thousands of American soldiers and Vietnamese civilians. At that point, the Catholic Worker Movement and anti-war activists like Daniel and Philip Berrigan (the Berrigan brothers) ignited a vibrant movement within the church, even as leadership remained divided and largely silent.[16]

Similarly, throughout the first half of the twentieth century, prominent Catholics had remained, by and large, on the sidelines of the civil rights issue, especially when it came to segregation in the American South. Catholic leadership there had been all too content to tolerate—even implicitly accommodate and support—segregationist practices. One notable example was Thomas J. Toolen, bishop of Mobile, Alabama, who explicitly forbade clergy from challenging segregation, instead calling on parishioners to "bring God to the negro" through separate churches and missions.[17] Yet, as the civil rights movement evolved, so did Catholic leadership, across the country and in the Deep South, where, even as Toolen refused to consider integration, other Catholics, like Father Albert Foley, worked to desegregate businesses in the state. Catholic leadership's seemingly inconsistent stance reflected the church's complicated place in American society. Catholics were a minority in the South, still viewed with suspicion and often treated as belonging outside the Christian mainstream. In this context, church leadership faced serious constraints, which coupled with its hierarchical structure, made universal pronouncements tricky, leading to reluctance to speak out about racial injustice. But as early as 1958, national leadership, perhaps anticipating the success of civil rights movements, attempted to get ahead of the issue. That year, US Catholic bishops issued a statement of profound and unprecedented moral clarity, stating that "the heart of the race question is moral and religious" and stating in unequivocal terms that "segregation cannot be reconciled with the Christian view" of humanity. By the time of Martin Luther King's martyrdom in 1968, the Catholic position had become much more explicit in its support for integration and civil rights, with Pope Paul VI calling King "a Christian prophet for racial integration" and vowing to "lift up the burden of the poor and oppressed in our land" during his Angelus address in St. Peter's Square.

For an increasing number of Catholics, that promise also meant taking up the cause of newcomers, especially Mexican immigrants, though others as well (especially Cuban refugees) at a time when doing so was hardly popular. It is true, of course, that Catholic leaders had previously spoken in support of immigrant groups, especially waves of late nineteenth-century, Polish, Italian, German, and Irish.[18] But the church had also been complicit, at least through sins of omission, in the deportation of immigrants earlier in the century, when one million Mexicans were expelled in 1954 during Operation Wetback. One writer has characterized the early to mid-twentieth-century American Catholic Church as, at best, a "formidable but inconsistent ally" of ethnic Mexicans in the United States.[19]

In many ways, the church's (and its members') changing attitudes reflected the dilemma of Mexican Americans. In fact, even Mexican Americans had complicated feelings about braceros and the undocumented, with opinions ranging from ambivalent at best to downright hostile at worst, and this hostility was hardly new in the 1960s. Mexican Americans had long found the immigration issue to be a central, and vexing, problem, and during the 1950s, some of the most prominent organizations and leaders in the community endorsed the mass deportation of Mexican immigrants.[20] Yet some Catholics had denounced the deportations and continued to advocate for the rights of immigrants, and groups like Católicos por La Raza helped solidify the connection between Catholic activism and the Mexican American struggle, which itself quickly became intertwined with questions about immigration and the role of Mexican immigrants in the Chicano movement.[21]

Among Mexican Americans, the immigration question came to a boiling point during the farmworker mobilization of the late 1960s and early 1970s, as César Chávez led mostly Mexican American workers through a prolonged struggle against growers, the state, and along the way, Mexican immigrants, whom he viewed as essential to strikebreaking efforts, not without reason. Still, to many of those who were part of the movement and to many others who saw themselves as allies to the cause, the optics of rejecting immigrants—sometimes violently—proved deeply troubling.[22]

When we consider the religious dimension of both the farmworker movement and Chicano identity, the quandary for Mexican Americans becomes even more evident. Chávez's movement was partly a labor struggle, but partly a Catholic mystical movement that saw itself as fulfilling a religious mission.[23] Catholic imagery and rhetoric were everywhere in the movement, from the banners of the Virgin Mary that adorned the head of processions (including the massive and iconic one from Delano to Sacramento, California, in September 1965) to Chávez's public fasts, which transformed him from a minor regional organizer to a national figure and the patron saint of all oppressed brown people in the Southwest. But Catholics—Chicano and otherwise—who supported him were stuck in a difficult position. On the one hand, they worked to support and promote the cause he was championing, and that meant adapting a hard line on strikebreakers. On the other hand, Chávez was in direct conflict with an increasingly pro-immigrant Catholic stance on immigrants, including that of his "devoted mentors," like Bishop Joseph Donnelly and Monsignor George Higgins, as well as Pope Paul VI's proclamations in the late 1960s calling on church leadership to "more aptly respond to the needs of migrant people in these times."[24]

Sustained pressure forced Chávez to shift his position in 1975, when opposition to his anti-immigrant posture had become so divisive that it threatened to destroy the movement. It was then that he openly disavowed his previous strategy and admitted mistakes, which were made, he said, "in the heat of the struggle."[25] This shift led to countless other Chicanos taking up the cause of the undocumented as well. Seeing in them their own social struggles, Chicanos emerged as the foremost defenders of the undocumented. If in the 1950s Mexican Americans viewed immigrants as economic competitors and in the 1960s as obstacles to unionization, by the 1970s most Chicanos had come to see themselves and immigrants as "one people without borders."[26] This is not to suggest that this view was unanimous or static. Certainly, well into the 1980s and beyond, divisions among Mexican Americans remained.[27] But hostility toward immigrants was increasingly rare by the mid-1970s, when pro-immigrant sentiment had become the norm among Mexican Americans.[28]

The costs of this shift would become evident in the decades that followed, but for Mexican American activists in the 1970s, the Chicano struggle for social, cultural, and economic rights and the fight for self-determination could not be reconciled with anti-immigrant views. No one was more important in the movement for immigrants' rights than Humberto "Bert" Corona, a labor organizer from California. In defiance of César Chávez and the old guard of the Mexican American community, Corona had worked to organize undocumented people and build a movement for their rights, seeing such unity as essential to the cause of poor brown people in the United States. In 1968, along with Soledad "Chole" Alatorre, he established the Centro de Acción Social Autónomo (CASA). CASA activists sought to organize Mexican workers and educate them about their civil rights, their labor rights, and their human rights. CASA also focused on empowering immigrants on practical subjects like reading, writing, and driving.[29]

Corona was a revolutionary figure in the history of immigrants' rights, but he did not engender this movement alone. Though rarely credited with helping to spur and shape the immigrants' rights movement, a young priest named Mark Day proved essential to the movement. Day worked with Corona to publicize the plight of immigrants and helped him make the case that Catholics and all people of conscience had a moral and ethical obligation to fight for the rights of the foreign-born, including those in the country without documents. Together, Corona and Day drafted the "Immigrants' Bill of Rights," which asserted that immigrants had the rights to be free from deportation, to normalize their status, and to have access to equal pay and protections on the job.[30]

Other prominent Catholic leaders were also instrumental in providing the nascent immigrants' rights movement with moral authority. Among them was Father Sean O'Malley, an outspoken priest who was among the first to call on Catholics to consider the struggle of immigrants as a religious duty. O'Malley was especially insistent on calling on Chicanos to think of the undocumented as their brethren. O'Malley consistently used the pulpit to remind the faithful that immigrants were not threats, but instead, people who did valuable work for society. Another such Catholic leader was Bishop Juan Arzube of Los Angeles, who called immigrants a "hunted species" who deserved protection rather than hate.[31] Father Allan Figueroa Deck, another influential priest in the region, urged Catholics and Christians to see in Mexican immigrants a test of their faith and of their willingness to welcome the stranger. Writing in the Catholic paper the *Southern Cross*, Deck demanded the humane treatment of immigrants. Until this time, most Catholics who spoke about the immigration issue were content to call for the toleration of immigrants, or at most, their humane treatment. But by the late 1970s, the rhetoric had shifted, at times reflecting anti-capitalist sentiment, which although historically present in the Catholic tradition, was becoming much more unambiguous, even confrontational. Deck, for example, blamed "international elites and multinational corporations" for the immigrant crisis.[32] Catholic leadership's increasingly vocal defense of immigrants was sincere, but it was not isolated from its social context. Growing migration to the Southwest meant a growing Catholic population, since Mexican immigrants were overwhelmingly adherents of the faith. Attacks on immigrants were, essentially, attacks on Catholics.[33]

By the mid- to late 1970s, the immigration issue was inescapable. Dick Reavis, a journalist who wrote extensively about immigration at the time, remembers that through the 1950s and 1960s, immigration was an issue of regional concern, largely confined to the Southwest, especially Texas and California.[34] But in the 1970s, debates about immigration were everywhere, from small-town chatter to national newspapers, and eventually, Washington, DC. Toward the end of the decade, doing nothing seemed politically implausible. Both Democrats and Republicans spoke regularly of "immigration reform" and the need to address the immigration problem.

After his election in 1976, President Jimmy Carter promised to tackle immigration, placing it, in terms of importance, just below the oil crisis. But the Carter administration initially fumbled through the issue, apparently misjudging just how divisive it would prove. In order to study and evaluate the problem, Carter pressed Congress for the creation of an independent commission, eventually named the Select Commission on Immigration and Refugee Policy (SCIRP), which was formed in October 1978. From the beginning, the goal of the commission was to arrive at a compromise between opposing and competing factions. Significant debate about the composition and goal of the commission took place. Some suggested a narrow focus, others a broad debate. Some thought that the best way to arrive at a workable compromise was to include only moderate voices. Ultimately, the commission chose to tackle the issue comprehensively, including questions about trade policy, labor, population and demographics, and even the environment.

Carter initially chose Reuben Askew, an attorney and the former governor of Florida, to chair the commission. In 1979, however, Askew resigned to take the post of trade adviser for the Carter administration. Carter then asked Father Theodore "Ted" Hesburgh to lead the commission. Hesburgh was a respected theologian and scholar who served as president of the University of Notre Dame and who was widely respected by politicians across the political spectrum. More importantly, Hesburgh was thought to be someone who could balance the growing demands for respect for the human rights of migrants with the "national interest," or as he himself put it, the needs of "our own poor and unfortunate."[35] Hesburgh was widely estimated to be capable of producing "humane and even-handed" policy recommendations for immigration reform.[36]

Even so, Hesburgh could not have anticipated just how difficult it would be for the commission to arrive at recommendations that satisfied all parties. Balancing the interests of organized labor, employers, restrictionists, and ethnic groups proved all but impossible. Lawrence Fuchs, who was tasked with serving as the lead intermediary between these groups, later wrote that the job consisted of pure and utter frustration. Labor groups rejected the idea of including a guest worker program. Restrictionists outright dismissed the notion of supporting anything that included an amnesty provision. Mexican Americans and employers both rejected any consideration of sanctions on the use of undocumented labor, the latter worrying that it would eat into their profits and the former concerned that sanctions would lead to discrimination against people of Mexican descent.[37]

The commission did ultimately succeed in putting together a series of recommendations that, while hardly satisfying all parties, managed to draft a three-pronged approach that gave something to everyone: legalization for immigrants already in the country, employer sanctions to punish users of undocumented labor, and a "steady supply" of H-2 agricultural laborers through a managed guest worker program.[38]

After Ronald Reagan beat Carter in the 1980 election, it became his administration's task to ensure that the commission's recommendations would be shaped into a passable bill. The commission's fears that the various interest groups would clash proved inevitably true. Over the next five years, the bill appeared dead several times, though each time, "Lazarus" miraculously rose from the dead.[39] And considerable debate and negotiation eventually led to a bipartisan push to pass the bill, with Wyoming Republican senator Alan K. Simpson and Democratic Kentucky congressman Romano L. Mazzoli, the bill's sponsors, leading the effort. The bill found enough support and fought off enough opposition by 1986 to pass in the Senate on September 19, 1985 (69 to 30) and in the House of Representatives on October 9 (230 to 166). President Reagan signed the bill into law shortly thereafter in early November.

If the law managed to give every interest group something it wanted, it hardly satisfied any of them. For the nearly three million people who benefited from the amnesty provision, however, life changed dramatically. The fear that undocumented immigrants constantly felt was wiped away, and now they could live with a degree of dignity, gain access to the benefits of American society, and even become citizens in time.[40] The security that the "Reagan amnesty" brought to those who benefited from it—mostly men—also led to new patterns of migration, as men brought their families to the United States to remain here, disrupting the pattern of circular migration that had characterized the decades prior.[41]

This new form of migration, combined with the perceived failure to stop migration, led to a fierce backlash among conservative and nativist groups. It was true that IRCA did not stop migration. In fact, while the readjustment of three million undocumented people did initially reduce the number of "illegal" people in the country, in the years that followed, the number of unsanctioned immigrants crossing the border and living in the United States reached unprecedented levels. By the early 1990s, the number of undocumented immigrants in the United States was estimated to be around four million, causing American citizens and politicians to worry about the potential burden and "load" they caused to the economy.[42]

Of the millions of unsanctioned immigrants in the country, over one million were estimated to reside in California, and that is where the "new nativism" ignited a renewed restrictionist movement, largely fueled by resentment of both immigrants themselves and politicians, who, in the eyes of concerned citizens, had not only failed to stop unsanctioned immigration but actually encouraged it by legalizing millions.[43] Enraged, and taking advantage of the referendum system in the state of California, a group of anti-immigrant activists—led by Dick Mountjoy, an assemblyman representing Monrovia; Alan Nelson, the former commissioner of the Immigration and Naturalization Service (INS) under Ronald Reagan; Harold Ezell, a former regional director for the INS; and Ron Prince, an Orange County accountant—worked to get on the ballot an initiative aimed at severely restricting undocumented immigrants' access to social services, eventually doing so after collecting more than half a million signatures.[44] Proposition 187, as it came to be known, called on citizens to "Save Our State." The SOS initiative cleverly evoked a serious emergency caused by immigrants, who, its proponents claimed, cost California taxpayers millions. Whether this was the case remains a matter of debate. It is true, of course, that immigrants used social services like schools, hospitals, and roads. But it is also true that their contributions likely offset most of the burden they placed on the state.[45]

From the beginning, however, it was clear that although proponents of Proposition 187 portrayed the immigration issue as a fiscal matter the underlying driver was a concern with demographic changes, cultural anxiety, white resentment, and outright xenophobia. As numerous scholars have observed, the law was presented and couched in color-blind language but was "motivated by racism, nativism, and ethnocentrism" and reflected a particularly nefarious and difficult to confront form of racism: one expressed through the ballot box, anonymously and (at least nominally) democratically.[46]

For immigrants and immigrants' rights groups, which included Catholic bishops, clergy, and laypeople, the threat loomed large.[47] This was especially true after it became clear that the bill, even if crafted and sponsored by some of the most extreme voices in the state, had substantial public support. Because the initiative coincided with the gubernatorial race (surely by design), the two contenders were forced to take sides. Kathleen Brown, the Democratic challenger to incumbent Pete Wilson, the Republican governor of the state, offered a paltry defense of immigrants' rights, while Wilson saw in 187 a tremendous political opportunity. As a central voice in the Senate's debates about IRCA in the 1980s, Wilson had urged the government to open the door to guest workers; now he strongly supported the anti-immigrant proposition, making it the central issue in his campaign. Wilson ran television ads with ominous images of "illegals" who "keep coming" and implied that the state was being overwhelmed by hordes of nameless criminals.[48] An anti-immigrant posture, Wilson thought, was a winning strategy, and he was right. Polls consistently found strong support for the anti-immigrant proposition. This was true even among minority groups, including Mexican Americans: a quarter of them voted in favor of Proposition 187, and some polls suggested that the number could have been much higher if not for the relentless organizing efforts of pro-immigrant activists.[49]

Still, immigrants fought back, taking to the streets and organizing on the job and in their communities. For many of them Proposition 187 was a wake-up call, and rather than squash their visibility and strength as intended, it instead fueled both. As one woman explained, "I ended up becoming more involved in my community. I became more aware of the things that were going on."[50] And they did not do it alone. Mexican American groups, once ambivalent at best about immigrants and immigrants' rights, now stood squarely on the side of the undocumented seeing in the rhetoric about them a dangerously racist streak. Labor unions, too, were much more receptive to immigrants' rights than they had been in previous years and decades. The AFL-CIO, though still ambivalent about the role of immigrants in the labor movement, felt enough pressure to urge the defeat of 187. And some unions went further. The United Farm Workers, though largely defeated after the 1970s, and though previously hostile toward undocumented immigrants, now made it their issue. Dolores Huerta embraced a leading role, taking the union's pro-immigrant message door-to-door.[51]

And as before, Catholic clergy and leadership emerged as central moral voices in the debate. Perhaps none was more active in the fight against Proposition 187 than Cardinal Roger Mahony, who, as Mario García has noted had long "championed immigrant rights."[52] Mahony warned that Christians were facing, in the debates about immigration, a "test" of their "relationship with God." Mahony, who had long been active in the fight for immigrants' rights, urged Catholics to see Christ in the struggle of the immigrants, and to remember the church's teaching on the proper treatment of "the poor, the widow, and the alien."[53] Other Catholics took aim at the law as an immoral, mean-spirited development.[54] The California Catholic Conference, led by Mahony, was joined by other Christian groups, including the Southern Christian Leadership Conference, whose executive director, Joe Hicks, said, "We've got to send a message to the rest of the nation that California will not stand on a platform of bigotry, racism, and scapegoating."[55]

Unfortunately for immigrants and immigrants' rights activists, Hicks was wrong, and moral opposition and political mobilization—much of it taking place in Catholic churches across California, where clergy and activists rallied and organized against the initiative, from the pulpit and the pews—were not enough to prevent the passage of Proposition 187. In the end, the initiative was successful, passing easily by a margin of almost two to one.[56] And despite Mahony's and the church hierarchy's strong stance opposing "a devastating assault on human dignity," a majority of white Catholics, 58 percent, supported the proposition.[57] In fact, among the many lessons of Proposition 187 was the revelation that Catholic laypeople, despite the historical accusations of deference to church hierarchy, could prove stubbornly resistant to pastoral guidance. One man among the 777,122 Catholics who supported Prop 187 rejected Mahony's call to consider "our sisters and brothers who will suffer because of this law," responding as thousands of others did by asking, "Is it our moral obligation to feed and clothe illegals, to give them free medical and social services while our own senior citizens and multiple thousands of homes are without these services?"[58]

Despite its overwhelming victory at the polls, 187 did not survive legal challenges, which were submitted almost immediately after the law passed. In the days that followed, Judge W. Matthew Byrne issued a temporary restraining order against the law, and in December Judge

Mariana Pfaelzer placed a permanent injunction on the law's provisions. In March 1998, the law was found unconstitutional. Over the following years, Latinos and progressive allies came to respond to the nativist wave in remarkable ways. The ugliness of the law and the movement that created it led to the political mobilization of Latinos on a scale never previously seen. One of the ways this manifested itself was in the rise of Latino politicians. More broadly, many have credited the law with creating a sustained progressive response, one that, they argue, has "turned California blue."[59]

To think about Proposition 187 as a failure, however, ignores its significance in inspiring a renewed nativist movement that produced a bevy of copycat laws, from Arizona's SB 1070 in 2010 to Georgia's House Bill 87 the following year, and of course, the rise of Donald Trump, whose election to the presidency was largely fueled by a reaction to continued immigration and demographic and cultural changes across the country. If California failed to criminalize immigrants—at least to the extent that many of the supporters of 187 had hoped—it did provide lessons to anti-immigrant activists, including the enduring power of xenophobia, the utility of coded language, and the ways democratic institutions and norms could be weaponized to craft anti-democratic, discriminatory outcomes. The rights of immigrants and refugees suffered severe setbacks in the age of Obama and especially under Trump, whose administration made family separation, indefinite detention, and border militarization cornerstones of his tenure.[60]

But neither did immigrants and their allies remain quiet or accept the status as passive victims. In response to the policies of Obama—"the deporter-in-chief"—and Donald Trump, perhaps the most agressively anti-immigrant president since Dwight D. Eisenhower, activists fought back, creating grassroots organizations, raising money for migrant defense, and taking direct action in the streets across the country.[61]

The convergence of Catholic history and immigration history in the twentieth-century United States was a dynamic and complicated one—a story of change and diversity, of contradictions and paradoxes. But there have also been continuities—namely, the presence and voices of activist Catholics who viewed their faith as a calling to speak for those most vulnerable, to welcome the stranger. To see this activist tradition at work today, one need only look to the efforts of Catholic activists like the seventy people who were arrested in July 2019 for demonstrating in the Senate Office Building against the draconian policies of the Trump administration. Before being arrested, the activists made noise, disrupting business as usual by loudly offering up the Lord's Prayer and performatively forming a cross on the floor with their bodies, quite literally engaging in bodily politics with a religious edge. Emulating the symbol of Christ on the cross, suffering for the sins of others, activists were willing—eager, in some cases—to "put our bodies on the line," as Sister Marge Clark of the Sisters of Charity of the Blessed Virgin Mary told the *Washington Post*, in the service of immigrants, "to go beyond words, to put your body where your words are, where you beliefs are."[62] Like those who came before them, these Catholics felt compelled by their faith to act, to speak out against the injustices of their day, and to continue the long tradition of dissent and resistance—and of immigrants' rights advocacy—that has characterized the progressive American Catholic tradition since the beginning of the twentieth century.

NOTES

1. Mary Thornton, "Agreement Reached on Aliens Bill," *Washington Post*, October 15, 1986.
2. Ronald Reagan, "Statement on Signing the Immigration Reform and Control Act of 1986," November 6, 1986, American Presidency Project, www.presidency.ucsb.edu.
3. Maura Jane Farrelly, *Anti-Catholicism in America, 1620–1860* (Cambridge: Cambridge University Press, 2018); Shaun Casey, *The Making of a Catholic President: Kennedy vs. Nixon, 1960* (Oxford: Oxford University Press, 2009).
4. Jon Gjerde, *Catholicism and the Shaping of Nineteenth-Century America* (Cambridge: Cambridge University Press, 2012), 18; Farrelly, *Anti-Catholicism in America*, xi; Keith Somerville, *Radio Propaganda and the Broadcasting of Hatred: Historical Development and Definitions* (New York: Palgrave Macmillan, 2012), 37.
5. Philip Gleason, "Catholicism and Cultural Change in the 1960s," *Review of Politics* 34, no. 4 (October 1972): 91–107.
6. Pastoral Constitution on the Church in the Modern World *Gaudium et Spes*, Promulgated by His Holiness, Pope Paul VI, December 7, 1965.
7. Dan Kanstroom, *Deportation Nation: Outsiders in American History* (Cambridge: Harvard University Press, 2007), 221.
8. David Reimers, *Other Immigrants: The Global Origins of the American People* (New York: New York University Press, 2005), 5.

9 Eleanor M. Hadley, "A Critical Analysis of the Wetback Problem," *Law and Contemporary Problems* 21, no. 2 (Spring 1956): 334.

10 Significant debate has taken place—and continues to take place—about the terminology used to describe immigrants and Americans of Latin American descent. The vast majority being historically ethnic Mexicans, until the middle of the twentieth century, they were often called simply "Mexican" or, for those who held US citizenship, "Mexican American." As increasingly radical activists embraced new identities grounded in ethnic pride and self-determination beginning in the 1960s, a new term came into existence: "Chicano/a." Then, in the 1980s, as other Spanish-speaking groups grew in numbers and influence alongside ethnic Mexicans and as the Chicano movement declined, "Latino" and "Hispanic" became commonly used terms, even as many Chicanos rejected the terms as homogenizing and politically destructive. Recently, numerous scholars and activists have preferred to use "Latinx" in order to accommodate various gender identities. While I applaud the goals of the latter, in this chapter I generally choose to use terms based on the context of the community, group, or time period being examined.

11 William Korcik, "The Wetback Story," *Commonweal*, July 1951, 328.

12 David Fitzgerald, *A Nation of Emigrants: How Mexico Manages Its Migration* (Berkeley: University of California Press, 2008), 83.

13 "Concentration Camps USA," Box 1, Folder "ACPFB 1969–1974," American Committee for the Protection of the Foreign Born Records, Tamiment Library and Robert F. Wagner Labor Archives, New York University.

14 Joseph G. Morgan, "A Change of Course: American Catholics, Anticommunism, and the Vietnam War," *US Catholic Historian* 22, no. 4 (Fall 2004): 117–30.

15 Gallup Organization, "Catholics More Dovish on Vietnam, Poll Shows," *Indianapolis News*, May 12, 1990, A3; David E. Settje, *Faith and War: How Christians Debated the Cold and Vietnam Wars* (New York: New York University Press, 2011), 9; Geoffrey Shaw, *The Lost Mandate of Heaven: The American Betrayal of Ngo Dinh Diem, President of Vietnam* (San Francisco: Ignatius Press, 2015).

16 Nancy L. Roberts, *Dorothy Day and the Catholic Worker* (Albany: State University of New York Press, 1984), 172.

17 Keith R. Claridy, "'Bring God to the Negro, Bring the Negro to God': Thomas Joseph Toolen, Archbishop of Mobile (1927–1969), His Culture, His Religion, and His Mission" (MA thesis, Auburn University, 2006).

18 Kim Voss and Irene Bloemraad, *Rallying for Immigrant Rights: The Fight for Inclusion in 21st Century America* (Berkeley: University of California Press, 2011), 120.

19 Roberto R. Treviño and Richard V. Francaviglia, *Catholicism in the American West: A Rosary of Hidden Voices* (College Station: Texas A&M University Press, 2007), 133.

20 American GI Forum of Texas and Texas State Federation of Labor, *What Price Wetbacks?* (Austin: Texas Federation of Labor and the American GI Forum of Texas, 1953).

21 Mario T. García, *Católicos: Resistance and Affirmation in Chicano Catholic History* (Austin: University of Texas Press, 2010); David Gutiérrez, *Walls and Mirrors: Mexican Americans, Mexican Immigrants, and the Politics of Ethnicity* (Berkeley: University of California Press, 1995).
22 Frank Bardacke, "The UFW and the Undocumented," *International Labor and Working Class History* 83 (Spring 2013): 162–69.
23 Stephen R. Lloyd-Moffett, "The Mysticism and Social Action of César Chávez," in *Latino Religions and Civic Activism in the United States*, ed. Gastón Espinosa, Virgilio Elizondo, and Jesse Miranda (Oxford: Oxford University Press, 2011), 35–51.
24 Victor Riesel, "Bishops Confer on Chavez' Boycott," *Times* (San Mateo), December 23, 1974, 1; Pope Paul VI, "New Norms for the Care of Migrants, Apostolic Letter, August 15, 1969"; "Sacred Congregation for Bishops, Instructions on the Pastoral Care of People Who Migrate," August 22, 1969, Herman Baca Papers (MSS 649), Special Collections and Archives, UC San Diego.
25 "An Open Letter to Farm Workers from Cesar Chavez," *El Malcriado*, July 7, 1975, Box 17, Folder 24, Bert Corona Papers, Department of Special Collections and University Archives, Stanford University.
26 Resolution passed at the National Chicano Immigration Conference, May 24, 1980, Box 43, Folder 1, Herman Baca Papers.
27 Frank del Olmo, "Chicanos Divided by Sympathy for Aliens, Fear of Own Jobs," *Los Angeles Times*, March 25, 1972.
28 David Gutiérrez, "Sin Fronteras? Chicanos, Mexican Americans, and the Emergence of the Contemporary Mexican Immigration Debate, 1968–1978," *Journal of American Ethnic History* 10, no. 4 (Summer 1991): 5–37.
29 "What Is CASA? How Does it Function? How Was It Started?," ca. 1968, Box 11, Folder 2, Corona Papers.
30 Mark Day, "A Charter of Rights for Immigrant Workers," ca. 1973, Box 11, Folder 8, Corona Papers.
31 Juan Arzube, "Illegal Aliens—Refugees from Hunger," March 26, 1975, talk at the Embassy Auditorium, Box 9, Folder 23, Corona Papers.
32 Allan Figueroa Deck, "Talking Point: Seeing Christ in Mexican Aliens," *Southern Cross*, February 23, 1978, 10.
33 David G. Gutiérrez, "The New Turn in Chicano/Mexicano History: Integrating Religious Belief and Practice," in *Catholics in the American Century: Recasting Narratives of US History*, ed. R. Scott Appleby and Kathleen Sprows Cummings (Ithaca: Cornell University Press, 2012), 109–34.
34 Dick Reavis, telephone interview with author, February 27, 2017.
35 Theodore Hesburgh, qtd. in Roger Daniels, *Guarding the Golden Door: American Immigration Policy and Immigrants since 1882* (New York: Hill and Wang, 2004), 221.
36 UPI, "Hesburgh: On Immigrants," *Indianapolis News*, April 28, 1981.

37 Lawrence H. Fuchs, "The corpse that would not die: The Immigration Reform and Control Act of 1986," *Revue Européenne des Migrations Internationales* 6, no. 1 (1990): 111–27.
38 Muzaffar Chishti and Charles Kamasaki, "IRCA in Retrospect: Guideposts for Today's Immigration Reform," January 2014, Migration Policy Institute, Washington, DC.
39 Daniel J. Tichenor, *Dividing Lines: The Politics of Immigration Control in America* (Princeton: Princeton University Press, 2002), 261.
40 Juan Báez Barragán, interview with Mireya Loza, July 27, 2005, Item #477, Bracero History Archive, http://braceroarchive.org.
41 Ana R. Minian, *Undocumented Lives: The Untold Story of Mexican Migration* (Cambridge: Harvard University Press, 2018), 104.
42 Deborah Sontag, "Illegal Aliens Put Uneven Load on States, Study Says," *New York Times*, September 15, 1994.
43 Robin Dale Jacobson, *The New Nativism: Proposition 187 and the Debate over Immigration* (Minneapolis: University of Minnesota Press, 2008).
44 Thomas Elias, "'Save Our State' May Do Opposite," *North County Times*, July 19, 1994.
45 National Research Council, *The New Americans: Economic, Demographic, and Fiscal Effects of Immigration* (Washington, DC: National Academies Press, 1997).
46 Jacobson, *New Nativism*, 5.
47 Holly Selby, "US Bishops Condemn California Anti-Immigrant Law, Euthanasia," *Tech* (MIT), November 18, 1994.
48 Tanya Maria Golash-Boza, *Immigration Nation: Raids, Detentions, and Deportations in Post-9/11 America* (New York: Routledge, 2015), 155.
49 Lina Y. Newton, "Why Some Latinos Supported Proposition 187: Testing the Economic Threat and Cultural Identity Hypotheses," *Social Science Quarterly* 81, no. 1 (March 2000): 180.
50 Leonel Sanchez, "Latino Activists Vow to Prevent Future '187s,'" *San Diego Union-Tribune*, July 30, 1999, A16.
51 Randy Shaw, *Beyond the Fields: Cesar Chavez, the UFW, and the Struggle for Justice in the 21st Century* (Berkeley: University of California Press, 2008).
52 García, *Católicos*, 239.
53 "Unofficial Translation of Cardinal Mahony's Immigration Address at Hispanic Evangelization Conference," July 28, 1994, Herman Baca Papers, https://library.ucsd.edu.
54 John S. W. Park, "Race, Discourse, and Proposition 187," *Michigan Journal of Race and Law* 2 (Fall 1996): 175–204.
55 Patrick J. McDonnell and Robert Lopez, "LA March against Prop. 187 Draws 70,000," *Los Angeles Times*, October 17, 1994.
56 John Dart, "187 Shows Clergy's Weak Influence on Electorate," *Los Angeles Times*, November 19, 1994, B1.

57 Patrick J. McDonnell, "Mahony to Fight Ballot Measure on Immigrants," *Los Angeles Times*, July 24, 1994, B4; Tim Tesconi, "Mean-Spirited or Timely Message (Con: It Will Increase Hate, Discrimination)," *Press Democrat* (Santa Rosa), October 30, 1994, A10.

58 Walter Sheasby, "Did Only Racists Vote for Proposition 187?," Herman Baca Papers (digital collection), https://library.ucsd.edu; "Cardinal Mahony's Address Opposing Proposition 187," July 28, 1994, Herman Baca Papers; Leonel Sanchez, "Angry Latinos Line Up against 187," *San Diego Union-Tribune*, September 12, 1994, B1–B4.

59 Nicole Hemmer, "Republican Nativism Helped Turn California Blue. Trump Could Do the Same for the Whole Country," *Vox*, January 20, 2017, www.vox.com.

60 Sarah Pierce and Andrew Selee, "Immigration under Trump: A Review of Policy Shifts in the Year since the Election," December 2007, Migration Policy Institute, www.migrationpolicy.org.

61 Mirren Gidda, "When It Comes to Trump vs. Obama, Who's the Real Deporter-in-Chief?," *Newsweek*, April 18, 2017, www.newsweek.com.

62 Marissa J. Lang, "70 Catholics Arrested in DC Protest over Trump Immigration Policies," *Washington Post*, July 20, 2019, www.washingtonpost.com.

11

The Spiritual Is Political

The Pilsen Via Crucis as a Path to Resistance

ANNE M. MARTÍNEZ

On the afternoon of December 24, 1976, fire erupted in a three-story apartment building in Pilsen, a predominantly Mexican neighborhood west of downtown Chicago.[1] On the third floor, neighbors and relatives who were celebrating the eleventh birthday of Jesús García were trapped by flames roaring through the stairwells of the building. When firefighters arrived, desperate mothers were dropping children from third-floor windows to the waiting arms of adults below. Ten children and two women perished in the fire, and eight others were seriously injured. Charles Pierce, of the Chicago Fire Department, reported that the "bodies were so badly burned we have not been able to identify them." He continued, "Nobody around here seems to know who they are."[2] Witnesses reported at the time that the fire department was slow to respond to the fire, "could not give directions [in Spanish] to panicking tenants amidst the hysteria," and did not understand bystanders yelling that there were still children in the building.[3]

Community members gathered two blocks away at St. Vitus Catholic Church, a social, religious, and political hub of Pilsen, for a prayer service for the deceased at the start of midnight Mass that night. After Mass, parishioners stayed to comfort those who had lost family members and homes. The following afternoon, Christmas Day, representatives from other Catholic parishes joined St. Vitus parishioners to plan a funeral for the victims of the fire. In the days that followed, neighbors gathered funds to support the victims and pay for the funeral. Their anger grew as news reports suggested that the carelessness and ignorance of the residents rather than poor coordination and communication with and within the fire department and unsafe housing conditions were the

In Loving Memory Of BERTHA CASTRO Age 4 LINO CASTRO Age 4 LETICIA CASTRO Age 2 HERMINIA REYES Age 24 JUAN R. REYES Age 4 JULISA REYES 11 months ADELIDA REYES 1 month OTILIA GARCIA Age 30 JUANITA GARCIA Age 10 MICHELLE MARTINEZ Age 5 MICHAEL MARTINEZ Age 3 SERGIO MIRANDA Age 5	At Rest December 24, 1976 Mass of the Resurrection St. Vitus Church Tuesday, December 28, 1976 at 10:00 a.m. Interment St. Mary Cemetery ORACION Reconoce, Señor, tu criatura, obra no de dioses extraños, sino tuya, Dios ùnico, vivo y verdadero, porque no hay otro Dios más que tú, y nadie te iguala en las obras. Haz, Señor, que tu dulce presencia le llene el alma de alegria; Olvida sus iniquidades pasadas y los extravios a que fué arrastrada por sus pasiono ha renunciado a la fé del nes; Porque aùn cuando pecó padre, del Hijo y del Espiritu Santo, sino que ha conservado el celo del Señor y adorado fielmente a Dios, creador de todas las cosas. Amen.

Figure 11.1. Funeral card for victims of Pilsen fire, 1976. Reproduced by permission from the Archdiocese of Chicago.

cause of the deaths. A mass funeral with twelve white caskets lining the aisles of St. Vitus in the form of a cross took place with donations from neighbors, businesses, and city officials. St. Vitus banned photographers from the funeral Mass to protest media representations of the community in the wake of the fire. In his homily, Father James Colleran urged those present "to mourn the dead by struggling for the living."[4]

The living—families of those who perished in the fire—made the extraordinary decision to mourn their lost family members as a group, rather than individually, signaling solidarity among the families and making the funeral a community event. "In the context of migration, a funerary ritual . . . offers an opportunity to enhance an identity and an origin that is under pressure from the surrounding culture."[5] The year that ended with the devastating fire had been a busy one for Latines pushing back against city indifference and hostility.[6] In the spring, Latines protested the hiring practices of the Chicago Transit Authority,

St. Luke's Hospital, and Rush-Presbyterian Hospital. One protest flyer circulated at St. Vitus read, "How can Latinos who make up over 50% of the hospital's immediate service area expect to receive adequate health care if St. Luke's hospital does nothing to employ persons who are competent in both English and Spanish???" This was about jobs, to be sure, but also about the treatment Pilsen residents received in their daily lives at neighborhood businesses and services hostile toward the majority Spanish-speaking population.[7]

The Christmas Eve fire and another apartment fire a few days later served to catalyze ongoing activism with spiritual fortitude to produce an enduring commemoration of the lives of the twelve in the first Pilsen Via Crucis on Good Friday 1977.[8] Mexicans in Pilsen politicized their spirituality by using the Via Crucis to call out neglect and abuse by city officials. Participants stopped for an "Our Father" in front of the burned-out building of the Christmas Eve fire, reminding participants and observers that the impetus for this ritual was the loss of a dozen lives at the hands of unscrupulous landlords and underperforming city services.[9] This politicized spirituality, which "is realized collectively in a public venue and is directed at social and political issues but yet resonates with religious beliefs," is renewed annually through the Pilsen Via Crucis.[10] Subsequent years have targeted immigration and labor issues, gentrification and displacement, and archdiocesan neglect in Pilsen. The Pilsen Via Crucis challenges the sacred/secular divide by taking a religious commemoration to the streets of Chicago.

The repetition of the ritual annually not only serves to re-sacralize the neighborhood but also serves as a critical pedagogy to remind younger generations, as well as newer inhabitants of Pilsen, that this is a Mexican Catholic space.[11] The first Pilsen Via Crucis in 1977 was a community response to the discrimination and chronic housing problems Mexicans experienced; its annual reenactment commemorates the decades-long struggle for the soul of Pilsen. For Mexican Catholics in Chicago this is not just a matter of faith, but indeed a political practice. Though the Via Crucis is attended by thousands, now including non-Latines and residents of other neighborhoods and cities, it remains an annual reminder of the religious face of Latine resistance in Chicago: the spiritual is political. Mexicans in Pilsen have forged a spiritual fortitude to resist gentrification, governmental and archdiocesan neglect and hostility, and other forms of violence against the community. The embodiment of Christ in the streets of Pilsen remakes Catholicism as a source of solidarity and comfort for Mexicans in Chicago. I begin with a brief consideration of the Living Stations of the Cross as a Catholic ritual and embodiment as a theological and practical concern, before analyzing the multilayered politicized spirituality in action in Pilsen.

From the Embodiment of Christ to the Embodiment of Mexican Pilsen

Theologians continue to wrestle with the meaning of Jesus' body, often neglecting the bodies of his believers. Though the Passion Play has a long history in Europe, Mexicans in Pilsen have reinvented the tradition in the context of their circumstances in Chicago. The Passion of Christ, Stations of the Cross, Via Dolorosa (Way of Sorrow), or Via Crucis (Way of the Cross) tells the story of Jesus' trial, crucifixion, and entombing, commemorated each year on Good Friday in anticipation of His resurrection on Easter Sunday. In the fifteenth and sixteenth centuries, Franciscans built outdoor shrines in Europe reproducing Holy Land sites that commemorated Jesus' journey, usually highlighting six major events. In the late seventeenth century, Spanish Franciscan communities made the Stations of the Cross part of their annual liturgical calendars, including plaques inside churches marking the events or stations. Within a century, the number of stations was fixed at fourteen and they became common in Catholic churches around the world. The fourteen stations usually appear as plaques, carvings, paintings, or even stained-glass windows around the interior perimeter of churches. The stations are as follows: I. Jesus is condemned to death; II. Jesus is made to carry the cross; III. Jesus falls for the first time; IV. Jesus meets his mother; V. Simon of Cyrene helps Jesus carry the cross; VI. Veronica wipes the face of Jesus; VII. Jesus falls for the second time; VIII. Jesus meets the women of Jerusalem; IX. Jesus falls a third time; X. Jesus is stripped; XI. Jesus is placed on the cross; XII. Jesus dies on the cross; XIII. Jesus is removed from the cross; and XIV. Jesus is laid in the tomb. During Good Friday services, the celebrant, sometimes accompanied by actors playing out the events at each station, makes his way from station to station reciting or performing the steps of Jesus' journey. It is a somber service, which has been embraced by artists, musicians, and believers for centuries, marking one of the most important and meaningful days of the Christian calendar. It is a day of mourning and reflection on the meaning of Jesus' sacrifice, in contrast to the celebratory nature of Easter and Christmas.

The Living Stations of the Cross, the live reenactment of Christ's journey, began in the first half of the seventeenth century and had regional popularity in parts of Europe and Spanish and Portuguese colonies.[12] In the early twentieth century traditionalists eschewed turning the Stations of the Cross into "an occasion for idle sightseeing" or turning religion into spectacle.[13] This perspective echoes centuries-old critiques by Northern European Christians of the emotive practices of Southern Europeans and nonwhite believers, reproduced in the twentieth-century United States as Irish and German Catholic priests criticized Italian and Mexican Catholic practice as laden with superstition and idolatry.[14] Mexican Catholics in Chicago have reproduced the Mexican custom of the Via Crucis to perform their faith and their culture in a hostile setting.

The revival of the Living Stations of the Cross in the late twentieth-century United States reflects a broader shift in theology and practice. In the post–Vatican II era, and as other social movements reshaped many denominations, the participatory element of the Living Stations of the Cross appeals to many liturgists and laypeople.[15] The Via Crucis "allows people to engage with the ritual in ways that they don't get to engage with other types of experience."[16] In many instances, much of that focus, however, is still on the afterlife—on reminders that believers will be redeemed, and that Jesus died for their sins. Joseph Donnella, a Lutheran evangelical pastor, writes, "As they gazed on him who was tormented," referring to Jesus on the cross, "they understood the Lord, their God, to be fashioning a people who were able to look ahead, to look beyond the here and now, to the ultimate transformation of this world and their world."[17] The transubstantiation enacted in the Last Supper, along with Jesus' resurrection, are the focal point of Christian belief and skeptics' disbelief. The Stations of the Cross also center Jesus as the embodiment of God. "It is on the cross that God identifies with those who are suffering; the cross discloses God's weakness and vulnerability. Because of love, God volunteers to suffer with other suffering people, giving them hope and strength."[18] In the twenty-first century, many Christian communities have performed the Living Stations of the Cross in an effort to bring themselves closer to Jesus and his suffering.[19] The contemporary Living Stations are often characterized as "remind[ing] people of Jesus' suffering and devotion."[20] But this coverage fails to address the theological and political value of the Pilsen Via Crucis. The politicized spirituality of the Pilsen Via Crucis connects Jesus' suffering and that of his community to the suffering of Mexicans in Chicago.

Theologians have delved more into the bodies of believers in recent decades, but with scant attention to race. Embodiment theology covers "the creation of the body, the gendered body, the sexual body, the disciplined body, the sanctification of the body, the clothing of the body, the body and the worship of God, the suffering and healing of the body, the death of the body, and the future of the body."[21] The theological approach to embodiment, defined by Pope John Paul II, has limits. "The body, and it alone, is capable of making visible what is invisible, the spiritual and divine," according to Pope John Paul II. "It was created to transfer into the visible reality of the world, the invisible mystery hidden in God from time immemorial, and thus to be a sign of it."[22] What John Paul and most theologians neglect is the ways that human bodies are marked as lesser or different by race, national origin, gender, and sexuality, making the experience of lived religion distinctly different, even within the universal church.

These ethereal elements of faith belie the suffering of Mexican Catholics, whose enactment of the Via Crucis is tied to their current, lived reality, rather than a historic understanding of Christ's suffering or a commitment to the afterlife. Catholics of color have brought together body and soul by drawing attention to their own experience and making it Jesus' experience, as well.[23] "At the center of Jesus' praxis were the bodies of common people, peasants, economic and political refugees, and poor and destitute."[24] Praxis, action informed by reflection and based in a community of believers, captures not only the physical body, but the social body as well, marked by race, the economy, and politics, as well as religion. In performing their sorrow through the Via Crucis, these faith communities resist the powerful forces shaping their lives, creating a safe—if fleeting—space of their own. In the context of neglect, racism, and displacement, ethnic Mexican solidarity explicitly tied to Pilsen reminds those forces that Mexicans are in Chicago, and Pilsen, to stay. The body, M. Shawn Copeland writes, "provokes theology."[25] Copeland's focus is on African American women's bodies, but here I turn our attention to Mexican bodies in Chicago. The Via Crucis makes embodied religious practice—that practice centered around the individual body—communal and thus political, as an act of solidarity among community members, and an act of resistance in defense of Mexican Pilsen. By re-sacralizing the streets of Chicago, and performing an act of solidarity with the families of the twelve who were lost in the fire in 1976, and those who have continued the struggle for social justice since, the *Via Crucis* brings Jesus to Pilsen in an act of solidarity with his Mexican followers.

Beyond other Mexican parish performances in San Antonio and New York, the Via Crucis as protest is drawing attention in other Latine communities.[26] Since 2014, Central American migrants have walked the Via Crucis del Migrantes (The Way of the Cross of Migrants), marking the dangerous path their countrymen and countrywomen had travelled from the Guatemala-Mexico border to the Mexico-US border. The migrants called for "the creation of an institute that promotes human security instead of national security."[27] The 2018 version, called a caravan in the US press, again drew international attention to the rightlessness of migrants from Honduras and elsewhere, seeking the most basic of human needs. By drawing attention to their journey with press releases, and making the trek from Tenosique, Tabasco, to Reynosa, Tamaulipas, en masse, these migrants subverted the Mexican government's and drug cartels' efforts to capitalize on their plight with legal and extralegal tolls. "Although largely unsuccessful in their attempts to reform US and Mexican border policies, religious leaders have been quite effective in delivering their plea to local clergy, lay workers, and parishioners who counsel and provide for the poor and potential migrant."[28] Similar protests have taken place in defense of migrants and refugees in South America.[29] This Catholic praxis in defense of migrants reaffirms Jesus' commitment to migrants and others who are suffering.

In Pilsen, the insistence on Jesus walking the same streets and facing the same suffering that Mexicans in Chicago face remakes Catholicism not as the religion of the conqueror or of colonialism, but as a source of comfort, strength, and solidarity with those resisting the daily hostilities experienced on the streets of Chicago. Racism, poverty, and police brutality are all invoked during the Via Crucis. Paul Shelton, associate pastor of St. Procopius Catholic Church in Chicago, described the Pilsen Via Crucis as "their own journey with Jesus in the way of the cross," emphasizing the ways the crucifixion "still speaks to our lives" in the twenty-first century.[30] Mexicans in Chicago see their own suffering in Jesus' crucifixion, and that of witnesses to the events of the Passion. The Pilsen Via Crucis reflects the embodiment of not just Jesus, but Mary, Veronica, and the people of Jerusalem—or Pilsen—who witness the journey. The Via Crucis is not just an individual reflection or meditation; rather, it is a shared spiritual experience—Eucharistic solidarity, as Copeland calls it.[31] In this solidarity, as in 1976, Mexicans in Pilsen share the burdens of community losses. Nellie Quintana notes that Pilsen is largely silent during the Via Crucis. "We're all praying in unity."[32] This praxis of solidarity strengthens the community through mutual support and resistance.

The Pilsen Via Crucis: The Spiritual Is Political

The Via Crucis marks not only a religious devotion, but also a social and political practice that uses the scriptures to acknowledge the suffering that Mexicans experience in their daily lives in a racially divided city. The faith that carried Mexicans in Pilsen through difficult times and dangers lurking in the neighborhood was not just in a God who was distant, but also in surrounding community members and this collaborative project. This "enfleshing of the spirit" brings Jesus into solidarity with Mexican believers.[33] The first Via Crucis drew attention to shoddy housing conditions and city services in Pilsen, adding to a long list of residents' grievances expressed in the previous year. Margaret Ramírez writes that the first Via Crucis connected "the loss of the people who perished with the death of Jesus."[34] This embodied practice is not just about accompanying Jesus in his suffering, but also about accompanying each other in enduring the social ills of Mexicans in Chicago.

Subsequent processions have used Jesus' suffering as a window into the challenges facing the community, including labor concerns, drug abuse and gun violence, the displacement of ethnic Mexicans from the neighborhood, and struggles with the Archdiocese of Chicago. Small community gains, like the naming of the Pilsen post office after César Chávez, are minimized when employees of that post office refuse to serve Spanish speakers, as was reported in February 2020. "A spokesperson for USPS admitted that following a summer retirement, there are no full-time bilingual clerks at the Pilsen post office, which they said they are currently trying to correct."[35] In a city that seeks the elimination, removal, or relocation of Mexicans, survival is a form of resistance. The Pilsen Via Crucis serves to remind government officials who, under the Trump administration, had increased license to discriminate that Pilsen is still Mexican.

Beyond re/claiming space, the Pilsen Via Crucis resists the incursion of gangs and gun violence through a communal callout of crimes in the community. "A praxis of solidarity arises from apprehension and heartfelt response to accounts of historic and contemporary abuse and violence directed against," in this case, Mexicans in Chicago.[36] In 2019 the role of Mary was portrayed by Denice Coronel, who lost her teenage son to gun violence earlier that year. Graciela Guzman, who played Mary in 2005, said, "When I look up at Jesus on that cross, I think about my children. How can I protect them from all the evil in the world today?"[37] Guzman and Coronel embodied not just the mother of Christ, historically, but the mothers of Pilsen in the present. "The Via Crucis is something we live in the barrio," María Hernández confirmed. "The Virgin Mary cried for her son and now the mothers cry for their sons who use drugs and are in gangs. It's real."[38] The Via Crucis airs grievances of individuals so they can share their burdens among the community. In 2018 at Station VI, Veronica wipes the face of Jesus, the narrator related Veronica comforting Christ to the comfort community members provide family and neighbors who are struggling with drug addiction or gun violence. This Eucharistic solidarity helps to sustain community in the face of grave conditions when city and federal authorities fail to serve Mexican residents.

Taking this practice into the streets imbues the neighborhood with Jesus' and the community's own loss and pain, sacralizing the very city that contains their suffering. In the 1990s Del Rey Tortillería was notorious for its abuse of undocumented workers.[39] Patricia Luz, one of the organizers of the Via Crucis, indicated, "We must be Christlike. He fought [against] injustices. We should also fight [against] injustices, to make our

Figure 11.2. Station VI, Veronica wipes the face of Jesus, at the 2018 Via Crucis, Pilsen. Photo by the author.

life and our world a better place to live." In 1994 the Via Crucis stopped in front of Del Rey Tortillería to draw attention to the plight of its workers and pray for them.[40] For Mexicans in Chicago, the Via Crucis is a regular marker of their roles in a community of believers, and their commitment to care for each other when immigration legislation continues to make migrants vulnerable to exploitation. The imagery invoking various "stops" on Christ's journey illustrates his suffering but, as performed in Chicago, emphasizes not just community ills but solidarity, too.

The Via Crucis is an important act of reclamation of Pilsen for Mexicans. Longtime Pilsen resident Vicky Romero remarked that her sense of Mexicana American self "is threatened every day that I walk down the street and see a new [housing] development."[41] Pilsen Alliance, an anti-gentrification organization with which Romero has been affiliated, is the latest in a long line of grassroots organizations resisting "renewal" and "development" projects in Pilsen. Casa Aztlán, a community center founded in 1970, closed in 2013 when the city auctioned the property to pay back taxes. The building, which was adorned with Mexican-themed murals, was whitewashed by the new owner in 2017 as part of his redevelopment of the gutted building into upscale apartments.[42] Residents protested the move, demanding that the murals be restored and that the building be used for affordable housing. Their efforts led to a renewed art program for neighborhood children, including repainting the building with murals, but they were unable to stop the luxury loft apartments from being built.[43] Pilsen resident Vicky Romero reports, "Within the past 10 or 15 years my mom and I have consistently received solicitations and letters from different developers, people offering cash to buy our homes—about four to five letters per month, that obviously we just toss in the garbage."[44] As blocks of housing are eliminated or sold off piece by piece, the sense of belonging, mutual assistance, and material exchange among longtime residents is lost, eroding their sense of security.[45] Elaine Peña argues that past religious performances, "in particular the embodied acts that have previously imbued a space with the sacred, are always active."[46] Davalos notes the Mexican altars that dot Pilsen as year-round sacred markings of the neighborhood. As further evidence, Pilsen is watched over by the Virgin of Guadalupe, as seen in figure 11.3, a 2018 photo on the route of the Via Crucis. The Pilsen Via Crucis is one of many acts that reassert Mexican social power in Pilsen, by being present, by shutting the streets of Pilsen for half a day for a Mexican communal gathering.

Despite increased attention to the destruction of local neighborhoods in the media and local politics, Mexicans in Pilsen still face the same racist tropes in the twenty-first century as they did in 1976. In her 2019 mayoral campaign, Lori Lightfoot promised to protect working-class neighborhoods from the rampant development encouraged by her opponent, then-mayor Rahm Emanual (2011–2019). After taking office, Lightfoot remarked at the *Economist*'s Innovation Summit in 2020, "If you think about it, and you may have been here at the time, what's the difference between Pilsen now and Pilsen 10 years ago? Pilsen 10 years ago was a neighborhood we all would have been a little concerned about being in after dark." Lightfoot's remark echoed the racialized claims that have plagued communities of color for decades. This dog whistle is especially disturbing given that Lightfoot is African American. She continued, "Pilsen now is a vibrant, thriving neighborhood. What's the

Figure 11.3. Mexican Catholic markers are present throughout the Via Crucis. Pilsen, 2018. Photo by the author.

difference? The difference is economic development."⁴⁷ Pilsen alderman Byron Sigcho-López led the questioning of Lightfoot's neoliberal framing of "development" in Pilsen. "Thriving for Whom?," read a headline in the *Chicago Tribune* reporting on the summit and its fallout. The *Chicago Tribune* itself had identified Pilsen as "Chicago's ground zero for gentrification" two years earlier. The editorial board suggested that "exotic," "claustrophobic," Mexican Pilsen can either thrive by inviting gentrification or "build a figurative wall around Pilsen . . . to expedite the neighborhood's demise," perhaps invoking Donald Trump's dog whistle border wall.⁴⁸ This kind of discursive racialization of a neighborhood is used by developers, city officials, and media to justify their interventions to "save" neighborhoods targeted for "renewal."⁴⁹

Through the Via Crucis, Mexicans annually occupy public space in Pilsen to remind the casual observer or new occupants that these streets are an important religious site. Sigcho-López wrote an open letter to Lightfoot exclaiming, "We can no longer stomach the displacement of families and the erosion of the character of the community."⁵⁰ The displacement the alderman spoke of was the so-called urban renewal brought by the University of Illinois Chicago since the 1960s and the gentrification that has rapidly accelerated in twenty-first-century Pilsen. Lightfoot appeared at a ribbon-cutting ceremony for an affordable housing development in Old Town, another neighborhood fighting displacement of low-income residents, the day after the Innovation Summit. Asked about the Pilsen incident, she said, "We are living with a history of development, whether it's housing or otherwise, happening in neighborhoods without any intentionality around that. And what that's led to is displacement."⁵¹ Alderman Sigcho-López challenged that interpretation. In spite of Pilsen's international reputation for Mexican art and culture, "We still have small businesses struggling and empty storefronts. We still have homeowners, especially the most vulnerable, struggling to pay their property taxes. . . . We have a community that is still the victim of violence," he told the *Chicago Sun-Times*.⁵² Davalos noted that during her research in the 1990s, residents posted signs in their street-facing windows reading, "¡Esta Casa NO Está Por Venta!/This House is NOT for sale!"⁵³ These attempts to keep development at bay have been marginally successful in retaining the Mexican character of Pilsen. The Via Crucis temporarily reverts "ownership" of Pilsen back to Mexicans.

The Pilsen Via Crucis announces the Mexican Catholic presence in an area where the Archdiocese of Chicago has been steadily reducing services. In November 1994, Cardinal Joseph Bernardin closed St. Francis of Assisi, which had served Mexican Catholics since 1925. After the pews and stained-glass windows had been removed, Mexican parishioners occupied the shell of a church to prevent its demolition, taking embodied spirituality to an even more visceral level. After a year and a half of protests, parishioners succeeded in convincing the archdiocese to keep St. Francis open. "Ultimately, the archdiocese came around to much of the parishioners' reasoning.... St. Francis of Assisi has a unique history and role in the Hispanic community, and it was stronger and more fiscally solvent than most parishes that are merged or closed, according to the archdiocese's statement."[54] The Via Crucis sustains a community of faith in Pilsen, even when the archdiocese fails in this mission.

In 2015 Blase Cupich, newly appointed archbishop of Chicago, spoke at St Adalbert Church, where Jesus is entombed at a Mass at the end of the Pilsen Via Crucis. Cupich said, "Jesus is there. Every time someone has escaped violence in their own country, only to be exploited and humiliated in the United States because they lack papers, Jesus, too, is insulted."[55] Cupich's solidarity with Mexicans in Pilsen evaporated a year later when he announced the closing of St. Adalbert and two other churches in Pilsen. Efforts to save St. Adalbert and Providence of God churches from closure failed. Even the historical significance of Pope John Paul II having visited Providence of God in 1979 was not able to preserve the church. "This is where they taught us to be a church, and it is a pillar in our community," said Julie Contreras, who graduated from Providence of God School.[56] In addition to the churches, the Mexican community has supported Catholic schools in Pilsen for decades. Latines are recognized as the future of the Catholic Church in the United States, yet the Archdiocese of Chicago has steadily eliminated parishes for their worship.[57] Four and a half decades after the first Via Crucis, Mexicans in Pilsen have transformed Good Friday into a day of protest and resistance in Chicago. The archdiocese sought to exploit this connection starting in 2017 with the Peace Walk, and in 2018 with the March for Our Lives, which was commemorated by the Archdiocese of Chicago six days later than the national March for Our Lives organized by survivors of the Parkland High School mass shooting.

The politicized spirituality conveyed in the Via Crucis has outlasted numerous popes and archbishops of Chicago; it has been appropriated by the archdiocese to address broader social ills in Chicago, signaling how powerful the Via Crucis has been in reshaping the meaning of Good Friday in Catholic Chicago. The Pilsen Via Crucis is a reminder that Mexican Catholicism is not dependent on clergy; community leaders and community solidarity reproduce the church in the absence of diocesan leadership.

Generations of Mexicans from Pilsen return on Good Friday to support their community through Eucharistic solidarity. The Via Crucis is a communal engagement in the suffering and crucifixion of Christ, with period costumes sewn by women parishioners, stages and props built by men in the parish, and roles for children and adults, including the elderly. This devotional labor permeates the unofficial parish, including their oldest and youngest members in this politicized project.[58] Martina Mancilla, who has come to the Via Crucis since she moved to Pilsen in 1995, described it as a defining tradition for the community. "It's also great to see different generations coming out," including her own daughter and granddaughters, who came from northwestern Indiana to bear witness in 2019.[59] For those who move out of Pilsen, returning for the Via Crucis every year marks a return to their Mexican roots in Pilsen. The Pilsen Via Crucis serves as a critical pedagogy of liberation for generations of Mexicans who have lived in Chicago, and learned that the spiritual is political.

NOTES

My thanks to Erika Bsumek, Maggie Elmore, Sergio González, and Felipe Hinojosa for comments on a previous version of this chapter.

1. According to the US census, Pilsen was 77.6 percent Latine in 1980.
2. "Chicago Fire Kills Twelve at Christmas Party; Eight Others Are Injured," *New York Times*, December 25, 1976.
3. Charles Heinrich, "Profile of a Priest—Father James Colleran—Activist and Pastor," Archdiocese of Chicago Archives and Records, n.d., https://archives.archchicago.org.
4. Robert H. Stark, "Religious Ritual and Class Formation: The Story of Pilsen St. Vitus Parish, and the 1977 Via Crucis" (PhD diss., University of Chicago, 1981), 201–2.
5. Eva Reimers, "Death and Identity: Graves and Funerals as Cultural Communication," *Mortality* 4, no. 2 (1999): 149.

6 I use "Latine" to denote people of Latin American descent in the United States regardless of national origin or gender identity. I prefer "Latine" to "Latinx" as it is more linguistically accessible in Spanish and English.
7 Protest flyer, in Stark, "Religious Ritual and Class Formation," 190.
8 Daryl J. Van Tongeren, Jamie D. Aten, Stacey McElroy, Don E. Davis, Laura Shannonhouse, Edward B. Davis, and Joshua N. Hook define spiritual fortitude as "a confidence that one has sufficient spiritual resources to face and grow in the face of a stressor, . . . a spiritual depth and capacity for authentic spiritual engagement in the wake of hardship." "Development and Validation of a Measure of Spiritual Fortitude," *Psychological Trauma: Theory, Research, Practice, and Policy* 11, no. 6 (2019): 589.
9 "Anonymous First-Hand Account of the *Via Crucis* from 'Reflecting on a Call to Mission,' 1977," Archdiocese of Chicago Archives and Records Center, https://archives.archchicago.org.
10 Pierrette Hondagneu-Sotelo, Genelle Gaudinez, Hector Lara, and Billie C. Ortiz, "'There's a Spirit Transcends the Border': Faith, Ritual, and Postnational Protest at the US-Mexico Border," *Sociological Perspectives* 47, no 2 (Summer 2004): 154.
11 Karen Mary Davalos, "'The Real Way of Praying': The Via Crucis, *Mexicano* Sacred Space, and the Architecture of Domination," in *Horizons of the Sacred: Mexican Traditions in US Catholicism*, ed. Timothy Matovina and Gary Riebe-Estrella (Ithaca: Cornell University Press, 2002), 41–68. Davalos argues that the Via Crucis sacralized the streets of Pilsen. This argument is echoed by Deborah E. Kanter, *Chicago Católico: Making Catholic Parishes Mexican* (Urbana: University of Illinois Press, 2020), 127–28. On public ritual as critical pedagogy, see Christopher D. Tirres, *The Aesthetics and Ethics of Faith: A Dialogue between Liberationist and Pragmatic Thought* (Oxford: Oxford University Press, 2014), 158.
12 I refer to "Living Stations of the Cross" to discuss the general performance of the Stations of the Cross; following the lead of the organizers, I call the Pilsen version the Via Crucis. Over the next couple of centuries the Living Stations seemed to die out in much of Europe, but remained strong in former Spanish colonies, particularly Mexico. Pampanga, Philippines, is famous for its annual crucifixions as part of this reenactment; Oberammergau, Germany, is known for "the world's largest, longest running and most famous passion play," according to Anne Lisa Ohm, "Oberammergau: Germany's 376-Year-Old Passion Play before and after the Holocaust, Vatican II, and Ongoing Research into Early Christianity," *Headwaters* 27 (2010): 4. Edilson Pereira discusses the social and political challenges to "updating" performances of Christ's Passion in Brazil in "The Bodies of Christ: Performances and Agencies of Passion in Ouro Preto," *Vibrant* 14, no. 1 (2018): 1–20.
13 Eric Gill, "The Stations of the Cross in Westminster Cathedral," *New Blackfriars* 1, no. 5 (August 1920): 257. See also Mátyás Varga, "Stations of the Cross: Júlia Néma," *Ceramics Art and Perception* 79 (March–May 2010): 36–38; and Ulrike

Kistner, "The Passion of *The Passion*—Return of the Public Spectacle?," *Journal of Literary Studies* 21, nos. 1–2 (June 2005): 143–54.
14 See Jeffrey D. Burson and Ulrich L. Lehner, eds., *Enlightenment and Catholicism in Europe: A Transnational History* (Notre Dame: University of Notre Dame Press, 2014). On tensions between Catholicism and the Enlightenment, see Juan Pablo Domínguez, "Introduction: Religious Toleration in the Age of Enlightenment," *History of European Ideas* 43, no. 4 (2017): 273–87. On tensions among Euro-American Catholics, see Rudolph J. Vecoli, "Prelates and Peasants: Italian Immigrants and the Catholic Church," *Journal of Social History* 2, no. 3 (Spring 1969): 217–68. Catholic nativism continues into the present. See Paul Moses, "White Catholics and Nativism: The Church's Future under Trump," *Commonweal*, September 1, 2017, www.commonwealmagazine.org; and Julia G. Young, "'We Were Different': Why Nativism Persists among US Catholics," *Commonweal*, March 5, 2018, www.commonwealmagazine.org.
15 Other Christian denominations also faced calls for change in light of the social movements of the 1960s. See, for example, Felipe Hinojosa, *Latino Mennonites: Civil Rights, Faith, and Evangelical Culture* (Baltimore: Johns Hopkins University Press, 2014), esp. chap. 2; and Joel L. Alvis Jr., *Religion and Race: Southern Presbyterians, 1946–1983* (Tuscaloosa: University of Alabama Press, 1994), chaps. 5 and 6. John C. Green offers a fascinating analysis of the activism of "the preeminent liberal denomination," Unitarian Universalists, in "A Liberal Dynamo: The Political Activism of the Unitarian-Universalist Clergy," *Journal for the Scientific Study of Religion* 42, no. 4 (December 2003): 577.
16 Chris Tirres in Jesse Remedios, "Via Crucis on US Streets: Faithful Accompany Jesus in His Suffering," *National Catholic Reporter*, April 18, 2019, www.ncronline.org.
17 Joseph A. Donnella II, "A Lenten Pilgrimage: Doing the Stations of the Cross," *Liturgy* 17, no. 3 (2002): 75.
18 Pieter van Niekerk and Nelus Niemandt, "The Radical Embodiment of God for a Christology of a New Era," *HTS Teologiese Studies/Theological Studies* 75, no. 1 (2019), https://hts.org.za.
19 This twenty-first-century revival is likely inspired, in part, by Mel Gibson's controversial 2004 film *The Passion of the Christ*. The film was widely criticized by theologians and film critics, in part because of its portrayal of Jews, but was embraced by many conservative Christian groups. See Ohm, "Oberammergau"; Frances Flannery-Daily, "Biblical Scholarship and the Passion Surrounding *The Passion of the Christ*," *Journal of Religion & Film* 8, no. 1 (February 2004), article 10; and Gordon R. Mork, "Christ's Passion on Stage: The Traditional Melodrama of Deicide," *Journal of Religion & Film* 8, no 1 (February 2004), article 3.
20 Kari Beal, "Thousands Gather for Living Stations of the Cross," KATC News, Lafayette, LA, April 2, 2015, www.katc.com.

21 Greg Allison, "Toward a Theology of Human Embodiment," *Southern Baptist Journal of Theology* 13, no. 2 (Summer 2009): 4–17, 5.
22 February 20, 1980, in Christopher West, "The Theology of the Body: An Education in Being Human," n.d., www3.nd.edu. Pope John Paul II made embodiment the focus of his Wednesday audiences from 1979 to 1984, which turned significant theological attention toward the body.
23 People of color have made explicit theological interventions since at least the 1960s, when stirrings of liberation theology, Black theology, womanist theology, Latine theology, and mujerista theology developed in conjunction with or in response to civil rights movements across the United States and around the world. Tirres argues that Latine theology centers popular religion, in place of the Christian base communities of liberation theology, in search of liberation. Tirres, *Aesthetics and Ethics*, 158. In the twenty-first century, radical and postcolonial theologies are continuing this pushback against White Western-centric bases of Christianity.
24 M. Shawn Copeland, *Enfleshing Freedom: Body, Race, and Being* (Minneapolis: Fortress, 2010), 60.
25 Copeland, *Enfleshing Freedom*, 7.
26 On San Antonio, see Tirres, *Aesthetics and Ethics*. On New York, see Alyshia Gálvez, *Guadalupe in New York: Devotion and the Struggle for Citizenship Rights among Mexican Immigrants* (New York: New York University Press, 2010).
27 Martha Pskowski, "Via Crucis: Migrants Step out of Shadows into the Streets," *Americas Program: A New World of Action and Communication for Social Change*, June 3, 2014, www.cipamericas.org.
28 Jacqueline Hagan, "Making Theological Sense of the Migration Journey from Latin America: Catholic, Protestant, and Interfaith Perspectives," *American Behavioral Scientist* 49, no. 11 (July 2006): 1556.
29 See, for example, Comisión Equitoriana de Refugiados, "Via Crucis de Jesús Migrante y Refugiado," Quito, 2003, organized by the Society of the Divine Word missionaries. There has been an explosion of work on Central America, in particular, and the religious organizations and individuals pushing for the rights and protections of migrants.
30 "Pilsen Via Crucis" *Catholic Chicago*, April 14, 2015, https://www.youtube.com/watch?v=8rBMVUAGneo.
31 Copeland, *Enfleshing Freedom*, 124.
32 Remedios, "Via Crucis on US Streets."
33 Copeland, *Enfleshing Freedom*, 5.
34 Margaret Ramírez, "Reliving the Passion in Pilsen," *Chicago Tribune*, March 25, 2005, www.chicagotribune.com.
35 Diane Pathieu and Michelle Gallardo, "Cesar Chavez Post Office in Pilsen Accused of Denying Service to Spanish Speaking Customers," ABC7 Eyewitness News, https://abc7chicago.com.
36 Copeland, *Enfleshing Freedom*, 125.

37 Ramirez, "Reliving the Passion."
38 Constanza Montana, "Passion Play Unites Pilsen," *Chicago Tribune*, March 26, 1991, www.chicagotribune.com.
39 See John F. Barmon, "The Seventh Circuit Explains Why There Is No Harm in Exploiting Undocumented Workers: Del Rey Tortilleria, Inc. v. NLRB, 976 F.2d 1115 (7th Cir. 1992)," *University of Miami Inter-American Law Review* 24, no. 3 (1993), https://repository.law.miami.edu.
40 Davalos, "'Real Way of Praying,'" 60–63.
41 Jessica Pupovac, "Pilsen Develops New Tools to Fight Gentrification," WTTW Chicago, n.d., https://interactive.wttw.com.
42 Hinda Seif, "Visualizing Spaces of Empowerment in Chicanx/Mexicanx Chicago with Arts and Cultural Organizer Diana Solís," *Diálogo* 21, no. 1 (Spring 2018): 72.
43 Jacqueline Serrato, "'Casa Aztlán' Mural Repainted, Plus Kids' Art Program but No Affordable Units," *Chicago Tribune*, December 14, 2017, www.chicagotribune.com.
44 Romero quoted in Christian Belanger, "Can Rent Control Stem Gentrification in Pilsen?," *Chicago Magazine*, September 8, 2017, www.chicagomag.com.
45 Winifred Curran, "'Mexicans Love Red' and Other Gentrification Myths: Displacements and Contestations in the Gentrification of Pilsen, Chicago, USA," *Urban Studies* 55, no. 8 (June 2018): 1714.
46 Elaine A. Peña, *Performing Piety: Making Space Sacred with the Virgin of Guadalupe* (Berkeley: University of California Press, 2011), 43.
47 John Byrne, "Mayor Lori Lightfoot Says Chicago's Pilsen Community Now Thriving. Alderman Wonders, 'Thriving for Whom?,'" *Chicago Tribune*, March 5, 2020, www.chicagotribune.com.
48 Chicago Tribune Editorial Board, "Renewing Pilsen: When Chicago's History and Future Collide," *Chicago Tribune*, April 9, 2018, www.chicagotribune.com.
49 Curran, "'Mexicans Love Red.'"
50 Sigcho-López quoted in John Byrne and Gregory Pratt, "Lightfoot Defends Neighborhood Housing Strategy after Pilsen Comments Draw Fire," *Chicago Tribune*, March 6, 2020, www.chicagotribune.com.
51 Byrne and Pratt, "Lightfoot Defends Neighborhood Housing Strategy."
52 Fran Spielman, "Lightfoot's Pilsen Remark Irks Local Alderman," *Chicago Sun-Times*, March 5, 2020, https://chicago.suntimes.com.
53 Davalos, "'Real Way of Praying,'" 62.
54 Stephen Lee, "St. Francis Envisions Resurrection of Its Own," *Chicago Tribune*, April 8, 1996, www.chicagotribune.com.
55 Blase Cupich, "Good Friday Reflection," *Catholic Chicago*, April 5, 2015, https://www.youtube.com/watch?v=odXuOk8nKZM.
56 "Pilsen Catholic Church Slated for Consolidation Seeking to Stay a Full-Time Parish," CBS 2 Chicago, February 19, 2016, https://chicago.cbslocal.com.
57 David Crary, "US Hispanic Catholics Are Future, but Priest Numbers Dismal," AP, March 14, 2020, https://apnews.com.

58 For more on devotional labor, see Elaine A. Peña, *Performing Piety*.
59 Mauricio Peña, "Hundreds Watch Stations of the Cross in Pilsen as Via Crucis Good Friday 'Brings People Together,'" *Block Club Chicago*, April 19, 2019, https://blockclubchicago.org.

12

"Two Churches in One Building"

Holy Cross Catholic Church, Latino Immigration, and New Geographies of Resistance, 1988-1997

YURIDIA RAMÍREZ

Having just finished celebrating Sunday mass, Father David Barry—the White pastor at Holy Cross, a historically Black Catholic church in Durham—readied himself to announce to the congregation on October 13, 1996, that the bilingual mass celebrated at Holy Cross would be terminated. As he launched into his announcement, a group of Latino immigrant parishioners who had made Holy Cross their home for eight years stood from their pews. Some Latino parishioners had prepared themselves for this announcement and had decided to walk out of the church, situated on Durham's Alton Avenue at the edge of North Carolina Central University (NCCU), an institution that—like the community in which it was located—was historically Black. As they stepped into the sunlight on that warm October day, a local journalist photographed and questioned the marchers. This moment in Durham history grabbed media attention for weeks.[1]

The walkout was the culmination of drastic changes taking place in Durham by the end of the 1980s. Telling confrontations between Black and Latino residents occurred across the city as more and more Latinos—increasingly immigrants—settled in historically Black neighborhoods. Though the census recorded only two thousand "Hispanics" in 1990, the population numbered above seventeen thousand in the 2000 census.[2] Within a decade, the city of Durham had become an all-minority municipality, where no racial or ethnic group could claim a majority.[3] In a city whose historic Black leadership was celebrated through the recognition of places like downtown Durham's "Black Wall Street," the arrival of Latino migrants threatened to undermine the progress African Americans had made in attaining and establishing their own cultural and geographic spaces, but also the figurative spaces that the African American community had come to occupy. The Holy Cross walkout reflected this demographic shift in Durham, as it was the first of various subsequent events that forced the Catholic Church in North Carolina to respond to the mass migration of Latinos. In North Carolina, spaces of social interaction proved critical to how newly arrived immigrants engaged with residents and developed ideas about their own race.

Holy Cross Catholic Church became a site of contestation and political resistance as Latino newcomers developed a sense of community based on language and religious practice, while African Americans defended their legacy and histories of struggle as Black Catholics. For their part, various media outlets chronicled the walkout using racial terms. Scholars have found that though confrontations between Latinos and African Americans have been narrated in ways that hyperbolize racial tensions, their relationships were more nuanced.[4] These newspaper accounts downplay the pervasiveness of White institutions and their leaders who established the foundations for tensions to arise between minority groups. My analysis highlights the historic complexity of the Catholic Church in the US South and its Black and Latino parishioners to understand the nuances of these two seemingly homogeneous minority groups.

The communities at the heart of the Holy Cross walkout were quite extraordinary for 1980s North Carolina. On the one hand, to be Black *and* Catholic in the United States, much less in the US South, where Bible Belt southerners regarded the Catholic Church with hostility and suspicion, seemed an anomaly and for many was itself a political act of resistance. On the other hand, unlike other regions of the United States, North Carolina was a new immigrant destination for Latinos. Though African Americans and Latinos throughout the twentieth century have been neighbors in places like California, New York, Florida, Texas, and Illinois, their settlement in the US South unsettled the supposed Black/White binary of the area.

Indigenous migrants from Latin America complicated the Black/White binary even further. By the 1980s, an increasing number of migrants, immigrants, and refugees from Puerto Rico, the Dominican

Republic, Colombia, Cuba, and Mexico called North Carolina home. Of those Mexican immigrants, an increasing number of Indigenous P'urhépecha migrants from Cherán, Michoacán, were settling in Durham, people who until then had rarely identified as Mexican, much less as Latinos. The legacy of colonialism and slavery in Latin America had marginalized Afro-descended and Indigenous peoples, ridiculed for being backward, uncivilized, and unwelcome citizens of the nation. However, as the Latino immigrant community emerged in North Carolina, newly arrived Indigenous Mexican migrants created a sense of home and community by establishing relationships with their non-Indigenous Mexican counterparts. They set aside their indigeneity in favor of their national identification as Mexicans.

The fact that journalists, church officials, and even other Latino parishioners were unaware that some of those walking out of Holy Cross Catholic Church on October 13, 1996, were Indigenous Mexican immigrants demonstrates the complexity of identity. In her work, anthropologist Bianet Castellanos argues that indigeneity is "an intersectional and relational category of analysis that engages with dominant racial, gendered, and class structures to construct, produce, and at times erase difference."[5] Castellanos found in her work with Maya women in the United States that, in particular contexts, "indigeneity becomes obscured and strategically resurfaces" in their immigration narratives.[6] In much the same way, I contend that Indigenous Mexican immigrants recognized the saliency and power of "Mexicanness" in 1980s North Carolina and engaged that identity to organize with other Latino parishioners. To honor this strategy, this chapter will examine how Mexican and other Latino parishioners organized as a united front to assert a space of their own.

Building on a new field of scholarship known as Critical Latinx Indigeneities, I argue that where Latino migrants are bringing ideas of anti-Blackness with them to the United States, and where there is a history of Black struggle, like in the US South, Indigenous migrants—like those involved in the Holy Cross walkout—used their identities as Mexicans as a way to exercise power.[7] This chapter shows how Latin American structures of coloniality and racial domination (anti-Blackness and anti-Indianness) confront US racial and settler colonial structures through migration. In the late 1980s and 1990s US South, "indigeneity" became secondary to a "Mexican" identity employed to challenge what they understood to be a structure of disempowerment. Holy Cross Catholic Church, like so many other churches throughout the US South, became a critical site of contestation and resistance as southerners reacted to the arrival of Latinos in search of community and a religious home.

Black and Catholic in the US South: The Historical Context of Holy Cross

There are three million African American Catholics in the United States, outnumbering the members of the African Methodist Episcopal Church.[8] Although most assume that Catholics in the United States are White and African Americans are Protestant, Black Catholics are not an anomaly. As Matthew Cressler points out, "from a hemispheric perspective, Black Christianity in the Americas has been and continues to be majority Catholic, just as Catholicism in the Americas has been and continues to be majority non-White," evidenced by the Catholics in Brazil, Haiti, Mexico, and other Latin American countries.[9] It is true that most twentieth-century Catholics in the United States were the grandchildren of European immigrants, and that the majority of religious African Americans were Protestant. However, the Great Migrations of African Americans from the rural South to the urban North and West introduced African Americans to Catholicism and its missionaries, leading to the conversion of tens of thousands. Though their numbers were small in the early twentieth century, there were nearly a million Black Catholics by 1975.[10] As their numbers increased, Black Catholics' style of worship also transformed. While the Catholic Church during the first half of the twentieth century welcomed Black people to a solemn and quiet Latin mass, the 1960s and 1970s ushered in a revolution that led many Black Catholic churches to adopt the aesthetics and worship styles of Black evangelicals. This period, which Cressler argues set out to define what it meant to be both Black and Catholic, drew from the Black Power tradition and called for self-determination.[11] By positioning the Holy Cross walkout within this broader movement, we can begin to understand the nuances of Black Catholic identity in the US South.

Early twentieth-century relationships within the Catholic Church reflected greater societal trends. Just as with the broader Black population,

Black Catholics were viewed as morally and intellectually inferior relative to their White counterparts. Well into the twentieth century, the Catholic Church had excluded all but a handful of African Americans from its clergy. Instead, White priests had been placed as the pastors of Black Catholic congregations for decades. Even the most well-intentioned White priests oftentimes developed paternalistic relationships with their congregation and reinforced Black Catholics' feelings of inferiority.[12] Places of worship were segregated just as other spaces had been during the Jim Crow era.[13] Rather than challenge the social system or racial hierarchy, the Catholic Church chose instead to conform to the area's existing racial ideologies and practices.[14] Even as African Americans joined the Catholic Church, its hierarchical structure and culture reflected society's prevalent racism.

The establishment of Holy Cross in Durham reflected the Catholic Church's desire to minister to African Americans while upholding segregation. In 1938 there were only 8,585 Catholics in North Carolina—less than one-third of 1 percent of the state's population.[15] Holy Cross was established in 1939 specifically to serve the small but prominent Black Catholics predominantly associated with the historically Black North Carolina Central University. Though the community was educated and middle-class, they were not allowed to attend White Catholic churches during Jim Crow.[16] For decades, the Black Catholic community claimed Holy Cross as theirs and as a reserved, safe space for Black Catholics. As one journalist put it, "members of the Holy Cross Catholic Church know their church has a mission worth preserving: reaching out to African American Catholics, whose needs were neglected during the days of segregation."[17]

Ironically, integration in North Carolina led to the closing of most Black Catholic churches. Nearly a year before *Brown v. Board of Education*, Bishop Vincent Waters declared in 1953 the end of segregation within the Diocese of Raleigh, to which the Holy Cross parish belonged. Pastors in churches across the diocese were instructed on June 21 to read aloud a letter written by Waters, who declared his position on racism and segregation:

> Let me state here as emphatically as I can, that there is no segregation of races to be tolerated in any Catholic Church in the Diocese of Raleigh. . . .

> Equal rights are accorded, therefore, to every race . . . and within the church building itself. Everyone is given the privilege to sit or kneel wherever he desires.[18]

How integration took shape in North Carolina, however, proved more difficult than Waters had anticipated. Though the expectation was that neighboring, segregated Catholic churches in the diocese would combine, in practice Black Catholic churches were absorbed into all-White churches, where African Americans held no authority. Holy Cross in Durham, however, endured, its congregation unmoved because it was the only parish not under the direction of the diocese, but rather the Jesuit order. This separation allowed Holy Cross to remain intact, despite attacks that might threaten its existence.[19]

A fundamental structural shift within the Catholic Church led to a growing sense of Black awareness and self-determination among Black Catholics in the United States. Convened from 1962 to 1965 by Pope John XXIII, the Second Vatican Council addressed relations between the Catholic Church and the modern world. An ecumenical council—an assembly of Roman Catholic religious leaders meant to settle doctrinal issues—had not been convened in nearly a hundred years. Introducing a spirit of change and modernization in the church, Vatican II announced that mass should be celebrated in people's native languages and allowed laypeople to take leadership roles within the church.[20] Though the pastors at Holy Cross would continue to be White, parishioners finally felt that they could control and democratize some aspects of their church.

The emergence of the civil rights and Black Power movements following Vatican II spurred what Matthew Cressler calls the "Black Catholic Revolution."[21] In his work, Cressler argues that "the ways Black Catholics understood and engaged [Vatican II] became indecipherable apart from debates about Black Power." Black Catholics interpreted Vatican II "as an opportunity to incorporate Black Power in Catholic life."[22] Understood best perhaps as a set of ideas and practices, Black Power embraced Black self-determination, the idea that African Americans should have the political, economic, and social power to control their community resources and thereby determine their own fortune. Those involved in the Black Catholic Revolution especially challenged ecclesial authority, or the power to determine church leadership and control religious institutions, which were predominantly under the jurisdiction of White men at all levels of the church hierarchy.[23] Founded in 1968, the National Black Catholic Clergy Caucus (NBCCC) declared that "the Catholic Church in the United States, primarily a White racist institution, has addressed itself primarily to White society and is definitely part of that society."[24] The NBCCC demanded that the Catholic Church recruit Black men for priesthood, with the expectation that Black priests control Black Catholic institutions whenever possible. Unlike White priests, Black Catholic priests could serve as representatives for the Black community and promote changes that acknowledged Black Catholics and honored their rightful place in the church.

The Black Catholic Revolution also called for the development of a Black consciousness, an intellectual transformation of what it meant to be Black *and* Catholic, embracing Black spirituality and incorporating traditions of Black worship into the liturgy.[25] Unlike White Catholic churches, Holy Cross's choir sang in gospel style, while the altar at the front of the church was draped with elaborate, traditional African cloths, symbolic touches that made all the difference to parishioners. "The other churches were just a little too cold for us," said Ronald Patterson, a Black parishioner of Holy Cross for nearly thirty years, to a journalist. "You just didn't feel like anybody wanted you there."[26] Patterson worried that if Holy Cross lost its heritage as an African American church, as had so many others, Black Catholics would "disappear from the face of the Earth."[27] Patterson's fear was justified. By 1996, Holy Cross was one of four historically Black churches remaining in a diocese of eighty-seven. For longtime parishioners, that theirs was a Black Catholic parish was both historically and culturally significant. Black parishioners, who had endured decades of systemic oppression in the US South for being Black and Catholic, were invested in defining and maintaining Holy Cross's identity as a Black Catholic church.

A White priest from Michigan, Father Bruce Bavinger, arrived as pastor of Holy Cross in 1985, just as changes in both the Catholic Church and the state were transforming religious and racial geographies. Even in a Black Catholic church like Holy Cross, White pastors historically had controlled the church's organization.[28] In the absence of a Black priest, Holy Cross maintained its identity as a Black Catholic church through its laity. African Americans organized the ministries, and a parish council, comprised predominantly of African Americans, governed the church. Though White Catholics had been Holy Cross parishioners since its foundation in 1939, they honored the church's identity as a Black parish and understood that their Black counterparts held the authority. The ideals established by the Black Catholic Revolution encouraged parishioners at Holy Cross to fight for their Black Catholic church, an identity that—in spite of challenges—would not be erased.[29]

Spanish in the Black Catholic Church

Holy Cross was not prepared to face the demographic changes taking place in North Carolina by the 1980s. As he faced the congregation and delivered his homilies from the ambo, Father Bruce began to notice a new group of people attending Sunday masses. In 1987 these newcomers—predominantly Mexican immigrants hoping to continue their religious practice in the United States—approached Father Bruce after services and asked whether he would consider celebrating a bilingual mass in Spanish and English. Father Bruce earnestly contemplated their request. Though he had worked in a Puerto Rican school in New York City prior to commencing his theology studies, Father Bruce's Spanish was elementary at best, so he was unsure of how to proceed. Joining forces with a Catholic priest from another church in Durham, they decided to offer a bilingual mass once a month, alternating parishes.[30] By the end of the decade, the growing Latino immigrant community had secured places to worship in a language and a religious cultural tradition that reminded them of home.

Logistical issues with distance and transportation led Father Bruce to continue as the sole celebrant of the Latino masses after just a few months. As Holy Cross gradually became a spiritual home to more and more Spanish-speaking immigrants, the parish's vanguard Black community took notice. Members of the parish council approached the pastor with their concerns in the fall of 1992, five years after Father Bruce had celebrated his first bilingual mass. According to Father Bruce, the Black parishioners worried that their church was becoming a church of misfits, a church to which other churches sent their undesirables. While Father Bruce did not believe this to be the case, he honored how their emotions were contingent on a much longer history. "We talked about it at the parish council meeting, and they said, 'Well, what bothers us is that everybody has their own Mass ... and that sounds like separate but equal to us, where it sounds good but we always wound up at the bottom."[31] The celebration of mass, even if only partly in Spanish, disturbed the parish council and subverted its attempts to maintain the church's African American legacy.

For the Black community at Holy Cross, the secrecy, intimacy, and illegibility of masses under one roof harkened to a time of trauma and pain. Father Bruce, a priest who had devoted his religious life to uplifting Black Catholics and their struggles, told them that he would celebrate a bilingual mass once every two weeks and would invite all Holy Cross parishioners to attend this English and Spanish mass. The parish council accepted those terms.[32] The parish council and Father Bruce walked out of their meeting with a renewed emphasis to be more accessible to all members of the church while remaining faithful to Holy Cross's African American heritage.

Despite attempts by the parish council to imbue the church with a Black Catholic identity, Holy Cross's Latino membership during the 1990s outwardly, if unintentionally, challenged this character. By 1996, it was impossible to ignore the Latino community who attended mass, since they accounted for 30 percent of the parishioners. The Latino—mostly Mexican—community purchased and imported from Mexico a statue of the Virgen de Guadalupe, which they were allowed to display at Holy Cross. Unlike the English mass at Holy Cross, the bilingual mass also featured traditional songs and instruments, like guitars, from the Mexican Catholic tradition.[33] Because most of the Latinos did not speak English, and some were illiterate, they could not attend a monolingual English mass, read from printed sheets that translated the service from English to Spanish, or build relationships with their Black counterparts. Bilingual masses, Mexican Catholic relics and sounds, and the inability to foster dialogue between the English- and Spanish-speaking communities slowly eroded Holy Cross's Black Catholic legacy.

For eight years, Father Bruce led a bilingual mass and Latino ministry in Holy Cross with the blessing of both the bishop and the parish council. Despite the presence of Latino members, Black churchgoers continued to serve as the leaders in most of the church's ministries, thereby not disrupting the organizational structure of the church and in some ways appeasing the Black Catholics who felt threatened or at the very least undermined by the Spanish-speaking community. Even so, tensions remained. Some felt that Holy Cross had transformed into an integrated Catholic church at the expense of its Black Catholic heritage. Though it had stood firm in the face of mid-century integration efforts, Holy Cross and its parishioners could not fight North Carolina's transforming demographics. As the years passed, the strain on these relationships gave way to a dramatic end.

Father Bruce's departure from Holy Cross underscored his pivotal role in the continuation of the bilingual mass. When he was reassigned to serve in Berkeley in 1994, the Jesuit order and Father Bruce searched for a replacement pastor for two years. With his replacement finally secured by June 1996, Father Bruce also recruited the help of a retired priest to continue the bilingual masses in his absence, since the new pastor, Father David E. Barry, did not speak Spanish.[34] Father David was pastor at Holy Cross for only a short term, but his leadership had a lasting effect on Holy Cross's parishioners, as the discontent felt among Black Catholics erupted.

Just months after Father Bruce's departure, the parish council—which included no Latino parishioners—approached Father David with their concerns regarding the bilingual masses. New to the parish, Father David was unaware of past deliberations and tensions regarding the bilingual mass, so he listened to the council's petition and explanation. During a parish council meeting sometime in the fall of 1996, the council and new pastor agreed to eliminate the bilingual masses at Holy Cross. Father Bruce, who was in Berkeley, heard what happened next through rumors. Apparently, the parish council agreed that Father David would make an announcement during mass that services at Holy Cross from then on only would be celebrated in English. "The people had gotten word that this was going to be announced at this mass," remembered Father Bruce, "so they got the cameras and newspaper people there, and they had planned to make a very dramatic exit from Holy Cross at that point."[35] On October 13, as Father David made the announcement, the Spanish-speaking parishioners approached the sacristy and grabbed their statue of Our Lady of Guadalupe.[36] Sensing that they were losing the church they had once called home, many of the Latino members walked out of the church, some in tears, and carried with them the one thing that did belong to them: their statue.[37]

Spanish-speaking parishioners involved in the walkout, however, recounted another tale. Ann-Marie Villasana, a White woman married to an Indigenous Mexican man and who together with her husband had attended the bilingual mass since 1987, said that Father David called her and another leader in the Spanish-speaking community into his office in the fall of 1996. The parish council had decided to discontinue the bilingual mass, he said to the unsuspecting women, and he wanted *them* to announce it during the following service. Refusing Father David's directive, Villasana and the other parishioner explained that if the parish council and pastor had unilaterally decided to terminate the bilingual mass without consulting any member of the Latino community, then it was *their* obligation to inform the congregation.

The women left their meeting with Father David devastated, and discussed the encounter at their daily evening rosary with a few other Latino parishioners. After some deliberation on how to proceed, they agreed they would walk out, but planned no other details. According to Villasana years later, as Father David made the announcement on October 13, every subsequent action was spontaneous. As Latina parishioner Irma Aguirre grabbed the statue of Our Lady and made her way out of the church, those few Latinos who had been at the rosary and knew the resistance plan stood and followed. Because most Latino parishioners did not attend the daily rosaries, they remained seated in the pews, confused.[38] Years later, priests like Father Bruce would continue to believe that the walkout had been a strategically organized event intended to make waves in the Durham community.

Employees, students, teachers, parishioners, politicians, and many others have employed walkouts as a form of social protest, using them as a strategic action, a form of disruption, or a refusal to participate. In the case of the Latino parishioners who agreed to walk out of Holy Cross that Sunday, their actions were definitely intended to disrupt the celebration of mass and draw attention to their anger and frustration. However, the walkout was not an outcome of Latino parishioners refusing to participate in the debate regarding the bilingual mass; they had never been consulted. Feeling powerless and left with no other options, the Latino parishioners employed a walkout, drawing on the most basic power they had: their unity as a Spanish-speaking community.

While rumors presumed that members of the Latino community had notified the press, Ann-Marie Villasana also negates that claim. Though someone at the rosary had suggested notifying the press, it had not been a Latino parishioner; it had been the retired White priest who celebrated the bilingual mass after Father Bruce's departure from Holy Cross. While the Latino parishioners appreciated his input, all at the rosary decided against the idea. That a reporter from the *Herald-Sun*—a daily Durham newspaper—was waiting outside as they exited Holy Cross on October 13 had taken them completely by surprise. The sensational story and accompanying image of Irma Aguirre carrying the Our Lady statue made front-page news the next day. In the aftermath, Villasana and many Latino parishioners were distraught and angry. They had never intended for the walkout to become a "newspaper thing," much less for it to become city, state, and national news. The walkout only was intended to communicate their sense of betrayal. "The parish council didn't talk to us. They had the priest talk to us! We knew people in the parish council," Villasana explained. Especially during Father Bruce's time as pastor, the communities had organized celebrations together, and the Latinos even helped build a community center behind the parish. The sense of betrayal among parishioners and leaders in the Spanish-speaking community like Villasana was palpable. "I don't know why they didn't just talk to us."[39]

Latinos who walked out of Holy Cross insisted that they never meant to undermine the church's identity; quite the contrary, they told reporters that they had embraced African American culture. Displaying a photograph depicting Latino children during a First Communion celebration to reporters from the *News & Observer* (*N&O*), a daily newspaper serving the area of Durham, Chapel Hill, and Raleigh with the largest circulation in the state, Villasana explained that although the children in faith formation were mostly Latino, they performed a traditional African dance during their First Communion mass, and everyone loved it. "We want to share cultures," Villasana told the reporter. "I guess they feel like we're taking over, but that was never our intention."[40] Because of the community's language and literacy limitations, the Latinos who marched out of Holy Cross on that October day asserted that they were "kicked out."⁴¹ Days after the walkout, the Latino parishioners of Holy Cross drafted a petition that they presented to the vicar general of the Catholic diocese in Raleigh, the Reverend Jerald Lewis, who together with Teresa Soto, director of Hispanic Ministry, promised to find a peaceful solution to the problem.⁴² The diocese vowed that their worship and language needs would be met.

The original *Herald-Sun* article spurred both local and national media coverage on the walkout. With so many requests for public comment, the Holy Cross parish council released a public statement, upholding its mission to promote "an African American cultural approach to Catholicism." While "Holy Cross has become an increasingly diverse parish, we see the need to retain that which is fundamental to our foundation, the African American culturally based mass. We plan to more aggressively address cultural diversity in the programming of Parish activities."⁴³ According to Father David and the parish council, the bilingual mass was terminated to build a more unified parish community. "They fought very hard to get this church," said Fred Boadu, a member of Holy Cross's parish council. "And if they want to maintain it, they ought to be able to."⁴⁴

Efforts to build a more unified parish at Holy Cross would have in many ways replicated the forced integration of churches decades before. Because few Latino parishioners spoke English, they would have been unable to join the parish's ministries or hold positions of leadership. The bilingual mass had afforded the Spanish-speaking community some authority, and their catechism classes allowed them to teach religious education in a culturally specific way. With no future plans to encourage or facilitate English-language learning among its Latino parishioners, the parish's decision to terminate the bilingual mass without consulting the Spanish-speaking community essentially did impose integration with no attention to how this would essentially be understood as elimination.

Public discourse emphasized animosity and discord. National publications characterized the Holy Cross walkout as an interracial conflict between two minority groups. Just two days after the walkout, *USA Today* described the walkout in a short blurb that detailed how "Holy Cross Catholic Church, known for its efforts to attract Black members, has angered some of its Hispanic members by dropping a bilingual Sunday afternoon service," which Latinos saw as an "effort to push them out."⁴⁵ With little context, the story read as another tale of victimization and discrimination from the US South.

Within days, the *N&O* also reported on the walkout and situated race at the crux of the incident. "Black, Hispanic Cultures Clash at Durham Church," read the October 15 headline. Unlike previous stories on the walkout, this *N&O* article was the first to describe the Holy Cross walkout as a conflict, its headline underscoring the oppositional and perhaps even combative nature of the event.⁴⁶ A few days later, the *N&O* published another article contextualizing the walkout, situating the narrative within the history of African American segregation in Durham. This article downplayed the conflict and examined instead the long, nuanced trajectory of Black Catholics and their struggles in the US South, highlighting how Holy Cross represented a physical marker of triumph against integration and elimination, serving as a sanctuary for Black Catholics. The journalist also tied this history to the current challenges facing Latinos, who had lacked a spiritual home in Durham and, at least since 1987, had found one within Holy Cross.⁴⁷

Latinos who spoke to the Spanish-language press of the Durham area, *La Voz de Carolina*, did so with more candor than they had with the English-language presses of the region. An unnamed Latina organizer and participant in the walkout told the press that "the resolution of the [parish] council of this church is inoperative and racist." They were never consulted, she continued, and their opinions or feelings were never considered.⁴⁸ Her claims that the move was "racist" not only shows how she positioned the Latino community as oppressed victims, but also demonstrates her understanding that racism can exist between oppressed groups. Her explanation affirms Natalia Molina's proposal of "racial scripts" as a term that "emphasize[s] the ways in which we think, talk about, and act toward one racialized group based on our experiences with other groups whose race differs from our own."⁴⁹ In this case, we can assume that the unnamed woman is drawing from a vocabulary and lessons she has learned and experienced as a Latina in the post–Jim Crow US South.

Sociologist Regine O. Jackson has described the shifting nature of racism in the US South in the wake of these new Latino immigrant arrivals. Jackson argues that the portrayal of southern race relations has shifted from a focus on vertical racism to horizontal racism, which "operates as part of the new South mythology."⁵⁰ According to Jackson, the rhetoric of horizontal racism works to mask continued anti-Black discrimination, suppress White racism, and normalize the redefinition of racism that then mediates relationships between new Latino immigrants and southern Blacks. Horizontal racism effectively positions Black southerners as the main actors subordinating Latino immigrants. However, as Jackson points out, "the idea of fractured minority communities which puts subordinate racial groups into conflict with one another, also keeps Whites safely out of the firing line."⁵¹ Understood this way, horizontal racism is simply a new form of old racism that blames the victims for their own oppression.

Editorials published in local Durham newspapers provided some insight into how some community members not involved understood the Holy Cross walkout. Presumably a Durham resident, Stacey Humphreys wrote to the *Herald-Sun* on October 20, stating that the Holy Cross walkout had unnerved her. Humphreys wondered, "What good is a church that touts diversity but that is essentially two churches in one building?" Humphreys contended that "it is wrong to take something from one group to appease another, or to dilute the very thing that makes Holy Cross unique so much that it doesn't matter anymore."⁵² For Humphreys, the walkout and its consequences could have been avoided had more emphasis been placed on educating Latinos on traditional Black Catholic traditions and vice versa. According to Humphreys, understanding was key to demystifying the supposed differences between the groups and encouraging unity.

Transforming the Catholic Church in the US South

The complications that arose in Durham were symptomatic of greater transformations occurring across the country's Catholic churches and specifically churches with Spanish-speaking Catholics. Just as Vatican II responded to the racial and civil rights movements of the 1960s and opened up new opportunities for Black Catholics, it also allowed Latino Catholics to openly challenge the discrimination they faced in the United States, a period religious scholars Ana María Díaz-Stevens and Anthony M. Stevens-Arroyo have dubbed "the Latino resurgence in US religion." Latinos' call for the institutionalization of progressive policies led to three national meetings (1972, 1977, and 1985) that reunited Latino Catholics from across the country to develop solutions for the problems facing Hispanic ministries, namely, discrimination and neglect. As a result, in 1983 the National Council of Catholic Bishops (NCCB) issued a pastoral letter called "The Hispanic Presence: Challenge and Commitment," which reiterated dedication and commitment to honoring the cultural practices of Latino Catholics and welcoming these and their Latino brothers and sisters into the mainstream Catholic Church.[53] Within five years, the NCBB approved the National Pastoral Plan for Hispanic Ministry, "thus indicating a separate and special dimension to Latino Catholicism as compared to Euro-American Catholicism."[54] The plan reversed previous policies that had promoted assimilation to instead make the US Catholic Church a more welcoming place, introducing, for example, a Spanish text for the celebration of mass.[55] While archdioceses and parishes across the country did not universally implement the plan, it established a precedent through which Latino Catholics could demand equal treatment within their local churches and parishes.

Latino Catholic parishioners across the country pushed for changes within their churches, though the work of Latino Catholics in the US South is particularly salient because theirs was a new, mostly immigrant community challenging an already minority religion in the region.[56] Work on Latino Catholics in the US South is burgeoning; historian Mary Odem has found similar transformations to those occurring in Durham underway in Atlanta. Prior to the arrival of Latinos in the 1980s, Catholic leaders in Atlanta were mostly White US citizens with European ancestry. These leaders before the 1980s had directed their diversity efforts toward supporting their Black Catholic parishioners, who, like their North Carolina counterparts, understood integration as erasure. With the 1980s settlement of mostly Mexican immigrants in Atlanta, church officials, priests, and parishioners revisited what integration meant with regard to these Spanish-speaking newcomers. Some assumed that Latino immigrants eventually would adapt and assimilate to their ways of worship, while others concluded that the celebration of a Spanish-language mass would be enough to meet immigrants' needs. A third group argued that, in fact, significant structural changes would need to be implemented to meet the particular needs of these new Latino immigrant communities.

Though faced with cultural and class barriers and transportation issues, Latino immigrants in Atlanta desired to find a spiritual home. Together, Latino immigrants reached out to allies in the Archdiocese of Atlanta to establish a Spanish-language mass geared toward their new community.[57] Odem's study demonstrates how grassroots struggle by Spanish-speaking immigrants led to the establishment of a dedicated space where they could both practice their faith and "find the material, social and spiritual resources to deal with hardships of migration and adaptation to life in the United States."[58] By the end of the century, Latino Catholic parishioners would outnumber White Catholics in Atlanta and Georgia.[59]

More than any other time in its history, the Catholic Church also was facing unprecedented growth in North Carolina, due not only to the significant influx of Latino immigrants, but also to relocating northerners who settled to work in the area.[60] Though the state's Catholic population did not even comprise 1 percent of the population prior to the 1990s, by the end of the decade, more than 300,000 people identified as Catholics.[61] The demographics of North Carolina Catholics, however, could not have represented more disparate experiences. On the one hand, affluent White northerners arrived amid the state's technology and industrial boom and broadening white-collar employment opportunities. On the other hand, working-class, Spanish-speaking migrants flocked to the state, some settling in rural areas to labor in agriculture or meat and poultry processing, while others established themselves in cities and worked in restaurants, hotels, and construction.[62] An *N&O* article published on October 25, "Catholic Welcome of Latinos Uneven," detailed the discrepancies with which North Carolina clergy handled the influx of Spanish-speaking parishioners. While about a dozen churches from the eastern region of the state embraced the Latino newcomers and welcomed them into every facet of church life, others ignored this new community and focused their efforts on attracting the northern arrivals. "Hispanic ministry is kicked like a football from parish to parish, based on the local pastor's interest or lack of interest," said James Garneau, former pastor of Our Lady of Guadalupe in Newton Grove. "We're more comfortable dealing with White people from the North than brown people from the South."[63] While the Catholic Church in North Carolina was quick to meet the needs of relocated White northerners, its vacillation with regard to Latino immigrants suggests at the very least a structural and cultural deficiency in ministry outreach.

Cultural and class differences threatened the role of the Catholic Church within the Latino community in the United States. Catholic priests, unlike many Latino immigrants, were predominantly White and educated. While 30 percent of Catholics in the United States were Latino during the 1990s, only 2,450 priests of the nation's 49,000 spoke Spanish, and only 400 were born in Latin America. In North Carolina, Catholic priests had never been required to speak a foreign language. By the 1980s, however, the Diocese of Raleigh required all newly ordained priests to spend a summer in Latin America to learn how to celebrate mass in Spanish. Some White priests who had lived mostly privileged lives were resentful of this new language requirement, effected to allow priests to minister to a group so culturally different from them. For some clerics, it became easier to just feign ignorance. "We've got some pastors who will tell you there are no Latinos living in their area," said Joe Vetter, pastor of Sacred Heart Catholic Church in Southport. "But you drive around and see them and you know the pastor's wrong. He just doesn't hang out where the people are."[64] Though the Catholic Church had previously been much more evangelical in its early outreach efforts to Latino migrants, especially during the 1970s, the walkout from Holy Cross represented a greater concern that many Catholic pastors in North Carolina shared. Vetter maintained that the church was now more concerned with maintenance than evangelism. "We've become too institutional," Vetter said to the *N&O*. "We've turned in on ourselves too much."[65]

Latino immigrants' status as working-class people also might have exacerbated tensions between African Americans and Latinos at Holy Cross. Durham was renowned for its Black middle class, reputed as being the heart of the Black bourgeoisie. The success of the North Carolina Mutual Life Insurance Company, the largest Black financial institution in the world, allowed for a number of surrounding African American–owned businesses to flourish. These significant accomplishments were facilitated by ongoing negotiations between the Black middle class and White power brokers. As a result, a *de facto* social order emerged—especially during the Jim Crow era—that maintained the racial hierarchy of the US South: Whites financially supported the business endeavors of African Americans, while they in turn guaranteed peace and deference.[66]

For the most part, Holy Cross parishioners belonged to this educated, middle-class Black elite of Durham, who since the civil rights movement had, in their own way, fought for their rights and interests. Though civil rights and Black Power leaders often have criticized the Black elite for complacency and accommodationism, historian Christina Greene challenged these ideas in her work on Durham women's organizing during the civil rights movement. Greene argued that Black women's organizing had been class-based, with middle-class Black women employing a more formal style of organizing.[67] While these women might not have participated in marches or in acts of civil disobedience, they challenged the status quo within their social clubs, literary societies, and church groups. While the desire to ensure that Holy Cross remained a Black Catholic church was crucial for longtime parishioners, on another level it also might have been an attempt to maintain the socioeconomic identity of the church. Working-class Latino immigrants, many of them uneducated and from rural Mexico, threatened the parish's—and its parishioners'—fidelity to a particular reputation within Durham and North Carolina as bourgeois Black Catholics. The decision of Holy Cross's parish council to terminate the bilingual mass was part of a much longer trajectory in which middle-class Black Catholics fought for respect, recognition, and belonging amid challenges to their existence as a Black and Catholic educated community.

A Time of Reckoning

Though the Diocese of Raleigh had attempted to mend the damage that resulted from the Holy Cross walkout, its efforts were to no avail; the Spanish-speaking community no longer felt welcomed by the Holy Cross parish. Just three days after the walkout, the *Herald-Sun*'s front page announced that Immaculate Conception, the mother church of Catholic congregations in the Durham area, would begin ministering to Latinos in a few weeks through the celebration of its first bilingual mass.[68] Immaculate Conception was just three miles away from Holy Cross, and the parish had recently come under the pastoral leadership of the Order of Friars Minors from Holy Name Province. One of the Franciscan friars, Father John Heffernan, had experience ministering to Latino communities, and he agreed to celebrate bilingual masses. Since then, the Spanish-speaking Catholic community of Durham has made Immaculate Conception their religious home, with Latino parishioners outnumbering all other demographics.

Sitting in his office eighteen years later, Father David McBriar—who served as pastor of Immaculate Conception in 1996—remembered some of the events from the Holy Cross walkout differently. For one, he remembered Father Bruce as pastor of Holy Cross at the time of the walkout, when it had been Father Bruce's replacement, Father David Barry. Father David also suggested that the walkout occurred because the mass time changed from 4:00 p.m. to 1:00 p.m., which would have been inconvenient for Latinos who worked Sunday mornings. While a change in mass times did accompany the end of the bilingual mass, dozens of newspaper articles reported that parishioners on both sides of the debate felt that the issues were predominantly about racial, cultural, and language differences. Even so, Father David warned not to make "too much of this Holy Cross, Immaculate Conception thing." He warned to avoid the "sensationalism" of the walkout and its legacy. When asked whether there was a racial aspect to it, he did not disagree. "Sure, but when I say 'racial,' here again, you have to be very careful," Father David said. "You're on quicksand to say the African American community ejected the Latino community. They were unhappy, though, with it, and they didn't have the resources to provide for it."[69] Holy Cross's pastor, Father David Barry, had the responsibility of celebrating all masses and overseeing all of the church's ministries, and he did not speak Spanish. On the other hand, the three friars at Immaculate Conception did have the means to serve the community since they shared the responsibilities of the parish. Father John's language skills allowed him to take on the responsibility of ministering to the Spanish-speaking parishioners.

Father Bruce, the Jesuit who initiated the bilingual masses at Holy Cross, also believed that the walkout was indirectly a racial issue. "To say you want Holy Cross to identify as a Black Catholic church is kind of a racial statement, you know," Father Bruce said. Years later, Holy Cross modified its mission statement on its website to declare itself *historically* African American, which allowed for the presence of a more diverse community to join their parish.[70] Even so, "they still wanted to have the character of it being a Black church."[71]

The reticence of the Catholic priests to define the Holy Cross walkout as a racial issue underscores the role that White actors had in the incident. To label it as such would be to admit that there existed structural racism within the Catholic Church and its organization that still needed to be addressed and confronted. Instead, the priests decided that the problem concerned resources and services, so the "Band-Aid" was to move the Spanish-speaking community to another church, thereby safely evading more critical discussions of race, culture, and language at the core of the walkout. Meanwhile, Holy Cross continues to identify as a historically Black Catholic church, even though its pastors (with only one exception) continue to be White. For their part, although Latinos found a permanent spiritual home at Immaculate Conception, the critique that their parish is two separate communities within one church endures.

While the Holy Cross walkout has been narrated and remembered in terms that emphasize racial conflict and discord between African American and Latino Catholics, constructed as an incident between two already marginalized groups divided by language, ethnicity, and immigrant status, a broader historical analysis reveals a more complicated story. Black Catholics in the United States have struggled for recognition and representation within a broader religious and predominantly White community. The influx of immigrant, Spanish-speaking Latinos has forced the Catholic Church to reevaluate its commitment to ministry and evangelism. Implicated in both of these stories are continuous and interlocking historical and social structures of Whiteness that have governed the interactions of these Catholics of color on many scales, from global forces (Catholicism, migration, etc.) to quotidian spiritual practices (language of mass, church leadership, etc.). The legacy of racism in the US South and Latin America and lived racism in the present must inform how we examine questions of "racial division" as a phenomenon that is created, rather than something that *is*. We also need to acknowledge that what we call "racial division" oftentimes obscures class and cultural conflict subtext.

We also cannot ignore the ideas of race that Latinos bring with them from their homelands and how those influence their relationships in the United States. While the majority of scholarship on Latino immigration to the US South has emphasized the victimization of Latinos by African Americans, the history of race in Latin America shows how anti-Blackness and anti-Indigenous prejudices have been prominent components of popular and official discourses.[72] Whiteness throughout Latin America historically was privileged and posited as the epitome of the modern nation-state, as traces of indigeneity or Blackness were debased. These widely assumed beliefs are the remnants of hundreds of years of historical erasure and racial suppression.[73] Indigenous Mexican parishioners at Holy Cross joined in solidarity with their non-Indigenous counterparts as one homogeneous Latino community. Because no one identified them as Indigenous, P'urhépecha migrants from Cherán, Michoacán, were able to themselves avoid racial animus and disappear within the narratives as they joined their Latino comrades in an exercise of resistance and power against African Americans.[74] More work is needed that investigates how indigeneity can sometimes be articulated within Latinidad as resistance against Blackness.

The parishioners' desire to maintain the Black identity of Holy Cross should not be understood as reactionary or oppressive. Black Catholics have endured segregation and historical erasure in society for being Black, and they have been culturally ostracized and systematically oppressed within the religious institution in which they have placed their faith. Theirs is a resiliency to survive and thrive amid changes that seem to threaten their identity. At the crux of the Holy Cross incident is not interracial distrust or animus, but rather the irony of the southern Catholic Church, which has attempted to move toward a more unifying consciousness without confronting its anti-Black history and structurally addressing it in real ways that transform the US Catholic Church amid the ongoing demographic transformation of our society.

By situating the Holy Cross walkout within the larger historical trajectory of Black Catholics in general, Black Catholics in the US South, the Latino resurgence of the 1960s in the US Catholic Church, and the 1980s and 1990s Catholic Church in North Carolina, this chapter builds on a longer history of Latino engagement in religious politics that—though grounded in faith—are not limited to the realm of the "religious" but build from various experiences of injustice. Like many of the histories presented in this volume, this chapter shows ordinary Latinos living and struggling within various systems of power, their eventual resistance, and their ultimate attempts at scratching out a place for themselves in a seemingly familiar place but one with a long and yet unaccounted-for legacy of racism and racist practices. My research on the intersections between faith spaces, grassroots organizing, and Latino identity highlights the variety of identities and historical narratives created and erased as a result of significant Latino immigration to the US South.

NOTES

1 Kammie Michael, "Catholic Church to Drop Bilingual Service," *Herald-Sun*, October 14, 1996.
2 I employ "Latino" when describing immigrants from Latin America and refer to them as "Hispanics" only when citing from the original source. Latino Migration Project at UNC-Chapel Hill, "Durham's Immigrant Communities: Looking to the Future," 2013.
3 Thomas A. Tweed, "Our Lady of Guadeloupe Visits the Confederate Memorial: Latino and Asian Religions in the South," in *Religion in the Contemporary South: Changes, Continuities, and Contexts*, ed. Corrie E. Norman and Don S. Armentrout (Knoxville: University of Tennessee Press, 2005), 144.
4 See, for example, Brian D. Behnken, ed., *The Struggle in Black and Brown: African American and Mexican American Relations during the Civil Rights Era* (Lincoln: University of Nebraska Press, 2011); Lauren Araiza, *To March for Others: The Black Freedom Struggle and the United Farm Workers* (Philadelphia: University of Pennsylvania Press, 2014); Max Krochmal, *Blue Texas: The Making of a Multiracial Democratic Coalition in the Civil Rights Era* (Chapel Hill: University of North Carolina Press, 2016); and Brian D. Behnken, *Fighting Their Own Battles: Mexican Americans, African Americans, and the Struggle for Civil Rights in Texas* (Chapel Hill: University of North Carolina Press, 2011).
5 M. Bianet Castellanos, "Rewriting the Mexican Immigrant Narrative: Situating Indigeneity in Maya Women's Stories," *Latino Studies* 15, no. 2 (July 2017): 220.
6 Castellanos, "Rewriting the Mexican Immigrant Narrative," 220.
7 Maylei Blackwell, Floridalma Boj Lopez, and Luis Urrieta, "Special Issue: Critical Latinx Indigeneities," *Latino Studies* 15, no. 2 (July 2017): 126–37.
8 Matthew J. Cressler, *Authentically Black and Truly Catholic: The Rise of Black Catholicism in the Great Migration* (New York: New York University Press, 2017), 5.
9 Cressler, *Authentically Black and Truly Catholic*, 8.
10 Cressler, *Authentically Black and Truly Catholic*, 5.
11 Cressler, *Authentically Black and Truly Catholic*, 2–17.
12 Stephen J. Ochs, *Desegregating the Altar: The Josephites and the Struggle for Black Priests, 1871–1960* (Baton Rouge: Louisiana State University Press, 1990), 2.
13 Jamie T. Phelps, ed., *Black and Catholic: The Challenge and Gift of Black Folk: Contributions of African American Experience and Thought to Catholic Theology* (Milwaukee: Marquette University Press, 1997), 26–27.

14 Ochs, *Desegregating the Altar*, 2.
15 William F. Powers, *Tar Heel Catholics: A History of Catholicism in North Carolina* (Lanham, MD: University Press of America, 2003), 235.
16 Lindsay Ruebens, "Black and Catholic in North Carolina," *Endeavors*, June 2, 2011.
17 Ben Stocking, "Changing Times Divide Durham Congregation: Church Struggles to Serve Latinos, Remain True to Blacks," *News & Observer*, October 21, 1996.
18 "Religion: Cure for the Virus," *Time*, June 29, 1953.
19 Father Bruce Bavinger, interview with author, March 11, 2015.
20 Mary A. Ward, *A Mission for Justice: The History of the First African American Catholic Church in Newark, New Jersey* (Knoxville: University of Tennessee Press, 2002), 84–86, 114.
21 Cressler, *Authentically Black and Truly Catholic*, 129.
22 Cressler, *Authentically Black and Truly Catholic*, 121.
23 Cressler, *Authentically Black and Truly Catholic*, 120–28.
24 "A Statement of the Black Catholic Clergy Caucus," in *Black Theology: A Documentary History*, vol. 1, 1966–1979, ed. James H. Cone and Gayraud S. Wilmore (New York: Orbis, 1993), 230–32.
25 Cressler, *Authentically Black and Truly Catholic*, 16.
26 Stocking, "Changing Times."
27 Stocking, "Changing Times."
28 Ochs, *Desegregating the Altar*, 1.
29 Bavinger, interview.
30 Bavinger, interview.
31 Bavinger, interview.
32 Bavinger, interview.
33 Stocking, "Changing Times."
34 Bavinger, interview; Ann-Marie Villasana, interview with author, February 29, 2020.
35 Bavinger, interview.
36 Michael, "Catholic Church to Drop Bilingual Service."
37 Michael, "Catholic Church to Drop Bilingual Service."
38 Villasana, interview.
39 Villasana, interview.
40 Stocking, "Changing Times."
41 Gloria Quintanilla and Ernesto Quintanilla, interview with author, April 26, 2015.
42 Luis Arturo Alvarenga, "Cancelan Única Misa en Español en Durham," *La Voz de Carolina*, October 16, 1996.
43 Michael, "Catholic Church to Drop Bilingual Service."
44 Stocking, "Changing Times."
45 "Across the USA: News from Every State," *USA Today*, October 15, 1996.
46 Ben Stocking, "Black, Hispanic Cultures Clash at Durham Church," *News & Observer*, October 15, 1996.
47 Stocking, "Changing Times."

48 Alvarenga, "Cancelan Única Misa en Español."
49 Natalia Molina, "The Power of Racial Scripts: What the History of Mexican Immigration to the United States Teaches Us about Relational Notions of Race," *Latino Studies* 8, no. 2 (June 2010): 157.
50 Regine O. Jackson, "The Shifting Nature of Racism," in *Being Brown in Dixie: Race, Ethnicity, and Latino Immigration in the New South*, ed. Charles A. Gallagher and Cameron D. Lippard (Boulder: FirstForumPress, 2011), 27.
51 Jackson, "Shifting Nature of Racism," 36–47.
52 Stacey Humphreys, "One Church, or Two?," *Herald-Sun*, October 20, 1996.
53 Ana María Díaz-Stevens and Anthony M. Stevens-Arroyo, *Recognizing the Latino Resurgence in US Religion: The Emmaus Paradigm* (London: Routledge, 1997), 120–28; Mary E. Odem, "Our Lady of Guadalupe in the New South: Latino Immigrants and the Politics of Integration in the Catholic Church," *Journal of American Ethnic History* 24, no. 1 (Fall 2004): 29–30.
54 Díaz-Stevens and Stevens-Arroyo, *Recognizing the Latino Resurgence*, 189–90.
55 Díaz-Stevens and Stevens-Arroyo, *Recognizing the Latino Resurgence*, 190.
56 Odem, "Our Lady of Guadalupe," 31–34.
57 Odem, "Our Lady of Guadalupe," 28–38.
58 Odem, "Our Lady of Guadalupe," 27.
59 Odem, "Our Lady of Guadalupe," 50.
60 Powers, *Tar Heel Catholics*, xii; Leoneda Inge, "Standing Room Only at NC Catholic Churches," WUNC, Durham, NC, March 29, 2013; Rebecca Tippett, "Religion in North Carolina: Southern Baptists Dominate, Catholicism and Non-Denominational Affiliation Rising," *Carolina Demography* (blog), June 2, 2014; Lindsay Ruebens, "The Catholic Boom in North Carolina: A Priest's Perspective," *Endeavors*, June 7, 2011.
61 Powers, *Tar Heel Catholics*, xi.
62 Owen J. Furuseth and Heather A. Smith, eds., *Latinos in the New South: Transformations of Place* (Burlington, VT: Ashgate, 2006), 46–47.
63 Yonat Shimron, "Catholic Welcome of Latinos Uneven," *News & Observer*, October 25, 1996.
64 Shimron, "Catholic Welcome of Latinos."
65 Shimron, "Catholic Welcome of Latinos."
66 Christina Greene, *Our Separate Ways: Women and the Black Freedom Movement in Durham, North Carolina* (Chapel Hill: University of North Carolina Press, 2005), 8–9.
67 Greene, *Our Separate Ways*, 7–8.
68 Flo Johnston, "Mother Church to Offer Durham Bilingual Mass: Immaculate Conception Adds Ministry for Area's Spanish-Speaking People," *Herald-Sun*, October 16, 1996.
69 Father David McBriar, interview with author, May 15, 2015.
70 Italics mine. "About Our Parish," Holy Cross Catholic Church, n.d., http://holycrossdurham.org.

71 Bavinger, interview.
72 Hannah E. Gill, *The Latino Migration Experience in North Carolina: New Roots in the Old North State* (Chapel Hill: University of North Carolina Press, 2010); Chenoa A. Flippen and Emilio A. Parrado, "Perceived Discrimination among Latino Immigrants in New Destinations: The Case of Durham, NC," *Sociological Perspectives* 58, no. 4 (December 2015): 666–85; Helen B. Marrow, *New Destination Dreaming: Immigration, Race, and Legal Status in the Rural American South* (Stanford: Stanford University Press, 2011); Helen B. Marrow, "'The White Americans Have Always Been Very Friendly': Discrimination, Racial Expectations, and Moral Hierarchies in the Black-White Binary," in *New Destination Dreaming*; Helen B. Marrow, "Intergroup Relations: Reconceptualizing Discrimination and Hierarchy," in Gallagher and Lippard, *Being Brown in Dixie*; Fran Ansley and Jon Shefner, eds., *Global Connections and Local Receptions: New Latino Immigration to the Southeastern United States* (Knoxville: University of Tennessee Press, 2009); Raymond A. Mohl, "Globalization, Latinization, and the Nuevo New South," *Journal of American Ethnic History* 22, no. 4 (Summer 2003): 31–66.
73 Nancy P. Appelbaum, Anne S. Macpherson, and Karin Alejandra Rosemblatt, "Introduction: Racial Nations," in *Race and Nation in Modern Latin America*, ed. Nancy P. Appelbaum, Anne S. Macpherson, and Karin Alejandra Rosemblatt (Chapel Hill: University of North Carolina Press, 2003), 1–31.
74 Villasana, interview.

Afterword

GERALDO L. CADAVA

As a historian of Latinos in the United States, I've known for a long time that I needed a better understanding of the topic covered in this book: the ways that faith and politics intersect and in many ways are inseparable.

When I was a child, I watched my great-grandmother in Safford, Arizona, move her amber-colored rosary beads through her fingers, her lips mouthing inaudible words. Her daughter, my grandmother, used to go to church regularly, but these days she mostly stays home. Still, she stands daily in front of her sliding-glass door in Tucson, praying as she looks into her back yard at the small statue of the Virgen de Guadalupe. I myself was baptized but not confirmed, and I probably could count on two hands the number of times I've attended a mass that wasn't part of a wedding ceremony. Whenever my grandmother says "God bless you" at the end of a phone call, or when she explains her belief that seeming coincidences are part of a divine plan, I say thank you and listen patiently, but have never internalized her words; I thought her faith was a part of her life that was somehow separate from the others, and didn't touch me.

I've come to understand, though, that my grandmother's faith touches every part of her life, and also touches me. Her prayers to the Virgen de Guadalupe in her backyard are her way of continuing to look after everyone in our family: my grandfather, who stays at the VA home a few miles away from her; my great-aunt in Minnesota; my father and stepmother, who live on the East Coast, thousands of miles away; my uncle who sorts mail for the US Postal Service and had to go to the warehouse throughout the pandemic; my cousin who recently moved to Texas, the first time in thirty years that he has lived anywhere but Tucson; my small family in Chicago; and many others.

My grandmother prays for our health, happiness, security, and professional success. Whenever I've told her that I had a job interview, was applying for graduate school, had a doctor's appointment, or that we're freezing in Chicago, she said a prayer for me. It made me feel better, not necessarily because it meant that God was looking after me, but that my grandma continued to do so. In addition to our family, she has prayed for a less-divided country. Her prayers give her an opportunity to express, at least to herself, all of her best hopes for the world; they've shaped her sense of all that is good and just. They've shaped her sense of identity, and the circumstances of her life, our lives, and the world have shaped how she goes about practicing her faith.

Having spent years watching my grandmother praying to the Virgen de Guadalupe, I might have approached my research and writing with the knowledge that faith was an integral part of one's sense of self as an actor in the world, and that an understanding of one's sense of self was an integral part of one's faith. But I haven't always.

In my first book, *Standing on Common Ground*, about the Arizona-Sonora border region since World War II, I wrote about a conservative Mexican American department store owner named Alex G. Jácome. I understood his life and career as a reflection of Arizona's post–World War II economic growth, which was part of the broader development of the Sun Belt stretching from Florida to California and the blossoming of political conservatism represented by the likes of Jácome's friend Barry Goldwater.[1]

I sent a copy of my book to the department store owner's son, Felipe Jácome, whom I'd interviewed probably a dozen times, and who responded to my gift with a hurtful, scathing review of my book. He said I'd made his father seem like an immoral businessman, a two-dimensional character whose main motivations were the growth of his business, maintaining his family's class position, and his proximity to politically powerful men. Instead, Felipe Jácome argued, everything his father did stemmed from his Catholic faith, even his amassing of a fortune that allowed him to give back to his community. He sent a follow-up email to say that his wife wanted me to know that I'm a bad person headed for hell.

That was in 2013, and in the years since, I've drawn many conclusions from the meaning and intention behind the email, including that

Felipe Jácome had a point. I don't know that there is anything an author could write about a father that his son would read and appreciate as an accurate representation of someone so important to him in all of his complexity. But I could very well have paid more attention—I should have paid more attention—to his Catholicism as an integral part of his sense of self, and as one motivator among many for everything he did during his life and career. It was all over the documents in the Jácome family papers at the University of Arizona.

Alex Jácome went to church regularly; the logo for his department store showed a Spanish missionary blessing a kneeling Indian; and he and his wife, Estella, chose the governor of Sonora's son, Ignacio Soto Jr., as the godfather of their children, who went to Salpointe Catholic High School. Setting aside a deeper analysis of the colonial imagery, and how Jácome saw himself as a *patrón* to his employees, I chose to focus on Jácome the businessman, with his political connections and his privileged class standing. In other words, I did what many other, though certainly not all, historians have done: I saw business, politics, and faith as separate instead of as intertwined concerns. I did the exact thing that this book makes it much harder for historians to do.

And I did it again in my second book! Whenever I talked with audiences—of one or many—about the research I'd done for *The Hispanic Republican*, the near-unanimous response was, oh, you must be writing a lot about Cuban exiles and religion, mainly Catholicism. I responded that those were important parts of the story, but hardly all of it. Perhaps as a bit of knee-jerk contrarianism, I downplayed religion and instead focused on issues such as Cold War politics (and not only US-Cuban relations), patriotism, capitalism, or intra-ethnic divides over immigration, for example.[2]

I certainly noted when one of my actors said that their religious upbringing had shaped their politics, but religion stood alongside other issues, instead of infusing, and being infused by, all others. It was one of four or five or six other issues I pointed to as part of the story of Latino conservatism, but one that I understood on its own terms, not as an indistinguishable part of the whole.

The beauty, or rather one of the beauties, of *Faith and Power* is how it so thoroughly blurs the lines between religion and politics, giving us a fabulous roadmap for how we can better integrate these important subjects into all of the stories we tell about the Latino past. It's not that there isn't theology, communion, and devotion. It's that theology, communion, and devotion have particular settings, within specific communities, and are expressed at specific historical moments, for reasons that have to do with politics in its broadest sense. It's also not that there's no such thing as worldly concerns or secular spaces. It's that worldly concerns and secular spaces are shared by individuals and communities whose faith is an important part of their self-definition.

It is also not the case that historians of religion haven't merged faith and politics before. In their own books, the contributors to *Faith and Power* have done or will do just that. Before them, moreover, historians such as Timothy Matovina and Gastón Espinosa have written excellent books about Catholicism and Pentecostalism, respectively, titled *Latino Catholicism* and *Latino Pentecostals in America* (among many others), that effectively blend religion and politics.[3]

Yet what I find so impressive about *Faith and Power* is the sheer diversity of sects, nationality groups, and contexts presented: Catholicism, Evangelicalism, Mormonism; Mexican Americans, Indigenous Mexicans, Cuban Americans, Puerto Ricans, Dominican Americans, Central Americans; in institutional settings, in dialogue with government agencies, out in the streets, within families. The works by other historians are sweeping, but, collectively, the chapters in this volume are pervasive, finding their way into practically every corner of Latino life in the United States.

There has always been a danger in seeing religion and public life as separate, and in seeing religious life as existing on a higher moral plane than public life. Sometimes, faithful Latinos and other religious Americans have argued that their religious views are unquestionable because they are deeply personal. That argument has justified positions on a range of issues from opposition to abortion and same-sex marriage, to biblical defenses of racial discrimination. And when individuals or communities have their religious beliefs challenged—when they are asked to consider how the protection of their religious freedom might infringe on the liberty and equality of others—they have often responded that their views cannot be called into question because they are motivated by faith. To foreground all of the ways that religion and politics are connected is to deny the ability to justify controversial political beliefs on religious grounds alone.

The ways that religion has intervened in politics and vice versa need to be understood in all of their complexity. Religious organizations helped wage diplomacy between the United States and Latin America. Local parishes helped newly arrived immigrants find work and integrate into their communities. Individual congregants stood up to the discriminatory leaders of their churches to argue forcefully in defense of immigrants' rights, and churches took in refugees out of love and in protest of the ways that US economic, political, and military interventions destabilized their home countries.

These social justice motivations of many religious organizations provide an important counterweight to the widespread narrative that religion is an important source of Latino conservatism. And instead of a wholly economic, material, social, and political explanation for what has motivated much Latino activism, *Faith and Power* demonstrates conclusively that many movements have been guided by their conviction that a better world was and remains possible, and that their religious faith will help guide them toward it.

As much as *Faith and Power* accomplishes, I'm sure the editors and authors would agree that their volume is only the beginning of a conversation. It offers a clear perspective: that Latino religion and politics—or Latino religion and all aspects of Latino life, really—are deeply connected. That vantage point for seeing political movements as religiously motivated, and religious subjects engaged in politics, will reshape our work as Latino historians going forward. *Faith and Power* has set an agenda for the rest of us. And much work remains to be done, especially, to my mind, in the area of Latino religion and electoral politics.

In the months after the 2020 election, the topic of Latino religious politics became increasingly urgent. Or, rather, it was always urgent, but the election foregrounded how important it was. As the contributors to *Faith and Power* note, religion was one of the main dividing lines between different groups of Latino voters, yet the depth of these divisions was often misunderstood by the media and other political analysts, or reduced to issues like abortion and school prayer. Post-election analysis also presented religious belief as something like unshakeable faith, or ingrained cultural belief. There might be some truth to that, but religious politics are also a matter of human history, the story of particular communities figuring out how to act based on a combination of spiritual and secular concerns.

Before our next elections, political analysts, journalists, and scholars should take to heart *Faith and Power*'s main point, that all of the ways faith and politics are intertwined—across the country, by many different ethnic and nationality groups, in many different settings—are incredibly diverse and haven't been fully understood before. At the same time, historians, political scientists, sociologists, and other scholars should deepen their studies of the role that religious beliefs and practices among Latinos have played in their electoral decision making about which parties and candidates they decide to support.

The deep faith of Latinos—that they are more churchgoing than non-Latino Americans—is thought to be of greatest benefit to the Republican Party. On the one hand, the chapters in *Faith and Power* demonstrate that this has never been true. The faith-based motivations of Latinos have perhaps just as often led them to fight for economic justice, immigrants' rights, or social and gender equality. Yet even here, we should know more about how the Democratic Party, and other liberal and progressive civic or political organizations, have tapped into, and crafted policies in response to, the desires of the vast majority of Latinos for justice, rights, and equality. I don't believe that conservative Latinos would concede that these are inherently liberal values, just as liberal Latinos wouldn't concede that family values are inherently conservative. Still, the Republican Party has often appealed to Latino religiosity in order to advance an anti-abortion, anti-LGBTQ+, pro-school prayer agenda. We should know more about this, too. *Faith and Power* might need a sequel to elaborate on the few places in the volume where its authors touch on these themes.

As crazy as it sounds—since the standard bearer of the Republican Party was hardly a model of piety and rectitude—Donald Trump's support for religious freedom was one of his main appeals to Latinos across the United States. From early on in his presidency, Trump's Latino surrogates made inroads with evangelical churches across the United States, and some of his Latino advisers were evangelical pastors. Trump's evangelical vice president, Mike Pence, was often the face of the Trump administration when it came to Latino churchgoers. So was the vice president's Spanish-speaking nephew, John Pence, who stumped for Trump in Latino communities across the United States.

After the Latinos for Trump campaign officially launched in the late spring of 2019, Trump himself visited with Latino evangelical leaders, especially in Florida. During one visit with Latino evangelicals in Miami, Trump said, "America was not built by religion-hating socialists," but, rather, "by churchgoing, God-worshipping, freedom-loving patriots."[4] His words underscored the main point of *Faith and Power*, that religion and politics are always intertwined. The fear of socialism—sparked by Democratic candidates like Bernie Sanders, national leaders like Alexandria Ocasio-Cortez, and even the idea that Joe Biden was a "Trojan horse" for socialism, meaning that once in office he would be beholden to the far-left members of his party—resonated with many Latinos, and not only in Florida.[5]

Trump's talk about socialism, moreover, wasn't only about politics or the economy, because, right or wrong, it tapped into the sense among many Latino evangelicals that socialism is a god-hating ideology, as Trump suggested. Similarly, Trump's support for school choice was also about religious politics, since charter schools can have denominational affiliations. Following the main argument advanced in *Faith and Power*, Trump's positions on the economy, education, or the role of government in American life all got knotted and raveled together in a ball of yarn that also included the politics of religion.

To be sure, it is not the case that all Latino evangelicals are conservative. The fabulous Latino Religions and Politics National Survey, overseen by Gastón Espinosa, found that Latino evangelicals were about evenly divided in their support for Joe Biden and Trump—with 46 percent supporting Biden, and 48 percent supporting Trump.[6] Similarly, the *New York Times* reporter Jennifer Medina interviewed an evangelical pastor in Arizona named Jose Rivera, who said that Latino evangelicals were "politically homeless."[7] Finally, Gabriel Salguero, president and founder of the National Latino Evangelical Coalition (NaLEC), has long referred to evangelical Latinos as swing voters. But a near 50–50 split among Latino evangelicals who support Republicans and Democrats is, for Republicans, better odds than the 25–75 percent or 33–67 percent split between Latino support for Republicans and Democrats in general. Courting Latino evangelicals simply amounts to Republicans hunting where the ducks are, as the conservative Arizona senator Goldwater described it. Moreover, Latino evangelicalism in the United States is a religion practiced by many recent immigrants from Latin America, and Republicans are well aware that in order to continue winning elections in the future, they need to reach out to youth and new Americans instead of continuing to rely on their aging base of white voters.

More than anything else, the 2020 election revealed how diverse the Latino population in the United States has become, and in many ways has always been. It has become cliché to say that Latinos are not a monolith, but the political analysts who've said this have mainly meant that we come from many different national backgrounds. But that's just the beginning of the story. Latinos live in every state, and in rural and urban areas. Latino men and women may be as divided now as they've ever been, and the same could be said of new Americans and those who've been citizens for generations.

Latino conservatives have postulated that Trump appealed in particular to Latinos from rural, working-class backgrounds, who are by nature more culturally conservative than the woke Latinos who live in cities. They've said that the GOP is becoming the party for nonwhite, working-class Americans. I understand this as posturing, as the GOP tries to figure out what direction it should go after Trump, what elements of Trumpism it should embrace, and which it should leave behind. We'll see whether its assertion turns out to be true, but I don't like it for the way it essentializes rural, working-class communities of faith. The chapters in *Faith and Power* are an antidote to such speculation not grounded in, or supported by, research and data. They demonstrate the potential that historical scholarship has to explain the past, present, and future of Latinos in the United States, in all of their diversity and complexity. They are a clarion call for even more work on the ties between religion and politics.

NOTES
1 Geraldo Cadava, *Standing on Common Ground: The Making of a Sunbelt Borderland* (Cambridge: Harvard University Press, 2013).
2 Geraldo Cadava, *The Hispanic Republican: The Shaping of an American Political Identity, from Nixon to Trump* (New York: Ecco, 2020).
3 Timothy Matovina, *Latino Catholicism: Transformation in America's Largest Church* (Princeton: Princeton University Press, 2014); Gastón Espinosa, *Latino Pentecostals in America: Faith and Politics in Action* (Cambridge: Harvard University Press, 2014).
4 Donald Trump during speech in Miami, January 3, 2020. Clip available at https://www.air.tv/watch?v=bpIvTNeLQoKfFztTD_sPog.

5 Dominick Mastrangelo, "Tom Cotton: Joe Biden Is a 'Trojan Horse for the Far Left,'" *Washington Examiner*, August 3, 2020, www.washingtonexaminer.com.
6 Alejandra Molina, "Latino Evangelicals Narrowly Favor Trump," *Christianity Today*, October 6, 2020, www.christianitytoday.com.
7 Jennifer Medina, "Latino, Evangelical, and Politically Homeless," *New York Times*, October 11, 2020.

ACKNOWLEDGMENTS

This book started, as many edited volumes do, with a simple conversation among friends. We had come together for a panel presentation at the Western History Association Conference in San Antonio, Texas, in the fall of 2018. Our panel, "Redefining Activism: New Directions in Latina/o Religious History," generated robust conversation among the presenters and the audience members who had generously trudged to the hotel conference room for an 8:30 a.m. presentation. Afterwards, sipping overpriced coffee in the hotel lobby, Felipe broached the idea of expanding our conversations about the individual interventions we hoped to make in Latino studies and religious history and turning them into an edited volume. Excited about the possibility of working together, we laid out a plan to bring together some of the most innovative historians working in the field, scholars across generational cohorts who were actively engaged in exploring the intersections between Latino political power, faith, and religious institutions. With contributors lined up and then a contract for publication from New York University Press in hand, we set off to develop our volume.

Then the world changed. A week before we were to meet at Texas A&M University in March 2020 to exchange ideas, critique each other's drafts, and listen to our ideas about Latino religion and politics, COVID-19 stopped us in our tracks. One participant, already at the airport and preparing to board their international flight to the United States, made the quick decision to stay home. Of course, after those chaotic first days in March 2020, we all had to stay home and learn how to live entirely new lives: socially distant, masks on, and with daily Zoom meetings. In the late spring and early summer months of 2020, as we adjusted to our new realities and focused on keeping our families safe, our editorial team lost touch with our contributors. The possibility of this project falling apart felt very real as we shifted our energies to learning how to teach virtually from home, how to care for sick loved ones, and where to find hand sanitizer and toilet paper. Somehow, however, we found the will (the faith?) to push forward and continue the work. Part of it, we think, is that as co-editors of this collection, we genuinely enjoyed collaborating with each other—it's not every day that you have an opportunity to build a project with people you enjoy spending time with. Perhaps just as important was the simple fact that we couldn't shake the feeling that the underlying questions we were asking in this book—how do Latinos build community, how do they find a sense of belonging, where are the spaces where they can most feel empowered and full—could help address some of the most pressing issues facing Latino communities today. And then, as we finalized the manuscript, Texas faced a winter weather event that left millions without power and water, long lines at the gas pump, and grocery stores with empty shelves, throwing the lives of many of our contributors into new disarray. To call the eighteen months leading up to the submission of this manuscript unprecedented does not even come close. Somehow, through all of that, this work came to fruition. And for that, we are forever grateful to all of our colleagues, our editorial team, and our families who supported us along the way.

That this volume exists at all is a testament to its contributors and their willingness to collaborate virtually in the middle of a global pandemic. Each contributor had agreed to join our project in early 2020, and perhaps luckily for the editors, each of them had diligently submitted their contribution just weeks before our worlds shut down. In the midst of the chaos of the spring of 2020, they participated in creating and fostering an intellectual community through virtual spaces, emails, and various drafts of our chapters. Their ability to help us complete this project is also a testament to their own commitments to addressing the pressing questions raised by this volume.

We would like to express our appreciation for Jennifer Hammer and the entire editorial staff at New York University Press, who saw the promise of this volume in its earliest stages and encouraged us to push it across the finish line, even in the midst of a pandemic. We would also like to thank the reviewers of our initial manuscript, who provided invaluable guidance on how to continue to reach across disciplinary strands within and beyond Latino studies and religious studies. And we would like to thank the staff at Texas A&M University who helped plan our (someday to be rescheduled) conference. Finally, we'd like to thank our families—Maribel, Alejandro, and Ariana (Felipe); Luis and Grayce (Maggie); and Laura and Penelope (Sergio)—who encouraged us and allowed us the time we needed to engage in countless strategy sessions, group writing retreats, and endless group text streams in the years we developed this volume from an idea to a finished project.

SUGGESTED READINGS

Aponte, Edwin David. *¡Santo! Varieties of Latino/a Spirituality*. Maryknoll, NY: Orbis, 2012.
Avalos, Hector. *Introduction to the US Latina and Latino Religious Experience*. Boston: Brill, 2004.
Badillo, David. "Catholicism and the Search for Nationhood in Miami's Cuban Community." *US Catholic Historian* 20, no. 4 (Fall 2002): 75–90.
———. *Latinos and the New Immigrant Church: A Comparative History of Urban Religion*. Baltimore: Johns Hopkins University Press, 2006.
———. "Religion and Transnational Migration in Chicago: The Case of the Potosinos." *Journal of the Illinois State Historical Society* 94, no. 4 (Winter 2001–2002): 420–40.
Banker, Mark T. *Presbyterian Missions and Cultural Interaction in the Far Southwest, 1850–1950*. Champagne: University of Illinois Press, 1992.
Barba, Lloyd. "Farmworker Frames: *Apostólico* Counter Narratives in California's Valleys." *Journal of the American Academy of Religion* 86, no. 3 (September 2018): 691–723.
———. "Latinx Christianities in North America." In *Bloomsbury Religion in North America*. London: Bloomsbury Academic, 2021. http://dx.doi.org/10.5040/9781350971073.0023.
———. "More Spirit in That Little Madera Church: Cesar Chavez and Borderlands Religious Soundscapes 1954-1966." *California History* 94, no. 1 (Spring 2017): 26–42.
Barba, Lloyd, and Tatyana Castillo-Ramos. "Sacred Resistance: The Sanctuary Movement from Reagan to Trump." *Perspectivas: Journal for the Hispanic Theological Initiative* 16 (2019): 11–36.
Barton, Paul. *Hispanic Methodists, Presbyterians, and Baptists in Texas*. Austin: University of Texas Press, 2006.
Busto, Rudy V. *King Tiger: The Religious Vision of Reies López Tijerina*. Albuquerque: University of New Mexico Press, 2005.
Calvillo, Jonathan. *The Saints of Santa Ana: Faith and Ethnicity in a Mexican Majority City*. New York: Oxford University Press, 2020.
Cameron, David Jeffrey. "Race and Religion in the Bayou City: Latino/a, African American, and Anglo Baptists in Houston's Long Civil Rights Movement." PhD diss., Texas A&M University, 2017.
Chávez, César. "The Mexican American and the Church." *Quinto Sol Publications* 1, no. 4 (Summer 1968): 9–12.

Coutin, Susan B. *The Culture of Protest: Religious Activism and the US Sanctuary Movement*. Boulder: Westview, 1993.

Cunningham, Hilary. *God and Caesar at the Rio Grande: Sanctuary and the Politics of Religion*. Minneapolis: University of Minnesota Press, 1995.

Dalton, Frederick John. *The Moral Vision of César Chávez*. Maryknoll, NY: Orbis, 2003.

Davalos, Karen Mary. "'The Real Way of Praying': The Via Crucis, Mexicano Sacred Space, and the Architecture of Domination." In *Horizons of the Sacred: Mexican Traditions in US Catholicism*, edited by Timothy Matovina and Gary Riebe-Estrella, 41–68. Ithaca: Cornell University Press, 2002.

Delgadillo, Theresa. *Spiritual Mestizaje: Religion, Gender, Race, and Nation in Contemporary Chicana Narrative*. Durham: Duke University Press, 2011.

Díaz-Stevens, Ana María. *Oxcart Catholicism on Fifth Avenue: The Impact of the Puerto Rican Migration on the Archdiocese of New York*. Notre Dame, IN: University of Notre Dame Press, 1993.

Díaz-Stevens, Ana María, and Anthony M. Stevens-Arroyo. *Recognizing the Latino Resurgence in US Religion: The Emmaus Paradigm*. London: Routledge, 1997.

Dolan, Jay P., and Allan Figueroa Deck, eds. *Hispanic Catholic Culture in the US: Issues and Concerns*. Notre Dame, IN: University of Notre Dame Press, 1997.

Dolan, Jay P., and Gilberto M Hinojosa. *Mexican Americans and the Catholic Church, 1900–1965*. Notre Dame, IN: University of Notre Dame Press, 1994.

Dolan, Jay P., and Jaime R. Vidal, eds. *Puerto Rican and Cuban Catholics in the US, 1900–1965*. Notre Dame, IN: University of Notre Dame Press, 1994.

Elizondo, Virgilio. *Galilean Journey: The Mexican-American Promise*. Maryknoll, NY: Orbis, 1983.

Elmore, Maggie. "Fighting for Hemispheric Solidarity: The National Catholic Welfare Conference and the Quest to Secure Mexican American Employment Rights during World War II." *US Catholic Historian* 35, no. 2 (May 2017): 125–49.

Embry, Jessie L. *In His Own Language: Mormon Spanish Speaking Congregations in the United States*. Salt Lake City: Signature Books, 1997.

Espinosa, Gastón. *Latino Pentecostals in America: Faith and Politics in Action*. Cambridge: Harvard University Press, 2014.

Espinosa, Gastón, and Miguel A. De La Torre, eds. *Rethinking Latino(a) Religions and Identity*. Cleveland: Pilgrim Press, 2006.

Espinosa, Gastón, Virgilio P. Elizondo, and Jesse Miranda, eds. *Latino Religions and Civic Activism in the United States*. New York: Oxford University Press, 2005.

Espinosa, Gastón, and Mario T. García, eds. *Mexican American Religions: Spirituality, Activism, and Culture*. Durham: Duke University Press, 2008.

Fernández, Eduardo C. *La Cosecha: Harvesting Contemporary United States Hispanic Theology (1972–1998)*. Collegeville, MN: Liturgical Press, 2000.

Floyd-Thomas, Stacey M., and Anthony B. Pinn, eds. *Liberation Theologies in the United States: An Introduction*. New York: New York University Press, 2010.

Gálvez, Alyshia. *Guadalupe in New York: Devotion and the Struggle for Citizenship Rights among Mexican Immigrants*. New York: New York University Press, 2010.

García, Ignacio M. *Chicano While Mormon: Activism, War, and Keeping the Faith.* Madison, NJ: Fairleigh Dickinson University Press, 2015.
García, Mario T. *Católicos: Resistance and Affirmation in Chicano Catholic History.* Austin: University of Texas Press, 2008.
———. *Chicano Liberation Theology: The Writings and Documents of Richard Cruz and Católicos por La Raza.* Dubuque, IA: Kendall Hunt, 2009.
———. *Father Luis Olivares, a Biography: Faith Politics and the Origins of the Sanctuary Movement in Los Angeles.* Chapel Hill: University of North Carolina Press, 2018.
———. *The Gospel of César Chávez: My Faith in Action.* Lanham, MD: Sheed and Ward, 2007.
González, Sergio M. "'Juntos en el Nombre de Dios': Milwaukee's Mexican Mission Chapel of Our Lady of Guadalupe, 1924–1929." *Journal of American Ethnic History* 36, no. 1 (Fall 2016): 5–30.
———. "Refugees, Religious Space, and Sanctuary in Wisconsin." In *Building Sustainable Worlds: Latinx Placemaking in the Midwest,* edited by Theresa Delgadillo, Claire F. Fox, Ramón Rivera-Servera, and Geraldo L. Cadava. Urbana: University of Illinois Press, forthcoming.
———. "The Sanctuary Movement." In *Oxford Research Encyclopedia of American History.* New York: Oxford University Press, 2020.
Gutiérrez, David G. "The New Turn in Chicano/Mexicano History: Integrating Religious Belief and Practice." In *Catholics in the American Century: Recasting Narratives of US History,* edited by R. Scott Appleby and Kathleen Sprows Cummings. Ithaca: Cornell University Press, 2012.
Gutiérrez, Ramón A. "The Religious Origins of Reies López Tijerina's Land Grant Activism in the Southwest." In *A New Insurgency: The Port Huron Statement and Its Times,* edited by Howard Brick and Gregory Parker, 109–34. Ann Arbor: University of Michigan Publishing Services, 2015.
Hagan, Jacqueline. "Making Theological Sense of the Migration Journey from Latin America: Catholic, Protestant, and Interfaith Perspectives." *American Behavioral Scientist* 49, no. 11 (July 2006): 1554–73.
Hendrickson, Brett. *The Healing Power of the Santuario de Chimayó: America's Miraculous Church.* New York: New York University Press, 2017.
Hidalgo, Jacqueline M. *Revelation in Aztlán: Scriptures, Utopias, and the Chicano Movement.* New York: Palgrave Macmillan, 2016.
Hinojosa, Felipe. *Apostles of Change: Latino Radical Politics, Church Occupations, and the Fight to Save the Barrio.* Austin: University of Texas Press, 2021.
———. "The Catholic Interracial Council and Mexican American Civil Rights in Davenport, Iowa, 1952–1974." In *The Religious Left in Modern America: Doorkeepers of a Radical Faith,* edited by Leilah Danielson, Marian Mollin, and Doug Rossinow, 163–84. New York: Palgrave Macmillan, 2018.
———. "Católicos por La Raza and the Future of Catholic Studies." *American Catholic Studies* 127, no. 3 (Fall 2016): 26–29.

———. "Latina/o Religious Studies since the 1970s." In *The Oxford Handbook of Latino Studies*, edited by Ilan Stavans. New York: Oxford University Press, 2020.
———. *Latino Mennonites: Civil Rights, Faith, and Evangelical Culture*. Baltimore: Johns Hopkins University Press, 2014.
———. "Religious Migrants: The Latino Mennonite Quest for Community and Civil Rights in the American Midwest." In *The Latino Midwest Reader*, edited by Omar Valerio-Jiménez, Santiago Vaquera-Vásquez, and Claire F. Fox, 213–28. Urbana: University of Illinois Press, 2017.
———. "Sacred Spaces: Race, Resistance, and the Politics of Chicana/o and Latina/o Religious History." In *A Promising Problem: The New Chicana/o History*, edited by Carlos Kevin Blanton, 111–34. Austin: University of Texas Press, 2016.
———. "The Sanctuary Movement, 1980s." In *50 Events That Shaped Latina/o History: An Encyclopedia of the American Mosaic*, edited by Lilia Fernández, 729–53. Santa Barbara, CA: ABC-CLIO, 2018.
Hiraldo, Samiri Hernández. *Black Puerto Rican Identity and Religious Experience*. Gainesville: University Press of Florida, 2006.
Hondagneu-Sotelo, Pierrette. *God's Heart Has No Borders: How Religious Activists Are Working for Immigrant Rights*. Berkeley: University of California Press, 2008.
———, ed. *Religion and Social Justice for Immigrants*. New Brunswick: Rutgers University Press, 2006.
———. "Religion and a Standpoint Theory of Immigrant Social Justice." In *Religion and Social Justice for Immigrants*, edited by Pierrette Hondagneu-Sotelo, 3–15. New Brunswick: Rutgers University Press, 2007.
Hondagneu-Sotelo, Pierrette, Genelle Gaudinez, Hector Lara, and Billie C. Ortiz. "'There's a Spirit That Transcends the Border': Faith, Ritual, and Postnational Protest at the US-Mexico Border." *Sociological Perspectives* 47, no. 2 (2004): 133–59.
Hoover, Brett C. *The Shared Parish: Latinos, Anglos, and the Future of US Catholicism*. New York: New York University Press, 2014.
Kanter, Deborah E. *Chicago Católico: Making Catholic Parishes Mexican*. Urbana: University of Illinois Press, 2020.
———. "Making Mexican Parishes: Ethnic Succession in Chicago Churches, 1947–1977." *US Catholic Historian* 30, no. 2 (Winter 2012): 35–58.
———. "Mexican Priests and Migrant Ministry in the Midwest, 1953–1969." *US Catholic Historian* 39, no. 1 (Winter 2021): 93–112.
Lara-Braud, Jorge. "The Status of Religion among Mexican Americans." In *La Causa Chicana: The Movement for Justice*, edited by Margaret M. Mangold and Family Service Association of America, 87–94. New York: Family Service Association of America, 1972.
León, Luis D. *La Llorona's Children: Religion, Life, and Death in the US–Mexican Borderlands*. Berkeley: University of California Press, 2004.
———. *The Political Spirituality of César Chávez: Crossing Religious Borders*. Oakland: University of California Press, 2015.
Levitt, Peggy. *The Transnational Villagers*. Berkley: University of California Press, 2001.

Lin, Tony Tian-Ren. *Prosperity Gospel Latinos and Their American Dream*. Chapel Hill: University of North Carolina Press, 2020.
Lorentzen, Robin. *Women in the Sanctuary Movement*. Philadelphia: Temple University Press, 1991.
Lozano, Nora O. "Faithful in the Struggle: A Historical Perspective on Hispanic Protestant Women in the United States." In *Los Evangélicos: Portraits of Hispanic Protestantism*, edited by Juan Francisco Martínez and Lindy Scott, 120–40. Eugene, OR: Wipf and Stock, 2009.
Lucas, Isidro. *The Browning of America: The Hispanic Revolution in the American Church*. Chicago: Fides/Claretian Books, 1981.
Machado, Daisy L. *Of Borders and Margins: Hispanic Disciples in Texas, 1888–1945*. New York: Oxford University Press, 2003.
Martínez, Anne. *Catholic Borderlands: Mapping Catholicism onto American Empire, 1905–1935*. Lincoln: University of Nebraska Press, 2014.
———. "Catholic Monroeism: US Support for the Catholic Church during the Mexican Revolution, 1914–1929." *US Catholic Historian* 39, no. 1 (Winter 2021): 49–69.
Martínez, Juan Francisco. *Sea la Luz: The Making of Mexican Protestantism in the American Southwest, 1829–1900*. Denton: University of North Texas Press, 2006.
———. *The Story of Latino Protestants in the United States*. Grand Rapids, MI: Eerdmans, 2018.
Martínez, Richard Edward. *PADRES: The National Chicano Priest Movement*. Austin: University of Texas Press, 2005.
Martínez-Vázquez, Hjamil. *Made in the Margins: Latina/o Constructions of US Religious History*. Waco, TX: Baylor University Press, 2013.
Matovina, Timothy. *Guadalupe and Her Faithful: Latino Catholics in San Antonio, from Colonial Origins to the Present*. Baltimore: Johns Hopkins University Press, 2005.
———. *Latino Catholicism: Transformation in America's Largest Church*. Princeton: Princeton University Press, 2014.
———. "Representation and the Reconstruction of Power: The Rise of PADRES and Las Hermanas." In *What's Left? Liberal American Catholics*, edited by Mary Jo Weaver and R. Scott Appleby, 220–37. Bloomington: Indiana University Press, 1999.
———. *Tejano Religion and Ethnicity: San Antonio, 1821–1860*. Austin: University of Texas Press, 1995.
Matovina, Timothy, and Gary Riebe-Estrella, eds. *Horizons of the Sacred: Mexican Traditions in US Catholicism*. Ithaca: Cornell University Press, 2002.
McCarthy, Malachy Richard. "Which Christ Came to Chicago: Catholic and Protestant Programs to Evangelize, Socialize and Americanize the Mexican Immigrant, 1900–1940." PhD diss., Loyola University Chicago, 2002.
McEvoy, Gráinne. "'Operation Migratory Labor': Braceros, Migrants, and the American Catholic Bishops' Committee for the Spanish Speaking." *US Catholic Historian* 34, no. 3 (Summer 2016): 75–98.
Medina, Lara. *Las Hermanas: Chicana/Latina Religious Political Activism in the US Catholic Church*. Philadelphia: Temple University Press, 2004.

Medina, Nestor, and Sammy Alfaro, eds. *Pentecostals and Charismatics in Latin American and Latino Communities.* New York: Palgrave MacMillan, 2015.
Mulder, Mark, Aida Ramos, and Gerardo Martí. *Latino Protestants in America: Growing and Diverse.* Lanham, MD: Rowman and Littlefield, 2017.
Nabhan-Warren, Kristy. *The Virgin of El Barrio: Marian Apparitions, Catholic Evangelizing, and Mexican American Activism.* New York: New York University Press, 2005.
Nieto, Adriana Pilar. "From 'Black-Eyed Girls' to the MMU (Mujeres Metodistas Unidas): Race, Religion and Gender in the US-Mexico Borderlands." PhD diss., University of Denver, 2009.
Nieto, Leo D. "The Chicano Movement and the Churches in the United States/El Movimiento Chicano y las Iglesias en los Estados Unidos." *Perkins Journal*, no. 29 (Fall 1975): 32–41.
———. "The Chicano Movement and the Gospel: Historical Accounts of a Protestant Pastor." In *Hidden Stories: Unveiling the History of the Latino Church*, edited by Daniel R. Rodríguez-Díaz and David Cortés-Fuentes, 143–57. Decatur, GA: AETH, 1994.
Odem, Mary E. "Our Lady of Guadalupe in the New South: Latino Immigrants and the Politics of Integration in the Catholic Church." *Journal of American Ethnic History* 24, no. 1 (Fall 2004): 26–57.
Oropeza, Lorena. *The King of Adobe: Reies López Tijerina, Lost Prophet of the Chicano Movement.* Chapel Hill: University of North Carolina Press, 2019.
Paik, A. Naomi. "Abolitionist Futures and the US Sanctuary Movement." *Race & Class* 59, no. 2 (October–December 2017): 3–25.
Peña, Elaine A. *Performing Piety: Making Space Sacred with the Virgin of Guadalupe.* Berkeley: University of California Press, 2011.
Pitti, Gina Marie. "A Ghastly International Racket: The Catholic Church and the *Bracero* Program in California, 1942–1964." Working Paper Series, Cushwa Center for the Study of American Catholicism, University of Notre Dame, series 33, no. 2 (Fall 2001): 1–21.
———. "To Hear about God in Spanish: Ethnicity, Church, and Community Activism in the San Francisco Archdiocese's Mexican American Colonias, 1942–1965." PhD diss., Stanford University, 2003.
Poyo, Gerald Eugene. *Cuban Catholics in the United States, 1960–1980: Exile and Integration.* Notre Dame, IN: University of Notre Dame Press, 2007.
Poyo, Gerald Eugene, and Timothy M. Matovina, eds. *Presente! US Latino Catholics from Colonial Origins to the Present.* Maryknoll, NY: Orbis, 2000.
Prouty, Marco G. *César Chávez, the Catholic Bishops, and the Farmworkers' Struggle for Social Justice.* Tucson: University of Arizona Press, 2006.
Pulido, Alberto L. "Are You an Emissary of Jesus Christ? Justice, the Catholic Church and the Chicano Movement." *Explorations in Ethnic Studies* 14, no. 1 (January 1991): 17–34.
Ramírez, Daniel. *Migrating Faith: Pentecostalism in the United States and Mexico in the Twentieth Century.* Chapel Hill: University of North Carolina Press, 2015.

Rivera, Orlando. "Mormonism and the Chicano." In *Mormonism: A Faith for All Cultures*, edited by F. LaMond Tullis, 115–26. Provo: Brigham Young University Press, 1978.

Rodríguez, Jeanette. *Our Lady of Guadalupe: Faith and Empowerment among Mexican-American Women*. Austin: University of Texas Press, 2010.

Rodríguez, Jorge Juan, V. "The Neoliberal Co-Optation of Identity Politics: Geo-Political Situatedness as a Decolonial Discussion Partner." *Horizontes Decoloniales/Decolonial Horizons* 5 (January 2019): 101–30.

Romero, Roberto Chao. *Brown Church: Five Centuries of Latina/o Social Justice, Theology, and Identity*. Downers Grove, IL: Intervarsity Press, 2020.

Ruiz, Carlos. "The Question of Sanctuary: The Adorers of the Blood of Christ and the US Sanctuary Movement, 1983–1996." *US Catholic Historian* 38, no. 4 (Fall 2020): 53–70.

Sagarena, Roberto Lint. *Aztlán and Arcadia: Religion, Ethnicity, and the Creation of Place*. New York: New York University Press, 2014.

Sánchez, David A. *From Patmos to the Barrio: Subverting Imperial Myths*. Minneapolis: Fortress, 2008.

Sánchez-Walsh, Arlene. "Emma Tenayuca, Religious Elites, and the 1938 Pecan-Shellers' Strike." In *The Pew and the Picket Line*, edited by Christopher D. Cantwell, Heath W. Carter, and Janine Giordano Drake, 145–66. Champaign: University of Illinois Press, 2016.

———. *Latino Pentecostal Identity: Evangelical Faith, Self, and Society*. New York: Columbia University Press, 2003.

Sandoval, Moises. *Fronteras: A History of the Latin American Church in the USA since 1513*. San Antonio, TX: Mexican American Cultural Center, 1983.

———. *On the Move: A History of the Hispanic Church in the United States*. Maryknoll, NY: Orbis, 1990.

Smith, Christian. *The Emergence of Liberation Theology: Radical Religion and Social Movement Theory*. Chicago: University of Chicago Press, 1991.

———. *Resisting Reagan: The US Central America Peace Movement*. Chicago: University of Chicago Press, 1996.

Stevens-Arroyo, Anthony M. "From Barrios to Barricades: Religion and Religiosity in Latino Life." In *The Columbia History of Latinos in the United States since 1960*, edited by David G. Gutiérrez, 303–54. New York: Columbia University Press, 2004.

Tirres, Christopher D. *The Aesthetics and Ethics of Faith: A Dialogue between Liberationist and Pragmatist Thought*. Oxford: Oxford University Press, 2014.

Treviño, Roberto R. *The Church in the Barrio: Mexican American Ethno-Catholicism in Houston*. Chapel Hill: University of North Carolina Press, 2006.

Treviño, Roberto R., and Richard V. Francaviglia. *Catholicism in the American West: A Rosary of Hidden Voices*. College Station: Texas A&M University Press, 2007.

Tweed, Thomas A. *Crossing and Dwelling: A Theory of Religion*. Cambridge: Harvard University Press, 2008.

———. *Our Lady of the Exile: Diasporic Religion at a Cuban Catholic Shrine in Miami.* Oxford: Oxford University Press, 1997.

———. "Our Lady of Guadeloupe Visits the Confederate Memorial: Latino and Asian Religions in the South." In *Religion in the Contemporary South: Changes, Continuities, and Contexts*, edited by Corrie E. Norman and Don S. Armentrout, 139–58. Knoxville: University of Tennessee Press, 2005.

Vásquez, Manuel A., and Marie Friedman Marquardt. *Globalizing the Sacred: Religion across the Americas.* New Brunswick: Rutgers University Press, 2003.

Vázquez, Luis. "Go and Make Disciples: An Analysis of the Salsa Evangélica Movement in Puerto Rico." *Centro Journal* 16, no. 2 (Fall 2004): 194–225.

Vega, Sujey. *Latino Heartland: Of Borders and Belonging in the Midwest.* New York: New York University Press, 2016.

Vidal, Jaime R. "The American Church and the Puerto Rican People." *US Catholic Historian* 9, nos. 1–2 (Winter–Spring 1990): 119–35.

Villareal, Aimee. "Sanctuaryscapes in the North American Southwest." *Radical History Review* 135 (2019): 43–70.

Walker-Jones, Randi. *Protestantism in the Sangre de Cristos, 1850–1920.* Albuquerque: University of New Mexico Press, 1991.

Watt, Alan J. *Farm Workers and the Churches: The Movement in California and Texas.* College Station: Texas A&M University Press, 2010.

Wilson, Catherine. *The Politics of Latino Faith: Religion, Identity, and Urban Community.* New York: New York University Press, 2008.

Young, Julia G. *Mexican Exodus: Emigrants, Exiles, and Refugees of the Cristero War.* Oxford: Oxford University Press, 2015.

Yukich, Grace. *One Family under God: Immigration Politics and Progressive Religion in America.* Oxford: Oxford University Press, 2013.

ABOUT THE EDITORS

MAGGIE ELMORE is Assistant Professor of History at Sam Houston State University in Huntsville, Texas. She is a historian of US religion and politics, human rights, and Latinx history.

SERGIO M. GONZÁLEZ is Assistant Professor of Latinx Studies at Marquette University. He is a historian of US immigration, labor, religion, and Latinx communities in the Midwest. He is the author of *Mexicans in Wisconsin*.

FELIPE HINOJOSA is Associate Professor of History at Texas A&M University in College Station, Texas. He serves as Director of the Carlos H. Cantu Endowment and is editor of the interdisciplinary, peer-reviewed, and online moderated forum *Latinx Talk*. He is the author of *Latino Mennonites* and *Apostles of Change*.

ABOUT THE CONTRIBUTORS

LLOYD D. BARBA is Assistant Professor in the Department of Religion and core faculty in Latinx and Latin American Studies at Amherst College. His book, *Sowing the Sacred: Mexican Pentecostal Farmworkers in California* is forthcoming. He earned his BA in History and Religion from the University of the Pacific and his PhD in American Culture from the University of Michigan.

ELADIO B. BOBADILLA is Assistant Professor of History at the University of Kentucky. He received his PhD at Duke University in 2019. He was awarded the 2020 Herbert G. Gutman Dissertation Prize and is the author of a forthcoming book on the history of the modern immigrants' rights movement.

GERALDO L. CADAVA is Professor of History and Latina and Latino Studies at Northwestern University. He is the author of *Standing on Common Ground* and *The Hispanic Republican*.

LILIA FERNÁNDEZ is the Henry Rutgers Term Chair in the Department of Latino and Caribbean Studies and the Department of History at Rutgers University in New Brunswick, New Jersey. She is a scholar of twentieth-century Latina/o urban and Immigration history and the author of *Brown in the Windy City: Mexicans and Puerto Ricans in Postwar Chicago*, a history of the migration and settlement of Latina/os in Chicago in the years after World War II.

DELIA FERNÁNDEZ-JONES is Assistant Professor of History at Michigan State University. Her research centers on Latina/o placemaking in the Midwest and how Latina/os transform the places they live in to suit their political, economic, and social needs. Her forthcoming book is in press with the University of Illinois Press.

ANNE M. MARTÍNEZ is Assistant Professor of American Political Culture and Theory at Rijksuniversiteit Groningen in the Netherlands. She is the author of *Catholic Borderlands: Mapping Catholicism onto American Empire, 1905–1945* and numerous articles and chapters on race, religion, and nation. She is currently working on projects on American Indians and Catholic missionaries, and religious practice among Catholics in Chicago.

LARA MEDINA is Professor in the Department of Chicana and Chicano Studies at California State University, Northridge, where she teaches Chicanx history and courses on religion and spirituality in Chicanx communities. Her recent co-edited publication is *Voices from the Ancestors: Xicanx and Latinx Spiritual Expressions and Healing Practices.*

YURIDIA RAMÍREZ is Assistant Professor in the Department of History at the University of Illinois at Urbana-Champaign. She is currently working on her book manuscript, tentatively titled *Indigeneity on the Move: Transborder Politics from Michoacán to North Carolina*, a historic and interdisciplinary analysis of a diasporic Indigenous community and its transforming sense of indigeneity.

JORGE JUAN RODRÍGUEZ V is the son of two Puerto Rican migrants and grew up outside Hartford, Connecticut. He holds degrees in biblical studies, social thought, liberation theologies, and history and currently serves as Associate Director for Strategic Programming at the Hispanic Summer Program in New York City.

SUJEY VEGA is Associate Professor in Gender Studies and Faculty Lead of American Studies at Arizona State University. She is the author of *Latino Heartland: Of Borders and Belonging in the Midwest.*

INDEX

Note: Page numbers in italics indicate figures.

181st General Assembly, United Presbyterian Church in the USA (UPCUSA), 166, 174, 175, 183n5
287(g) agreements, 227

ABC Agreement, 226
Academia de la Nueva Raza, 173
Acción Cívica Evangélica, 177, 178–80, 182
activism, 9, 184n11, 202–3; Catholic, 4, 166–87, 184n11, 202–3, 234–36, 238–40; Central American, 223; Chicano, 193; faith-based, 214–15; farmworker, 121–44; gay and lesbian, 189; Latina spiritual political activism, 188–89; Latino, 145–65; Mormon, 94–119; Protestant, 4, 166–87; religious, 3; student, 166, 171, 193–94. *See also specific organizations and movements*
advocacy groups, 179–80. *See also specific organizations*
AFL-CIO, 245
African Americans, 6, 7, 24, 26; in Durham, North Carolina, 273–74, 276–80; in Grand Rapids, 77, 84, 86; Great Migrations and, 276; in New York City, 149; self-determination and, 276, 278–79
African Methodist Episcopal Church, 276
African traditions, 7, 8
agricultural workers, 31. *See also* farmworker movement; farmworkers
Agricultural Workers Organizing Committee (AWOC), 138
Aguirre, Irma, 283, 284

Alatorre, Soledad "Chole," 240
Albertelli, Domnic, 126
Alianza Ministerial Evangélicos Nacionales (AMEN), 179–80
Alinsky, Saul, 50, 51–52, 131
Alvarez, Luis, 6
Alvarez, Robert Lee, 77
Alvarez, Santos, 77
Amado, Catherine, 77
Amado, Frank, 77
American Board for Catholic Missions, 47
American Committee for the Protection of the Foreign Born, 236
American dream, 151, 157, 159
American Indian Movement, 152
Americanization, 173
Anderson, Carol, 7
anti-Blackness, 294
anti-Catholicism, 234
anti-immigrant sentiment, 112, 114. *See also* nativism
anti-Indigenous prejudice, 294
anti-Latino sentiments, 9
antiwar movement, 57, 189, 193, 237
Anzaldúa, Gloria, 8
Aparicio, Ferdinand, 148–49
Apostólico music, 128–30
Apostólicos, 126–27, 131, 134, 137, 138–41, 141n4, 143–44n3; Pentecostals and, 135–36; self-proclaimed prophets among, 143–44n3; Tijerina's influence on, 132–38

325

Archdiocesan Latin American Committee (ALAC), 58, 61, 69n61
Archdiocese of Atlanta, 289
Archdiocese of Chicago, 42–69, 260, 265, 266
Archdiocese of San Antonio, 28–29
Arizona, 96, 97, 112, 217; Mormons in, 96–100; SB 1070 bill, 94, 101, 247
Armendáriz, Ruben, 171
Arpaio, Joe, 101
Arzube, Juan, 177, 241
Askew, Reuben D., 242
Asociación Cubana, 54
Assemblies of God, 134
assimilation pressures, 110
asylum, denied, 215–18, 232n44
asylum seekers, 202–3, 211, 215–18, 220–21, 222–25, 226. *See also* sanctuary movement
Atencio, Tomás, 173
Atlanta, Georgia, 289
Austin, Texas, 173
Austin Presbyterian Theological Seminary, 173
Ayala, Carlos, 76
Ayala, Priscilla, 76
Ayala, Saturnino, 76

Badillo, Herman, 156
Balassiano, Katia, 71
baptisms, 77–78, 81, 82, 96
Barba, Lloyd, 161
Barrett, James, 63n14
barrios, 109, 145–65, 177, 178, 182. *See also specific locations*
Barry, David E., 273, 282–83, 285, 292
Basso, Theresa, 190, 203–4
Bavinger, Bruce, 279–83, 292
belonging, LDS politics of, 98–102
Benedict XVI, Pope, 201
Berle, Adolf, Jr., 21, 26
Bernardin, Joseph, 266
Berrigan, Daniel, 237

Berrigan, Philip, 237
Bérrios, Dionicio, 85
Bérrios, Michael, 81
Bérrios family, 79
the Bible, 133–34, 136, 192
Biden, Joe, 305
Bishops' Committee for the Spanish Speaking (BCSS), 22, 27, 29–31, 32, 33, 34–35, 47–50, 65n25, 65n28
Black Active and Determined (BAD), 174
Black Catholic churches, 276–80; closing of, 277; Spanish in, 280–87
Black Catholic Clergy Caucus (NBCCC), 279
"Black Catholic Revolution," 278–79
Black Catholics: Latino Catholics and, 273–98; mass and, 276; traditions of, 285, 287. *See also* African Americans
Black civil rights movement, 168, 193
Black consciousness, 278, 279
Black evangelicals, 276
Black freedom movement, 7, 171–72
Black identity, 294
"Black Manifesto," 183n5
Black middle class, 290–91
Black Panthers, 152, 174–75
Black Power movement, 276, 278–79
Black theology, 270n23
Boadu, Fred, 285
Board of Christian Social Concerns, 171–72
Boff, Leonardo, 219
Book of Mormon, 95, 102–3, 104, 106–7
borderlands, 215–18
Border Patrol, 215, 227
Borella, Victor, 27, 28
boycotts, 56, 193–94
Bracero Program, 30–34, 39–40n27, 47, 64n19, 69n67, 235, 236, 238
Brigham Young University, 103
Brotherhood of Sleeping Car Porters, 24
Brown, Jerry, 178

Brown, Kathleen, 245
"Brown Manifesto," 167
"Brown Revolution Manifesto," 183n5
Budzynski, Susan, 84
Buff, Rachel, 228
bureaucracy, language of, 36
Bureau of Employment Services, 33
Burke, Edward M., 51
Burke, John J., 48
Bush administration, 180, 227
Busto, Rudy, 139
Byrne, W. Michael, 246–47

California, 30, 121–31, 176, 177, 182, 216, 217, 241, 244; Proposition 8 campaign in, 100–101; Proposition 187, 244–45, 246–47
California Catholic Conference, 246
California Migrant Ministry (CMM), 168–74, 181, 182, 186n32
Calvinism, 72–73, 90n8
Cámara, Helder, 192
campesino literacy campaigns, 220
Cantu, Rafael, 35
Cantú family, 79
Caraballo, José, 178
Cardinal's Committee for the Spanish Speaking (CCSS), 43–44, 50–58, 61, 66–67n37, 171
Carrazana, Humberto, 151–55, 156
Carroll, Gilbert A., 51
Carter, Jimmy: administration of, 233, 241–43; immigration and, 241–43
Cary, Leland P., 149–50
Casa Aztlán, 262–63
Castañeda, Carlos, 2
Castellanos, Bianet, 275
Castillo, Daniel, 82
Castillo, David, 82
Castillo, Mario, 82
Castillo, Raquel, 82
Castillo family, 82
Castro, Fidel, 49, 56, 67–68n51

Catholic activism, 4, 166–87, 184n11, 202–3; immigration reform and, 234–36; Mexican Americans and, 238–40. *See also specific organizations and movements*
Catholic Charismatic Renewal, 86
Catholic Charities USA, 22, 43, 50, 54, 66–67n37
Catholic Church, 107–8, 173; advocacy for Latino immigrants and, 233–52; in Chicago, 42–69; clergy of, 57–58, 233–52; discrimination against Latino priesthood in, 59–60; federal government and, 21–41; in Grand Rapids, 90n8; hierarchy of, 47–60, 233–52, 277; immigrants and, 42–69, 168–69, 273–98; immigration history and, 247–48; Immigration Reform and Control Act of 1986 and, 233–52; importance of, 2–3; as Irish-dominated, 49, 63n14; Latino priesthood in, 59–60; Latino religious leaders in, 196; Latino resurgence in, 294; leaders of, 21–41; Mexican Americans and, 21–41; modernization of (*see* Second Vatican Council reforms); patriarchy in, 197; race and, 273–98; reform in, 234; segregation and, 277–78; in the South, 273–98; as tool of empire, 2; transformation of in the South, 287–91. *See also specific locations*
Catholicism, 8; in the Americas, 276; colonialism and, 8; Latin American, 191–92; reframed as source of comfort, 259–60
Catholic organizations, 21–41, 188–89. *See also specific organizations*
Catholics, 7, 21–41, 181; civil rights movement and, 237–38; farmworker movement and, 239; in Grand Rapids, 70–93; immigrant rights and, 241, 246; immigrants' rights and, 233–52; Mexican-descent, 2; Native Americans and, 211;

Catholics (cont.)
    in North Carolina, 273–98; Protestants and, 171, 182; social justice and, 236–37; in the South, 237–38; undocumented immigrants and, 241; in US South, 12
Catholic Worker Movement, 237
Catholic Youth Organization (CYO), 50
Católicos por La Raza, 175, 238
"Celebration for the People's Church," 145, 146
Celler, Emmanuel, 233–34
Central America, wars in, 215–18, 221–22
Central American activists, 223
Central American refugees, 176, 179, 182, 211, 211–32
Centro de Acción Social Autónomo (CASA), 240
Centro Hispano Católico, 49
Cerda, Maria, 42
chapels, 116n16
Chapman, Robert, 159
Chappell, David, 7
Charismatic movement, 86
Chavarria, Vicente, 35
Chávez, César, 8, 57, 121–44, 169–71, 175, 193, 239–40, 261
Chavez, Gloria, 178
Chavez, Gregorio, 75
Chávez, Tomás, 167, 183n5
Chevere brothers, 52
Chicago, Illinois, 152, 167, 253–72; Catholic Archdiocese of, 42–69; Catholic Church in, 42–69, 260, 265, 266; estimated weekly attendance of Spanish-speakers at mass, 1961, 55t; Latinos in, 42–69, 152, 174–75, 253–72; Mexican Americans in, 253–72; Pilsen Via Crucis in, 253–72; Puerto Ricans in, 152, 174–75
Chicago Public Schools, 58
Chicago Religious Task Force on Central America (CRTF), 212, 214, 217, 220, 226
Chicago Transit Authority, 254–55

Chicana feminism, 189, 193, 197
Chicanismo, 106
Chicano, terminology used to describe, 141n5
Chicano/a, terminology used to describe, 249n10
Chicano activism, 193
"Chicano Apocalypse," 131
Chicano civil rights movement, 124, 139–40
Chicano freedom movement, 12
Chicano historical scholarship, religion's absence from, 2
Chicano identity, 109–10
Chicano movement, 131, 167, 168, 173, 174, 176, 182, 204; Las Hermanas and, 193–205; Mexican immigrants and, 238–40; role of religion in, 121–44; terminology used to describe, 249n10
Chicano nationalism, 106–7, 109–10, 114
Chicano Power movement, 131
Chicano self-determination, 2
Chicano student mobilization, 193–94
Chicano studies, 2
Chicanx studies, 139
Christian base communities (*comunidades eclesiales de base*, or CEBs), 220
Christianity: colonialism and, 157; romanticized view of, 2; sanctuary movement and, 213–15; "Social Gospel" and, 168. *See also specific denominations*
Christianity and Crisis, 170
church boards, 176
church curricula, Spanish-language, 176
church identity politics, 107–8
church leaders, human rights and, 7
church occupations, 174–80, 181
Church of God of Prophecy, 181
Church of the Saviour, New York, 148–50
church reform movements, 3
church-state collaboration, 21–41
Church World Service, 227
civil rights, of Mexican Americans, 23

civil rights era, rise of Latino religious politics in, 166–87
civil rights leaders, 6, 27, 29. *See also specific leaders*
civil rights movement, 57, 82–83, 124–31, 152, 180–81, 189, 270n23, 278–79, 287, 291; Black civil rights movement, 168, 193; Catholics and, 237–38; Chicano civil rights movement, 6–7, 24, 124, 139–40; in the South, 237–38. *See also specific organizations and movements*
Claretian Fathers, 46, 57, 59
class, 109, 151, 157, 159, 275, 290–91
class mobility, 151, 157, 159
clergy: of Catholic Church, 57–58, 233–52; Cuban immigrant, 67–68n51; Latino, 2–3; native, 8; nationalities among, 63n14; Spanish-speaking, 81, 85, 89, 196; stereotypes held by, 57–58. *See also specific people*
Clínica Santa María, 88
coalitions, 202–3
Cody, John, 57–58, 69n61
Cody, Michael, 53
Cold War, 57, 137, 152, 215
collective ethno-religious identity, 104
Colleran, James, 254
Colombian immigrants, 275
Colón, Gilbert, 160
Colón, María, 160
colonialism, 2, 7; Catholicism and, 8; Christianity and, 157; interna, 107; legacy of, 275
comadrazgo, networks of, 94–119
Commission on Migratory Labor, 31
common good, 5
common-law marriages, 67n43
Commonweal, 236
communism, attacks against, 6–7
Communities Organized for Public Service (COPS), 177–78, 179, 181–82
community, meaning and, 161

community activism, Mormons and, 94–119
community formation, 299–308; religion and, 2; rituals and, 253–72
Community Service Organization (CSO), 125–27, 129, 140, 169–70
compadrazgo, 75–76
Concerned Citizens of Lincoln Park, 174–75
Conference of Major Superiors of Men, 202
Conference of Major Superiors of Women Religious, 195
Conference on Spanish-Speaking People of the Southwest, 29
Congress of Racial Equity (Core), 171
conservatism, 180, 182, 214, 243–44, 299–308
conservative Latino voters, faith commitments of, 299–308
Contreras, Julie, 266
Cook, Vincent, 66–67n37
Copeland, M. Shawn, 259, 260
Cordi-Marian Sisters, 46
Corona, Humberto "Bert," 240
Coronel, Denice, 261
Cortés, Ernie, 177
Costas, Orlando, 2–3
Coughlin, Charles, 234
COVID-19 pandemic, 35–36
Cressler, Matthew, 276, 278
Cristero Wars, 62–63n11
Critical Latinx Indigeneities, 275–76
cross disciplinary approach, 4–5
cross disciplinary studies, 3
Cuba, 152, 215
Cuban Americans, Las Hermanas and, 189
Cuban immigrants, 56, 151, 275; in Chicago, 42–69; clergy among, 67–68n51; exceptionalism of, 54, 67–68n51; in Grand Rapids, 79, 80, 83, 88
Cuban Resettlement Committee, 54

Cuban Revolution, 151
cultural differences, 273–98
cultural nationalism, 106
cultural production, religion and, 2
cultural studies, 3
Cunningham, Hilary, 222
Cupich, Blase, 266
cursillos, 53

Dale, Dan, 225–26
Daley, Richard J., 58
D'Amico, Antoinette, 77
Davalos, Karen Mary, 263
Day, Mark, 240
DC Catholic Coalition, 202
death penalty, 180
deindustrialization, 12, 152
Delano Ministerial Association, 170
Del Rey Tortillería, 261–62
democracy, 7
Democratic Party, 304, 305–6
deportation, 211–32, 238
De Prada, Joaquin, 57
DeQuattro, Jo'ann, 178
desegregation, 237, 277–78
Deseret, 95, 97
Díaz-Stevens, Ana María, 287–88
Di Giorgio Corporation, 174
dignity, 8
Diocese of California, 171
Diocese of Grand Rapids, 74–75, 85–87
Diocese of Raleigh, 273–98
Diocese of San Bernardino, 197
Diocese of San Diego, 197
discrimination, 7, 24, 25, 287–88. *See also* racism
Dolan, Timothy, 36
domestic violence, 197
Dominican immigrants, 274–75
Donnella, Joseph, 256
Donnelly, Joseph, 239
dress codes, 136
Dudek, Seven, 85

Durham, North Carolina, racial tensions in, 273–98
Dutch Catholicism, 76–80
Dutch immigrants, 72–73, 90n8

economic justice, 4
economic subjugation, 7
educational programs, 184n12
Eisenhower, Dwight D., administration of, 31
"El Corrido de Cananea," 128–29
electoral politics, 8; 1960s elections, 234; 1980 election, 243; 2016 election, 227; 2020 election, 181, 303–5
el grito de Dolores, 8
Elizondo, Virgilio, 2
El Salvador, 213, 215–18, 220, 221, 222, 223–24, 226
El Teatro Campesino, 130
El Valle de Paz, 132–38, 140–41, 219
Emanuel, Rahm, 263
embodiment theology, 256–60
Embry, Jessie L., 109, 110
empire, Catholic Church as tool of, 2
employment, 30, 31, 33. *See also* labor
employment discrimination, 24
Encarnación Padilla de Armas, 168–69
encuentros, 198
English classes, 58
English-only approaches, 110–11
equality, rhetoric of, 25–26
Ernades, Ricardo, 216
Escobedo, Elizabeth, 6
Espinolda, Rosalia, 79
Espinosa, Gastón, 2, 305
Espinoza, Carmelita, 192
ethnic lineage, Mormons and, 102–9
ethnic movements, 189
ethnic studies, 3
ethno-racial identity, religious identities and, 104, 176–77
Eucharistic solidarity, 260, 261–62
evangelicals, 180, 181, 305–6

evangelism, 305–6
Excot, Elena, 211
Excot, Felipe, 211, 224–25, 226
Excot family, 211–12, 213
exploitation, 2
Ezell, Harold, 244

Fair Employment Practice Committee, 30
faith, 3, 299–308; immigration and, 3, 8–9; instrumental, 121–44; law and, 113; politics and, 301–3; in postwar America, 5–9; role of, 2–3
faith-based activism, 214–15
faith-based organizations, 174–80, 184n12; Pentecostal, 178–79; Protestant, 176–79; rise of, 166–87. *See also specific organizations*
faith leaders, in postwar America, 6–7
faith politics, progressive strain of, 5
faith spaces, 273–98
family detention policies, 227
family separation, 202, 247
farm labor advocates, 33
Farm Security Administration, 30
farmworker movement, 8, 12, 31–32, 56, 121–44, 167–68, 170–72, 174, 175, 176, 193, 239; Catholics and, 166–87, 239; CMM and, 169–70; Pentecostalism and, 121–44, 161; Protestants and, 166–87
farmworkers, 31, 33, 39–40n27, 82, 85, 121–44, 170. *See also* farmworker movement
federal government: Catholic organizations and, 21–41; civil rights movement and, 6; Mexican Americans and, 21–41; rhetoric of equality and, 25–26; War on Poverty, 58
feminist movement, 189; Chicana, 189; Latina, 188–209
Fernández, Arturo, 171
Fernandez, Cirilo, 79

Fernández, Johanna, 147, 151
Fernández, Lilia, 71
Fernandez, Luísa, 78
Fernandez, Pío, 78
Figueroa, Guadalupe, 75
Figueroa Deck, Allan, 200, 241
Filipino farmworkers, 170
fires, at Latino churches, 179
The First People's Church Offensive, 153–56; fifty years after, 160; weeks leading up to occupation, 158–59
First Presbyterian Church, Fresno, 170
First Spanish United Methodist Church (FSUMC), 8–9, 162n2, 163n22, 175; fire at, 150–51; history of, 145–65; occupation of, 145–65; rebuilding of, 151; weeks leading up to occupation, 158–59
Fitzpatrick, Joseph P., 48, 49
Flores, Francisco, 135
Flores, John, 62–63n11
Foley, Albert, 237
Forman, James, 167; "Black Manifesto," 166, 183n5
Francis, Pope, 200; *Christus vivit*, 200–201; *Evangelii Gaudium*, 200–201
Franciscans, 256
freedom movements, 8, 12
Freire, Paulo, 192
Frenken, Henry, 76
Fuchs, Lawrence, 242

Galarza, Ernesto, 32, 33, 36
Galewski, Mary, 77
Galewski, Raymond, 77
Gallardo, Gloria, 194–95
Gallegos, Alfredo, 94, 95
Gallegos, David, 57
Gallegos, Father, 113
Gálvez, Alyshia, 94–95
García, Ignacio, 109–11, 114
García, Jesús, 253
García, Mario T., 2, 106, 246

García, Pedro, 85, 86–88
Garneau, James, 289
Gaudium et spes, 190–91
gay and lesbian activism, 189
gay marriage, opposition to, 180
gender, 275; gender roles, 58; liberation theology and, 192
General Motors Fisher I plant, 88
Georgia, 289; House Bill 87, 247
Gleason, Philip, 234
global protest movements, 234
Goddard, R. A., 34
godparents, choice of, 75–76
Goizueta, Roberto, 213–14, 224, 229
Goldwater, Barry, 300, 305
Gómez, Isabel, 171
González, Justo, 2
Good Neighbor Policy, 23–24
Granados, Roger, 166–67, 168, 171, 174, 182–83
Grand Rapids, Michigan: African Americans in, 77, 84, 86; Cuban immigrants in, 79, 80, 83, 88; demographics of, 72–73, 76–80, 91–92n26; Dutch immigrants in, 72–73, 90n8; history of churches in, 90n8; housing in, 78; Latino im/migrants in, 70–93; Protestants in, 72–73, 89; Puerto Ricans in, 73–74, 78–79, 80, 83, 88; segregation in, 78, 91–92n26
grassroots community movements, 182. *See also specific movements*
Great Depression, 22, 47, 169
Great Migrations, 276
Greene, Christina, 291
growers, 33
Guatemala, 211–12, 215–18, 220, 221, 222
Guatemalans, 226
guest work programs, 242
Gutiérrez, Gustavo, 219, 223, 225
Gutiérrez, Ramón, 132
Guzman, Graciela, 261
Guzmán, Yoruba, 154–55, 157–58

Haas, Francis, 29, 74–75
Harlem, New York, 145–65
Hart, Philip, 233–34
Hartmire, Chris, 170, 171, 181, 186n32
Headley, Donald J., 42, 51, 52–53, 57, 58, 61, 61n1, 66–67n37
Heffernan, John, 291, 292
hemispheric politics, Latinos and, 23
Herald-Sun, 284, 285, 287
hermandad, 111
Hermanos en la Familia de Dios, 52–53
Hernandez, Lydia, 171
Hernandez, María, 261
Hesburgh, Theodore "Ted," 233, 234, 242
Hicks, Joe, 246
Hidalgo y Costilla, Miguel, 8
Higgins, George, 239
Hinojosa, Felipe, 109, 147
Hispanic American Institute (HAI), 173, 176
Hispanic Apostolate, 85
Hispanic Center of West Michigan, 86
Hispanic Pastoral Encuentros, 196–97
"The Hispanic Presence: Challenge and Commitment," 288
historical context, 3, 12
Hoffman, Nick, 51
Holy Cross Catholic Church, Durham, North Carolina, 50, 273–98; historical context of, 276–80; press coverage of walkout, 284–87, 292
Holy Name Cathedral—St. Joseph, Chicago, Illinois, 42, 50, 51, 56
Holy Name Province, 291
Homeland Ministries of the United Church of Christ (UCC), 171
Honduras, 221
housing, 33, 70–93, 169, 174
Houston, Hough, 148–49
Huerta, Dolores, 170, 175, 193, 245
Hull House, 50
human dignity, 5
humanism, 147

Humanitarian Respite Center, Sacred Heart Church, 1
human rights, 7
Humphreys, Stacey, 287
Hunt, Lester, 50, 51

Iberian traditions, 7, 8
Idaho, 96
identity, 183, 275–76; church identity politics, 107–8; collective ethno-religious identity, 104; complexity of, 275; ethno-racial identity, 104, 176–77; identity politics, 109; Latino religious identity politics, 109. *See also specific identities*
III Hispanic National Encuentro, 198
Illinois, Mormons in, 97
Illinois Federation of Mexican Americans (IFOMA), 53
Immaculate Conception Church, Durham, North Carolina, 291–92
Immaculate Heart Vicariate, 46, 47
immigrant freedom movement, 12
immigrants, 42–69, 238–40, 275; advocacy for, 233–52; Catholic Church and, 42–69, 273–98; deportation of, 238; faith and, 8–9; in Grand Rapids, Michigan, 70–93; Mexican Americans and, 238–40; race and, 293–94; terminology used to describe, 249n10; undocumented, 94–95, 100–102, 211–32, 238, 241, 242; unsanctioned, 244; violence against, 23
immigrant sanctuary, 211–32
"Immigrants' Bill of Rights," 240
immigrants' rights, 161, 188–209, 233–52, 246; advocacy for, 248; Catholics and, 241, 246; labor movement and, 240; labor unions and, 242, 245; setbacks in, 247
immigrants' rights movements, 8. *See also specific organizations*
immigration, 4, 12, 121, 168, 180, 273–98; after World War II, 8; Catholic Church and, 273–98; criminalization of undocumented immigrants, 94–95; faith and, 3; labor movement and, 239–40; politics of, 4; theology and, 4
Immigration Act of 1990, 226
Immigration and Customs Enforcement, 227
Immigration and Nationality Act of 1965 ("Hart-Celler"), 233–34
Immigration and Naturalization Service (INS), 216
immigration history, Catholic history and, 247–48
immigration policy, 214, 232n44, 233–52
immigration politics, 94–119, 253–72
Immigration Reform and Control Act of 1986, 233–52
imperialism, 224
independence movements, religion a source of inspiration for, 8
Indigeneity, 109, 275–76, 294
Indigenous identity, Latino, 273–98
Indigenous peoples, 274–75; Catholics and, 211; migrants, 274–75, 294; Mormons and, 97–98, 102–8, 114
Indigenous traditions, 7, 8
Industrial Areas Foundation, 51–52, 125
Industrial Arts Foundation (IAF), 177
inequality, 28–29
INS, 57
institutional power, religious organizations and, 4
integration, 4, 277–78, 281–82
Interfaith Office on Accompaniment, 221
"internal colonialism" model, 107
interracial justice, 184n12
intersectionality, 275, 295
In Yaotlapixqui, 104–5
Isasi-Díaz, Ada María, 2, 192

Jackson, Regine O., 286–87
Jácome, Alex G., 300, 301
Jácome, Estella, 301

Jácome, Felipe, 300–301
Jaredites, 95
Jericho Walks, 228
Jesuits, 221
"Jewish Indian Theory," 102–8
Jews, 7, 213–15
Jim Crow, 6, 7, 168, 277–78, 290. *See also* racism; segregation
Jiménez, José "Cha Cha," 152
Jímenez, Pedro, 171
John Paul II, 60, 258, 266
John XXIII, Pope, 278
Jones, Daniel Webster, 97–98
"Juan Crowism," 6
Juan Marcos Presbyterian Church, Houston, Texas, 175
Juffer, Jane, 214
justice, 2, 5; social justice, 56, 196, 200, 205, 219, 236–37, 303; through religion, 133

Kanter, Deborah, 62–63n11, 71
Kelley, Dean, 159
Kelliher, Thomas, 45
Kennedy, John F., 234, 236
Kennedy, Robert, 131
King, Dempsey, 34
King, Martin Luther Jr., 131, 238
Knights of St John, 171
Know-Nothings, 234, 235
Kozlowski, Ted, 75, 76, 80–85

labor: economics of, 2. *See also* wages; working conditions
labor camps, conditions in, 34
labor force, 23; Latinos and, 23
labor movement, 28, 30–32, 56, 124–25, 182, 239–40
labor unionism, 31, 32
labor unions, 30, 31, 32, 174; immigrant rights and, 242, 245
"La Iglesia de la Gente, The People's Church," 145–65, 162n2

"La Iglesia y La Raza Unida," 167–68, 183n8
La Luz del Mundo, 138
Laman, 102–3, 108
Lamanites, 99, 102–8, 114
"Lamanite Temple," 99
Lamarre, Theodore, 82
Larabee, Peter, 216
Lara-Braud, Jorge, 173, 176
Las Hermanas, 161, 173–74, 176; bicultural identity and, 195; history of, 207n43; legacy of, 188–209; liberation theology and, 204; parish national survey conducted by, 196–97; Proyecto Mexico and, 196; radical and transformative politics of, 188–209; self-reflection by, 194–96, 204; "spirituality of transformative struggle" and, 199
Las Hijas de Maria, 53
Latin America, US pledge of nonintervention in, 23–24
Latin American Conference of Bishops (CELAM—Congreso Episcopal Lationamericano), 191
Latin American Council (LAC), 80–81, 85
Latin American Defense Organization (LADO), 175
Latin American Methodist Action group, 173
Latin American Services, 86
Latin American Youth Committee, 27
Latinas: Latina feminist movement, 188–209; Latina spiritual political activism, 188–89; needs of, 197; rights of, 198–99. *See also* women
Latinidad, 109
Latino, terminology used to describe, 89n1, 249n10, 295n2
Latino activism, 145–65
Latino advocacy, 21–41
Latino Catholicism, 8, 76–80
Latino Catholics: Black Catholics and, 273–98; discrimination against, 287–88; in the South, 273–98

Latino churches, nationwide network of, 179–80
Latino communities: scholarship of, 299–308; in Southwest, 21–41
Latino evangelism, 305–6
Latino freedom movements, 2–3
Latino history, 3, 94–119
Latino identity, 167, 168, 183, 295
Latino politicians, rise of, 247
Latino population: diversity of, 306; multiethnic, 42–69
Latino priesthood, 67–68n51; in Catholic Church, 59–60; discrimination against, 59–60
Latino Religions and Politics National Survey, 305
Latino religious communities, political movements of, 3
Latino religious history, 94–119; future of, 299–308
Latino religious identity politics, 109
Latino religious leaders, 21–41, 180; in Catholic Church, 196; in Civil Rights era, 166–87; nationwide network of, 179–80; Pentecostal, 178–80; Protestant, 178–79; questioning status quo, 171; white religious leaders and, 172–74, 175–76. *See also specific leaders*
Latino religious politics, 3–5, 161, 177, 188–209, 301–3; mapping the field, 1–17; what constitutes, 5
Latino religious resurgence, 3, 287–88, 294
Latino religious scholarship, 71
Latinos: hemispheric politics and, 23; political mobilization of, 247; subjugation of, 2; terminology used to describe, 13n2, 37n3, 61n3, 141n5, 162n5, 249n10
Latino Saints, 103–10, 112, 113–14, 114n11
Latinos for Trump, 304–5
Latino studies, 3
Latino theological studies, 176, 181
Latino theology, 270n23

Latinx Catholic Leadership Coalition, 202–3
Latter-day Saints wards, 4
Latvians, 74
La Virgen de Caridad del Cobre, 83
La Voz de Carolina, 286
law: faith and, 113; LDS Church and, 100–101. *See also specific laws*
lay leaders, 52, 53
Lazarus, 233, 243
LDS Church, 94–119, 114n11; community formation in, 115n12; doctrinal populations in, 108–9; immigration politics and, 94–119; Lamanite narrative and, 102–8; law and, 100–101, 113; national image as mainstream religion open to all, 100–101; politics of belonging and, 98–102; Spanish-speaking wards and, 111–12. *See also* Mormons
LDS Living, 112
Leadership Conference of Women Religious (LCRW), 201
League of United Latin American Citizens (LULAC), 24
Lehi, 99, 102–3, 108
Lemuel, 102
Leo XIII, Pope, 184n11; *Rerum novarum*, 236
Lewis, Jerald, 285
Liohona, 104–6
liberation theologians, 2–3
liberation theology, 4, 57, 151, 189, 192, 197, 202, 204, 270n23; Las Hermanas and, 191–92; rise of Latino religious politics in, 8; sanctuary movement and, 218–20, 222
Lightfoot, Lori, 263–64, 265
Lipsitz, George, 115n5, 218
lived religion, 146, 147–52, 158–61
Lopez, Angelo, 79
López, Ellen Mary, 84
López, Lydia, 178
Lopez, Mario, 79

López, Obed, 167, 175
Lopez, Severíno, 59
López Tijerina, Reies, 121, 123, 131, 132–38, 138–41
Los Angeles, California, 177, 178
Los Caballeros de San Juan, 51–53, 52
Los Heraldos de la Paz, 134
los valientes, 135, 137–38
Lu, Linda, 77
Lucas, Isidro, 42, 60
Lucey, Robert, 26, 27, 28, 29, 30–31, 36, 39–40n27, 47, 49, 59, 65n25
Luciani, Rafael, 201–2
Luciano, Felipe, 153, 155, 157, 158
Luz, Patricia, 261–62

MACC, 197
Machado, Antonio, 213, 229
Madera, California, 121–31, 140
Mahon, Leo, 50, 51
Mahony, Roger, 246
Malave, Dorlimar Lebron, 160
Malcom X, 131
Maldonado, Marta María, 71
Mancilla, Martina, 266
Mañes, Antonio, 53
Manpower Development Training Act, 58
Manuel Ramos Memorial Building, 174
March for Our Lives, 266
Márez, Rodolfo, 135, 138
Marín, Mariano, 121, 122, 125–26, 127
Marsh, Charles, 7
Martínez, Joel, 171
Martínez, Vicente, 135, 136–37
Marxism, 2
Maryknolls, 221, 222
Masó, Marta, 43
mass: African American culturally based, 285; bilingual, 281–85, 288, 291–92; Black Catholics and, 276; English-only, 79–80; estimated weekly attendance of Spanish-speakers at, 1961, 55; Second Vatican Council reforms and, 56; in Spanish, 83–84, 85, 281–85, 288, 291–92
Mata, Manuel, 135
Mata family, 136
Mathew 25 Movement, 232n46
Matovina, Timothy, 203
Mazzoli, Romano L., 243
McAllen, Texas, 1
McBriar, David, 292
McCalister, Nelda, 112–13, 114
McCarthy, Eli, 202
McCormick Theological Seminary, Chicago, 167, 174–75, 182
McDonald, Dan, 216
McDonald, Ed, 34
McDonnell, Donald, 125–26
McFarland, W. B., 34
McGowan, Raymond, 28
McGuire, Meredith, 147–48
meaning, community and, 161
Medina, Jennifer, 305
Medina, Lara, 2, 161
Meléndez, Micky, 154–55
Mendoza, Carmen, 53
Mesa Arizona Temple, 99–100, 103
Methodism, 145–65, 173
Mexican American civil rights leaders. *See specific leaders*
Mexican American Cultural Center, 176, 196, 203
Mexican American Methodists, 173
Mexican American Program, Perkins School of Theology, 176
Mexican American religious experience, 2
Mexican Americans, 42–69, 64n21, 70–93, 253–72; Catholic activism and, 238–40; Catholic Church and, 21–41; civil rights of, 23; discrimination against, 21, 25, 59–60, 242; federal government and, 21–41; Las Hermanas and, 189; Mexican immigrants and, 238–40; terminology used to describe, 249n10; violence against,

23; World War II racial landscape and, 25
Mexican-American War, 97
Mexican American Youth Organization (MAYO), 175
Mexican Apostolate, 72–76
Mexican Baptist Church, Fresno, 171
Mexican civil rights, 23–24
Mexican civil rights organizations, 24
Mexican identity, 273–98
Mexican Revolution, 44, 46, 62–63n11, 99
Mexico: Bracero Program and, 30–31; missionaries in, 99, 101, 115n15; Mormons and, 97, 98–99
Meyer, Samuel B., 51, 54, 57
Miami, Florida, 151
Midwest, 8–9, 12, 70–93, 211–32. *See also specific locations*
migrant labor advocacy groups, 31
migrant ministries, 168–74, 184n12
migrants, 42–69, 82, 85, 125–31, 184n11, 273–98; faith and, 8–9; indigenous, 274–75; needs of, 233–52. *See also* immigrants
migration: economics of, 2; Mormon identity and, 95. *See also* immigration
Miranda, Jesse, 2, 179–80
missionaries, 1, 99, 101, 103–10, 115n15, 184n12, 221–23
Missionaries of Jesus, 1
Missouri, 97
Mitchell, H. L., 32
Mitchell, James, 31–32, 33–35
mobilization, 3, 8–9, 193–94, 247
modesty, principle of, 136
Molina, Natalia, 286
Montavon, William, 26, 27, 28
Morales, Iris, 155–56
Moral Majority, 214
moral obligation, 214, 224–25
moral vision, 233–52
Moreno, Luis, 135
Moreno, Lupe, 85

Moreno, María, 138
Moreno family, 136
Mormon Church, women and, 94–119
Mormon Corridor, 95–97, 99–100, 102
Mormons, 114n1; in Arizona, 96–100; community activism and, 94–119; ethnic lineage and, 102–9; growth of Spanish-speaking population among, 113; immigration politics and, 102; Latino, 94–119; Mexico and, 97, 98–99; Native Americans and, 97–98, 102–8, 114; politics and, 94–119; Whiteness and, 97, 98, 109, 113–14, 115n5
Mormon studies, 94–119
Moulton, Kristen, 94
Mountjoy, Dick, 244
Movement for Grassroots Education (MEB—Movimiento para Educación de Base), 192
Moyet, Gabino, 52, 53
Moyn, Samuel, 7
mujerista theology, 192, 199, 204–5, 270n23
multiethnic coalitions, 182
multiethnic neighborhood organizations, 168
Mundelein, George, 46
Muñoz, Irene, 193–94
Murrieta, Sara, 197
mutual aid organizations, 176–77
mutuality through sanctuary, ethic of, 213–14
My Lai massacre, 237

Narbutas, Titus, 74
National Agricultural Workers Union, 32
National Association for the Advancement of Colored People (NAACP), 24, 26
National Black Economic Development Conference, 166
National Catholic Reporter, 170
National Catholic War Council, 25

National Catholic Welfare Conference (NCWC), 4, 25–31, 47
National Conference of Catholic Charities, 25
National Council of Brazilian Bishops (CNBB—Conferencia Nacional Episcopal Brazileño), 192
National Council of Catholic Bishops (NCCB), 288
National Council of Churches, 157, 159
National Farm Workers Association (NFWA), 129, 138, 170
National Hispanic Christian Leadership Conference (NHCLC), 180
National Latino Evangelical Coalition (NaLEC), 180, 305
National Negro Congress, 24
national organizations, 24–26. *See also specific organizations*
National Pastoral Plan for Hispanic Ministry, 288
Native Americans. *See* Indigenous peoples
nativism, 7, 234, 235, 243–44, 247
Navarro, Mike, 78
Nazi Germany, 6
Nazism, 22, 23
Nelson, Alan, 244
Nephi, 108–9
Nephites, 95, 102–3
New Deal, 28
New Mexico, 131–38
new nativism, 244
News & Observer (*N&O*), 284, 286, 289, 290
New Sanctuary Movement, 211–32
New York City, 149, 168–69, 177; demographics of, 149; Department of Social Services, 156; fires at Latino churches in, 179; Young Lords Organization in, 145–65
New York Methodist City Society, 150, 156; New York Methodist Conference, 151
Ngo Dinh Diem, 237

Nicaragua, 221
Nicgorski, Darlene, 222
Nieto, Leo, 171
Nixon, Richard, 234
normative assumptions, disentangling, 299–308
North Carolina, 273–98
North Carolina Central University (NCCU), 273, 277
North Carolina Mutual Life Insurance Company, 290
Northside Coopeerative Ministry (NSCM), 174

Obama, Barack, 247
Obama administration, 180, 227, 247
Ocasio-Cortez, Alexandria, 305
O'Conner, William, 34
Office of the Coordinator of Inter-American Affairs (OCIAA), 23–24, 26–27, 28, 29–30
O'Grady, John, 21, 26, 28
O'Leary, Kathy, 202
Olivares, Luis, 178
O'Malley, Sean, 240–41
Operation Peter Pan, 54
Operation Wetback, 121, 238
Orbis books, 222
Order of Friars Minors, 291
organizing, 273–98. *See also* mobilization
Orsi, Robert, 147
Ortega, Gregoria, 194
Ortega-Aponte, Elías, 147
Ortegón, Samuel, 2
Our Lady of Guadalupe, 46, 47, 55, 72–76, 282–83, 284
Our Lady of Guadalupe Chapel, Grand Rapids, Michigan, 79–80, 81, 82
Our Lady of Sorrows, 56

PADRES (Padres Asociados para Derechos Religiosos, Educativos, y Sociales), 173, 174, 176, 194, 196, 197

padrinos, 75–76
Palma, Natividad, 77
pan-Latino placemaking, 80–85
pan-Latino religious community, 80–85
pan-Latino religious spaces: history of, 72–76; saving, 86–89
parishes, transitions of, 76–80
Passion of the Christ, 256, 268n12, 269n19
Passion Play, 256, 268n12
patriarchy, 197
Patterson, Ronald, 279
Paul VI, Pope, 238, 239
Pawel, Miriam, 169
Paycheck Protection Program, 36
Paz, Frank, 57
Peace Walk, 266
Pearce, Russell, 100–101, 102, 116n19
Peña, Elaine, 263
Pence, John, 304
Pence, Mike, 304
Pentecostalism, 3, 12, 121–44, 141n1, 178–80; dress codes and, 136; farmworker movement and, 161; power of the sonic and, 127–31; rise of, 180
Pentecostals, Apostólicos and, 135–36
The People's Church, 145–65, 162n2
"peregrinos," 156, 160
Perelli Minnetti Vineyards, 174
Pérez, Manuel, 132, 135–36
performances, 253–72
periodicals, 104–6, 170. *See also specific periodicals*
Perla, Héctor Jr., 223
Pfaelzer, Mariana, 247
Pierce, Charles, 253
Pietri, Carmen, 154
Pilsen Alliance, 262
Pilsen barrio, 60
Pilsen fire, 253–54, 254, 255
Pilsen Via Crucis, 253–72, 262, 264
Pima, 97
Pimentel, Sister Norma, 1, 2
Pius XI, Pope, 184n11

placemaking, 70–93
placemaking scholarship, 71
Pledge of Resistance, 221
police brutality, 152, 260
political fellowship, 211–32; practices of, 218–27
political movements. *See specific movements*
political oppression, 2
political parties. *See* Democratic Party; Republican Party
politics, 3; faith and, 301–3; Mormons and, 94–119; political consciousness, 179, 193; political engagement, 2; political movements, 211–32; political parties, 299–308; political will, 233–52; postwar, 168; progressive, 299–308; reformist politics, 182; theology and, 4. *See also* electoral politics; immigration politics; Latino religious politics
Poor People's Coalition (PPC), 174
Portillo, Hilda, 42, 59
poverty, 174, 176, 180, 181, 191, 200, 260
power, 3, 188; alternative, 121–44; in postwar America, 5–9. *See also* politics
Precious Blood, 56
Prendergast, Walter, 27, 28
Presbyterian Latin American Council, 176
Presbyterian Life, 170
Presbyterians, 166, 174, 175
President's Commission on Migratory Labor, 31, 39–40n27
Prieto, Jorge, 57
Primer Encuentro Hispano de Pastoral, 169
Prince, Ron, 244
Program for the Analysis of Religion Among Latinos (PARAL), 3
Programming Committee of the Presbyterian Church US Synod of Texas, 173
progressive politics, 299–308
progressive religious movements, 168. *See also specific movements*

pro-life movement, 180
Protestant activism, 4, 166–87
Protestants, 7, 72–73, 89, 107, 178–79; Catholics and, 171, 182; farmworker movement and, 126–27; Latino immigrants and, 168–74; Mexican-descent, 2; in Midwest, 12. *See also specific denominations*
Proyecto Mexico, 196
Public Religion Research Institute (PRRI), 181
public space, 8
Puerto Rican nationalism, 2, 8, 12, 151, 158–59, 168
Puerto Ricans, 42–69, 274–75; in Chicago, 42–69, 152, 174–75; in Grand Rapids, 80, 83, 88; Las Hermanas and, 189; in New York City, 149, 168–69
Puerto Rican studies, 2
Puerto Rican Young Lords, revolutionary politics of, 145–65
P'urhépecha migrants, 275, 294

Quinn, William J., 65n25
Quintana, Nellie, 260

race, 2, 174, 176, 275; Catholic Church and, 273–98; race relations, 6, 23, 109, 273–98; "racial division," 293; racial ideology after World War II, 5–6. *See also* segregation
racial liberalism, 6
racial movements, 287
racial nativism, 7. *See also* nativism
racial tensions, in Durham, North Carolina, 273–74, 276–80, 285–87, 292–93
racial violence, 6, 24
racism, 181, 260, 286–87, 293, 295. *See also* discrimination
Ralston Purina Company, 69n61
Ramírez, Margaret, 260
Reagan, Ronald, 215, 233, 244; administration of, 216, 224; immigration reform and, 243; "Reagan amnesty," 233, 243
Reavis, Dick, 241
reformist politics, 182
Refugee Act of 1980, 215, 226
refugee admittance, politics of, 4
refugee movements, 211–32
refugee policies, 12
refugees, Central American, 176, 179, 182, 211–32
refugee sanctuary, 211–32
regional organizations, 24. *See also specific organizations*
relics, Mexican Catholic, 281–83, 284
religion, social uplift and, 2
religiopolitical accompaniment, practices of, 211–32
religious activism, 3
religious diversity, 7, 8
religious identities, 3, 176–77
religious orders, missionaries, 221–23
religious organizations, 4, 303. *See also specific organizations*
religious performance, 253–72
religious politics. *See* Latino religious politics
religious societies, 52–53
Republican Party, 304, 305–6
resistance, 8; new geographies of, 273–98; Pilsen Via Crucis as path to, 253–72
retreats, 53
revolutionary politics, 145–65, 182. *See also* activism
Reyna, Juan, 135
Ring, John D., 57
Rio Grande Annual Conference, 171
Ríos, Elizabeth, 179
Risco, Eliezer, 167, 183n5
rituals, 253–72
Rivera, Cesar, 52
Rivera, Jose, 181, 305
Rivera, Orlando, 106–7, 109–10, 114
Rivera, Raymond, 179, 180

Riverside Church, New York City, 166
Rocha Ramirez, Rosa, 82
Rockefeller, Nelson, 26–27
Rodriguez, Benita, 153
Rodriguez, Edmundo, 194
Rodriguez, Gloria, 82
Rodriguez, Jesus, 52
Rodriguez, Justa, 53
Rodriguez, Peter, 57
Rodriguez, Samuel, 180
Rodriguez, Sara, 82
Roediger, David, 63n14
Romero, Oscar, 197, 212, 217, 219
Romero, Vicky, 262
"Romero Refugee Express," 212
Roosevelt, Franklin: administration of, 21; Good Neighbor Policy and, 23–24; New Deal coalition and, 24; pledge of hemispheric collaboration, 23–24
Rosa Gloria, "El Campesino," 128–29
Ross, Fred, 125
Ross, Rosetta, 7
Ruiz, Manuel Jr., 27
Rush-Presbyterian Hospital, 255
Ryan, John, 28

safe harbor, 217–18. *See also* sanctuary movement
Salguero, Gabriel, 180, 305
Salinas, California, 135, 136–37
Salinas Valley, California, 132, 134
Salvadoran Humanitarian Aid, Relief, and Education Foundation (SHARE), 221
Salvadorans, 226
San Antonio, Texas, 28–29, 174, 177
"San Antonio Shakedown," 166
Sánchez, Santa, 75
Sánchez-Walsh, Arlene, 107
sanctuary movement, 176, 211–32; liberation theology and, 218–20, 222; today, 227–29
Sanders, Bernie, 305
Sandoval, Moises, 3

Sandoval-Strausz, A. K., 183–84n9
San Francisco Presbytery, 171
San Joaquin Valley, 171
San Juan, Puerto Rico, first diocese in, 8
Sayeed, Marta (née Masó), 54, 56, 58, 61
School Sisters of Saint Francis, 222
Schultz, Kevin, 7
Second Annual Mexican-American Conference, 193
second-class citizenship, 6
Second Vatican Council reforms, 4, 56–60, 82–83, 140, 171, 189–92, 200, 218, 234, 236, 278, 287
Secretariat of the Spanish Speaking, 196
Secure Communities, 227
segregation, 2, 78, 91–92n26, 168, 237, 277–78, 290, 294
Segundo, Juan Luis, 219
Select Committee on Immigration and Refugee Policy (SCIRP), 242
self-determination, 2, 276, 278, 302
Serna, Simón, 135, 137–38
Shaw, Howland, 21
Shelton, Paul, 260
Shiel, Bernard James, 50
sidewalk shrines, 8
Sigcho-López, Byron, 265
Simpson, Alan K., 243
slavery, legacy of, 275
Snarr, Melissa, 226
Sobrino, Jon, 219
social engagement, 184n11
"Social Gospel," 168
socialism, 2, 305
social justice, 56, 196, 200, 205, 219, 236–37, 303
social movements, 2, 4, 57, 211–32
social uplift, religion and, 2
Sociedad Guadalupana, 73
solidarity, praxis of, 223, 226, 261
solidarity coalitions, 223, 226
Sosa, Juan, 52, 53
Soto, Ignacio Jr., 301

South Central Organizing Project (SCOP), 178
Southern Christian Leadership Conference, 246
Southern Cross, 241
Soviet Union, 7, 215
space, reclaiming of, 261
Spanish-American Outreach, 167
Spanish Catholic Action, 169
Spanish Claretian brothers, 46
Spanish language: church curricula in, 176; LDS Church and, 111–12; worship in, 83–84, 85, 109–13, 280–87, 288, 291–92
Spanish Speaking Committee, 50
the spiritual, as political, 260–67
spiritual fortitude, 268n8
Spreckels Sugar Company, 132
St. Adalbert, Chicago, Illinois, 266
St. Andrew's Cathedral, Grand Rapids, Michigan, 74, 78
STAR (Street Transvestite Action Revolutionaries), 156
Stations of the Cross, 253–72, 268n12
St. Basil's Catholic Church, Los Angeles, California, 175
Stevens-Arroyo, Anthony M., 2–3, 287–88
St. Francis of Assisi, Chicago, Illinois, 42, 46, 47, 57, 59, 266
St. Ignatius High School, 43
Still, Doug, 169
St. Joseph Mission Program, 84
St. Joseph the Worker Parish, Grand Rapids, Michigan, 70–93
St. Luke's Hospital, Chicago, Illinois, 255
St. Michael's, Chicago, Illinois, 56
Stonewall riots, 156
storefront churches, 8
St. Procopius Catholic Church, Chicago, Illinois, 260
Strauss, James, 35
strikebreakers, 239

Stritch, Samuel A., 47, 51, 57, 65n28
student activism, 166, 171, 193–94. *See also specific organizations*
Student Nonviolent Coordinating Committee (SNCC), 166, 171
Students for a Democratic Society, 174
St. Vitus Catholic Church, Chicago, Illinois, 253, *254*, 255
syncretism, 7, 8
Synod of Bishops for the Amazon, 201

Tarango, Yolanda, 190, 199, 203
Teague, Charles, 33
Temples, 99, 116n16
temporary protected status (TPS), 226
terminology, 13n2, 37n3, 61n3, 89n1, 141n5, 162n5, 249n10, 295n2
testimonios, 153, 223–26
Texas, 30, 171, 176, 177, 182, 194, 241
Texas Council of Churches, 171
Texas Employment Commission, 35
theology, 3, 4, 159, 168, 176; theological interventions, 270n23
theopolitics, 168, 180
Tirres, Christopher D., 270n23
Tohono-O'odham, 97
Tolbert, William, 33
Tomlinson, Barbara, 218
Toolen, Thomas J., 237
Toribio, Abbie, 53
Torres, Jerry, 127
Torres, Lucia, 78–79
Torres, Pedro, 171
Torres, Robert, 78–79
Torres, Sallie, 127
Tort, Father, 46
transformative spirituality, 199
transnational cultures, 184n11
transnational networks, 8
Treaty of Guadalupe Hidalgo, 131, 138
Treviño, Roberto, 104
tribalism, 7
"tri-faith America," 7

Truman, Harry, 31, 39–40n27
Trump, Donald, 36, 101, 180, 181, 202, 232n44, 304–5, 306; administration of, 227, 247, 261; family separation and, 247; rise of, 247

undocumented immigrants, 94–95, 100–102, 211, 227, 238, 241, 242
unemployment, 152
United Farm Workers, 4, 56, 58, 129, 245
"United Nations of Latino Catholics," 86–89
United Neighborhood Organization (UNO), 177–78, 179, 181–82
United Presbyterian Church in the USA (UPCUSA), 181st General Assembly, 166, 174, 175, 183n5
United States: Bracero Program and, 30–31; foreign policy of, 214, 221; immigration policy of, 214, 215–18, 229, 232n44, 233–34; imperialism of, 224; pledge of non-intervention in Latin America, 23–24; race re Latinos in, 5–6
United States Employment Services, regional representatives, 32
University of Chicago, 50
unsanctioned immigrants, 244
urban crisis, 167–68, 171–72, 181, 183–84n9
urban religious institutions, politics of, 3
USA Today, 285
US Catholic Conference of Bishops, 197, 198, 203
US House of Representatives Western Hemispheric Affairs Sub-Committee, 221
US Labor Department, 22, 31–32, 33–35
USPS, 261
US South, 273–98; Black and Latino Catholic parishioners in, 273–98; Catholic Church in, 237–38, 273–98; Catholics in, 12; civil rights movement in, 237–38; race in, 237, 273–98

US Southwest: Latino communities in, 21–41; Latter-day Saints wards in, 4
US State Department, 21, 216
USWA Local 65, 58
Utah, 94–97, 100, 112
Utah Compact, 101–2

Valdéz, Facundo, 173
VanDrunen, Lois, 77
VanDrunen, Peter, 77
Vargas, Daniel, 73
Vargas, Gaudalupe, 73
Vásquez, Consuelo, 73
Vásquez, Daniel, 73, 76
Vatican II. *See* Second Vatican Council reforms
Velasquez, Arturo, 53
Vetter, Joe, 290
Via Crucis (Way of the Cross), 256, 259–60, 268n12
Via Crucis del Migrantes (Way of the Cross of Migrants), 259
Via Dolorosa (Way of Sorrow), 256
Vietnam War, 152, 237. *See also* antiwar movement
Villasana, Ann-Marie, 283, 284
Virgen de Altagracia of the Dominican Republic, 89
Virgen de Caridad del Cobre of Cuba, 89
Virgen de Guadalupe, 8, 83, 89, 104, 263, 281, 282–83, 299, 300
Virgen del Rosario of Guatemala, 89
Virgen de Providencia of Puerto Rico, 89
vocational training, 58
Von Hoffman, Nichoals, 50

wages, 25, 30, 31, 33, 49, 125, 128, 133, 169, 171–72, 197
Wagner, John A., 48, 49
walkouts, 194, 273–98
Wanzer-Serrano, Darrel, 147
War on Poverty, 58
Washburne Trade School, 58

Waters, Vincent, 277–78
"welcoming the stranger," 214–15
Welfare and Working Mothers of Wicker Park, 175
West, 94–119
Weston Priory Monastery, Vermont, 211
White Catholics, 26, 279–81, 289
white flight, 76–80; "White flight," 149, 150
Whiteness: in Latin America, 294; Mormons and, 97, 98, 109, 113–14, 115n5; social structures of, 293
white religious leaders, Latino religious leaders and, 172–74, 175–76
White supremacy, 102, 108
Wilson, Pete, 245
Witness for Peace, 221
womanist theology, 270n23
women: liberation theology and, 192; Mormon Church and, 94–119; needs of, 197; role in The People's Church, 155–56. *See also* Latinas
women's rights, 161, 188–209
worker organization, 30
working conditions, 34, 49, 125, 169, 171–72
World War I, 25

World War II, 5, 6–7, 21–41, 235; church-state collaboration and, 22–23; war economy, 6; war effort, 6
worship, in Spanish, 83–84, 85, 109–13, 280–87, 288, 291–92
Wyoming, Michigan, 88

xenophobia, 247

Yapias, Tony, 94, 95, 113
Yaquis, 97, 103
Ybarra, María de Jesús, 192
Young, Brigham, 96–97, 98–99
Young Lords Organization (YLO), 4, 8–9, 163n22, 167, 174–75; Gay and Lesbian caucus in, 156; New York chapter of, 145–65, 175; theology and, 159; women's role in, 155–56
Young Patriots, 152

Zamora, Emilio, 6
Zapata, Hilario, 70, 89
Zapata, Katie, 70
Zapata, Lucia, 82–83, 84, 85, 89
Zárate, Rosa Martha, 188, 197, 204, 205
Zavela, Martha, 110
Zubovich, Gene, 7

www.ingramcontent.com/pod-product-compliance
Lightning Source LLC
Chambersburg PA
CBHW020351080526
44584CB00014B/983